CompTIA A+
Rapid Review
(Exam 220-801 and
Exam 220-802)

Darril Gibson

Published with the authorization of Microsoft Corporation by:
O'Reilly Media, Inc.
1005 Gravenstein Highway North
Sebastopol, California 95472

ISBN: 978-0-735-66682-5

1 2 3 4 5 6 7 8 9 LSI 8 7 6 5 4 3

Printed and bound in the United States of America.

Microsoft Press books are available through booksellers and distributors worldwide.
If you need support related to this book, email Microsoft Press Book Support at
mspinput@microsoft.com. Please tell us what you think of this book at *http://www.
microsoft.com/learning/booksurvey*.

Microsoft and the trademarks listed at *http://www.microsoft.com/about/legal/en/us/
IntellectualProperty/Trademarks/EN-US.aspx* are trademarks of the Microsoft group of
companies. All other marks are property of their respective owners.

The example companies, organizations, products, domain names, email addresses,
logos, people, places, and events depicted herein are fictitious. No association with
any real company, organization, product, domain name, email address, logo, person,
place, or event is intended or should be inferred.

This book expresses the author's views and opinions. The information contained in
this book is provided without any express, statutory, or implied warranties. Neither
the authors, O'Reilly Media, Inc., Microsoft Corporation, nor its resellers, or distributors will be held liable for any damages caused or alleged to be caused either directly
or indirectly by this book.

The CompTIA Marks are the proprietary trademarks and/or service marks of CompTIA
Properties, LLC used under license from CompTIA Certifications, LLC through partici-
pation in the CompTIA Authorized Partner Program. More information about the program can be found at *http://www.comptia.org/certifications/capp/login.aspx*.

Acquisitions and Developmental Editor: Kenyon Brown
Production Editor: Kristen Borg
Editorial Production: nSight, Inc.
Technical Reviewer: Brian Blum
Indexer: BIM Indexing
Cover Design: Karen Montgomery
Cover Composition: Best & Company Design
Illustrator: Rebecca Demarest

Contents at a Glance

Contents

What do you think of this book? We want to hear from you!

Microsoft is interested in hearing your feedback so we can continually improve our
books and learning resources for you. To participate in a brief online survey, please visit:

microsoft.com/learning/booksurvey

PART II   EXAM 220-802

What do you think of this book? We want to hear from you!

Microsoft is interested in hearing your feedback so we can continually improve our
books and learning resources for you. To participate in a brief online survey, please visit:

microsoft.com/learning/booksurvey

What do you think of this book? We want to hear from you!

Microsoft is interested in hearing your feedback so we can continually improve our
books and learning resources for you. To participate in a brief online survey, please visit:

microsoft.com/learning/booksurvey

Introduction

This Rapid Review is designed to assist you with studying for the CompTIA A+ exams 220-801 and 220-802. The Rapid Review series is designed for exam candidates who already have a good grasp of the exam objectives through a combination of experience, skills, and study and could use a concise review guide to help them assess their readiness for the exam.

The A+ certification is aimed at an entry-level IT professional who has a minimum of 12 months of hands-on experience with computers. This can be either classroom or lab experience, or on-the-job experience, or a combination of both. To earn the A+ certification, you need to pass two exams:

- CompTIA A+ 220-801 covers the fundamentals of computer technology, installation and configuration of PCs, laptops and related hardware, and basic networking.
- CompTIA A+ 220-802 covers the skills required to install and configure PC operating systems, as well as configuring common features (for example, network connectivity and email) for mobile operating systems Android and Apple iOS.

Successful candidates will have the knowledge required to assemble components based on customer requirements. They can install, configure, and maintain devices, PCs, and software for end users, and they understand the basics of networking and security/forensics. They can provide appropriate customer support by applying appropriate troubleshooting skills to properly and safely diagnose, resolve, and document common hardware and software issues. Successful candidates will also understand the basics of virtualization, desktop imaging, and deployment.

This book will review every concept described in the following exam objective domains from exam 220-801:

- 1.0 PC Hardware
- 2.0 Networking
- 3.0 Laptops
- 4.0 Printers
- 5.0 Operational Procedures

This book will also review every concept described in the following exam objective domains from exam 220-802:

- 1.0 Operating Systems
- 2.0 Security
- 3.0 Mobile Devices
- 4.0 Troubleshooting

This is a Rapid Review and not a comprehensive guide such as the CompTIA A+ Training Kit. The book covers every exam objective on the 220-801 and 220-802 exams but will not necessarily cover every exam question. CompTIA regularly adds new questions to the exam, making it impossible for this (or any) book to provide every answer. Instead, this book is designed to supplement your existing independent study and real-world experience with the topics.

If you encounter a topic in this book that you do not feel completely comfortable with, you can visit the links described in the text, in addition to researching the topic further by using other websites and by consulting support forums. If you review a topic and find that you don't understand it, you should consider consulting the CompTIA A+ Training Kit from Microsoft Press. You can also purchase practice exams, or you can use the exams available with the Training Kit, to further determine whether you have need further study on particular topics.

NOTE The Rapid Review is designed to assess your readiness for the 220-801 and 220-802 exams. It is not designed as a comprehensive exam preparation guide. If you need that level of training for any or all of the exam objectives covered in this book, we suggest the *CompTIA A+ Training Kit* (ISBN: 9780735662681). The Training Kit provides comprehensive coverage of each exam objective, along with exercises, review questions, and practice tests.

CompTIA professional certification program

CompTIA

CompTIA professional certifications cover the technical skills and knowledge needed to succeed in a specific IT career. Certification is a vendor-neutral credential. An exam is an internationally recognized validation of skills and knowledge and is used by organizations and professionals around the globe. CompTIA certification is ISO 17024 Accredited (Personnel Certification Accreditation) and, as such, undergoes regular reviews and updates to the exam objectives. CompTIA exam objectives reflect the subject areas in an edition of an exam and result from subject matter expert workshops and industry-wide survey results regarding the skills and knowledge required of a professional with a number of years of experience.

MORE INFO For a full list of CompTIA certifications, go to *http://certification .comptia.org/getCertified/certifications.aspx*.

Training materials given the CAQC seal have gone through a rigorous approval process to confirm the content meets exam objectives, language standards, necessary hands-on exercises and labs and applicable Instructional Design standards.

Certification helps your career

Certification can help your career in the following ways:

- The CompTIA A+ credential provides foundation-level knowledge and skills necessary for a career in PC repair and support.
- CompTIA A+ Certified individuals can earn as much as $65,000 per year.
- CompTIA A+ is a building block for other CompTIA certifications such as Network+, Security+ and vendor-specific technologies.
- More than 850,000 Individuals worldwide are CompTIA A+ certified.
- Mandated/recommended by organizations worldwide, such as Cisco and HP and Ricoh, the U.S. State Department, and U.S. government contractors such as EDS, General Dynamics, and Northrop Grumman.

It pays to get certified

In a digital world, digital literacy is an essential survival skill. Certification proves you have the knowledge and skill to solve business problems in virtually any business environment. Certifications are highly-valued credentials that qualify you for jobs, increased compensation and promotion.

IT is Everywhere	IT Knowledge and Skills Get Jobs	Job Retention	New Opportunities	High Pay-High Growth Jobs
IT is mission critical to almost all organizations and its importance is increasing.	Certifications verify your knowledge and skills that qualifies you for:	Competence is noticed and valued in organizations.	Certifications qualify you for new opportunities in your current job or when you want to change careers.	Hiring managers demand the strongest skill set.
• 79% of U.S. businesses report IT is either important or very important to the success of their company	• Jobs in the high growth IT career field • Increased compensation • Challenging assignments and promotions • 60% report that being certified is an employer or job requirement	• Increased knowledge of new or complex technologies • Enhanced productivity • More insightful problem solving • Better project management and communication skills • 47% report being certified helped improve their problem solving skills	• 31% report certification improved their career advancement opportunities	• There is a widening IT skills gap with over 300,000 jobs open • 88% report being certified enhanced their resume

Some of the primary benefits individuals report from becoming A+ certified are:

- More efficient troubleshooting
- Improved career advancement
- More insightful problem solving

Four steps to getting certified and staying certified

If you want to get certified and stay certified, follow these steps:

1. **Review exam objectives** Review the Certification objectives to make sure you know what is covered in the exam. Visit *http://www.comptia.org/certifications/testprep/examobjectives.aspx* for information.

2. **Practice for the exam** After you have studied for the certification, take a free assessment and sample test to get an idea of what type of questions might be on the exam. Go to *http://www.comptia.org/certifications/test prep/practicetests.aspx* for additional information.

3. **Purchase an exam voucher** Purchase exam vouchers on the CompTIA Marketplace, which is located at *www.comptiastore.com*.

4. **Take the test** Select a certification exam provider and schedule a time to take your exam. You can find exam providers at the following link: *http://www.comptia.org/certifications/testprep/testingcenters.aspx*.

Stay certified! Take advantage of continuing education

All new CompTIA A+ certifications will be valid for three years from the date the candidate is certified. After three years, those certifications must be renewed. For more information, go to *http://certification.comptia.org/getCertified/steps_to_certification/stayCertified.aspx*.

How to obtain more information

You can obtain more information about CompTIA in several ways:

- **Visit CompTIA online** Go to *www.comptia.org* to learn more about getting CompTIA certified.
- **Contact CompTIA** Call 866-835-8020 ext. 5 or email *questions@comptia.org*.
- **Join the IT Pro Community** Visit *http://itpro.comptia.org* to join the IT community and get relevant career information.
- Connect with us:
  - **LinkedIn** *http://www.linkedin.com/groups?home=&gid=83900*
  - **Facebook** *http://www.facebook.com/CompTIA*
  - **Twitter** *https://twitter.com/comptia*
  - **Flickr** *http://www.flickr.com/photos/comptia*
  - **YouTube** *http://www.youtube.com/user/CompTIATV*

Support & feedback

The following sections provide information about errata, book support, feedback, and contact information.

Errata

We've made every effort to ensure the accuracy of this book and its companion content. Any errors that have been reported since this book was published are listed on our Microsoft Press site at oreilly.com:

http://aka.ms/CompTIARapidReview/errata

If you find an error that is not already listed, you can report it to us through the same page.

If you need additional support, email Microsoft Press Book Support at *mspinput@microsoft.com*.

Please note that product support for Microsoft software is not offered through the addresses above.

We want to hear from you

At Microsoft Press, your satisfaction is our top priority, and your feedback our most valuable asset. Please tell us what you think of this book at:

http://www.microsoft.com/learning/booksurvey

The survey is short, and we read every one of your comments and ideas. Thanks in advance for your input!

Stay in touch

Let's keep the conversation going! We're on Twitter: *http://twitter.com/MicrosoftPress*.

Preparing for the exam

CompTIA certification exams are a great way to build your resume and let the world know about your level of expertise. Certification exams validate your on-the-job experience and product knowledge. Although there is no substitute for on-the-job experience, preparation through study and hands-on practice can help you prepare for the exam. We recommend that you augment your exam preparation plan by using a combination of available study materials and courses. For example, you might use the Rapid Review and another training kit for your "at home" preparation, and take a CompTIA professional certification course for the classroom experience. Choose the combination that you think works best for you.

CHAPTER 1

PC hardware

The Personal Computer (PC) Hardware domain covers approximately 40 percent of the A+ 220-801 exam. The first domain covers hardware components extensively and requires technicians to have a good understanding of computer hardware. This includes the motherboard, memory, expansion cards, disk and other storage media, the central processing unit (CPU), connection types, power supplies, monitors, and peripheral devices that connect to computers.

This chapter covers the following objectives:

- Objective 1.1: Configure and apply BIOS settings
- Objective 1.2: Differentiate between motherboard components, their purposes, and properties
- Objective 1.3: Compare and contrast RAM types and features
- Objective 1.4: Install and configure expansion cards
- Objective 1.5: Install and configure storage devices and use appropriate media
- Objective 1.6: Differentiate among various CPU types and features and select the appropriate cooling method
- Objective 1.7: Compare and contrast various connection interfaces and explain their purpose
- Objective 1.8: Install an appropriate power supply based on a given scenario
- Objective 1.9: Evaluate and select appropriate components for a custom configuration, to meet customer specifications or needs
- Objective 1.10: Given a scenario, evaluate types and features of display devices
- Objective 1.11: Identify connector types and associated cables
- Objective 1.12: Install and configure various peripheral devices

Objective 1.1: Configure and apply BIOS settings

The Basic Input/Output System (BIOS) is built into firmware in a computer and is the first code run when the computer starts. It provides information about what hardware is included in the system, and tests and initializes that hardware. The

BIOS also includes a program used to view and configure hardware settings. As a technician, you should know how to access the BIOS, view and manipulate the settings, and upgrade the BIOS (commonly called *flashing the BIOS*) when necessary.

Exam need to know...

- Install firmware upgrades—flash BIOS
  For example: When should the BIOS be upgraded? What is a significant risk related to flashing the BIOS?

- BIOS component information
  For example: How do you access the BIOS utility? What information can be obtained from a BIOS utility?

- BIOS configurations
  For example: What can be modified to overclock a CPU? What should be modified if a computer is unable to boot using a DVD?

- Use built-in diagnostics
  For example: What is the POST? What is the likely cause of a system that makes a buzzing sound when it's turned on?

- Monitoring
  For example: What is used to record when a computer case is opened? What is commonly reported in a BIOS monitoring tool?

Install firmware upgrades—flash BIOS

The BIOS is considered firmware because it includes software code that is embedded in a hardware chip. This software code sometimes needs to be upgraded by using a process referred to as *flashing the BIOS*.

True or false? Computers should be plugged into a UPS while flashing the BIOS.

Answer: *True.* If the computer loses power during the BIOS upgrade, it can corrupt the BIOS, but using an uninterruptible power supply (UPS) protects the system against an unexpected power loss.

The BIOS is needed to boot the system, so if it becomes corrupted due to a power failure during the upgrade process, the computer might no longer boot. Typically, the only repair options are to replace the motherboard or return the motherboard to the manufacturer.

BIOS manufacturers provide free software programs that are used to upgrade the BIOS. You can download the programs from their websites, and many BIOS upgrade programs can be started from within Windows. After running the program, the BIOS is upgraded and the computer is rebooted with the new BIOS installed.

> **EXAM TIP** The primary reason to flash the BIOS is to add a capability. For example, if the current version doesn't support virtualization but a newer version does support it, you can flash the BIOS to access virtualization capabilities. The computer should never be turned off during the flashing process, and plugging the computer into a UPS system prevents damage from an unplanned power outage.

BIOS component information

The BIOS includes information about components installed within the computer. You can look at this information to verify that your computer is recognizing installed hardware. If the computer doesn't recognize it, it might not be installed correctly or might be faulty.

True or false? The BIOS will show how much random access memory (RAM) is installed in a computer.

Answer: *True.* The BIOS includes information about installed hardware, including RAM, the CPU, hard drives, and optical drives.

Figure 1-1 shows a screen shot of BIOS on a computer. The main page lists disks and memory. Additional menu items can be selected to view other hardware and modify certain settings.

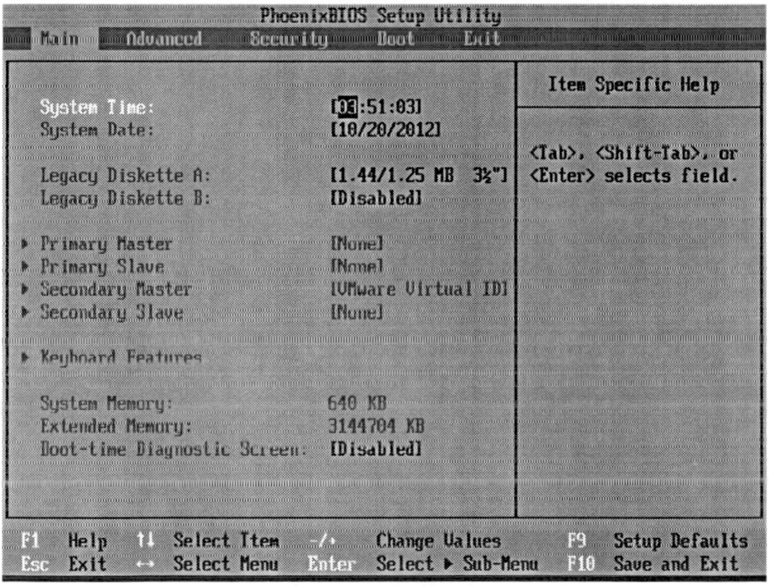

```
                    PhoenixBIOS Setup Utility
    Main      Advanced      Security      Boot      Exit

                                            |  Item Specific Help
    System Time:          [08:51:03]        |
    System Date:          [10/20/2012]      |
                                            |  <Tab>, <Shift-Tab>, or
    Legacy Diskette A:    [1.44/1.25 MB 3½"]|  <Enter> selects field.
    Legacy Diskette B:    [Disabled]        |

  ► Primary Master        [None]
  ► Primary Slave         [None]
  ► Secondary Master      [VMware Virtual ID]
  ► Secondary Slave       [None]

  ► Keyboard Features

    System Memory:        640 KB
    Extended Memory:      3144704 KB
    Boot-time Diagnostic Screen: [Disabled]


  F1   Help   ↑↓  Select Item   -/+    Change Values    F9   Setup Defaults
  Esc  Exit   ↔   Select Menu    Enter  Select ► Sub-Menu  F10  Save and Exit
```

FIGURE 1-1 BIOS screen showing basic hardware installed.

EXAM TIP The BIOS setup utility can be accessed by pressing a key or key combination when the computer is started. The key used to access BIOS is usually displayed during the boot cycle and is not the same on all computers. Some common keys or key combinations are as follows: F1, F2, F10, Del (delete key), or the Ctrl+Alt+Esc keys pressed at the same time. On some laptops, the key combination is the Fn+Esc keys or the Fn+F1 keys.

NOTE When technicians refer to BIOS, they are typically referring to one of two meanings. First, the BIOS is the startup program used during the boot process. Second, the BIOS is the utility program used to access and manipulate the settings. Both are correct. The BIOS is a software program contained within a hardware chip, so it is often referred to as firmware.

MORE INFO You can see pictures of BIOS displays and BIOS chips by searching on Bing.com/images using the search phrase "BIOS." Chapter 2 of the *CompTIA A+ Training Kit* (Exam 220-801 and Exam 220-802), ISBN-10: 0735662681, includes an extensive section on BIOS. It includes information about how to identify the current BIOS version by using the System Information tool (msinfo32) and a screen shot of a BIOS upgrade program during the flash process.

BIOS configurations

Many settings within the BIOS are configurable. As a technician, it's important that you know what can be configured and how to do so.

True or false? If a computer cannot boot from a bootable DVD-ROM disc, you can modify the BIOS to resolve the issue.

Answer: *True.* The boot sequence is an important setting within the BIOS and is used to determine what device the computer boots from first.

Computers can typically boot from a hard disk, an optical disc, the network interface card (NIC), a floppy disk (when installed), or a removable disk such as a Universal Serial Bus (USB) flash drive. When the computer is configured to boot to the hard disk first, other devices aren't checked. Even if the system is started with a bootable CD or DVD disc in the optical disc drive, the computer will boot to the hard disk. This is easily modifiable in the BIOS. Figure 1-2 shows the boot order screen from within a BIOS utility.

```
                    PhoenixBIOS Setup Utility
   Main     Advanced     Security     Boot     Exit

                                          Item Specific Help

  +Hard Drive
   CD-ROM Drive
  +Removable Devices                      Keys used to view or
   Network boot from Intel E1000          configure devices:
                                          <Enter> expands or
                                          collapses devices with
                                          a + or -
                                          <Ctrl+Enter> expands
                                          all
                                          <+> and <-> moves the
                                          device up or down.
                                          <n> May move removable
                                          device between Hard
                                          Disk or Removable Disk
                                          <d> Remove a device
                                          that is not installed.


  F1   Help    ↑↓ Select Item   -/+   Change Values    F9   Setup Defaults
  Esc  Exit    ↔  Select Menu   Enter Select ▶ Sub-Menu F10  Save and Exit
```

FIGURE 1-2 BIOS boot order.

EXAM TIP The boot order can be modified in any BIOS to cause a system to boot to a different device first. The computer will attempt to start by using each device in the list and will boot from the first device that has a bootable operating system. If you've never looked at the BIOS screens in your computer, now is the time. This is important for the exam and also on the job.

True or false? The graphics capability within a computer's motherboard can be disabled from the BIOS.

Answer: *True.* When a dedicated graphics card is added to a system, the onboard graphics capability should be disabled via the BIOS.

Most computers include many additional capabilities within the motherboard or the chipset on the motherboard. This includes graphics, USB controllers, FireWire (1394) controllers, audio, graphics, and network capabilities.

EXAM TIP Devices can be enabled or disabled by using the BIOS utility. For example, if an older USB 1.1 device needs to be used, you might need to enable the USB 1.1 hub in the BIOS. The most common reason to disable devices is when they cause a conflict with an added card. For example, the onboard sound capabilities should be disabled if a sound card is added.

True or false? If the clock is slow or keeps resetting, the CMOS battery should be replaced.

Answer: *True.* A common symptom of a failing battery is a slow clock.

The real-time clock in a computer keeps track of the current date and time. It is powered by the complementary metal oxide semiconductor (CMOS) battery when the computer is turned off, and if the battery is failing, the clock will either be slow or will reset to a default date/time.

NOTE In older computers, a CMOS chip was used to store settings and the BIOS held the firmware. However, most new computers do not have a CMOS chip. Instead, the CMOS settings are held in the same chip as the BIOS or sometimes in the same chip as the real-time clock. However, the term *CMOS* is still used. Today, it refers to the area where the configurable settings are stored.

EXAM TIP The CMOS battery is often used to provide power to memory used for configurable BIOS settings. If this battery is failing, the user might see errors related to the date and time or a slow clock. Additionally, if the battery is failing, the hardware settings for the computer will no longer be stored in the computer. The BIOS will be forced to rediscover the hardware each time the system is turned on, which might slow down boot times. After replacing the battery, settings return to the factory defaults and need to be reconfigured.

True or false? In some BIOS utilities, it's possible to manipulate the CPU to over-clock it.

Answer: *True*. Some BIOS utilities allow you to modify the clock speeds and over-clock the CPU.

Overclocking the CPU is done by modifying the crystal frequency, the multiplier, or the voltage used by the CPU. For example, a computer might have a 133-MHz clock with an x20 multiplier, resulting in a CPU speed of 2.66 GHz (133 × 20). This can be increased by modifying the clock to 140 MHz, resulting in a CPU speed of 2.8 GHz (140 × 20), or by changing the multiplier to 22, resulting in a CPU speed of 2.926 GHz (133 × 22), or even changing both, resulting in a CPU speed of 3.08 GHz (140 × 22). Similarly, increasing the CPU voltage causes the CPU to run faster.

EXAM TIP A CPU is sold based on its speed rating and has a guarantee that it will run at that speed. Running it faster by overclocking it is possible, but doing so will likely void the warranty and runs the risk of damaging the CPU from overheating. When a system is overclocked, additional steps need to be taken to keep the system cool.

MORE INFO PCPro has an informative article and tutorial showing how a BIOS can be overclocked. It includes several images of different BIOS screens that are modified when overclocking a system. You can access it here: *http://www.pcpro.co.uk/tutorials /367693/bios-guide-how-to-overclock-your-cpu*.

True or false? Computers that support hardware-assisted virtualization require a CPU that supports virtualization and a BIOS that supports virtualization.

Answer: *True*. Almost all CPUs shipped by Advanced Micro Devices (AMD) and Intel support virtualization.

MORE INFO Many CPUs include built-in support for hardware virtualization, and when available, it also needs to be enabled in the BIOS. The following page includes links to tools that you can use to see whether your system supports hardware virtualization and links to sample instructions to modify the BIOS for many computer manufacturers: *http://www.microsoft.com/windows/virtual-pc/support/configure-bios.aspx*.

True or false? You can restrict a user's ability to modify the BIOS by setting a password within the BIOS.

Answer: *True*. Most BIOS programs include the ability to set a password, which can be used to restrict access.

Some BIOS utilities include a single password, and some use two. A supervisor password unlocks full privileges to view and modify BIOS settings, while a basic user password gives the user only limited privileges. It's important to realize that these passwords can be bypassed by using a jumper on the motherboard. They restrict casual users but do not provide strong security. Anyone with a little knowledge can bypass them. Other security elements within some BIOS programs include the following:

- **Drive encryption**   Systems that include a Trusted Platform Module (TPM) can be enabled within the BIOS to encrypt the hard drive. Windows-based systems use a TPM with BitLocker to encrypt partitions.
- **LoJack for laptops**   Some laptops include LoJack for laptops. If available and enabled, it can be used to locate a stolen laptop.

EXAM TIP BIOS passwords can restrict access to a computer's BIOS. A supervisor's BIOS password can be set to prevent users from locking out an administrator from the BIOS.

Use built-in diagnostics

BIOS programs include built-in diagnostics that perform a power-on self-test (POST). POST will check the CPU, clock, RAM, graphics, the keyboard, and BIOS to ensure that they are installed and operational. If the computer passes POST, it continues to boot. If it fails POST, the boot process stops. Technicians refer to this as a computer that "does not POST."

True or false? A successful POST will always finish with two single beeps.

Answer: *False*. BIOS programs commonly use a single beep to indicate that POST completed without any errors.

Most systems also display a message on the screen when they fail POST. Of course, some failures prevent the computer from even displaying a message. The following two beep errors are common:

- **Continuous beeping**   This is a clear indication of a hardware problem and often indicates a problem with the motherboard or power supply.
- **Buzzing sound from quickly repeating beeps**   This usually indicates a problem with RAM.

Many BIOS programs also include additional diagnostics that can be used to check some hardware. The most common diagnostic is one that will check memory.

Monitoring

It's also common for a BIOS to have monitoring capabilities. These are used to monitor the health of the system based on the operations of the temperature, fan operation, and voltages, and they can also be used for basic security.

True or false? A biased switch is used with some computers to record when a case has been opened.

Answer: *True.* A biased switch is in the closed position when the case is closed, but it will record when the case has been opened.

An intrusion detection/notification or similar option can be enabled in the BIOS. This works with the biased switch and will record when a case has been opened after receiving the message from the switch. When recorded, the BIOS will report the event each time the computer is started until it is reset. Some other monitoring capabilities available with many systems include the following:

- **Temperature monitoring** This shows the current temperature and will commonly include the temperature inside the case and the temperature of the CPU. Some applications can read this data from the BIOS when the computer is booted into an operating system.

- **Fan speeds** These can be reported as the actual rounds per minute (RPM) or as a percentage of a fan's total speed capability. In addition to monitoring these speeds, you can sometimes manually configure the fan speeds through the BIOS.

- **Voltage** Important voltages to monitor are 3.3 V, 5 V, and 12 V. Many BIOS utilities also report the voltage used by the CPU reported as the CPU Vcore voltage.

- **Clock** While a clock is often listed as 100 MHz, 133 MHz, or something similar, it rarely runs at exactly this speed. The monitoring tool shows the actual speed.

- **Bus speed** The bus speed is a combination of the clock speed and the multiplier. It's common to list the CPU speed and the memory speed. Both use the same base clock but different multipliers.

Figure 1-3 shows the monitoring page from a BIOS utility. The intrusion detection/notification setting is labeled as Chassis Intrusion.

```
   CMOS Setup Utility - Copyright (C) 1985-2005, American Megatrends, Inc.
                              H/W Monitor

   Chassis Intrusion              [Disabled]              Help Item
   CPU Smart FAN Target           [55]
   CPU Min.FAN Speed (%)          [50]              Chassis Intrusion
   SYS FAN 1 Control              [100%]            function
   SYS FAN 2 Control              [100%]


              ----- PC Health Status -----
   CPU Temperature                56"C/132"F
   System Temperature             34"C/93"F
   CPU FAN Speed                  1516 RPM
   SYS FAN 1 Speed                2242 RPM
   SYS FAN 2 Speed                0 RPM
   CPU Vcore                      1.120 V
   3.3V                           3.360 V
   5V                             5.003 V
   12V                            11.880 V


   ↑↓→←:Move   Enter:Select   +/-/:Value  F10:Save  ESC:Exit  F1:General Help
   F4: CPU Spec   F5:Memory-Z   F8:Fail-Safe Defaults   F6:Optimized Defaults
```

FIGURE 1-3 BIOS monitoring page.

EXAM TIP The BIOS monitoring program allows you to monitor temperatures, fan speeds, and voltages used within the computer. Fans are often dynamically controlled to speed up as the heat increases, but they can also be set to run at a specific speed.

Can you answer these questions?

You can find the answers to these questions at the end of this chapter.

1. What should be done before flashing the BIOS to protect the computer from damage?

2. A technician installed RAM in a computer, but it isn't recognized in Windows. What can the technician use to see whether the computer recognizes the new memory?

3. What should be modified if a computer cannot boot using a known-good DVD?

4. What elements are commonly checked by POST?

Objective 1.2: Differentiate between motherboard components, their purposes, and properties

The motherboard is a central computer component, and technicians need to be able to differentiate between different components on the motherboard. Motherboards come in different sizes and support different components, such as expansion slots, RAM slots, and CPU sockets. They also have a variety of jumpers and connectors that technicians need to recognize and understand.

Exam need to know...

- Sizes
  For example: What type of case can a mini-ATX motherboard fit into? What are some common ITX-based motherboard types?

- Expansion slots
  For example: What are expansion slots used for in a computer? Are PCIe and PCI-X compatible with other?

- RAM slots
  For example: What is a formal name for a RAM stick? What type of RAM socket is used in a laptop?

- CPU sockets
  For example: What is the difference between PGA and LGA? What is used to secure a CPU in its socket?

- Chipsets
  For example: What is the difference between the north bridge and south bridge? Where is the north bridge on new systems?

- Jumpers
  For example: What types of jumpers are commonly found on motherboards? How can you connect pins if you don't have a jumper?

- Power connections and types
  For example: How many pins are in the P1 power connector? How many pins are in a typical CPU power connector?

- Fan connectors
  For example: How many pins will a fan connector include?

- Front panel connectors
  For example: What are some common connectors found at the front panel of a computer?

- Bus speeds
  For example: How does the speed of a bus impact the speed of PCIe devices?

Sizes

Motherboards come in different sizes but still follow basic standards so that they can be used in different computer cases. The two primary standard families are the Advanced Technology Extended (ATX) public standards and the ITX standards used primarily by VIA Technologies. ITX is not an acronym but instead is used as a name.

True or false? ATX-based motherboards are commonly used in desktop computers.

Answer: *True.* Advanced Technology Extended (ATX)–based motherboards are used in most desktop computers. They are based on the original AT motherboards and have been steadily improved and upgraded over the years.

The micro-ATX (also called mATX or µATX) is a smaller version of the ATX but will still fit in any ATX case and uses the same power connections. The mini-ITX, nano-ITX, and pico-ITX are the most commonly used ITX-based motherboards. Table 1-1 compares their sizes.

TABLE 1-1 Motherboard sizes

MOTHERBOARD TYPE	SIZE
ATX	12 × 9.6 in (305 × 244 mm)
Micro-ATX	6.75 × 6.75 in to 9.6 × 9.6 in (171.45 × 171.45 mm to 244 × 244 mm)
Mini-ITX	6.7 × 6.7 in (17 × 17 cm)
Nano-ITX	4.7 × 4.7 in (120 × 120 mm)
Pico-ITX	3.9 × 2.8 in (7.2 × 10 mm)

EXAM TIP The ATX motherboard is a standard size, but the micro-ATX motherboard size varies. However, both still follow the ATX standard and can be powered by similar power supplies. A micro-ATX motherboard can fit in an ATX case. ITX-based motherboards come in a variety of different sizes, and many are used in smaller devices.

MORE INFO The Wikipedia article on computer form factors (*http://en.wikipedia .org/wiki/Computer_form_factor*) includes some good drawings and pictures showing the different form factors side by side. Also, VIA Technologies has an extensive list of resources available on the different ITX-based motherboards here: *http://www.via .com.tw/en/initiatives/spearhead/mini-itx/.*

Expansion slots

Motherboards include many built in capabilities, and these can be expanded by adding additional cards. The types of cards that a motherboard supports are dependent on the expansion slots it includes.

True or false? PCI X is an upgrade to PCIe.

Answer: *False.* Peripheral Component Interconnect-Extended (PCI-X) is an upgrade to PCI, not PCI Express (PCIe).

PCI-X is backward compatible to PCI and is most commonly used in servers. That is, you can insert a PCI-X card into a PCI or a PCI-X slot. PCIe is a newer standard than PCI and PCI-X, and it is not backward compatible with these standards. That is, you cannot plug a PCIe card into a PCI or PCI-X slot.

True or false? You can plug a PCIe x2 card into a PCIe x4 slot.

Answer: *True.* You can plug smaller PCIe cards into larger PCIe slots.

The PCIe multiplier indicates how many two-way lanes are supported by a PCIe card or slot. Cards with more lanes are larger and require larger slots. Smaller cards can still plug into a larger slot—they just won't use all of the lanes available in the card. PCIe sizes include PCIe, PCIe x2, PCIe x4, PCIe x8, PCIe x16, and PCIe x32.

Mini-PCI and mini-PCIe cards are used in laptops. You cannot install these cards into a standard PCI or PCIe slot.

True or false? AGP slots are used for dedicated graphics cards.

Answer: *True.* Accelerated Graphics Port (AGP) is a dedicated expansion slot used for graphics cards.

AGP cards and slots have been largely replaced by PCIe cards in current systems. When available, they were steadily improved from AGP to AGP 2X, AGP 4X, and AGP 8X.

A Communications and Networking Riser (CNR) expansion card is used in some systems. These are smaller and are designed to accept an audio, modem, or network interface card (NIC) installed by the manufacturer.

RAM slots

Random access memory (RAM) circuit boards (also called memory sticks) plug into available RAM slots on the motherboard. A motherboard will typically have at least two RAM slots, and some have as many as six.

True or false? A motherboard used for a desktop system will include DIMM slots used for RAM.

Answer: *True.* Dual in-line memory modules (DIMMs) are memory sticks that plug into RAM slots.

A DIMM includes integrated circuit (IC) memory chips. In contrast, laptops use small outline DIMMs (SODIMMs), which also hold memory chips but are smaller than a normal DIMM and cannot fit into a DIMM slot.

RAM sticks use Synchronous Dynamic RAM (SDRAM) and come in three primary double data rate (DDR) versions (DDR, DDR2, and DDR3), and none of the versions are compatible with each other. An important consideration when replacing RAM is ensuring that the memory stick matches the RAM slot. Different DIMMs have a different number of pins, as shown in the following list:

- DDR DIMM: 184 pins
- DDR2 DIMM: 240 pins

- DDR3 DIMM: 240 pins
- DDR SODIMM: 200 pins
- DDR2 SODIMM: 144 pins or 200 pins
- DDR3 SODIMM: 204 pins

EXAM TIP Ensure that you know the number of pins used in different DDR types, especially for DDR3 DIMMs (240 pins) and DDR3 SODIMM (204 pins). DDR versions are not compatible with each other, and you cannot use SODIMMs in a desktop computer or traditional DIMMs in a laptop computer.

MORE INFO RAM types and their features are covered more extensively later in this chapter in Objective 1.3, "Compare and contrast RAM types and features."

CPU sockets

Central processing units (CPUs) plug into a CPU socket. The CPU is replaceable on most motherboards, but there are different socket types. When replacing a CPU, you need to ensure that you have a CPU that can fit into the existing socket. The two primary CPU manufacturers are Intel and Advanced Micro Devices (AMD), and their sockets are not compatible with each other.

True or false? Many current Intel CPUs use a land grid array (LGA)–based socket that doesn't include pin holes.

Answer: *True*. LGA sockets have small pins created as bumps or pads.

The matching Intel CPUs have identical bumps that line up with the bumps in the socket. This creates a strong electrical connection when the CPU is installed. Some other sockets use pin grid array (PGA), where pins on the CPU line up with holes in the socket. A ball grid array (BGA) chip uses balls of solder instead of pins or bumps. The CPU is mounted in the socket and heated to melt the solder balls and hold the CPU in place.

True or false? CPUs are locked into place with a ZIF socket or a flip top case.

Answer: *True*. Sockets commonly use either a zero insertion force (ZIF) socket or a flip top case. Both methods lock the CPU in place.

EXAM TIP Ensure that you understand the difference between PGA, LGA, and BGA when preparing for the exam. All CPUs are locked into place by some method, such as use of a ZIF socket or a flip top case.

MORE INFO CPU socket types are covered more extensively later in this chapter in Objective 1.6, "Differentiate among various CPU types and features and select the appropriate cooling method." Additionally, Chapter 3 of the CompTIA A+ Training Kit (Exam 220-801 and Exam 220-802), ISBN-10: 0735662681, includes some pictures and diagrams of sockets.

Chipsets

Motherboards include a chipset used as an interface between the CPU and the rest of the computer. These chipsets are one or more ICs and include additional capabilities such as audio, network, or USB interfaces. A chipset is designed to work with a specific family of CPUs.

True or false? The functionality of the north bridge is included on the CPU in most systems today.

Answer: *True.* Older chipsets included a north bridge and a south bridge, but most new CPUs include the north bridge functionality today.

The north bridge (also called the memory controller hub or MCH) provides the primary interface between the CPU and high-speed devices, such as RAM and a dedicated graphics card when it is used. The south bridge (also called the I/O controller hub or ICH) provides an interface to everything else.

When a north bridge is used, the bus between the CPU and the north bridge is called the front side bus. The bus between the north bridge and the south bridge is the internal bus (internal to the chipset). Figure 1-4 shows how this is laid out.

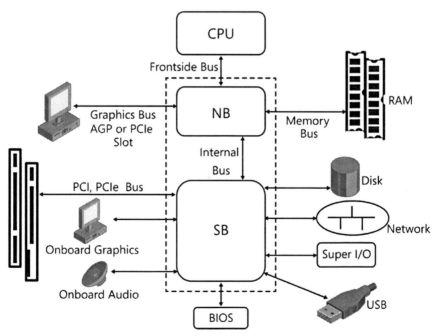

FIGURE 1-4 CPU using a chipset with a north bridge and a south bridge.

When the CPU includes the north bridge, it interacts directly with the RAM, the PCIe graphics card, and uses a direct memory interface (DMI) connection to the chipset. Figure 1-5 shows how this looks.

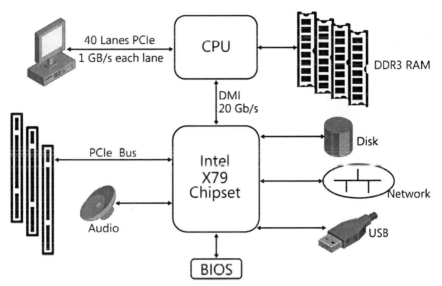

FIGURE 1-5 Chipset with the north bridge functionality included with CPU.

True or false? If a computer indicates that the date and time need to be reset each time the computer is turned on, replace the CMOS battery.

Answer: *True.* The CMOS battery powers the real-time clock when the computer is turned off, and this error indicates that the battery is faulty.

Check the CMOS battery if you find that the clock is running slow, CMOS settings are being reset, or the system is reporting CMOS errors. The CMOS battery is often circular, like a watch battery, but some motherboards use a barrel shaped battery similar to an AA battery though much smaller. In some chipsets, the real-time clock is integrated into the chipset. When the clock is in the chipset, these settings can also be stored there.

Jumpers

Motherboards include one or more jumpers used for different purposes. A jumper provides an electrical connection between two pins, also known as *shorting the connection*, because it creates an electrical short.

True or false? You can normally reset the BIOS password by connecting a jumper on the motherboard.

Answer: *True.* If the BIOS password has been reset or is not known, you can often reset it by connecting pins on the motherboard with a jumper.

In addition to pins for a BIOS jumper, motherboards commonly have pins that you can short to clear all the CMOS settings. This returns them to their factory defaults.

EXAM TIP You can also reset the BIOS password by shorting the two pins with any piece of metal, such as a screwdriver. This creates the same electrical short as the jumper. Before doing this, you should ensure that the computer is turned off and unplugged to prevent any damage.

Power connections and types

A computer power supply converts higher-voltage alternating current (AC) provided from a commercial power source to lower-voltage direct current (DC) needed by the computer. The power supply includes multiple cables with specific types of connections that plug into different computer components.

True or false? A 6+2 pin connector from the power supply plugs into an 8-pin port on the motherboard to provide power to PCIe components.

Answer: *True.* This might be provided as a single 8-pin connector or a 6+2 connector. Older systems used only 6 pins, so the 6+2 connector can be plugged into an older system.

In addition to the PCIe power connector, motherboards will have the following power connectors:

- **P1** This provides the primary power to the motherboard. It's rectangular, with two rows of pins, and comes in both 20-pin and 24-pin versions. It provides 3.3, 5, and 12 VDC to the motherboard.

- **Secondary motherboard power** This is a 4-pin connector used to provide 12-V power to the motherboard. Systems with multiple CPUs often use two 4-pin connectors (or an 8-pin connector) to provide power to the CPUs.

EXAM TIP Ensure that you know what type of power is provided to the motherboard (3.3, 5, 12 VDC) and the power connectors commonly found on a motherboard.

MORE INFO You can view a listing of the specific voltages provided on the different pins from a standard ATX-based power supply from the following page: *http://en.wikipedia.org/wiki/ATX12V*.

Fan connectors

Computers are kept cool with fans, and most fans plug directly into the motherboard. While it's rare, some fans plug directly into a power supply connector either directly or with an adapter.

True or false? A CPU fan will plug into a connector near the CPU.

Answer: *True.* Most CPUs require a fan to keep them cool, and these plug into a connector very close to the CPU.

Fan connectors are typically simple 2-pin, 3-pin, or 4-pin connectors. A 2-pin connector provides ground and 12 VDC power. A 3-pin connector adds a sensor to report the RPM of the fan. A 4-pin connector adds a pulse-width modulation (PWM) signal to vary the speed of the fan.

> **EXAM TIP** You can plug a 3-pin fan into a 4-pin connector. It should be plugged in so that the PWM signal is not used. It will still work and report the correct speed of the fan, but it will no longer function as a variable speed fan.

Front panel connectors

Several connectors go from the motherboard to the front panel. These are used for different purposes and will vary from computer to computer.

True or false? If the front panel light emitting diode (LED) is not lit, the computer does not have any power applied.

Answer: *False.* The LED indicates whether the computer is turned on. However, if the computer is plugged in but not turned on, the LED is not lit but the motherboard has power applied to it.

The front panel power button is connected to the motherboard, and when pressed, it causes the motherboard to provide full power to the computer. Some other front panel connectors on the motherboard include the following:

- **USB connectors** Most computers have one or more USB connectors at the front in addition to the rear of the computer.
- **Audio connectors** These accept tip ring sleeve (TRS) connections for headphones and/or microphones.
- **Drive activity LED** This flashes when the hard drive is reading or writing data.
- **Reset button** Pressing this button causes the system to restart. In contrast, pressing the power button causes the system to power down but not restart.

> **EXAM TIP** You should be familiar with the common connectors and indicators found on any computer and realize that these are connected to the motherboard. When replacing a motherboard, these need to be reinstalled correctly to ensure that they work just as they did before replacing the motherboard.

Bus speeds

The speeds of the different buses within a computer determine how fast the computer operates. These are important for technicians to understand when shopping for a computer and also when replacing components.

True or false? The speed of a bus provides a direct indication of how much data can be transferred over the bus.

Answer: *True.* Faster bus speeds transfer more data in the same time frame, often rated in megabytes per second (MB/s)

Many expansion card slots use a crystal, which provides a constant sine wave at a steady frequency. The rate of the sine wave is expressed as Hertz (such as MHz) and determines the data rate of the bus. Table 1-2 lists some common speeds and data rates of many expansion slot standards.

TABLE 1-2 Expansion card bus speeds

BUS	BUS SPEED	DATA RATES
PCI (32-bit)	33 and 66 MHz	133 and 266 MB/s
PCI (64-bit)	33 and 66 MHz	266 and 533 MB/s
PCI-X	66, 133, 266, and 533 MHz	533 and 1,064 MB/s, 2.15 and 4.3 GB/s
AGP (2X, 4X, 8X)	66 MHZ	266, 533, 1,066, and 2,133 MB/s

True or false? PCIe transmits data as a continuous stream of data without a clock.

Answer: *True.* PCIe isn't tied to a data clock.

PCIe uses multiple two-way lanes to send data. The number of lanes is identified with an x identifier. For example, PCIe x2 uses two lanes, PCIe x4 uses four lanes, and so on. PCIe standards include PCIe, PXIe x2, PXIe x4, PXIe x8, PXIe x16, and PXIe x32.

> **MORE INFO** The speed of the RAM and the CPU is directly related to the crystal used for the CPU and RAM. These speeds are covered in Objective 1.3 and Objective 1.6 later in this chapter.

Can you answer these questions?

You can find the answers to these questions at the end of this chapter.

1. What type of power supply is required for a mini-ATX motherboard?
2. Can you plug a PCIe x8 card into a PCIe x4 slot?
3. How many pins are in a DDR3 DIMM socket?
4. What does the CPU interact with directly when it includes north bridge functionality?

5. What can you use to reset the BIOS password?

6. What does the P1 power connector look like?

7. What is the difference between a 3-pin fan connector and a 4-pin fan connector?

Objective 1.3: Compare and contrast RAM types and features

A common task that PC technicians perform is upgrading the RAM in a computer. For example, a computer might have 2 GB of RAM, but a user wants to upgrade it to 4 GB of RAM or more. PC technicians need to know the different terminologies used with RAM so that they purchase the correct type. Additionally, they need to understand the features so that they don't spend extra money for RAM features that aren't needed.

Exam need to know...

- Types
  For example: What is the difference between DIMM, SODIMM, and RAMBUS? What is the difference between single-channel and dual-channel RAM?
- RAM compatibility and speed
  For example: What speed will RAM operate at if the speeds are mixed? What is the speed of the bus in a PC3-12800 memory stick?

Types

The primary type of random access memory (RAM) used in computers is Synchronous Dynamic RAM (SDRAM). It called synchronous because it operates with a clock, and the speed of the clock is the primary factor in the speed of the RAM. DDR, DDR2, and DDR3 are all types of SDRAM.

True or false? Double Data Rate 3 (DDR3) RAM uses double-pumping and is four times as fast as DDR.

Answer: *True.* DDR, DDR2, and DDR3 all use double-pumping. DDR2 is twice the speed of DDR, and DDR3 is twice the speed of DDR2 (or four times the speed of DDR). Double-pumping refers to using both the leading edge and the trailing edge of the clock, as shown in Figure 1-6.

Using Only The Leading Edge

Using Leading and Trailing Edge

FIGURE 1-6 Doubling the clock speed.

As mentioned earlier, RAM sticks come in DIMM versions for desktop computers and SODIMM versions for laptops. A less-used version is called RAMBUS. RAMBUS memory is easy to identify because it has a heavy metal covering over the ICs. This metal covering acts as a heat sink to dissipate the heat generated from RAMBUS sticks.

True or false? RAM labeled as using parity and ECC should be used whenever possible for desktop systems.

Answer: *False.* Memory that includes parity can detect errors, and memory that includes error correction code (ECC) features can detect and correct memory errors, but they are not needed in desktop systems.

RAM with parity includes an extra bit for each byte of RAM. This extra bit is used to detect errors but it adds to the cost of the RAM. Non-parity uses only eight bits for each byte of RAM making it less expensive, but it cannot detect errors.

RAM with ECC includes extra circuitry that can both detect and correct errors with RAM. This extra circuitry adds to the cost of the RAM. Non-ECC RAM does not include the extra circuitry and is less expensive.

Most applications and operating systems include software routines that can detect and correct some memory errors. The added cost for these features is not justified in desktop systems. However, these features are sometimes used in high-end servers.

EXAM TIP Parity and ECC memory improve the reliability of RAM. Parity memory adds an additional bit for every byte requiring more hardware for the same amount of RAM. ECC includes additional circuitry to detect and correct errors, and the additional circuitry adds to the cost. These features are often used in high-end financial servers and servers used in scientific applications but are not needed in desktop systems.

True or false? When installing RAM for a dual-channel system, the RAM should be purchased as a matched set and installed in the same bank.

Answer: *True.* Dual-channel RAM uses two slots combined as a single bank, and it should be purchased as a matched set for the best performance.

It's important to understand the following basic terminology when referring to single-, dual-, and triple-channel RAM:

- A slot is the physical slot in the motherboard. A DIMM plugs into the slot.
- A channel is a 64-bit communication path.
- A bank is used in dual-channel and triple-channel RAM and is composed of multiple channels.
- Dual-channel RAM has a bank of two channels and is 128 bits wide.
- Triple-channel RAM has a bank of three channels and is 192 bits wide.

When installing dual-channel or triple-channel RAM into a system, ensure that you use matched sets and install the matched set into the same bank. If the set isn't matched, the system will still operate but will use the slower speed. In some cases, the system will revert to single-channel RAM, being even slower. Also, the sticks in the bank should be the same size. If you install a 1-GB stick in one channel and a 2-GB stick in the other channel, it will operate as single-channel RAM or possibly not at all.

True or false? When installing two matched RAM sticks into a dual-channel motherboard, they should be installed in different color slots.

Answer: *False.* Dual-channel matched RAM should be installed in the same bank, and banks are identified by slots of the same color.

Figure 1-7 shows the layout of dual-channel RAM slots on Intel and many AMD motherboards. The Intel motherboard has bank 0 (B0) as slots 1 and 3 (S1 and S3), and these slots are blue. In contrast, AMD is using slots 1 and 2 for bank 0. Intel is using black slots 2 and 4 for bank 1 (B1), but AMD is using black slots 3 and 4 for bank 1.

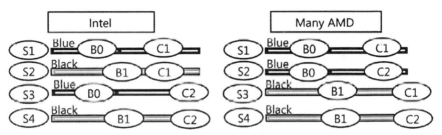

FIGURE 1-7 Identifying banks and channels based on slot colors.

Imagine two scenarios. In the first, the technician correctly plugs the two matched RAM sticks into the blue slots 1 and 3 of the Intel motherboard. The RAM will use channel 1 of bank 0 and channel 2 of bank 0 and perform optimally.

In the second scenario, the technician incorrectly plugs the RAM sticks into the blue slot 1 and the black slot 2. The computer will use channel 1 of bank 0 and channel 1 of bank 1. While the computer can access the RAM, it can't access 128 bits at a time through a single channel, and the computer will be slower.

Slots in the same bank will be the same color but won't necessarily be in the same order in different motherboards. They might be slots 1 and 3 on one motherboard, and they might be slots 1 and 2 on another motherboard. Dual-channel RAM should be plugged into the same bank.

True or false? Double-sided RAM has RAM separated into two groups called ranks, and the computer accesses only one rank at a time.

Answer: *True*. Double-sided means that the DIMM has two ranks.

The computer can access only one rank at a time. When it needs to access the second rank, it has to switch to the next rank. Double-sided RAM is slower than single-sided RAM (which uses a single rank) because the switching between ranks takes time.

A common misconception is that double-sided means that chips are on both sides of the DIMM, and single-sided means that the chips are only on one side. This is true in some cases, but the technical definition of dual-sided RAM is related to the ranks, not to the physical layout.

EXAM TIP Single-sided RAM uses a single rank and is faster than double-sided RAM.

RAM compatibility and speed

An important consideration when purchasing RAM is ensuring that you purchase the right RAM for your system. As mentioned previously, different DDR versions come in different configurations. They are not interchangeable, so if your computer has DDR3 slots, you can plug in only DDR3 RAM.

True or false? If you install a 1,333-MHz DDR3 RAM stick with a 1,600-MHz DDR3 RAM stick, the RAM will operate at 1,600 MHz.

Answer: *False*. Both RAM sticks will operate at the slower speed of 1,333 MHz, not the faster speed.

Also, the RAM will operate only as fast as the clock within the computer. If the computer has a 1,066-Mhz clock with the same two sticks of DDR3 RAM (1,333 MHz and 1,600 MHz), each stick will operate at 1,066 MHz.

Similarly, if a computer supports PC3-12800 RAM (using a 200-MHz clock) but you purchase PC3-6400 RAM (using a 100-MHz clock), the RAM will run at the slower speed of the PC3-6400 RAM stick.

EXAM TIP If your computer has a fast clock but you install slow RAM, the RAM will operate at the slower speed. If your computer has a slow clock but you install fast RAM, it will also operate at the slower speed. The slowest speed will be the limiting speed.

True or false? A system with a 200-MHz clock used for SDRAM requires a PC3-12800 memory stick.

Answer: *True*. DDR3 using a 200-MHz clock has a module name of PC3-12800 and a standard name of DDR3-1600.

The DDR module name always starts with PC and uses 2 for DDR2 (as PC2) or 3 for DDR3 (for PC3). The formula identifies how many bytes per second (B/s) that the RAM can process. The formula for each of the DDR module names is based on the double pumping (DP) of DDR and the clock multiplier (Clk Mult) used within the memory. DDR uses 64-bit channels, so it multiplies this by 64 and then divides it by 8 to convert the result to bytes. The following formulas apply for each of the DDR module names:

- **DDR** Clock × 2 (DP) × 64 (bits) / 8 (bytes)
- **DDR2** Clock × 2 (DP) × 2 (DDR2 Clk Mult) × 64 (bits) / 8 (bytes)
- **DDR3** Clock × 2 (DP) × 4 (DDR3 Clk Mult) × 64 (bits) / 8 (bytes)

With a 200-MHZ clock, the formula for a DDR3 module name is as follows:

- 200 × 2 × 4 × 64 / 8 = 12,800 MB/s
- 12,800 MB/s = DDR3 module name of PC3-12800 with 200 MHz clock

Notice that each formula uses 64 / 8. This always equals 8, so you can simplify the formula by just multiplying by 8, as follows:

- **DDR** Clock × 2 (DP) × 8
- **DDR2** Clock × 2 (DP) × 2 (DDR2 Clk Mult) × 8
- **DDR3** Clock × 2 (DP) × 4 (DDR3 Clk Mult) × 8

EXAM TIP You should be able to identify the DDR3 module name based on the clock. The basic formulas are as follows: DDR = Clock × 2 × 8, DDR2 = Clock × 4 × 8, DDR3 = Clock × 8 × 8. DDR and DDR2 exist in some older computers, but new computers use DDR3.

The DDR standard name starts with the DDR type (DDR, DDR2, or DDR3) followed by a dash and a number, such as DDR3-1600. The formula for each of the DDR standard names is based on the double pumping (DP) of DDR and the clock multiplier (Clk Mult) used within the memory, as follows:

- **DDR** Clock × 2 (DP)
- **DDR2** Clock × 2 (DP) × 2 (DDR2 Clk Mult)
- **DDR3** Clock × 2 (DP) × 4 (DDR3 Clk Mult)

With a 200-MHZ clock, the formula to identify a DDR3 standard name is as follows:

- 200 × 2 × 4 = 1,600
- 1,600 = DDR3 standard name of DDR3-1600 with 200 MHz clock

EXAM TIP You should be able to identify the DDR3 standard name based on the clock. A simpler method is to remember that DDR doubles the clock, DDR2 multiplies the clock times 4, and DDR3 multiplies the clock times 8. That is, the basic formulas are as follows: DDR = clock × 2, DDR3 = clock × 4, DDR4 = clock × 8.

True or false? You can install DDR3 in a DDR2 slot, but it will operate at the DDR2 speed.

Answer: *False*. DDR2 and DDR3 are not compatible, and it is not possible to install a DDR2 stick in a DDR3 slot or vice versa.

Can you answer these questions?

You can find the answers to these questions at the end of this chapter.

1. Where should you install a matched pair of RAM in a dual-channel motherboard?

2. What is the standard name and module name for a DDR3 RAM stick that uses a 400-MHz clock?

Objective 1.4: Install and configure expansion cards

You can add capabilities to most computers by adding expansion cards. For example, if a computer has a basic speaker, you can add an extensive sound system by adding a sound card. As a PC technician, you need to have a good understanding of the different types of expansion cards that are available and what is needed to install them. Many of the same concepts apply to all cards, but some cards have some special considerations.

Exam need to know...

- Sound cards
  For example: What cables need to be checked when adding a sound card?
- Video cards
  For example: What should be checked before adding a new video card to a system?
- Network cards
  For example: What is the benefit of adding a network card?
- Serial and parallel cards
  For example: What is the logical name of a parallel port?
- USB and FireWire cards
  For example: How can you clean contacts on expansion cards?
- Storage cards
  For example: What else needs to be done after adding a SATA card for a bootable disk?
- Modem cards
  For example: What type of connections are used with a modem?
- Wireless/cellular cards
  For example: What type of wireless cards are used in laptops?
- TV tuner cards
  For example: What is needed for a user to record one channel while watching another channel?
- Video capture cards
  For example: What is the purpose of a video capture card?
- Riser cards
  For example: What is the purpose of a riser card?

Sound cards

Users sometimes add sound cards to systems to improve the sound capabilities. Computers commonly come with some type of audio, but sound cards can improve it with 3.1, 5.1, and 7.1 sound systems.

> **MORE INFO** In x.1 sound systems, the number (3, 5, or 7) indicates how many speakers it uses and the .1 indicates that it's using a subwoofer. Later in this chapter, Objective 1.12, "Install and configure various peripheral devices," covers connecting the sound systems.

True or false? When adding a sound card to a system with onboard sound capabilities, you need to disable the onboard sound card in the BIOS.

Answer: *True*. The onboard device must be disabled to prevent conflicts.

The system won't work properly with two sound systems trying to play audio at the same time. The new sound card might not work properly or might not work at all.

This is also true for some other types of expansion cards, but there are some instances where you can use both devices. For example, if you add an additional USB card, you can use it along with existing USB connections.

Additionally, when adding any type of expansion card, ensure that you have up-to-date drivers for the new card.

> **EXAM TIP** When adding a sound card, ensure that existing sound card capabilities are disabled in the BIOS. Additionally, you need to ensure that any existing sound connections going to the front panel are connected to the new sound card. For example, many systems have a headphone jack at the front panel, and this should be connected to the new sound card.

Video cards

Video graphics continuously get better and better, and gamers often want the best video cards on the market. With that in mind, video cards are often added to systems even though chipsets commonly include good graphics capabilities.

True or false? Adding a video card can stop the computer from booting due to the extra draw on the power supply.

Answer: *True*. Video cards include powerful processors and onboard RAM and can draw a lot of power. If the power supply is already close to maximum capacity, adding a video card can stop the computer from booting.

Video cards include a powerful graphics processing unit (GPU) that draws as much power as a CPU. If the power supply is already close to capacity, this can actually stop the computer from booting.

Power for PCIe graphics card is provided by a 6-pin power connector from the power supply. In some power supplies, this is provided with a 6+2 power connector or an 8-pin power connector.

EXAM TIP When adding any expansion card, you should ensure that the power supply can handle the extra load and also ensure that you have an available expansion slot for the bus type of the card. For example, many graphics cards are PCIe x16, requiring an open PCIe x16 bus slot.

True or false? The best source for troubleshooting information about a new video card is the manufacturer.

Answer: *True*. If a new video card is not working correctly after installation, the manufacturer's website should be checked.

It's common for issues to be discovered after the card is released. The manufacturer will usually have addressed these issues, and they can commonly be corrected with a new driver. Of course, you should also ensure that you followed the procedures specified in the manual accompanying the new card for proper installation.

EXAM TIP In addition to drawing a lot of power, video cards also generate a lot of heat. Video cards often have at least a heat sink over the GPU, and many also have a fan over the heat sink. When installing the video card, you need to find an open slot with enough space to accommodate the extra components. It's also important to ensure that the system has adequate ventilation. Ensure that you check the manufacturer's website for the most up-to-date drivers.

MORE INFO You can view a listing of current video cards on *www.tigerdirect.com* by searching for "video cards." Chapter 6 of the CompTIA A+ Training Kit (Exam 220-801 and Exam 220-802), ISBN-10: 0735662681, covers video cards and display devices in depth and includes pictures of video cards.

True or false? When installing a video card, you rarely need to update the drivers.

Answer: *False*. Video cards are often at the leading edge of technology, and new video cards will almost always have newer drivers available from the manufacturer.

When adding any expansion card, you should ensure that you have the most up-to-date drivers. Drivers are often provided on a CD with the expansion card, and newer drivers are available either from Windows Update or from the manufacturer.

EXAM TIP PCIe cards provide significant performance gains over older PCI cards for graphics. AGP cards provide improved performance over PCI but aren't as fast as PCIe. Many quality graphics cards use PCIe x16.

Network cards

The most common reason to add a network interface card (NIC) is because the onboard NIC has failed or to increase the capacity of the system. For example, if an onboard NIC supports 100 Mbps but the local area network (LAN) is running at 1,000 Mbps, it's possible to add a faster NIC.

True or false? You always need to disable the onboard NIC when installing an additional NIC.

Answer: *False*. A computer can support two NICs and is referred to as a multihomed computer when it has two NICs.

You can use one NIC to connect to one network, and you can use the second NIC to connect to the second network. You can also use two NICs on some computers to increase the throughput. This is commonly called *NIC teaming* or *link aggregation*. NICs typically use 8P8C connections (which are commonly, but incorrectly, known as RJ-45 connections) with twisted-pair cables but can also use other types of connections.

> **EXAM TIP** When adding an additional NIC, you should get an up-to-date driver and install it to ensure that the NIC works properly.

Serial and parallel cards

Serial and parallel connections are rarely used in computers today, so it's unlikely that you'll need to add a serial or parallel card. Devices that have used these connections have largely been replaced with devices using USB connections. However, if you do need to add a card with these capabilities, ensure that the system has an open slot for the card and that you have the correct drivers.

True or false? You should install a parallel card if you want to connect a printer to an LPT1 port.

Answer: *True*. LPT is the logical designation for parallel ports, and if a system doesn't have a parallel port, you can add a parallel card to support it.

> **EXAM TIP** Parallel ports are designated as LPT1, LPT2, and so on. Serial ports are designated as COM1, COM2, and so on.

True or false? A common configuration for serial ports is 8-N1.

Answer: *True*. Serial ports are commonly configured to send data in a stream of eight data bits, no parity, and one stop bit. Additionally, each string of data starts with a start signal prior to each set of bits.

> **MORE INFO** Serial data is most commonly used with asynchronous modems. The following Wikipedia article provides a good explanation along with a picture of how these bits look: *http://en.wikipedia.org/wiki/Asynchronous_serial_communication*.

USB and FireWire cards

Computers commonly come with a wealth of USB ports on their front and rear panels. However, not all systems come with FireWire ports. If you need to add USB or FireWire ports, you can do so with an expansion card. Ports will be available at the card and accessible on the back of the computer.

True or false? You can clean connectors on FireWire cards with a pencil eraser.

Answer: *False.* Rubbing the contacts on any type of expansion card with a pencil eraser can cause electrostatic discharge (ESD) damage.

Contacts can develop oxidation over time, which is a form of rust. This oxidation can prevent a good connection, but cleaning the contacts removes the oxidation. You can clean contacts on any type of expansion card with isopropyl alcohol and a lint-free cloth.

> **EXAM TIP** You should clean expansion card contacts only with suitable cleaners. When handling any expansion card, you should take steps to avoid ESD damage.

Storage cards

Storage cards are added to support additional disk drives in a system. For example, if an existing system has only four serial ATA (SATA) drives but you want to add additional drives, you can add a SATA expansion card.

True or false? If you want to boot to a drive connected to a new SATA expansion card, you need to reconfigure the BIOS.

Answer: *True.* If you add a SATA expansion card and you want the computer to boot to a drive connected to it, you'll need to modify the boot order in the BIOS.

Depending on the BIOS version, you might also need to modify the BIOS to ensure that it identifies the new drive as a bootable device. Not all devices are bootable.

> **EXAM TIP** Additional hard drives can be added to a system by using either Parallel ATA or SATA expansion cards, although SATA is much more common today. As with many other expansion cards, you typically have to reconfigure the BIOS when adding an additional SATA card.

True or false? An external SATA (eSATA) expansion card can be installed in a computer to support internal RAID drives.

Answer: *False.* An eSATA card would provide a port for external SATA devices using eSATA.

If internal disks are needed to support a redundant array of independent disks (RAID) configuration, an internal SATA storage card could be added. Some disk controllers known as RAID controllers are specifically designed to support RAID configurations. Small Computer System Interface (SCSI) controllers are also used with RAID systems.

Modem cards

A modulator/demodulator (modem) card is used to connect a computer to a phone line. While most people have Internet access with a high-speed connection, there are still many people that don't have cable or fiber-optic connectivity and use a modem. If the computer doesn't have a built-in modem, you can add an internal modem via an expansion card. It's also possible to add external modems, and they typically connect to the computer via a serial or USB connection.

True or false? A modem has an RJ-45 jack to connect to the phone line.

Answer: *False.* A modem will have an RJ-11 jack to connect to the phone line. An RJ-45 jack is used for a network connection.

Modems may have two RJ-11 connections. One goes from the phone line to the modem, and the second line goes from the modem to a phone. This allows you to use the phone when the modem is not connected to the phone line.

NOTE Modems used with phone lines are considered asynchronous modems. They work differently than modems used with cable TV connections. A modem used with the cable TV connection filters out everything except for the Internet connection on incoming signals and adds the Internet signal back into the cable for outgoing connections.

EXAM TIP Modems connect to plain old telephone service (POTS) phone lines or digital subscriber line (DSL) connections with RJ-11 connectors. External modems connect to the computer with a serial connection or a USB connection.

True or false? If a modem card is not secured with a screw, it can cause random reboots.

Answer: *True.* This is true of any type of expansion card.

Over time, an expansion card expands and contracts due to heating and cooling. If the expansion card is not secured to the case, this expansion and contraction causes it to slowly move out of the slot. The card can be secured to the case with a screw or with a hinged block or panel that locks the card into place. If a computer is randomly rebooting and you notice that cards aren't secured, you can open the case and reseat the cards. This will often solve the problem. Of course, you should also ensure that the card is locked in place.

EXAM TIP All expansion cards should be secured in the case. If a computer does experience random reboots, it could be due to a loose card, a case that needs to be cleaned, overheating within the computer, or electrostatic discharge (ESD)–damaged components.

Wireless/cellular cards

You can add wireless or cellular cards into a computer to add that capability. Wireless cards connect with a wireless network, such as an 802.11g or 802.11n network. Cellular cards are used to connect to a cellular phone network, such as a 3G or 4G network that provides Internet access.

> **MORE INFO** Chapter 2, "Networking," covers networking topics in more detail. This includes common 802.11-based wireless networks.

While these types of cards exist, the most common way these capabilities are added to a desktop computer is with USB dongles. Software drivers are added, the USB dongle is plugged in, and the computer can connect to the wireless or cellular network. However, laptop computers often have a mini-PCIe wireless card for wireless capabilities.

True or false? If a computer stops working after installing a new wireless card, the first step should be to reseat the card.

Answer: *True*. This is true no matter what type of card you are installing.

If a computer stops working after you take an action, the first step is to check that action. The most likely reason is that the card isn't seated correctly in the slot. It's also possible that something else was affected when the card was installed.

TV tuner cards

TV tuner cards are used to convert video to digital data. They can typically accept National Television System Committee (NTSC) and/or Phase Alternating Line (PAL) signals used for video. These cards are used in home theater PCs, and by some users who want to record video on their computers.

True or false? When recording TV from a TV tuner, you need a tuner with two channels or two tuners if you want to record two channels at a time.

Answer: *True*. Basic TV tuners can decode a single channel, and some advanced tuners include two tuners in the same card. Only one TV station can be decoded for viewing or recording per channel of a TV tuner.

Tuners use an F type of connector, which is the same as that used to connect RG-6 coaxial cable to a TV.

> **EXAM TIP** Tuners will decode only a single channel. If a user wants to watch one channel on a computer and record a second channel, two tuners are required.

Video capture cards

Video capture cards are used to capture video from external sources. The type of connection needed varies depending on the external source.

True or false? A video capture card can be used to convert old VCR tapes to a digital format.

Answer: *True*. This can be used to preserve old home movies or any other type of old tapes.

> **EXAM TIP** Video capture cards can be used to capture and convert video from many different sources. In addition to capturing video from a VCR, you can also use these to capture video from another computer or a gaming console.

Riser cards

Riser cards are used in computers with small form-factor or low profile cases. They are used when there isn't enough space for the card to plug directly into the motherboard.

True or false? A riser card allows an expansion card to be positioned parallel with the motherboard.

Answer: *True*. The riser card plugs into the slot and includes an identical slot configured at a right angle.

After plugging the riser card into the slot, you can plug the expansion card into the riser card. When positioned parallel with the motherboard, it doesn't take as much space.

Can you answer these questions?

You can find the answers to these questions at the end of this chapter.

1. You have upgraded the sound system in a computer by adding a 7.1 sound card and hooking up the speakers. What else needs to be done?
2. If a computer no longer starts after correctly installing a new video card, what is the most likely problem?
3. What can you install to give a computer the ability to connect to two separate LANs?
4. What type of expansion cards will you typically install to add RAID capabilities for a computer?
5. What type of signals can a TV tuner capture?

Objective 1.5: Install and configure storage devices and use appropriate media

A common task for PC technicians is to install and configure storage devices. This includes optical drives such as CD, DVD, and Blu-Ray drives. It also includes hard drives, solid state drives, floppy drives, and tape drives. You need to have a good understanding of both internal and external connections used with any of these storage devices. This objective also includes RAID types, and you need to know the differences between RAID-0, RAID-1, RAID-5, and RAID-10.

Exam need to know...

- Optical drives
  For example: What are the different types of optical drives?

- Combo drives and burners
  For example: What does the -R designation mean for a DVD-R?

- Connection types
  For example: What are common connections used for external drives? What will prevent IDE drives from working?

- Hard drives
  For example: What are some common RPM speeds used by hard drives?

- Solid state/flash drives
  For example: What is a primary benefit of a solid state drive?

- RAID types
  For example: How many disks are in a RAID-1? What RAID configuration doesn't provide fault tolerance?

- Floppy drive
  For example: What type of power connector does a floppy drive use?

- Tape drive
  For example: What are tape drives primarily used for in computers?

- Media capacity
  For example: How much data can a DL DVD disc hold? How much data can a Blu-Ray disc hold?

Optical drives

Optical drives include compact disc read only memory (CD-ROM), digital versatile disc (DVD), and Blu-Ray disc (BD) drives. They all use a laser, which can read data from compatible discs.

Combo drives and burners

It's common for a single drive to support multiple discs. This saves space within a computer. Many desktop computers have at least one combo drive that supports CDs and DVDs.

True or false? Data can be burned onto a DVD-R disc multiple times.

Answer: *False.* The R in DVD-R indicates that it is recordable, but data can be written to the disc only one time.

Some optical drives can read optical discs and also burn (or write) data onto a disc. Disc burners have a laser that can write the data. Common designations for discs that can be written to include the following:

- **R (recordable)**   This is also referred to as write once read many (WORM), and it is used with CDs, DVDs, and Blu-Ray discs (as CD-R, DVD-R, and BD-R).

- **RW (rewritable)**   RW discs can be rewritten multiple times, and the RW designation is used with CDs and DVDs (as CD-RW and DVD-RW).
- **RE (recordable erasable)**   Only Blu-Ray discs use RE to indicate that the disc is rewritable.

EXAM TIP   Ensure that you understand the R, RW, and RE designations when preparing for the exam. You might run across CDs and DVDs with a plus (+) or minus (-) designation. These can be read and written to with most combo drives without any problem. However, some DVD players that are used to play movies recognize only one version or the other.

Connection types

Storage devices can be connected either internally or externally. Internal devices are always available, but external devices can be added when needed. External devices are hot swappable, meaning that they can be plugged in or removed while power is on. In contrast, internal devices are rarely hot swappable but instead can be removed only after removing the power from the computer.

True or false? External USB hard drives can be plugged into either a USB port or an eSATA port.

Answer: *False.* USB hard drives can be plugged into a USB port but not an eSATA port. Powered eSATA (eSATAp) ports support both USB and SATA drives, but not all eSATA ports are eSATAp ports.

EXAM TIP   The most common type of connections used for external drives are eSATA and USB. Other external connections include Firewire (IEEE 1394) and Ethernet. Disk drives with an Ethernet connection typically use an RJ 45 connection and are accessible to all users on the network. These are also known as Network Attached Storage (NAS) devices.

True or false? The end connector on an internal IDE drive is for the slave drive.

Answer: *False.* The end connector of an Integrated Drive Electronics (IDE) cable is for the master drive. The middle connector is for the slave drive.

IDE drives are also called parallel ATA (PATA) drives. A single IDE channel supports only two drives, and the drives have jumpers used to identify the hierarchy of the drives. Jumpers set on one drive identify it as the master, and jumpers set on the second drive identify it as the slave. Alternately, both drives can be configured with the cable select jumper. When cable select is used, the drive connected to the end connector of the cable is the master and the drive connected to the middle connector is the slave.

EXAM TIP   IDE or PATA drives are only used as internal drives. The most common reason why newly installed IDE drives don't work is due to incorrectly configured master and slave jumpers.

True or false? SCSI controllers should be assigned the highest priority SCSI identifier (ID) of 1.

Answer: *False.* The SCSI controller should be assigned the highest priority, but this is 7, not 1. SCSI can support eight devices (identified as 0 through 7) or 16 devices (identified as 0 through 15).

When eight SCSI devices are used, the priority order from highest to lowest is as follows:

- 7, 6, 5, 4, 3, 2, 1, 0

When sixteen SCSI devices are used, the priority order from highest to lowest is as follows:

- 7, 6, 5, 4, 3, 2, 1, 0, 15, 14, 13, 12, 11, 10, 9, 8

EXAM TIP In addition to knowing the priority order and the need to assign the SCSI controller the highest priority, you should also understand how these are assigned. Most SCSI devices include jumpers or switches to assign binary values. When three jumpers or switches are available, they can be configured to select any number between 0 and 7. When four jumpers or switches are available, they can be configured to select any number between 0 and 15.

Hard drives

Hard drives have platters that spin and read/write heads that move back and forth across the platters as they are spinning. The platters are covered with ferromagnetic material, and the read/write heads can write data by magnetizing the material. The data stays written on the drive even after it's powered off and can be read by the same read/write heads.

True or false? The rotational speed of a hard drive is a major factor in the overall performance of the hard drive.

Answer: *True.* Some faster hard drives spin as fast as 15,000 revolutions per minute (rpm). Higher rpms indicate a faster drive.

Other common speeds of hard drives are 5400 rpm, 7200 rpm, and 10,000 rpm. Other factors also influence the overall performance of a hard drive. For example, serial ATA (SATA) hard drives can transfer data much faster than the older parallel ATA (PATA) drives.

Another important characteristic of a hard drive is its size. Most current hard drives can hold hundreds of GB of data, and drives as large as 1 TB are common. As a reminder, be able to recognize the following byte terms:

- **B** byte or 8 bits
- **KB** kilobytes or 1,024 bytes
- **MB** megabytes or 1,024 KB
- **GB** gigabytes or 1,024 MB
- **TB** terabytes or 1,024 GB
- **PB** petabytes or 1,024 TB
- **EB** exabytes or 1,024 PB

NOTE There is a difference between 10 Mb and 10 MB or 10 Gb and 10 GB. When the b is lowercase, it indicates bits; and when it is uppercase (B), it indicates bytes.

Solid state/flash drives

Solid state drives (SSDs) use the same type of memory as a USB flash drive. They are used in some systems as the primary disk drive, but unlike hard disk drives, they don't have any moving parts. In contrast, a traditional hard disk drive has platters that spin and heads that move to different areas when reading and writing.

True or false? SSDs provide fast boot times for systems.

Answer: *True*. SSDs are significantly faster than traditional hard drives.

SSDs are commonly used in tablet devices. As SSDs have come down in price, they are being used more often as the primary drive for laptops and some desktop computers. These systems boot much quicker than they do with a traditional hard drive. A platter on a fast hard drive spins as fast as 15,000 revolutions per minute (rpm), but the SSD is still faster.

EXAM TIP SSD drives are much faster than traditional hard drives. Additionally, because they don't have any moving parts, they are less susceptible to damage if they are dropped. Hard drives often have shock-resistance protection, but SSDs are even more resistant to shock damage.

Many mobile devices, including cameras, video recorders, and smartphones, support flash memory. These are small, but some are available that can hold up to 128 GB of data. Some common types of memory used in these devices include the following:

- CompactFlash (CF) is manufactured by SanDisk. Type 1 CF devices are 36 × 43 mm and 3.3 mm thick. Type 2 CF devices are 5 mm thick.
- SD (Secure Digital) has replaced older MultiMediaCard (MMC) flash memory. They are 24 × 32 mm in size.
- Mini-SD is 20 × 21.5 mm in size.
- Micro-SD is the smallest SD memory. It is 11 × 15 mm in size.
- xD is an older version that was used in Olympus cameras. However, newer Olympus cameras use the SD cards instead.

MORE INFO Jamie Hyneman and Adam Savage (of MythBusters fame) have a good article on their Jamie & Adam Tested site comparing different flash devices. You can view it here: *http://www.tested.com/news/news/195-sd-vs-cf-vs-memory-stick-flash-memory-showdown/*.

RAID types

Two or more disks can be combined to work together as a redundant array of independent disks (RAID). There are two primary reasons to use RAID:

- RAID increases performance of the disk subsystem. This includes the speed of reading and writing on most RAID configurations.
- RAID protects against data loss. Most RAID configurations provide fault tolerance and can continue to operate after a drive fails. That is, a fault occurs, but the RAID subsystem can tolerate the failure without stopping the system.

True or false? A RAID-1 uses two disks.

Answer: *True*. A RAID-1 is also known as a mirror, and it uses two disks.

True or false? RAID-0 uses two or more disks and increases reliability.

Answer: *False*. RAID-0 does use two or more disks, but it does not increase reliability.

The following common RAID types, mentioned in the objectives, are summarized in Table 1-3:

- RAID-0 (also called striping) extends the size of a volume across two or more disks, but it does not increase reliability with fault tolerance.
- RAID-1 (also called mirroring) uses two disks. Data written to one drive is written to the other drive, so if one drive fails, the data is still available.
- RAID-1 with duplexing adds a second disk controller to a mirror. This eliminates the disk controller as a single point of failure.
- RAID-5 (also called striping with parity) uses three or more disks. The equivalent of one drive is used for parity data.
- RAID-10 (also called a stripe of mirrors) uses an even number of disks, such as four, six, eight, and so on. Drives are paired in mirrors (RAID-1), and those mirrors are then striped (RAID-0). This provides superb fault tolerance and speed of access, but with high costs.

TABLE 1-3 RAID types

TYPE	NUMBER OF DISKS	FAULT TOLERANCE	PERFORMANCE
RAID-0	2 or more	No	Increased read and write
RAID-1	2 only	Yes	Increased read
RAID-5	3 or more	Yes	Increased read and write
RAID-10	4 or more (even number only)	Yes (can survive failure of two disks)	Increased read and write

EXAM TIP RAID subsystems on desktop computers are normally created with SATA hard disk drives, but SCSI is also used. RAID-1, 5, and 10 all provide fault tolerance, but RAID-0 does not provide fault tolerance.

NOTE Most RAID-1 systems can read from both disks at the same time, increasing the read performance. However, the write performance isn't increased because the same data is written to both drives.

MORE INFO The following page has an easy-to-understand tutorial on different RAID levels: *http://www.acnc.com/raid.*

Floppy drive

Floppy drives are almost extinct on new computers, but you might see them on older computers. They're used with removable floppy disks that can hold 1.44 MB of data. Compared with common USB flash drives that commonly hold 8 GB of data or more, the usefulness of floppy disks has passed on most systems.

True or false? A floppy disk uses a mini-Molex power connector.

Answer: *True.* These are also called Berg connectors and sometimes just floppy drive mini connectors.

Tape drive

Tape drives can be internal or external, and they can read and write to removable tapes. The most common use of tapes is to create backups.

True or false? Tapes are used to create backups, but DVD-ROMs can typically hold more data so DVDs are used more often.

Answer: *False.* Tapes are commonly used to create backups and will hold more data than a DVD.

Digital Linear Tapes (DLTs) are often used for backups. They can transfer data as fast as 60 MB/s, and cartridges as large as 800 GB are available. Another standard is Linear Tape-Open (LTO), which can transfer data as fast as 140 MB/s and hold as much as 1.5 TB of data.

EXAM TIP Tapes are used to create backups. Tape drives can read and write to removable tapes.

Media capacity

Different optical discs can hold varying amounts of data. As technology improves, discs of the same physical size can hold more data.

True or false? Blu-Ray discs can hold 25 GB of data.

Answer: *True.* Blu-Ray discs can hold the most data of the different types of optical discs.

Some common capacities used with different discs include the following:

- **CD-ROM**   700 MB (mini CD-ROM holds 194 MB)
- **DVD-ROM**   4.7 GB
- **Dual-layer**   DVD-ROM 8.5 GB (sometimes rounded up to 8.6 GB)
- **Blu-Ray**   25 GB
- **Dual-layer Blu-Ray**   50 GB

- **Floppy**   1.44 MB
- **Tapes**   Varies depending on the type and brand but can hold as much as 1.5 TB of data

Data can be stored on both sides of any of the optical discs, doubling their capacity.

EXAM TIP   Know the capacities of each type of optical disc. For example, you should know that DL DVD-ROMs can hold 8.5 GB of data. Blu-Ray also comes in a triple-layer version holding 100 GB and a quad-layer version holding 128 GB per side.

Can you answer these questions?

You can find the answers to these questions at the end of this chapter.

1. What is the designation for a Blu-Ray disc that can be written to multiple times?
2. What type of internal drive is resistant to shock damage?
3. What is a benefit of a RAID-0?
4. How much data can be stored on a dual-sided dual-layer DVD-ROM?

Objective 1.6: Differentiate among various CPU types and features and select the appropriate cooling method

The central processing unit (CPU) performs the processing in the computer. The two primary manufacturers of CPUs are Intel and Advanced Micro Devices (AMD). They each have separate families of CPUs, and as a technician, you should know the sockets they use and also be aware of basic CPU characteristics. CPUs can generate quite a bit of heat, so it's also important to understand the different methods used to keep CPUs as cool as possible.

Exam need to know...

- Socket types
  For example: What are common socket types used by Intel CPUs? What are common socket types used by AMD CPUs?
- Characteristics
  For example: What is hyper-threading? What is an integrated GPU?
- Cooling
  For example: What methods are used to keep CPUs cool? What is the purpose of thermal paste?

Socket types

CPUs plug into CPU sockets located on a motherboard. Many motherboards are sold with an empty CPU socket, and the CPU is added when the motherboard is installed. Additionally, CPUs can be replaced on existing motherboards.

True or false? Intel sockets include the 1155 and 1366 sockets.

Answer: *True.* The 1155 and 1366 sockets are used by Intel CPUs.

The following list identifies many common Intel sockets. Notice that each is an LGA socket and that the name identifies the number of pins.

- **LGA 775 (775 pins)** Also called Socket T, and it replaces the older Socket 478.
- **LGA 1366 (1366 pins)** Also called Socket B, and it was designed to replace LGA 755 in high-end desktop computers.
- **LGA 2011 (2011 pins)** Also called Socket R, and it replaces LGA 1366 sockets in high-end desktop systems.
- **LGA 1156 (1156 pins)** Also called Socket H or Socket H1.
- **LGA 1155 (1155 pins)** Also called Socket H2, and it replaces LGA 1156 in basic desktop systems.

EXAM TIP Most Intel CPUs are in one of the Core i3 families (Core i3, Core i5, and Core i7). The sockets are commonly identified by just the number. For example, LGA 1156 is sometimes referred to as just 1156.

True or false? AMD sockets include the 940 and F sockets.

Answer: *True.* The 940 and F sockets are used by AMD CPUs.

The following list identifies many common AMD sockets. Most AMD sockets and CPUs are PGA based, in contrast to the LGA-based sockets used by Intel.

- **Socket 940** This is a 940-pin PGA socket.
- **Socket AM2** This is also a 940-pin PGA socket, but it is not compatible with Socket 940.
- **Socket AM2+** This 940-pin PGA socket replaces the AM2 socket. CPUs that can fit in an AM2 socket can also fit in an AM2+ socket.
- **Socket AM3** This 941-pin PGA socket replaces the AM2+ socket. CPUs designed for AM3 will also work in AM2+ sockets, but CPUs designed for AM2+ might not work in AM3 sockets.
- **Socket AM3+** This 942-pin PGA socket replaces the AM3 socket. CPUs that can fit in an AM3 socket can also fit in an AM3+ socket.
- **Socket FM1** This 905-pin PGA socket is used for accelerated processing units (APUs).
- **Socket F** This 1,207-pin LGA socket is used on servers. It has been replaced by Socket C32 and Socket G34.

EXAM TIP Some of the AMD families include Athlon, Opteron, Phenom, and Sempron. AMD sockets are often identified without "Socket." For example, Socket 940 is often referred to as just 940.

Characteristics

The characteristics of a CPU give an indication of how fast it is. These are important to understand when comparing different computers with different processors.

True or false? The primary type of memory used for CPU cache is static RAM.

Answer: *True*. Static RAM (SRAM) uses switching circuitry and is faster than SDRAM used in DIMM and SODIMM memory sticks.

SRAM is much faster than SDRAM, but it's also more expensive. The cost is justified when using it for CPU cache, but not for regular RAM.

> **NOTE** Many people confuse static RAM and synchronous dynamic RAM, thinking that they are the same thing. They aren't. SRAM uses different circuitry than SDRAM, making it much faster but also more expensive.

True or false? Hyper-threading makes a logical CPU core appear as two physical CPU cores.

Answer: *True*. Hyper-threading is used on some Intel CPUs, and it makes each CPU appear as two cores.

A single CPU can contain multiple cores, and this can be doubled with hyper-threading. It is used only on Intel CPUs. HyperTransport is used on AMD CPUs to increase the speed of the CPU, but it doesn't make the CPU appear as two cores.

Other characteristics of CPUs include the following:

- **Speeds** The speed refers to how many instructions the CPU can perform at a time. The speed is determined by a system clock (created from a crystal on the motherboard) and a multiplier. For example, a computer might have a 133-MHz clock with a 22x multiplier, giving the CPU a speed of 2.93 GHz.

- **Cores** A CPU can have multiple cores, with each core functioning as a separate CPU. For example, a dual-core processor has two CPU cores. When hyper-threading is used, it makes the two cores appear as four cores.

- **Virtualization support** Most CPUs support hardware assisted virtualization (HAV). Intel calls it VT-x, and AMD calls it AMD-V. When the CPU supports it, it might need to be enabled in the BIOS.

- **Architecture (32-bit vs. 64-bit)** 32-bit processors use 32 bits to address memory and support a maximum of 4 GB of RAM. 64-bit processors use 64 bits to address memory and can support as much as 17 EB of RAM, although it's rare for an operating system to support this much RAM.

- **Integrated GPU** Some CPUs include a graphics processing unit (GPU) on the CPU chip. Graphics require strong processing power, and the integrated GPU negates the need for an additional graphics card.

> **EXAM TIP** Ensure that you understand the basic characteristics of CPUs. Combined, these determine the overall performance of the computer. A 64-bit multiple-core CPU using hyper-threading is common in new systems today.

Cooling

CPUs generate quite a bit of heat. If cooling methods aren't used, they can easily overheat and fail. Almost all CPUs will have at least a heat sink attached to them to help dissipate heat.

True or false? Thermal paste is added on top of a CPU's heat sink to dissipate heat.

Answer: *False*. Thermal paste is not put on top of a CPU's heat sink but instead is placed between the CPU and the heat sink.

Thermal paste helps fill in microscopic gaps to create a solid connection between the heat sink and the CPU. It helps transfer energy from the CPU to the heat sink.

True or false? Liquid-based cooling is the quietest cooling option for CPUs.

Answer: *True*. Liquid-based cooling can be used instead of fans and is the quietest cooling method. Fans can generate quite a lot of noise.

A pump moves liquid through a closed-loop system. A special heat sink is attached to the pump with tubing, and as the liquid moves through the heat sink, it keeps the heat sink cool.

> **EXAM TIP** Methods of cooling a CPU include heat sinks, thermal paste, fans, or liquid-based cooling systems. Thermal paste is added between the CPU and the heat sink to create a solid connection. Fans are added on top of the heat sink to create an active cooling solution. Liquid-based cooling systems move liquid through the heat sink.

Can you answer these questions?

You can find the answers to these questions at the end of this chapter.

1. What type of CPU uses an 1155 or 1366 socket?
2. What type of CPU uses a 940 or F socket?
3. What is used on Intel CPUs to make each core appear as two cores?
4. Which cooling method is quietest?

Objective 1.7: Compare and contrast various connection interfaces and explain their purpose

Devices communicate with a computer through various interfaces, and these interfaces have different purposes and specifications. As a PC technician, you need to be aware of these connections and some details about the underlying standards. Several interfaces are listed in this objective, but some key standards you should understand are USB, Firewire, and SATA. This includes the connectors used by these interfaces and some key characteristics, such as their speeds and the maximum length of their cables. Other connector types include video connectors, audio connectors, and connectors used with twisted-pair cable, such as RJ-11 and RJ-45. This objective also includes some wireless standards.

Exam need to know...

- Physical connections
  For example: How fast is USB 2.0? How fast is SATA 2? What types of video connections use analog signals? What types use digital signals?
- Speeds, distances, and frequencies of wireless device connections
  For example: What is the maximum distance of Bluetooth Class 2? What can block IR signals?

Physical connections

External devices connect to a computer with different types of physical connections. The most common types of external connections are USB and Firewire, but there are different USB standards and Firewire standards.

True or false? USB 2.0 runs at 400 Mbps.

Answer: *False.* USB 2.0 runs at 480 Mbps. Firewire (also known as Firewire 400 or 1394a) runs at 400 Mbps.

Table 1-4 summarizes the maximum speeds and distances of the different standards.

TABLE 1-4 USB and Firewire characteristics

STANDARD	MAXIMUM SPEED	MAXIMUM DISTANCE
USB 1.1 (Low speed)	1.5 Mbps	5 m (about 16 ft)
USB 1.1 (Full speed)	12 Mbps	5 m (about 16 ft)
USB 2.0 (High speed)	480 Mbps (60 MBps)	5 m (about 16 ft)
USB 3.0 (Super speed)	5 Gbps (625 MBps)	Recommended 3 m (about 10 ft)
Firewire 400 (IEEE 1394a)	400 Mbps	Each cable max of 4.5 m (about 15 ft) Daisy-chained cables max of 72 m (about 236 ft)
Firewire 800 (IEEE 1394b)	800 Mbps	Optical connections 100 m (about 330 ft)

EXAM TIP Ensure that you know the speeds of USB and Firewire standards. This includes USB 1.1, 2.0, and 3.0 and Firewire 400 and 800. It's also important to know the maximum length of a cable that you can you use with the different standards.

True or false? You can install a 3.5-inch drive in an external enclosure and connect it to an eSATA port to access the data on the drive.

Answer: *True*. External enclosures are available for full-size 3.5-inch drives and smaller 2.5-inch drives used in laptops. Some enclosures use a USB connection, and others use an eSATA connection.

> **EXAM TIP** External enclosures are valuable for retrieving data from a drive on a computer that has failed. For example, if the power supply has failed on a computer and you need to access the data on the drive, you can remove it from the computer, install it in the enclosure, and access the data on another system.

True or false? You can identify USB 3.0 ports by their red color.

Answer: *False*. USB 3.0 ports are blue, not red.

USB connector types include the following:

- **Standard Type A**   Common rectangular connector.
- **Standard Type B**   Squarish connector used on larger devices such as printers and camcorders.
- **Mini-B, Micro-A, and Micro-B**   Smaller connectors used on mobile devices such as smartphones and cameras.
- **Mini-A**   Discontinued.
- **USB 3.0 Standard A**   Backward compatible with USB 2.0 Standard Type A but has more pins. Blue in color.
- **USB 3.0 Standard B**   Backward compatible with USB 2.0 Standard Type B but has more pins. Blue in color.
- **USB 3.0 Micro B**   Adds five more connections in an extra connector. USB 2.0 Micro-B devices can plug into a USB 3.0 Micro-B connector. Blue in color.

Figure 1-8 shows the outline of several USB ports. The only USB 3.0 port that is visibly different is the USB 3.0 Micro-B port. Notice that part of the USB 3.0 Micro-B port is the exact same size as the USB 2.0 Micro-B port. The extra connector includes additional pins. In other USB 3.0 ports, additional pins are added in the same size port, making them backward compatible with USB 2.0 devices.

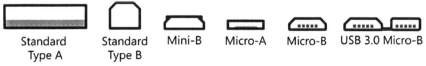

| Standard | Standard | Mini-B | Micro-A | Micro-B | USB 3.0 Micro-B |
| Type A | Type B | | | | |

FIGURE 1-8 USB ports.

Firewire connector types include the following:

- **4-pin**   Used on smaller devices that do not need power.
- **6-pin alpha**   Includes pins for data and power.
- **9-pin beta**   Adds pins for a ground shield for faster Firewire 800 devices.

MORE INFO Figure 1-12 in Objective 1.11, "Identify connector types and associated cables," later in this chapter, shows the outline of the Firewire connectors. Chapter 5 of the CompTIA A+ Training Kit (Exam 220-801 and Exam 220-802), ISBN-10: 0735662681, has additional pictures of USB and Firewire connectors.

True or false? Integrated Drive Electronics (IDE) drives are used inside a computer.

Answer: *True.* IDE hard drives are internal drives. They are also known as parallel ATA (PATA) drives.

True or false? SATA 3 drives can transfer data as fast as 6 Gbits/s.

Answer: *True.* SATA 3 drives have a maximum transfer speed of 6 Gbits/s.

Table 1-5 summarizes some of the common internal disk drive standards.

TABLE 1-5 Disk drive standards

STANDARD	MAXIMUM SPEED	ALSO CALLED
ATA-7	133 MBps	UDMA/133 or Ultra ATA 133
SATA 1	1.5 Gbits/s (150 MBps)	SATA 1.5G, SATA 1.5Gb/s, SATA 150
SATA 2	3 Gbits/s (300 MBps)	SATA 3G, SATA 3Gb/s, SATA 300
SATA 3	6 Gbits/s (600 MBps)	SATA 6G, SATA 6Gb/s, SATA 600

NOTE SATA versions are formally known as *generations* and have been informally called SATA 1G, SATA 2G, and SATA 3G, but this can be misleading. For example, SATA 2 has a speed of 3 Gbit/s and is sometimes called 3G. That is, SATA 3G might mean it is SATA 2 with a maximum speed of 3 Gbits/s, or it might mean that it is the third generation of SATA.

EXAM TIP Ensure that you know the difference between the different SATA versions. The speed of SATA has made PATA drives all but obsolete in new computers.

There are also many other connections used with computers. Table 1-6 provides details of many of these connections.

TABLE 1-6 Connector types

TYPE	NAME	COMMENTS
Serial	DE-9	Used with serial devices such as external modems. Commonly, but incorrectly, known as a DB-9 connector.
Parallel	DB-25	Used with older printers.
VGA	DE-15	Used with analog Video Graphic Array (VGA) displays. It has three rows of pins. Commonly, but incorrectly, known as a DB-15 connector.

TYPE	NAME	COMMENTS
HDMI	Type A common	Used with High-Definition Multimedia Interface (HDMI) displays. Includes digital video and audio signals.
DVI	Up to 29 pins	Digital Visual Interface (DVI) connectors. Can be analog (DVI-A), digital (DVI-D), or both (DVI-I).
Audio	Varies	Tip ring sleeve (TRS) connectors are common. Sony/Philips Digital Interconnect Format (S/PDIF) also used.
Network	RJ-45	Used with twisted-pair cable to connect to a network.
Phone	RJ-11	Used with twisted-pair cable for phones.

True or false? HDMI is backward compatible with VGA.

Answer: *False.* HDMI is not compatible with VGA but is backward compatible with DVI-D and DVI-I.

> **EXAM TIP** HDMI cables carry both video and 8-channel digital audio. They are backward compatible with DVI-D and DVI-I but not with VGA or DVI-A signals.

True or false? VGA connectors have 15 pins arranged in three rows.

Answer: *True.* VGA connectors have three rows with five pins in each row. This connector is often called a DB-15.

Figure 1-9 shows three common video ports on a graphics card.

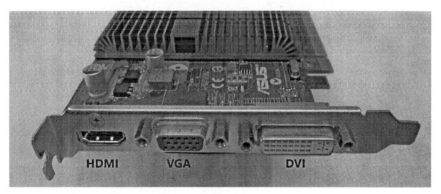

FIGURE 1-9 Video card with HDMI, VGA, and DVI ports.

> **EXAM TIP** You should be able to identify the type of any connector by sight. That is, if the exam shows you a picture of a connector, you should be able to identify what it is.

Speeds, distances, and frequencies of wireless device connections

Many devices use wireless technologies instead of connecting directly to the computer. Two important technologies to understand are Bluetooth and Infrared (IR).

True or false? Bluetooth networks are used to create a personal area network (PAN).

Answer: *True.* A PAN is a network centered around an individual, and Bluetooth is commonly used with PANs.

The three classes of Bluetooth are as follows:

- Class 1 has an approximate range of 100 meters (about 328 feet).
- Class 2 has an approximate range of 10 meters (about 33 feet).
- Class 3 has an approximate range of 5 meters (about 16 feet).

EXAM TIP If a Bluetooth device is not working, check the driver. This is true for most devices. If you have to reinstall an operating system, you might need to reinstall drivers. In some rare situations, you might have to reinstall a driver after updating an operating system because the original drivers can be overwritten.

IR devices use the same technology as remote controls used to operate televisions. Data is sent as subvisible light, and IR signals have a maximum range of about 38 meters (about 125 feet). The biggest challenge with IR signals is that they require a clear line of sight. A piece of paper can block the signal. Because of this, IR isn't commonly used.

Table 1-7 shows the speeds, distances, and frequencies of RF wireless device connections. The speed column reflects the maximum amount of data that can be transferred between two devices when they have an ideal connection. The distance column refers to the maximum indoor distance the RF signals can travel between two devices. However, you can often modify the range by increasing the strength of the signal, modifying the position of the antenna, and eliminating interference in the environment.

TABLE 1-7 Speeds, distances, and frequencies of RF wireless device connections

STANDARD	SPEED	DISTANCE	FREQUENCY
802.11a	54 Mbps	~30 m (100 feet)	5 GHz
802.11b	11 Mbps	~35 m (115 feet)	2.4 GHz
802.11g	54 Mbps	~38 m (125 feet)	2.4 GHz
802.11n	150 Mbps per stream, up to 600 Mbps (4 streams)	~70 m (230 feet)	2.4 GHz and 5 GHz

EXAM TIP You should know the maximum speeds and frequency bands of each of these wireless protocols. You should also know the relevant distances each can travel. For example, 802.11n has the maximum distance range and 802.11a has the minimum range.

Can you answer these questions?

You can find the answers to these questions at the end of this chapter.

1. What is the speed of SATA 2 devices?
2. What type of connector used by a VGA cable?
3. What is the difference between VGA and HDMI signals?

Objective 1.8: Install an appropriate power supply based on a given scenario

Every computer requires power, and it is provided by internal power supplies. These power supplies include multiple connectors to provide specific voltages to different components within the computer. PC technicians need to be familiar with common connectors used in a power supply and the voltages on these connectors. When a power supply fails and needs to be replaced, a technician should be able to identify a suitable substitute based on specifications such as how many watts it provides and how many 12-V rails it includes. You should also be aware of dual input voltage options included with many power supplies.

Exam need to know...

- Connector types and their voltages
  For example: What voltages are provided by a power supply?

- Specifications
  For example: How many rails will a power supply have? How is the load capability of a power supply identified?

- Dual voltage options
  For example: What are the two input voltage settings?

Connector types and their voltages

Power supply units (PSUs) provide multiple voltages to a computer. The PSU receives AC power from a commercial source, hopefully through a surge protector, and converts it to DC power needed by the components. Some power connectors plug in to the motherboard, and other connectors plug into individual devices.

True or false? A desktop computer power supply will normally provide 3.3 VDC, 5 VDC, 12 VDC, and 24 VDC for computer components.

Answer: *False.* Desktop computer power supplies do not provide 24 VDC to a system. They do provide 3.3 VDC, 5 VDC, and 12 VDC.

True or false? A power supply uses the same type of connector for an IDE-based CD-ROM and a SATA hard drive.

Answer: *False.* These connectors are different. IDE-based drives use a molex connector, and SATA drives use an *L*-shaped connector.

Some of the different connectors provided by a power supply include the following:

- **SATA (L-shaped connector)**   Provides 3.3 VDC, 5 VDC, and 12 VDC.
- **Molex connector used by PATA or IDE drives**   Provides 5 VDC and 12 VDC. Even though PATA drives are being phased out, PSUs still include a molex connector.
- **4/8-pin connector used by the CPU**   Single CPU motherboards use a 4-pin connector, and multiple CPU motherboards use an 8-pin connector. The connectors provide separate 12 VDC rails to the CPU.
- **PCIe 6/8-pin used by PCIe devices**   This can be plugged into the motherboard or, in some cases, into the PCIe graphics card. It provides 12 VDC.
- **20-pin or 24-pin primary power connector**   This is often called the P1 connector, and it provides 3.3 VDC, 5 VDC, and 12 VDC to the motherboard.
- **Mini (or sometimes mini-molex or Berg connector)**   These are used by old floppy drives and provide 5 VDC and 12 VDC.

EXAM TIP   PSUs provide 3.3 VDC, 5 VDC, and 12 VDC to a system via various connectors. SATA connectors are L shaped. PATA drives use molex connectors. The CPU has a separate 12 VDC rail, normally provided by a 4-pin connector. PCIe devices have a separate 12 VDC rail provided by a 6-pin, 6+2-pin, or 8-pin connector. The P1 connector is 20 or 24 pins and provides 3.3 VDC, 5 VDC, and 12 VDC.

MORE INFO   Tim Fisher has published multiple pinout tables for all of the connectors mentioned in this section. You can access it here: *http://pcsupport.about.com/od/ insidethepc/tp/atx-pinout-power-supply.htm*.

Specifications

The specifications of a power supply unit (PSU) identify its primary features and capabilities. Larger computers with more internal components require power supplies with larger capabilities. One of the primary specifications is the wattage of the PSU. A higher wattage indicates that it can provide power to more components.

True or false? A power supply for a desktop computer includes at least two 12 VDC rails.

Answer: *True*. At least one 12 VDC rail is dedicated to the CPU, and at least one 12 VDC rail is dedicated to disk drives.

By separating the 12 VDC rails, the power supply can provide a steady voltage and amperage to the different components. One of the challenges when additional hard drives are added is that they draw more current from one of the 12 VDC rails. If it is more than the 12 VDC rail can handle, it can cause damage to the hard drives.

True or false? ATX is the primary standard for power supplies used in desktop computers.

Answer: *True*. ATX is a standard defining the voltages and connectors included in a standard desktop computer. Some smaller computers use micro-ATX power supplies, which are physically smaller and supply a lower wattage.

Some common power outputs include the following:

- Micro-ATX PSUs typically provide between 180 and 300 watts, although they can be as small as 90 watts for some special-purpose power supplies.
- ATX PSUs have a typical range between 300 and 1,000 watts, although larger ones are available.

EXAM TIP When replacing a power supply, ensure that the new power supply at least meets the power output of the older power supply. If additional hard drives have been added to the computer, purchase a power supply with a higher wattage rating.

Dual voltage options

Many power supplies are designed to work in only a specific country/region, based on the commercial power provided locally. Other power supplies can be adjusted so that they will adapt to the supplied commercial power.

True or false? A power supply manually configured to use 230 VAC will not work in the U.S.

Answer: *True*. Commercial power in the U.S. is 115 VAC, so a power supply configured for 230 VAC will not work in the U.S.

Power supplies that can be manually configured have a switch labeled 115 for one selection and 230 for the other selection, accessible from the back of the computer. These need to be manually adjusted for the local power. Some PSUs can automatically adjust to the correct input voltage, but they are more expensive.

EXAM TIP A PSU configured for 230 VAC will not work if the commercial power is 115 VAC. In contrast, a PSU will be damaged if it is set at 115 VAC and it is plugged into a commercial power source providing 230 VAC. Countries/regions in Europe commonly use 230 VAC, and countries/regions in North America commonly use 115 VAC.

Can you answer these questions?

You can find the answers to these questions at the end of this chapter.

1. What type of connection would be used for a graphics card?
2. What should you look for in a power supply designed for a computer with an internal RAID?
3. What should you configure in a computer that was used in Europe but will be used in the U.S.?

Objective 1.9: Evaluate and select appropriate components for a custom configuration, to meet customer specifications or needs

PC technicians are viewed as computer experts. As experts, they are often asked what type of computer a customer should buy or what type of components the computer should include. The answer varies depending on what the customer plans on doing with the computer. However, there are some common guidelines related to components needed for different workstations. This objective expects you to know the primary components needed for several different workstations so that you can intelligently advise customers.

Exam need to know...

- Graphic/CAD/CAM design workstation
  For example: What are the hardware requirements for graphic design and CAD/CAM workstations?

- Audio/Video editing workstation
  For example: What is a concern related to monitors for professionals doing audio or video editing?

- Virtualization workstation
  For example: What architecture (32-bit or 64-bit) should be used for virtualization workstations?

- Gaming PC
  For example: How can a gaming PC be kept cool with the least amount of noise?

- Home Theater PC
  For example: What type of video is common with an HTPC?

- Standard thick client
  For example: What is meant by "thick client"?

- Thin client
  For example: How much RAM is needed by a thin client?

- Home Server PC
  For example: What are some benefits of a PC used as a home server?

Graphic/CAD/CAM design workstation

Computer aided design (CAD) and computer aided manufacturing (CAM) systems are used to create two-dimensional (2-D) and three-dimensional (3-D) drawings. These are often used to create drawings for buildings, machinery, and tools.

Graphics systems are used to create and process a wide variety of graphics. This includes graphics used for print layouts, such as for magazines and books, and also animated graphics used in programs.

True or false? PCs used for a CAD/CAM workstation require powerful processors and maximum RAM.

Answer: *True.* These systems require powerful processors and will often have multiple processors or at least multiple core processors. They also require a large amount of RAM and high-end graphics cards.

CAD/CAM systems repeatedly render (or draw) 2-D and 3-D drawings. If the system doesn't have a high-end graphics card, enough processing power, or enough RAM, these drawings can take a long time to render. Every time the user makes a minor change, it has to be drawn again, and the user will have to wait again.

High-end video cards will have their own graphics processing unit (GPU) on board, their own RAM, and will support fast refresh rates. PCIe graphics cards provide the performance needed by these systems, but older AGP and PCI graphics cards have trouble keeping up with the graphics requirements.

EXAM TIP CAD, CAM, and graphics workstations require a powerful processor, the maximum amount of RAM, and high-end video, such as a PCIe graphics card. This ensures that they can quickly render the drawing and allows the user to be more productive.

MORE INFO CompTIA lists the components that you should focus on for several different types of workstations. This is one of the objectives that you will benefit reading word for word in the objectives. Go to the CompTIA site (*http://certification.comptia .org/getCertified/certifications/a.aspx*), download and print the objectives, and high-light the entire 1.9 objective list. These are the items that CompTIA considers important for these workstations. As one of your final reviews, reread the highlighted items.

Audio/Video editing workstation

An audio/video editing workstation is used by artists creating or editing audio and video files. For example, many videos are created with a green screen background and given to a graphics artist to re-create the final product with stunning backgrounds.

True or false? A basic need for artists using a computer for audio/video editing is two or more monitors.

Answer: *True.* Audio/video editing workstations typically have dual monitors, specialized audio and video cards, and a large, fast hard drive.

EXAM TIP An audio/video editing workstation requires a specialized audio and video card to capture, display, and/or manipulate audio and video. These files can be very large, so a large, fast hard drive is necessary. Also, dual monitors are very useful so that users can modify files on one monitor while viewing the effects on the other monitor.

Virtualization workstation

A virtualization workstation is used to run multiple virtual machines (VMs) within a single physical host. For example, if you're running Windows 7 Professional, you can download Windows XP Mode for free and run applications within a virtual Windows XP environment. You can also run other virtual operating systems by using Windows Virtual PC, which is also available for free.

True or false? Virtual workstations should have powerful 64-bit multiple-core processors and a large amount of RAM.

Answer: *True.* Virtual workstations require powerful CPUs and a large amount of RAM.

Each VM consumes some RAM and CPU power from the host system, so the host needs enough to share. A 32-bit operating system supports only 4 GB of RAM, and only about 3.25 GB is actually available, so this is rarely enough to run VMs. In contrast, a 64-bit operating system supports a large amount of RAM (up to 192 GB on some Windows 7–based systems). A powerful multiple-core CPU provides enough processing power for multiple VMs along with the host.

> **EXAM TIP** Virtual workstations require a large amount of RAM and strong processors with multiple cores. A quad core processor with hyper-threading enabled appears as eight logical processors and is a good choice. The amount of RAM you need is dependent on the number of VMs you plan on running at a time and how much RAM you want to dedicate to each. If you want to create a virtual network with a server and two virtual desktop systems, 16 GB of RAM will meet your needs.

> **MORE INFO** You can access the free Virtual PC download and Windows XP Mode here: *http://www.microsoft.com/windows/virtual-pc/download.aspx*. Chapter 10 of the CompTIA A+ Training Kit (Exam 220-801 and Exam 220-802), ISBN-10: 0735662681, covers virtualization options in more depth.

Gaming PC

A gaming PC is a computer dedicated to playing games. Games can be quite sophisticated and consume a significant amount of processing power.

True or false? Liquid-based cooling is one way a gaming PC is kept cool.

Answer: *True.* A gaming PC will have a strong processor, which can generate a lot of heat. A liquid-based cooling system keeps the processor cool while also minimizing sound because the processor doesn't need a fan.

The key elements used in gaming PCs are as follows:

- Powerful processor
- High-end cooling such as liquid-based cooling
- High-end video using specialized GPU
- High-end sound card and speakers

Home Theater PC

A home theater PC (HTPC) is a dedicated computer used as a digital video recorder (DVR). It can capture and play television shows, play music, and play movies. HTPC systems commonly use a compact form-factor case that looks more aesthetically appealing than a computer case.

True or false? A home theater PC will typically include an HDMI output and an audio card supporting surround sound.

Answer: *True.* A home theater PC requires an HDMI output to connect to an HDMI-based television. Additionally, users who have a system like this will normally have a quality surround sound system requiring an eight-channel 7.1 sound card.

If the computer will be used to capture television shows, it requires a TV tuner. With more tuners, the system can record more than one show at a time or allow the user to record a show on one channel while watching a show on a different channel.

Standard thick client

A standard thick client refers to a computer that is used by a typical user. In comparison, most of the other computers described within objective 1.9 are used for a dedicated role.

True or false? A standard thick client should meet the hardware requirements for Windows and typical desktop applications.

Answer: *True.* A thick client (also called a standard PC) meets the minimum hardware requirements for Windows and standard applications.

The term *thick* in this context refers only to what is on the computer, not the size of the computer. A thick client will have an operating system installed along with various applications. Contrast it with a thin client, which is covered in the next section.

Thin client

A thin client is a good choice when the user will run only a minimum number of applications. In contrast, a thick client can run many different applications at a time.

True or false? A thin client is appropriate for users who want a light computer that can fit into a thin folder.

Answer: *False*. In this context, thin doesn't refer to the size but instead refers to the capabilities. Thin clients are not necessarily light or small.

If a user plans on using a computer only to surf the Internet, access email, and/or run a word processor application, a thin client is a good choice. The user doesn't need to invest in a computer with a powerful processor, a large amount of RAM, or fast disk drives.

Thin clients are also used in organizations that run applications remotely. For example, users might run thin clients at their desktops, but when they run applications, they connect to an application server over the network. The applications run on the server but appear on the users' desktops. In some cases, users use a thin client to connect to remote servers, and they run a full operating system from the server.

> **EXAM TIP** A thin client has a minimum amount of hardware to run Windows. It's appropriate for users who plan to run only a single application at a time, such as Internet Explorer to surf the Internet or Microsoft Word for simple word processing.

Home Server PC

A home server computer is a dedicated computer used to serve resources to users in the network. It can be used to store and share files and folders. This includes traditional files such as Microsoft Word documents, but it can also be used to store media files and stream media to other systems in the network. A home server can also be used as a print server.

True or false? Home servers used as file servers require a powerful CPU.

Answer: *False*. Serving files over a network does not require a powerful CPU.

The two primary resources that should be addressed in a home server are the network interface card (NIC) and the disk subsystem. For example, if the network supports 1,000 Mbps, the home server should have a Gigabit NIC installed. Also, a RAID array increases the speed and the reliability of the disk subsystem.

> **EXAM TIP** Home servers are useful for streaming media throughout a house and also to share files. Ensure that a home server has a NIC that matches the speed of the network and includes a powerful disk subsystem. A RAID-5 increases the speed of disk access and also increases the reliability, through fault tolerance.

Can you answer these questions?

You can find the answers to these questions at the end of this chapter.

1. Would an AGP-based graphics card be the best choice for a CAD workstation?

2. A user is planning on overclocking a new computer to be used as a gaming PC but wants to keep the system quiet. What type of cooling system should be used for the CPU?

3. What hardware requirements are needed for a computer that will connect to a high-quality LCD screen in a home theater?

4. What type of workstation is appropriate for Internet searches only?

5. What hardware requirements are needed for a home server?

Objective 1.10: Given a scenario, evaluate types and features of display devices

Display devices (also called monitors) are used to display data from a computer. There are several types of displays used with computers, and a PC technician should know the basics related to all displays and some of the features unique to each. Some common terms you should understand are *refresh rates, resolution,* and *lumens.* It's also important to recognize the difference between analog and digital signals. Privacy filters limit the view of a display, and multiple displays allow users to be more productive by viewing more data at a time.

Exam need to know...

- Types
  For example: What type of monitor draws the most power?
- Refresh rates
  For example: What is a typical refresh rate for an LCD display?
- Resolution
  For example: What is the resolution of HDMI?
- Native resolution
  For example: What type of displays have a native resolution?
- Brightness/lumens
  For example: When are displays with high lumens needed?
- Analog vs. digital
  For example: What types of signals can be converted with a passive adapter?
- Privacy/antiglare filters
  For example: How does a display filter provide privacy?
- Multiple displays
  For example: What is a benefit of using more than one display?

Types

All display monitors aren't the same, and there are several different types that a PC technician should know about. The older cathode ray tube (CRT) monitors are all but phased out, but others are very common.

True or false? Plasma-based monitors consume more power than LCD-based monitors.

Answer: *True*. One of the drawbacks of plasma-based monitors is that they draw more power than liquid crystal display (LCD)–based or light emitting diode (LED)–based monitors.

Following are descriptions of the types of monitors listed in this objective:

- CRT displays are older, bulkier monitors using an extremely large vacuum tube. They draw the most power and are commonly replaced by LED-based or LCD-based monitors.

- LCD monitors are thin and light flat-panel displays. They have liquid crystals that change colors based on how they are oriented in response to a voltage. These crystals do not emit light. A cold cathode fluorescent lamp (CCFL) is used as a backlight. It shines from the back, through the crystals, to the front of the monitor to display the data.

- LED monitors are LCD-based monitors that use LEDs as backlights instead of a CCFL. The LEDs provide better light and are more reliable than CCFLs.

- OLED (organic light emitting diode) displays are used on some small mobile devices. They can be thinner and lighter than other displays but are also more expensive. Unlike LCD and LED displays, an OLED display emits light, so a backlight is not needed.

- Plasma displays are also thin flat-panel displays, but they use millions of small cells filled with a gas that emits light. Because these cells emit light, a backlight is not needed. These displays draw more power and are more susceptible to screen burn-in than LCD-based and LED-based displays.

- Projector displays are used to project a display onto a large screen for viewing by an audience, such as in a conference room or classroom. Speakers or trainers connect a computer or laptop to the projector to display information from the computer.

NOTE If the same image is continuously displayed on some types of monitors, it will burn into the monitor. Even when the monitor is turned off, this image can be seen. CRT and plasma monitors are susceptible to this, but LCD-based and LED-based monitors are not.

EXAM TIP CRT monitors are being replaced due to the high cost of power associated with their use. When replaced, they should be disposed of properly. Plasma displays draw more power than LED and LCD displays but not anywhere near the amount of power required by CRT displays.

Refresh rates

The refresh rate of a monitor refers to how often the display needs to be redrawn to ensure that it stays visible. Refresh rates are typically stated in Hertz (Hz), such as 60 Hz. A refresh rate of 60 Hz indicates that the display is refreshed 60 times per second.

True or false? A refresh rate less than 72 Hz on an LCD-based display causes flicker and eyestrain.

Answer: *False.* LED-based and LCD-based displays do not have flicker problems and typically have a refresh rate of 60 Hz.

CRT monitors are highly susceptible to flicker problems, with a refresh rate of 72 Hz or less. When set lower than 72 Hz, users often experience eyestrain and headaches.

> **EXAM TIP** A refresh rate of 60 Hz is common for an LED-based or LCD-based monitor. CRT monitors needed faster refresh rates to reduce flicker and eye strain.

Resolution

The resolution of a monitor refers to the width and height of the display in picture elements (pixels). For example, VGA is expressed as 640 × 480.

True or false? The resolution of HDMI is 1920 × 1080.

Answer: *True.* HDMI has a resolution of 1920 × 1080.

Table 1-8 shows some common resolutions used by display monitors.

TABLE 1-8 Common resolutions

RESOLUTION NAME	RESOLUTION
VGA (Video Graphics Array)	640 × 480
SVGA (Super VGA)	800 × 600
XGA (Extended GA)	1024 × 768
EVGA (Extended VGA)	1024 × 768
SXGA (Super XGA)	1280 × 1024
UXGA (Ultra XGA)	1600 × 1200
WUXGA (Wide UXGA)	1920 × 1200
HDMI 1080	1920 × 1080
HDMI 780	1280 × 720

Native resolution

LED-based and LCD-based displays are designed to use a specific resolution, also called a native resolution. You can select different resolutions for these displays, but the native resolution is recommended.

True or false? Setting an LCD-based monitor to a resolution other than the native resolution will damage the monitor.

Answer: *False.* Setting the resolution to something other than the native resolution will distort the display, but it won't damage it.

> **EXAM TIP** Set LED-based and LCD-based displays to the native resolution for the best-quality display. This is identified as the recommended resolution on the Windows 7 Screen Resolution page.

Brightness/lumens

The brightness of a monitor can be adjusted to make it brighter or dimmer. *Lumens* refers to the brightness of an overhead projector.

True or false? A projector with high lumens is needed when doing presentations in a large room exposed to natural sunlight.

Answer: *True.* If a room has a lot of natural sunlight, a projector with high lumens is needed to ensure that participants can see the display.

> **EXAM TIP** All monitors have some type of adjustment to make them brighter and easier to see. As CRT monitors age, the display gets dimmer and more difficult to see, even when the brightness is turned up all the way. Projectors with higher lumens display are brighter and can be used in larger rooms and rooms with other lighting.

Analog vs. digital

Early displays used an analog input, but most modern-day monitors use a digital input. An analog signal uses a sine wave and modulates it with the data. In contrast, a digital signal uses 1s and 0s. One of the challenges with analog signals is that they are easily degraded when sent over a cable, resulting in a poor signal.

Older CRT monitors required analog inputs. Computers use digital data, so when a monitor needs analog data, the digital data is converted to analog by the graphics card.

Newer LCD and LED monitors require digital data. When the graphics card provides analog data, it is converted back to digital by the monitor. This wastes a lot of processing time and power because the digital data is converted to analog and then back to digital.

Newer graphics cards provide both analog and digital data connections. If an older CRT monitor is used, you can send an analog signal to it. If a newer LED or LCD monitor is used, you can send a digital signal to it.

True or false? An HDMI-to-DVI passive adapter will convert digital data to analog data.

Answer: *False.* A passive adapter will not convert analog and digital data. However, an HDMI-to-DVI adapter will allow you to plug an HDMI cable into a DVI port.

Key points to remember about video signals include the following:

- VGA signals are analog.
- DVI-A signals are analog.
- DVI-D signals are digital.
- HDMI signals are digital.

EXAM TIP Adapters are available to convert DVI-D to HDMI signals. However, an adapter to convert VGA to HDMI requires converting analog data to digital data and is too costly.

Privacy/antiglare filters

Filters are available for displays that can reduce glare and also reduce the viewing angle of the display. These are portable and available in many different sizes to match the sizes of available displays.

True or false? A privacy filter can prevent others from viewing data on a computer screen.

Answer: *True.* Privacy filters are often placed over screens to limit the viewing angle. The person directly in front of the display can view it, but someone looking at the display from the side cannot read anything on the display.

EXAM TIP Privacy filters are often used to prevent other people from viewing the data displayed on a screen. *Shoulder surfing* is the term used to describe someone trying to view through observation, and a privacy filter helps prevent its success.

Multiple displays

Many power users enjoy using more than one display with their computers. For example, users doing audio and/or video editing on a computer often use two displays. This allows them to be more productive. Similarly, many administrators use multiple displays. One display is used for monitoring key systems while the administrator does primary work with the other monitor. The administrator can check the status of systems with a quick glance at the second monitor.

True or false? You need at least two graphics cards to connect more than one display.

Answer: *False.* Most graphics cards have multiple outputs, allowing you to connect more than one display to a single graphics card.

Can you answer these questions?

You can find the answers to these questions at the end of this chapter.

1. What types of monitors require backlights?
2. What should the refresh rate of a CRT display be set at to reduce flicker?
3. What should you set the resolution to for an LCD-based display?
4. What type of data (analog or digital) is used by VGA, and what type of data is used by HDMI?

Objective 1.11: Identify connector types and associated cables

Along with their associated interfaces, several connections were introduced in Objective 1.7, "Compare and contrast various connection interfaces and explain their purpose." This objective expands on the information presented in that objective but focuses on the connectors and cables used for various displays, disk drives, and other devices. As a PC technician, you need to be aware of the various connectors and cables used to connect any device so that you can easily connect devices to a computer.

Exam need to know...

- Display connector types
  For example: What does a DVI connector look like? What does an HDMI connector look like?

- Display cable types
  For example: Can you identify a DisplayPort cable? What happens if cable carrying an analog signal is too long?

- Device connectors and pin arrangements
  For example: How can you identify a USB 3.0 port? What is the difference between a standard Type A USB 2.0 port and a standard Type A USB 3.0 port?

- Device cable types
  For example: What type of cable does an IDE drive use?

Display connector types

The interfaces for display monitors have changed over the years, and there are currently several different connectors available on computers. Several of the standards have been presented earlier in the chapter, but you should also be able to identify the connectors by sight.

True or false? You can plug a DVI-D cable into a DVI port.

Answer: *True.* A DVI connector will normally be able to accept either a DVI-D connection or a DVI-A connection.

DVI cables and connectors come in the following versions:

- DVI-A (analog) connectors supply only analog data on the cable.
- DVI-D (digital) connectors supply only digital data on the cable.
- DVI-I (integrated) connectors provide both analog and digital data on the cable.

Figure 1-10 shows an outline and the pins of the DVI port on a PC and various DVI connectors. You can see that the DVI port on the computer is designed to accept any type of DVI connector.

DVI (Port on PC)   DVI-A Connector   DVI-D (Connector)   DVI-I (Connector)

FIGURE 1-10 DVI port and connectors.

EXAM TIP DVI ports on computers typically have a connector that can accept any type of DVI. However, the connectors on the DVI cable will use only certain pins. For example, a DVI-A cable uses different pins than a DVI-D cable. However, either cable can plug into the same DVI port on a computer.

True or false? You can plug an S/PDIF cable into a DisplayPort connector.

Answer: *False.* A DisplayPort connector is used for a display monitor and is rectangular in shape, but an S/PDIF connector is used for audio and is round.

Figure 1-11 compares a DisplayPort and an HDMI connection.

DisplayPort   HDMI

FIGURE 1-11 DisplayPort and HDMI connectors.

You will need to understand the following basic information about other connector types listed in this objective:

- RCA connectors carry only analog audio or video signals.
- DB-15 connectors are also known as VGA connectors and have three rows of pins carrying analog video signals.
- BNC connectors are used with coaxial cables (similar to the cable used with cable TV) and carry analog signals.
- Mini HDMI (also called HDMI Type C) connectors are a smaller version of the standard Type A HDMI connector and carry both video and eight-channel audio digital signals.
- RJ-45 connectors are used with twisted-pair cables and can be used with displays, but that usage is rare.
- Mini-DIN 6-pin connectors are round connectors used for analog signals. A more common version is the 4-pin DIN connection, more commonly called S-Video.

Display cable types

In addition to being able to recognize the connectors, you should also be familiar with common cables used with the different display interfaces.

True or false? A DVI-D cable provides video and audio to a display.

Answer: *False*. The DVI-D cable provides digital video to a display but not audio.

True or false? HDMI cables provide both digital video and analog audio.

Answer: *False*. HDMI cables do provide digital video, but they also provide eight-channel digital audio, not analog audio.

True or false? The display on a monitor using a VGA cable will degrade with longer VGA cables.

Answer: *True*. VGA signals use an analog signal, and the signal quality degrades with longer cables. In contrast, DVI-D, HDMI, and DisplayPort use digital signals and don't suffer as much from signal degradation.

The cable types mentioned in the objectives include the following:

- HDMI cables carry digital video and eight-channel audio signals.
- DVI can be either analog (DVI-A) or digital (DVI-D), or both (DVI-I). DVI-D is compatible with HDMI, but it doesn't include audio. DVI-A is compatible with analog.
- VGA provides an analog signal and uses a three-row DB-15 connector.
- Composite cables use an RCA jack and provide an analog signal. They are used with audio more than video.
- Component cables use analog video signals across three separate cables, identified as YPBPR. Y is for green, PB is for blue, and PR is for red.
- S-video cables provide analog signals and use a 4-pin DIN connector.

- RGB cables use three RCA jacks to send analog video signals. One cable is for red, one for green, and one for blue.
- Coaxial cables are similar to what is used for cable TV and provide analog data to a display. They can use a twist-on BNC connector or a screw-on F-type connector.
- Ethernet display cables use a twisted pair cable and an RJ-45 connector. However, these are much less common than other display cable types.

Device connectors and pin arrangements

In addition to knowing the display connectors and cables types presented in the previous two sections, you should also be able to identify connectors used with other devices.

True or false? SATA power connectors provide 3.3 VDC, 5 VDC, and 12 VDC to SATA drives using *L*-shaped connectors.

Answer: *True.* The orange wire provides 3.3 VDC, the red wire provides 5 VDC, and the yellow wire provides 12 VDC. Black is used for ground.

SATA uses an *L*-shaped connector for both the power and the signal, but they are two different connectors. Common connectors used with disk drives include the following:

- SATA connectors are used for internal drives.
- eSATA connectors are used for external drives.
- PATA connectors are used for internal drives, and they use 40-wire or 80-wire ribbon cables with 40-pin connectors. PATA drives use the Integrated Drive Electronics (IDE) or Enhanced IDE (EIDE) interface. The red stripe on the cable goes to pin 1 of the connector.
- Floppy drives use a 34-pin ribbon cable similar to the 40-wire or 80-wire connectors used with PATA drives. The red stripe on the cable goes to pin 1 of the connector.
- Small Computer System Interface (SCSI) connectors are used with either internal or external disk drives.

EXAM TIP   SATA interfaces are used for internal disk drives, and eSATA interfaces are used for external disk drives. PATA drives (originally known as IDE and EIDE drives) are used internally but have been replaced with SATA technology in most new computers. Floppy drives have also disappeared in most computers due to the popularity of USB devices.

True or false? USB 3.0 ports are identified with a blue color.

Answer: *True.* Newer USB 3.0 ports and USB 3.0 devices have a blue color.

USB ports include pins for both data and 5 VDC power. USB 3.0 ports include five extra pins for ground and transmit and receive signals.

The characteristics of other connectors can be identified as follows:

- USB connectors are very common. Computers have several Type A connectors. Type B connectors are often used on printers and video recorders. Mini and micro connectors are used on smaller devices such as smartphones or digital cameras.

- IEEE 1394 (also known as Firewire) comes in two versions: 1394a (Firewire 400) and 1394b (Firewire 800). Figure 1-12 shows common Firewire connectors. The 4-pin connector does not provide power, but the 6-pin connector includes power. The 9-pin connector is used for Firewire 800.

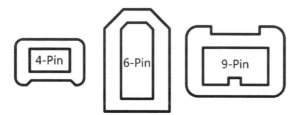

FIGURE 1-12 Firewire connectors.

- PS/2 is a round mini-DIN connector used for older mice. Most mice use USB ports today, so the PS/2 port is rarely used today.

- Parallel ports have a DB-25 female connector and were primarily used for printers. These parallel ports are logically called LPT (short for line printer) ports. Most printers today use a USB, Firewire, or a network connection. Network connections can be wireless or can use an RJ-45 connected to a twisted-pair cable.

- Serial ports commonly use a DB-9 male connector, but some use a DB-25 male connector. The underlying protocol used with serial ports is RS-232. Serial ports have been used for external modems, but it's more common to use a USB port with newer modems.

- RJ-45 connectors are used with twisted-pair cables in Ethernet networks.

- RJ-11 connectors are used with twisted-pair cables for telephones.

True or false? Sound systems use either RCA connections or TRS connections.

Answer: *True.* Many high-end sound systems use RCA connectors. Basic speakers often use tip ring sleeve (TRS) connectors. Some sound systems use a specialized S/PDIF connector.

> **EXAM TIP** TRS connectors are more common with computer sound systems, but some high-end sound systems use RCA connectors.

> **MORE INFO** You can view pictures of TRS, RCA, and S/PDIF connectors through Bing.com/images by searching on the type of connector. Chapter 5 of the CompTIA A+ Training Kit (Exam 220-801 and Exam 220-802), ISBN-10: 0735662681, covers sound cards and their connectors in more depth and includes pictures of various connectors.

Device cable types

This section covers additional cable types used within a computer. If you look at the objectives, you'll notice that many of these cable types are directly related to device connectors mentioned in the previous section. For example, an RJ-45 connector is used with twisted-pair cable on an Ethernet network.

True or false? IDE devices use 40-pin ribbon cables.

Answer: *True.* IDE (also called PATA) devices use 40-pin ribbon cables that plug into an IDE connection on the motherboard.

Newer cables have 80 pins in the cable but still use a 40-pin connector. The extra pins in the cable are connected to ground to provide better signals.

True or false? SCSI devices can use 25-pin, 50-pin, or 68-pin cables.

Answer: *True.* SCSI devices can use any of these types of cables.

SCSI-1 (also called narrow SCSI) typically used a 50-pin cable. SCSI-2 (also called fast SCSI) often uses 25-pin, 50-pin, or 68-pin cables. SCSI-3 (also called Ultra SCSI) often uses 50-pin, 68-pin, or 80-pin cables. Older SCSI cables are ribbon cables similar to the IDE cables, but some newer cables are round to allow better airflow inside the computer.

Characteristics of other cables can be identified as follows:

- SATA cables are thin, flat cables. Unlike the wide PATA cables, they allow better airflow inside the computer.
- eSATA cables are similar to SATA cables, but they have eSATA connections so that they can be connected externally.
- IDE and EIDE cables are broad ribbon cables with 40 pins on the connectors. A red stripe marks pin 1.
- Floppy cables are broad ribbon cables with 34 pins on the connectors. A red stripe marks pin 1.
- USB cables are small round cables.
- IEEE 1394 cables are small round cables.
- Parallel cables are thick round cables. They typically connect to the computer with a DB-25 connector and connect to the printer with a Centronics connector.
- Serial cables are round and follow the RS-232 standard for pin arrangement.
- Ethernet cables are round and include twisted pairs of wires. They use RJ-45 connectors.
- Telephone cables also use twisted-pair cable, but they use RJ-11 connectors.

Can you answer these questions?

You can find the answers to these questions at the end of this chapter.

1. Name three common connectors used for display devices.
2. What signals are included in an HDMI cable?

3. What type of cable and connector is used with Ethernet?
4. What type of cable and connector is used with phones?

Objective 1.12: Install and configure various peripheral devices

Computers accept input, complete processing, and then provide output. A variety of different peripheral devices are attached to the computer to provide input and output services. When working with computers, you need to have a good understanding of the different types of input and output devices, including how to install and configure them.

Exam need to know...

- Input devices
  For example: What is the most common method used to connect input devices? What input devices are commonly included with a multifunction printer?

- Multimedia devices
  For example: What should be done if another USB device stops working after connecting a camcorder? What is the purpose of a MIDI device?

- Output devices
  For example: What is the difference between a 5.1 sound system and a 7.1 sound system? How can you connect an HDMI monitor to a DVI graphics card?

Input devices

Input devices are used to provide an input to the computer. The most common input devices are the keyboard and mouse, but there are several additional types of devices used for input.

True or false? The Mouse applet can be used to swap the left and right buttons in a mouse.

Answer: *True.* The Mouse applet is available in the Control Panel and can be used to change the mouse buttons.

In addition to the buttons, it's also possible to change the speed of a recognized double-click, icons used by the mouse, and how the wheel operates. Many mice include additional capabilities and will enhance the Mouse applet based on the mouse's capabilities.

Similarly, you can change some settings for the keyboard. Some settings are in the Keyboard applet, but other settings are in the Ease of Access Center applet. For example, you can turn on Sticky Keys, which is useful for someone with a broken arm or some other physical issue affecting their ability to press two keys at the same time.

When Sticky Keys are enabled, you can use the Ctrl, Alt, and Del with another key, but you need to press only one key at a time. For example, to print something, you can press the Ctrl and P keys. With Sticky Keys enabled, you can press the Ctrl key and release it and then press the P key, and it works the same as if you pressed the Ctrl and P keys at the same time.

EXAM TIP Don't be surprised if you see a question related to the Mouse applet, Keyboard applet, or the Ease of Access Center. These questions are relatively simple to answer if you've taken the time to launch the applets from within the Control Panel and look at what they can do. If you haven't done this recently, now would be the perfect time to do so.

True or false? A KVM is used to use multiple monitors with a computer.

Answer: *False.* A keyboard video mouse (KVM) sharing device allows you to share a keyboard, monitor, and a mouse with multiple computers.

KVMs typically support a hot key combination to switch between computers. For example, you might need to press the Ctrl key or the Scroll Lock twice. The KVM recognizes the combination and automatically switches between the two computers.

A KVM used for two computers would have one USB mouse and one USB keyboard connected to it, along with a VGA or DVI cable going to a monitor. Each computer would connect to the KVM with USB cables for the mouse and keyboard and a VGA or DVI cable for the monitor.

EXAM TIP KVMs allow users to share a single monitor, keyboard, and mouse between two or more computers. They are often used with servers but can also be used with desktop computers.

True or false? A keyboard with a PS/2 connection should plug into the green mini-DIN connection.

Answer: *False.* Keyboards using the PS/2 connection plug into the purple (not green) mini-DIN connection.

A mouse using a PS/2 port plugs into the green mini-DIN connection. A mini-DIN connection is round and has 6 pins. Other mini-DIN connectors can have between 3 and 9 pins. For example, an S-Video connection uses a 4-pin mini-DIN connection.

EXAM TIP Most keyboards and mice plug into a USB connector, but some computers still use the older PS/2 connection. The mouse uses the green PS/2 connection, and the keyboard uses the purple connector.

True or false? Many multifunction printers include a scanner or digitizer used as an input device.

Answer: *True.* A printer is typically an output device, but multifunction printers include scanners or digitizers used as an input.

These printers include additional software that can be used with the printer to capture an image. Images can then be saved in a graphic format or as an Adobe PDF file, depending on the software.

When installing any additional input devices, it's important to ensure that the correct drivers are installed. The best source for up-to-date drivers is the manufacturer of the device.

EXAM TIP Stand-alone digitizers and scanners are available and work as input devices. Multifunction printers commonly include scanners or digitizers and can be used as input and output devices. If a multifunction printer prints but the scanner is not working, ensure that you have up-to-date drivers.

Additional input devices include the following:

- **Touch screen** These are commonly used with tablets but are also starting to be sold with regular desktop computers. The primary installation step when adding a touch screen is to install the driver provided by the manufacturer. External touch screens need another connection, such as a USB cable, to transmit the touch signals.

  EXAM TIP Many touch screens use an LCD monitor. In addition to connecting the video and power cables, you also need to connect a USB cable.

- **Microphone** A microphone captures voice and other audio. Many microphones plug into a USB connection. Some computers have a pink tip ring sleeve (TRS) connection on the front or rear of the computer for the microphone.

- **Bar code reader** Many organizations track their computers and other assets with a bar code–based inventory system. When the asset is purchased, a bar code is attached to it and the item is added to a database. The inventory is validated periodically by using the bar code reader to read the bar codes on inventory items. When in use, the bar code reader will typically plug into a USB port.

EXAM TIP Many bar code readers come with bar codes within the manual that you can scan to configure them. You can quickly configure the device by scanning these bar codes instead of manually configuring all of the settings.

- **Biometric devices** Advanced authentication methods use biometrics such as fingerprints, palm prints, or retina scan. A two-step process is required for these. First, users' biometric information (such as a fingerprint) is captured. Later, when users want to prove their identity, the biometric reader captures the information again and compares it against the previously captured information. If it matches, the user is authenticated.

- **Joysticks** These were commonly used with early computers but aren't as common today. They typically plugged into a two-row DB-15 port that was included with a sound card.

- **Game pads** These are handheld devices that have multiple controls, such as buttons and one or more analog sticks to provide similar functionality as a joystick. These typically plug into a USB connection, and some are available using a wireless connection.

EXAM TIP If an input device stops working after installing updates to the operating system, double-check the drivers for the device. It's possible for Windows Update to overwrite existing drivers in some situations.

Multimedia devices

Multimedia devices are used for audio and video input. They capture audio and video, which can be used in different applications by the user.

True or false? Computers with webcams and microphones allow users to communicate with friends and family over the Internet without a phone.

Answer: *True.* Webcams (short for web cameras) provide video, and microphones provide audio, and together they are used for online phone calls over the Internet without a phone connection.

Skype is a popular service that many people use for video conferencing. Additionally, Google+ supports video conferencing. A significant benefit is that long-distance phone line charges don't apply because only the Internet connection is used.

True or false? MIDI devices can play music by using a text file as an input.

Answer: *True.* Musical Instrument Digital Interface (MIDI) devices play synthesized music from a specially formatted text file.

Some MIDI connectors use a two-row DB-15 connection to plug into a sound card connection. This is the same port used by joysticks. Other MIDI connectors use the TRS connection.

Other multimedia devices include the following:

- **Digital cameras** Most digital cameras connect directly to a USB port on a computer. When connected, they are often accessible and can be browsed as an additional drive by using Windows Explorer.
- **Camcorders** These are digital recorders that can record and store videos with audio. A camcorder is a handheld device, but after recording the video, you can usually connect to a computer's USB or Firewire port to transfer the videos.

EXAM TIP Digital cameras and camcorders commonly plug into a standard Type A USB port on the computer. Digital cameras will often have a mini or micro connection on the camera, but a camcorder will use a larger Type B USB connection. If too many devices are plugged into a USB hub, the hub won't be able to provide power to all of them and one or more devices will stop working. This sometimes occurs when a camcorder is plugged in. The camcorder might work, but one or more other devices stop working. One solution is to provide power to the device separately or to use a powered hub.

Output devices

Output devices are used to provide information that users can see or hear. Common input devices are printers, speakers, and display devices.

True or false? Printers are commonly connected with a USB connection.

Answer: *True*. USB connections are the most common type connection used with printers.

In many situations, you can simply plug the USB cable from the printer into the computer and it will work. In some cases, you'll need to update or install the correct drivers for the printer.

True or false? A 5.1 sound system uses five speakers and a subwoofer providing surround sound capabilities.

Answer: *True*. A 5.1 sound system has left and right speakers in front of a user, left and right speakers behind the user, a central speaker in front of the user, and a subwoofer.

Sounds can be played within a 3-D sound space to give users the impression that sounds are around them. Common sound systems are 2.1 (stereo with a subwoofer), 5.1, and 7.1. A 7.1 sound system is a 5.1 system with an additional pair of speakers directly to the left and directly to the right of the user.

Some common connections used with sound cards include the following:

- **Lime green tip ring sleeve (TRS)**   Used for front speakers or headphones. This supports both right and left audio for stereo.
- **Brown TRS**   Used for middle speaker connection used in 7.1 systems. It supports both middle speakers.
- **Orange TRS**   Used for the center speaker and a subwoofer.
- **Black TRS**   Used for rear speakers. One connection supports both speakers.
- **Light blue TRS**   Used as a line in from another device.
- **Pink TRS**   Used for a microphone.
- **Sony/Philips Digital Interconnect Format (S/PDIF)**   This is a special connection that supports all channels used by a sound system.

True or false? A passive HDMI-to-DVI adapter can be used to plug an HDMI display into DVI port.

Answer: *True*. This type of adapter allows you to connect an HDMI cable into a DVI port. You can use it to connect an HDMI monitor to a DVI port without making any other changes.

> **EXAM TIP**   Both DVI and HDMI support digital, which is one reason why adapters are available. In contrast, passive adapters are not available to convert analog VGA signals to digital HDMI signals.

Can you answer these questions?

You can find the answers to these questions at the end of this chapter.

1. What is the purpose of a KVM?
2. What hardware is needed for video conferencing between two individuals using only an Internet connection?
3. What is an S/PDIF connection used for in a computer?

Answers

This section contains the answers to the "Can you answer these questions?" sections in this chapter.

Objective 1.1: Configure and apply BIOS settings

1. Computers should be plugged into an UPS to prevent damage from an unplanned power outage. If the computer loses power during the upgrade, it can corrupt the BIOS and prevent the computer from booting.
2. BIOS can be checked to see whether newly installed hardware (including RAM) is recognized. If the BIOS recognizes new hardware but the operating system doesn't, the technician needs to troubleshoot the operating system. If the BIOS doesn't recognize new hardware, the problem is with the computer or the new hardware, not the operating system.
3. The boot order (sometimes called boot sequence) in the BIOS should be modified if a computer is not booting to a bootable DVD disc.
4. POST will commonly check the CPU, clock, memory, graphics, and the keyboard. If POST fails, the computer stops and reports the error, often with a beep error code.

Objective 1.2: Differentiate between motherboard components, their purposes, and properties

1. A mini-ATX motherboard uses the same power connections specified in the ATX standard, so it needs an ATX-based power supply.
2. You cannot plug a larger PCIe x8 card into a smaller PCIe x4 slot. However, you can plug a smaller PCIe x4 card into a larger PCIe x8 slot.
3. A DDR3 DIMM socket has 240 pins.
4. CPUs that include north bridge functionality interact directly with memory and the PCIe graphics card (when used).
5. You can use a jumper or a screwdriver to reset the BIOS password.
6. The P1 power connector is a rectangular two-row connector with either 20 pins or 24 pins.
7. A 4-pin fan connector adds a pulse-width modulation signal used to vary the speed of a fan. 3-pin connectors don't have this capability.

Objective 1.3: Compare and contrast RAM types and features

1. A matched pair of RAM sticks should be installed in the same bank on a dual-channel motherboard. Banks are identified as slots of the same color, such as two blue slots or two black slots.

2. The standard name for a DDR3 RAM stick using a 400-MHz clock is DDR3-3200, and the module name is PC3-25600. The standard name is calculated as the clock × 2 × 4 (or the clock × 8). 400 × 8 = 3200, so DDR3-3200 is the standard name. The module name can be calculated as the clock × 2 × 4 × 64 / 8 (or the clock × 8 × 8). 400 × 8 × 8 = 25,600, giving a module name of PC3-25600.

Objective 1.4: Install and configure expansion cards

1. The original sound card needs to be disabled in the BIOS after adding a new sound card.

2. The most likely problem is the power supply if a computer no longer starts after adding a new video card. Video cards draw a lot of power, and if the computer is no longer able to start, it indicates that the power supply isn't providing enough power. It's possible that the video card is faulty, but if it's new, that isn't as likely. It's also possible that it wasn't installed correctly.

3. Assuming the computer has a NIC, you can add a second NIC to allow it to connect to an additional LAN. If the computer doesn't have a NIC, you can add two NICs.

4. SATA is commonly used for desktop systems, and a SATA expansion card can support additional drives used for a RAID. SCSI is also used.

5. TV tuners can capture NTSC and/or PAL video signals.

Objective 1.5: Install and configure storage devices and use appropriate media

1. A Blu-Ray disc that is rewritable will have the -RE designation.

2. Solid state disks (SSDs) are resistant to shock damage.

3. A RAID-0 provides increased read and write performance, but it does not add any reliability or fault tolerance. In contrast, RAID-1, RAID-5, and RAID-10 all provide fault tolerance.

4. A dual-sided dual-layer DVD-ROM can store 8.5 GB on each side for a total of 17 GB of data.

Objective 1.6: Differentiate among various CPU types and features and select the appropriate cooling method

1. Intel CPUs use LGA 1155 and LGA 1366 sockets. They also use LGA 775, LGA 2011, and LGA 1156 sockets.

2. AMD CPUs use Socket 940, AM2, AM2+, AM3, AM3+, FM1, and F.

3. Intel uses hyper-threading which effectively makes each core appear as two cores.
4. Liquid-based cooling systems are the quietest because they do not use fans.

Objective 1.7: Compare and contrast various connection interfaces and explain their purpose

1. SATA 2 devices have a maximum speed of 3 Gbits/s (300 MBps).
2. VGA cables use a three-row DB-15 connector.
3. VGA signals are analog, and HDMI signals are digital. Additionally, HDMI signals include both video and eight-channel audio, but VGA signals do not include audio.

Objective 1.8: Install an appropriate power supply based on a given scenarios

1. A 6-pin or 8-pin connector would be used for a PCIe graphics card, when it is used.
2. A RAID will use multiple hard drives, so the power supply should have enough 12 VDC rails to support it.
3. The power supply should be adjusted from 230 VAC, commonly used in European countries/regions, to 115 VAC, commonly used in North American countries/regions.

Objective 1.9: Evaluate and select appropriate components for a custom configuration, to meet customer specifications or needs

1. An AGP-based graphics card would be too slow for a CAD workstation. PCIe graphics cards provide better performance.
2. A liquid cooling system is the quietest and provides a high-end cooling solution for a gaming PC that will be overclocked. High-end fans can also be used, but they aren't as quiet as the liquid cooling system.
3. A home theater system needs a TV tuner, an HDMI output, and high-quality surround sound audio. The HDMI output would connect to the liquid crystal display (LCD) screen.
4. A thin client will meet the minimum requirements for the operating system and is appropriate for a user doing only Internet searches.
5. A home server should have a high-speed NIC (such as a Gigabit Ethernet NIC) and a high-speed, reliable disk subsystem (such as a RAID).

Objective 1.10: Given a scenario, evaluate types and features of display devices

1. LCD-based and LED-based displays require backlights. An LCD-based display uses a CCFL as a backlight, and an LED-based display uses LEDs as backlights.

2. CRT-based monitors should have a refresh rate of 72 Hz or more to reduce flicker and the associated eyestrain.

3. LCD-based displays have a native resolution that they are designed for, and the display should be set to the native resolution.

4. VGA uses analog data, and HDMI uses digital data. A VGA output cannot be used for an HDMI display.

Objective 1.11: Identify connector types and associated cables

1. Some common connectors used for display devices are VGA (DB-15), DVI, and HDMI. Some other connectors include DisplayPort and RCA.

2. An HDMI cable includes digital video and eight-channel audio.

3. Ethernet uses twisted-pair cable and an RJ-45 connector.

4. Phones use twisted-pair cable and an RJ-11 connector.

Objective 1.12: Install and configure various peripheral devices

1. A keyboard video mouse (KVM) device is used to share a single keyboard, video, and mouse with multiple computers.

2. The hardware needed for video conferencing between two individuals is a computer with a monitor, webcam, speaker, and microphone.

3. The webcam and microphone captures the video and audio of one user, and the monitor and speaker outputs the video and audio for the other user.

4. A Sony/Philips Digital Interconnect Format (S/PDIF) is used as a single connection for a sound system.

CHAPTER 2

Networking

The Networking domain covers approximately 27 percent of the A+ 220-801 exam. Almost every computer you'll service will be connected to a network, so it's important to understand some basic networking topics. This includes network cables and connectors, network devices such as routers and switches, wireless connections, and common protocols used to control traffic over a network. Many networks use both wired and wireless connections, along with a router for Internet access. Technicians are often asked to help configure connectivity for different types of networks, and they need to know the functions and features of various devices, along with appropriate networking tools.

This chapter covers the following objectives:

- Objective 2.1: Identify types of network cables and connectors
- Objective 2.2: Categorize characteristics of connectors and cabling
- Objective 2.3: Explain properties and characteristics of TCP/IP
- Objective 2.4: Explain common TCP and UDP ports, protocols, and their purpose
- Objective 2.5: Compare and contrast wireless networking standards and encryption types
- Objective 2.6: Install, configure, and deploy a SOHO wireless/wired router using appropriate settings
- Objective 2.7: Compare and contrast Internet connection types and features
- Objective 2.8: Identify various types of networks
- Objective 2.9: Compare and contrast network devices and their functions and features
- Objective 2.10: Given a scenario, use appropriate networking tools

Objective 2.1: Identify types of network cables and connectors

The first objective in this domain introduces the three most common types of cables used for networks: fiber, twisted-pair, and coaxial. The most important thing you should know for this objective is the types of connectors used with each type of cable. The next objective builds on these topics requiring you to know the characteristics of the cables.

Exam need to know...

- Fiber
  For example: What types of connectors are used with fiber cable?
- Twisted-pair
  For example: What types of connectors are used with twisted-pair cable? What standards are used when wiring a twisted-pair cable?
- Coaxial
  For example: What are the two common connectors used with coaxial cable?

Fiber

Fiber cable is made of a flexible glass material, and data is sent over the cable as light pulses. There are three primary connectors you'll see with fiber cables.

True or false? An LC is one of the common connectors used with fiber cable.

Answer: *True.* A Lucent Connector (LC) is used with fiber cable.

Some additional connectors commonly used with fiber cable include the following:

- **Square connector (SC)**   Just as its name implies, this connector is square shaped. The LC connector is a miniature version of the SC connector.
- **Straight tip (ST)**   This is a round connector with a straight tip.

EXAM TIP   Common connectors used with fiber cable are LC, SC, and ST. You should be able to identify each by sight.

MORE INFO   If you aren't familiar with the different fiber connectors, check out *http://www.bing.com/images*. Enter search words such as **fiber connectors, LC connector, SC connector**, and **ST connector**. You can use the same procedure to view pictures for any type connectors introduced in this section. Chapter 19 of the CompTIA A+ Training Kit (Exam 220-801 and Exam 220-802), ISBN-10: 0735662681, covers all of the cable types and connectors in more depth.

Twisted-pair

Twisted-pair cable includes multiple pairs of wires twisted around each other. These twists are precise and determine the frequency capabilities of the cable. Cables that support higher frequencies allow the cable to transmit more data at a time.

True or false? RJ-11 connectors are used with twisted-pair cables to connect network devices.

Answer: *False.* RJ-45 connectors are used with twisted-pair cables when connecting network devices.

RJ-11 connectors are used with phone-based twisted-pair cables. For example, RJ-11 connectors are used with a plain old telephone system (POTS) modem or even a digital subscriber line (DSL) modem.

> **MORE INFO** Modems can be used for Internet connectivity. Objective 2.7, "Compare and contrast Internet connection types and features," covers various methods of connecting to the Internet, including standard dial-up modems and DSL modems. Twisted-pair cables come in several different categories, such as CAT 5, CAT 6, and so on. These are discussed in Objective 2.2, "Categorize characteristics of connectors and cabling."

Twisted-pair cables used in networking have four pairs of wires. The colors of each pair are as follows:

- Blue wire and white wire with a blue stripe
- Orange wire and white wire with an orange stripe
- Green wire and white wire with a green stripe
- Brown wire and white wire with a brown stripe

Each wire should be connected to a specific pin on the RJ-45 connector, and there are two standards that can be used—T568A and T568B. When creating a standard cable, both ends should use the same standard. This ensures that the same wire is going to the same pin on each connector.

True or false? A cable wired with the T568A standard on one end and the T568B standard on the other end works as a crossover cable.

Answer: *True.* If different standards are used, certain wires are crossed over and the cable will function as a crossover cable. Crossover cables are used to connect similar devices together, such as two computers or two switches.

> **EXAM TIP** RJ-11 connectors are used for phone lines. RJ-45 connectors are used with network twisted-pair cables. When wiring RJ-45 connectors, you should use either the T568A or T568B standard on both ends of the cable.

Coaxial

Coaxial cable is commonly used to connect televisions with broadband cable, DVD players, and digital video recorders (DVRs). It isn't used as often with networks, but it has been used in the past.

True or false? F-type screw-on connectors are used with coaxial cable.

Answer: *True.* Coaxial cable uses F-type screw-on or BNC twist-on connectors.

Can you answer these questions?

You can find the answers to these questions at the end of this chapter.

1. What type of cable would an LC connector be used with?
2. What is the difference between an RJ-11 and an RJ-45 connector?
3. What type of cable is used with an F-type connector?

Objective 2.2: Categorize characteristics of connectors and cabling

In this objective, you're expected to know a little more about the cables and connectors introduced in Objective 2.1, "Identify types of network cables and connectors." In addition to being able to recognize the cables and connectors, you also need know about some of their characteristics, such as their speed and transmission limitations.

Exam need to know...

- Fiber
  For example: What is a benefit of fiber cable related to EMI? Which supports the maximum distance—SMF or MMF?

- Twisted-pair
  For example: What category of twisted-pair cable supports 1 Gbps? What is the maximum transmission speed of CAT 3?

- Coaxial
  For example: What is RG-6 cable used for?

Fiber

Fiber cable is more expensive and harder to work with than twisted-pair or coaxial cable. However, it has some significant advantages over other cable types, so it is being used in more and more networks.

True or false? Fiber cable is immune to EMI and RFI.

Answer: *True.* Fiber cable is not susceptible to signal loss from electromagnetic interference (EMI) or radio frequency interference (RFI).

Two common sources of EMI are from electric power cables or fluorescent light fixtures that are too close to signal cables. RFI interference comes from devices transmitting RF signals.

True or false? Data sent on a fiber cable can travel significantly farther than data sent on twisted-pair or coaxial cable.

Answer: *True.* Data sent on single-mode fiber (SMF) can travel the farthest without needing a repeater. Data sent on multi-mode (MMF) fiber can travel farther than data sent on twisted-pair or coaxial cable, but not as far as SMF cable.

For comparison, the maximum distances of different cables without using a repeater are as follows:

- SMF—up to 40 Km
- MMF—up to 2 Km
- Twisted-pair—up to 100 meters
- Coaxial—185 meters or 500 meters, depending on the cable type

NOTE A repeater receives and retransmits signals; it is used when distances exceed cable limitations. For example, to use twisted-pair cable to connect two devices that are 150 meters apart, you can use a repeater in the middle. One cable run can be about 75 meters and connect to the repeater. The repeater then "repeats" the signal onto the second cable run of about 75 more meters. Neither cable run is more than 100 meters.

EXAM TIP Fiber optic cable is immune to EMI and RFI. SMF cable supports the longest cable lengths without repeaters, and MMF cable supports longer cable lengths than twisted-pair and coaxial cable.

Twisted-pair

Twisted-pair cable comes in many different types and categories. All categories come in both unshielded twisted-pair (UTP) and shielded twisted-pair (STP) versions. The STP version provides some protection against EMI and RFI, but it isn't as effective as fiber cable against this interference.

True or false? If you need to run twisted-pair cable close to fluorescent lights, you should use UTP cable.

Answer: *False.* Fluorescent array lighting is a known source of interference, so STP cable is the best choice.

UTP cable is highly susceptible to signal loss from EMI and RFI. STP cable provides some protection against EMI and RFI, but it isn't as effective as fiber cable.

EXAM TIP STP protects against EMI and RFI. Use STP cable if you have to run cable near power cables or through a fluorescent lighting array.

True or false? CAT 5e cable supports a maximum transfer rate of 10 Gbps.

Answer: *False.* CAT 5e cable supports a maximum transfer rate of 1 Gbps.

The maximum transfer rates of various categories are as follows:

- CAT 3—10 Mbps
- CAT 5—100 Mbps

- CAT 5e—1000 Mbps (1 Gbps)
- CAT 6—10 Gbps

EXAM TIP Ensure that you know the maximum transmission speeds of each of the different cable categories. Even though some of the cable categories are rarely used today, they are specifically listed in the objectives.

True or false? Plenum rated cable is fire retardant and reduces hazardous fumes from a fire.

Answer: *True*. Plenum rated cable should be used when cable is run through a plenum. It is fire retardant and reduces hazardous fumes from a fire.

A plenum, or plenum space, is the open space where heated and/or air conditioned air is forced through a building. Cables are commonly routed through these plenum spaces. The standard jacket covering used for cables is made of polyvinyl chloride (PVC), and it will emit toxic fumes if it burns. PVC cable should never be used in a plenum space because the toxic fumes are sent through the building from the heating and ventilation system.

EXAM TIP Plenum-rated cable should be used when cable is routed through plenums. PVC cable emits toxic fumes, but plenum-rated cable is fire retardant.

Coaxial

The two types of coaxial cable mentioned in the objectives are RG-6 and RG-59. RG-6 cable commonly uses an F-type screw-on connector, and RG-59 normally uses a BNC twist-on connector, although both cable types can use either connector.

True or false? RG-6 cable is commonly used for cable television distribution and supports the transmission of both analog and digital data.

Answer: *True*. RG-6 supports both analog and digital data.

RG-59 supports analog or digital data, although it is susceptible to high-frequency losses, so it is not used for cable television transmissions. Cable TV companies often provide Internet access through the same cable used for television channels. RG-6 cable is often used for these connections. When customers subscribe to broadband Internet in addition to cable television, a splitter is used to send one output to televisions and another output to a cable modem for the Internet connection.

EXAM TIP RG-6 and RG-59 are two types of coaxial cable. RG-6 is used with broadband cable connections and supports both analog and digital transmissions.

Can you answer these questions?

You can find the answers to these questions at the end of this chapter.

1. Which cable type supports the longest cables without a repeater?

2. What is the maximum transfer rate supported by CAT 6 cables?

3. What type of data is transmitted on RG-6 cable?

Objective 2.3: Explain properties and characteristics of TCP/IP

The primary protocol suite used on networks is Transmission Control Protocol/ Internet Protocol (TCP/IP), and it includes several underlying protocols. You aren't expected to be an expert on everything related to TCP/IP, but you do need to be able to identify and explain many basic characteristics. This includes the class of an IP address, differences between IPv4 and IPv6, differences between private and public addresses, and differences between statically and dynamically assigned IP addresses. You should also know about basic services provided on a network.

Exam need to know...

- IP class
  For example: What class is 192.168.1.6? What class is 172.16.6.3?
- IPv4 vs. IPv6
  For example: How many bits does an IPv6 address use? How are IPv6 addresses displayed?
- Public vs. private vs. APIPA
  For example: What are the ranges of private IP addresses? When is an APIPA address used?
- Static vs. dynamic
  For example: Which method (static or dynamic) results in more IP address conflicts?
- Client-side DNS
  For example: What does DNS provide for a client?
- DHCP
  For example: What does DHCP provide for a client?
- Subnet mask
  For example: How is the subnet mask used with an IP address?
- Gateway
  For example: What is the difference between a gateway and a router?

IP class

Classful IP addresses are in certain predefined ranges. When you know the class of an IP address, you automatically know its subnet mask.

True or false? An address of 10.20.30.88 is a Class C address.

Answer: *False.* This address is a Class A address.

The class of an address is identified by the first number in the address. For example, in the 10.20.30.88 address, the first number is 10, which indicates that it is a Class A address. This also tells you that it has a subnet mask of 255.0.0.0. The ranges of each type of address are as follows:

- Class A—1 to 126 (subnet mask 255.0.0.0)
- Class B—128 to 191 (subnet mask 255.255.0.0)
- Class C—192 to 223 (subnet mask 255.255.255.0)

EXAM TIP Given an IP address, you should be able to identify if it is a Class A, Class B, or Class C IP address. Similarly, if you're given a specific class such as Class C, you should be able to identify all the IP addresses in a list that are in that class.

MORE INFO The Wikipedia article titled "Classful Network" includes more details on classful IP addresses, including specifically how many networks each supports and how many IP addresses can be used on each network. You can access it here: *http:// en.wikipedia.org/wiki/Classful_network.*

IPv4 vs. IPv6

IPv4 addresses use 32 bits and are displayed in dotted decimal format, such as 192.168.1.1. IPv6 addresses use 128 bits and are displayed in hexadecimal format separated by colons, like this: FC00:0000:0000:0000:042A:0000:0000:07F5.

True or false? The following two IPv6 addresses are identical: FC00::42A:0:0:7F5 and FC00:0000:0000:0000:042A:0000:0000:07F5.

Answer: *True.* IPv6 addresses can omit leading zeroes and use zero compression to shorten the way the address is displayed without changing the actual address.

IPv6 addresses use 32 hexadecimal characters. Each hexadecimal character represents four bits for a total of 128 bits (4 × 128).

MORE INFO Hexadecimal characters include the numbers 0 to 9 and the characters A to F. The following page shows how decimal, hexadecimal, and binary numbers compare side by side: *http://blogs.getcertifiedgetahead.com/comparing-decimal -hexadecimal-and-binary/.*

The IPv6 address is often represented as eight groups of four hexadecimal characters separated by colons. For example, in the IPv6 address of FC00:0000:0000:0000:042A:0000:0000:07F5, FC00 is one group of four hexadecimal characters, and the next group is 0000.

To understand how leading zeros are omitted, imagine you have 120 dollars. It could be represented as 0120 dollars, and it's still the same amount of money. However, we typically omit the leading zeros with money, and you can do the same thing with IPv6 addresses. The following example address is shown with leading zeros omitted: FC00:0:0:0:42A:0:0:7F5.

Trailing zeros are never omitted. For example, 120 dollars and 12 dollars are not the same amount of money. Similarly, FC00 is the not the same hexadecimal number as FC.

Zero compression is also used with IPv6 addresses. Instead of displaying groups of zeros, you can use a double colon to replace one or more such zero-value groups. For example, either of the following two IPv6 addresses represents the same address:

- FC00::042A:0000:0000:07F5
- FC00:0000:0000:0000:042A::07F5

An IPv6 address has eight groups of four hexadecimal characters. When you see a double colon, you can replace it with enough missing groups to get eight groups.

For example, in the first address, FC00::042A:0000:0000:07F5, five groups are showing (FC00, 042A, 0000, 0000, and 07F5), so you know that the double colon represents three groups of zeros (0000, 0000, and 0000).

In the second address, FC00:0000:0000:0000:042A::07F5, you can see six groups (FC00, 0000, 0000, 0000, 042A, and 07F5), so you know that the double colon represents two groups of zeros (0000 and 0000).

You cannot use two double colons in any IPv6 address. For example, if you did this FC00::042A::07F5, you would see that three groups are showing (FC00, 042A, and 07F5), indicating that five groups are missing. However, there's no way to tell how many groups should be used for each double colon. It could be FC00:0000:0000: 042A:0000:0000:0000:07F5 or FC00:0000:0000:0000:042A:0000:0000:07F5.

Both methods of omitting leading zeros and zero compression can be combined. For example, FC00:0000:0000:0000:042A:0000:0000:07F5 can be shortened to FC00::42A:0:0:7F5.

EXAM TIP IPv4 addresses use 32 bits and are commonly represented in dotted decimal format. IPv6 addresses use 128 bits and are commonly represented in hexadecimal format with eight groups of four hexadecimals. IPv6 addresses can be simplified by omitting leading zeroes in each group and using zero compression. With zero compression, a single string of zeroes is represented with a double colon.

MORE INFO IPv6 uses ::1 instead of 127.0.0.1 as the loopback address. Chapter 21 of the CompTIA A+ Training Kit (Exam 220-801 and Exam 220-802), ISBN-10: 0735662681, provides more detailed information about IPv6.

Public vs. private vs. APIPA

IP addresses used on the Internet are public IP addresses. IP addresses used on internal networks are private IP addresses. Automatic Private IP Addressing (APIPA) addresses are randomly selected private addresses that always start with 169.254.

True or false? An IP address of 172.16.10.5 is a public address.

Answer: *False*. This is a private IP address.

Private IP addresses are formally defined in Request for Comments (RFC) 1918, with the following ranges:

- 10.0.0.0 through 10.255.255.255 (Class A private IP addresses)
- 172.16.0.0 through 172.31.255.255 (Class B private IP addresses)
- 192.168.0.0 through 192.168.255.255 (Class C private IP addresses)

EXAM TIP   Given an IP address, you should be able to identify whether it is a public IP address or a private IP address. Similarly, you should be able to identify all the IP addresses in a list that are either public or private.

True or false? If you see a computer with an IP address of 169.254.6.3, you know that it was unable to get an IP address from a DHCP server.

Answer: *True.* An address starting with 169.254 is an APIPA address, and Dynamic Host Configuration Protocol (DHCP) clients can assign themselves an APIPA address if a DHCP server isn't available.

In many networks, administrators configure a DHCP server to provide clients with an IP address and other TCP/IP configuration information such as a subnet mask, a default gateway, and the address of a DNS server. If the DHCP server doesn't respond to the request for this information, the DHCP client assigns itself an APIPA address.

EXAM TIP   APIPA addresses always start with 169.254 and are assigned only when a DHCP client does not get a reply from a DHCP server for an IP address.

Static vs. dynamic

IP addresses can be statically assigned or dynamically assigned. A statically assigned address has been manually entered by a person, and a dynamically assigned address has been assigned through a service on the network or on the computer.

True or false? Statically assigned IP addresses often result in IP address conflicts.

Answer: *True.* When IP addresses are manually assigned, it's easy to assign the same IP address to two or more systems on the network, resulting in an IP address conflict.

IP address conflicts adversely affect the network communication of at least one client on the network and sometimes both. If you statically assign an IP address to one Windows-based computer named Win7 on a network and then later assign the same IP address to another Windows-based computer, the second computer recognizes the conflict and won't use the IP address. The Win7 computer continues to operate without problems, but the second computer can't communicate on the network.

However, printers aren't that smart. If you statically assign an IP address to a printer that was previously assigned to the Win7 computer, it adversely affects both the printer and the computer. Both will have network connectivity problems.

Client-side DNS

The primary purpose of a Domain Name System (DNS) server is to resolve computer and host names to IP addresses. DNS is used on the Internet and on internal networks.

True or false? DNS maps user-friendly names to network resources.

Answer: *True*. A DNS server stores computer names and their assigned IP address on a network.

Clients are configured with the IP address of a DNS server for name resolution purposes. Clients can query the DNS server by sending the user-friendly name of any host on the network (also called a host name), and the DNS server responds with the IP address. For example, when a user enters the user-friendly name of *www.bing.com* in the URL for a web browser, the user's computer queries DNS for the IP address of *www.bing.com* without any additional user intervention. Users don't need to memorize IP addresses but instead need only to remember names.

DHCP

Dynamic Host Configuration Protocol (DHCP) is a protocol that often runs on a DHCP server in a network. In small networks, routers often include DHCP, eliminating the need for a server to run DHCP.

True or false? DHCP assigns IP addresses to hosts on a network.

Answer: *True.* DHCP dynamically assigns IP addresses and other TCP/IP configuration to hosts within a network.

DHCP can assign much more than just the IP address, but assigning the IP address is a primary purpose. Other information commonly assigned by DHCP includes the following:

- Subnet mask
- Default gateway
- DNS server address

NOTE DHCP servers track which IP addresses are assigned to computers in the network so that the same IP addresses are not assigned to more than one client. They also have the ability to detect whether an IP address is already assigned within the network and, if so, can choose an alternate IP address to give to a client.

EXAM TIP The primary purpose of DHCP is to dynamically assign IP addresses and other TCP/IP configuration information to DHCP clients. DHCP clients that do not receive an IP address from DHCP assign themselves an APIPA address starting with 169.254.

Subnet mask

IPv4 addresses are matched with a subnet mask. For example, a Class C address of 192.168.1.5 has a subnet mask of 255.255.255.0. You don't always see the subnet mask, but it is being used.

True or false? The subnet mask defines what portion of an IP address is the network ID and what portion is the host ID.

Answer: *True.* IP addresses have two parts (the network ID and the host ID), and the subnet mask is used to differentiate the two.

Both IP addresses and subnet masks are composed of 32 bits. They are typically presented as four decimal numbers divided by dots (also known as dotted decimal notation), but they can also be represented in binary. For example, consider the IP address of 192.168.1.5 with a subnet mask of 255.255.255.0. Both can be represented in binary as follows:

- 192.168.1.5   = 1100 0000.1010 1000.0000 0001.0000 0101
- 255.255.255.0 = 1111 1111.1111 1111.1111 0000 0000

NOTE Numbers are easier to comprehend when they are grouped. For example 1,234,567,890 is easier to read and understand than 1234567890. Both are the same number, but it is easier to see that it is more than 1 million when grouping is used. Similarly, bytes are often grouped by putting a space between each set of four bits.

The subnet mask is used to determine which portion of the IP address is the network ID. When the subnet mask is a 1, that portion of the IP address is the network ID. In the following example, notice that the 1s in the subnet mask match up to only the first 24 bits in the IP address:

- 192.168.1.5 = 1100 0000.1010 1000.0000 0001.---- ----
- 255.255.255.0 = 1111 1111.1111 1111.1111 1111.0000 0000

If you convert these bits back to decimal, you have 192.168.1. However, you always add trailing zeros for the network ID, so the network ID is 192.168.1.0.

The host ID is whatever is left over. Because the first three decimal numbers are used for the network ID, the last number (5) is the host ID.

- 192.168.1.5 = ---- ----.---- ----.---- ----.0000 0101
- 255.255.255.0 = 1111 1111.1111 1111.1111 1111.0000 0000

NOTE When only 255 and 0 decimal numbers are used in the subnet mask, this can be simplified. When the subnet mask is a 255, that portion of the IP address is the network ID. When the subnet mask is a 0, that portion of the IP address is the host ID.

EXAM TIP The subnet mask is used to differentiate which portion of an IP address is the network ID and which portion of the IP address is the host ID. If the subnet mask bit is 1 (or the decimal number is 255), the corresponding portion of the IP address is the network ID. If the subnet mask is 0, the corresponding portion of the IP address is the host ID.

MORE INFO Chapter 21 of the CompTIA A+ Training Kit (Exam 220-801 and Exam 220-802), ISBN-10: 0735662681, goes into more depth about how the subnet mask is combined with the IP address to identify the network ID and the host ID portion.

Gateway

The gateway (or default gateway) is an IP address on a router, and it provides a path out of the network. A router will have more than one network interface, and each is assigned an IP address.

True or false? If a client is assigned an incorrect default gateway address, it will not be able to communicate with any systems on the network.

Answer: *False*. The gateway provides a path to other networks through a router, but even if it is configured incorrectly, clients on the network will still be able to communicate with clients on the same subnet.

Figure 2-1 shows a diagram of a network with a router. All clients in Network 1 use a network ID of 192.168.1.0 and a default gateway of 192.168.1.1 (label 1). If clients in Network 1 need to communicate with clients in Network 2 or the Internet, they send the traffic to the default gateway and the router sends the traffic to the correct path.

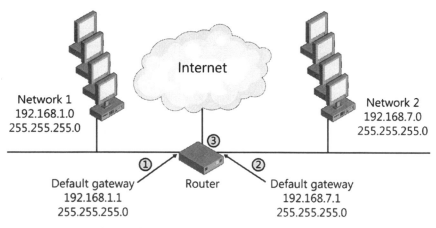

FIGURE 2-1 Router with two default gateways.

If the default gateway for any client on Network 1 is incorrect, this client will not be able to reach Network 2 or the Internet. However, it will still be able to communicate with other clients on Network 1.

In the diagram, you can see that the default gateway for Network 2 is 192.168.7.1 (label 2). All clients in Network 2 are assigned this address. Label 3 shows the interface card going to the Internet.

NOTE While many people call the default gateway the router, that is not completely accurate. It is the IP address of a network interface on the router, but the router is much more than just a single default gateway. Routers have multiple interfaces providing gateways, or paths, to other networks.

EXAM TIP The gateway provides a path out of a network, and all clients in the same subnet are assigned the same default gateway. The gateway is commonly assigned the first number in the subnet (such as 192.168.1.1), but this isn't a requirement.

Can you answer these questions?

You can find the answers to these questions at the end of this chapter.

1. What class is this IP address: 192.168.15.7?
2. What type of address is this: FC00::42A:0:0:7F5?
3. What type of address is this: 169.254.63.87?
4. What is the primary purpose of DNS?
5. What is the primary purpose of DHCP?

Objective 2.4: Explain common TCP and UDP ports, protocols, and their purpose

TCP and UDP are core protocols within the TCP/IP suite of protocols. They both use well-known port numbers to identify the type of traffic being sent to destination computers. Firewalls use these port numbers to allow or block traffic. Other protocols work within the TCP/IP suite for other purposes, and this objective expects you to know the primary purpose of some of these protocols. Also, you should know the primary differences between TCP and UDP.

Exam need to know...

- Ports
  For example: What ports are used for traffic in web browsers?
- Protocols
  For example: What is the difference between DHCP and DNS? What is SSH and SFTP?
- TCP vs. UDP
  For example: Which protocol (TCP or UDP) provides the best reliability?

Ports

TCP/IP packets include source IP addresses and ports, and destination IP addresses and ports. The IP address is used to get traffic from the source computer to the destination computer. When the packet reaches the destination, the destination computer uses the port to identify what to do with the traffic.

This is similar to how regular mail uses an address to get mail to a home. After it arrives, someone sorts the mail and determines who gets it. If it's addressed to you, you open and handle it. In this context, the mailing address is similar to the IP address, and the person the mail is addressed to is similar to the port.

For example, Hypertext Transfer Protocol (HTTP) uses port 80. When you use a web browser to browse the Internet, your computer sends a request to the web server using its IP address and a destination port of 80. When the web server receives it, it sees port 80 and sends the request to the service handling web requests.

If your web browser had a secure connection, it would use Hypertext Transfer Protocol Secure (HTTPS) and port 443. Instead of using a destination port 80, it uses a destination port of 443. Again, when the web server receives it, it recognizes port 443 and forwards the request to the web server.

True or false? Port 25 should be opened on a firewall to send email.

Answer: *True.* Port 25 is used by Simple Mail Transfer Protocol (SMTP) to send email.

Incoming email uses either port 110 with Post Office Protocol version 3 (POP3) or port 143 with Internet Message Access Protocol (IMAP).

True or false? Port 53 should be opened if a user wants to control a computer remotely with RDP.

Answer: *False.* Port 53 is used for DNS name resolution requests. Port 3389 should be opened when using the Remote Desktop Protocol (RDP).

> **EXAM TIP** There are several port numbers you should know for the exam. They are: FTP (20 and 21), Telnet (23), SMTP (25), POP3 (110), IMAP (143), DNS (53), HTTP (80), HTTPS (443), and RDP (3389).

> **MORE INFO** If you want to get more details on how ports are used, you can check out the following blog: *http://blogs.getcertifiedgetahead.com/understanding-ports -security/.* It was written for the Security+ exam, but the same principles apply for the ports in A+ and Network+. Chapter 20 of the CompTIA A+ Training Kit (Exam 220-801 and Exam 220-802), ISBN-10: 0735662681, covers the ports and protocols in more depth.

Protocols

Protocols provide the rules for transmitting traffic over a network. Most protocols are formally defined in Request For Comments (RFC) documents. For example, RFC 2131 defines how DHCP works, including the contents of packets sent back and forth between DHCP servers and DHCP clients.

True or false? SFTP is used to transfer large files in an encrypted format.

Answer: *True.* File Transfer Protocol (FTP) is used to transfer large files over a network, and Secure File Transfer Protocol (SFTP) uses Secure Shell (SSH) to encrypt the files.

You should know the primary purpose of the following protocols mentioned in this objective:

- **DHCP**   Assigns an IP address and other TCP/IP configuration to clients.
- **DNS**   Used to resolve user-friendly names of network resources (also called hosts or host names) to their IP addresses.
- **Lightweight Directory Access Protocol (LDAP)**   Used to interact with services such as Active Directory Domain Services in Microsoft domains.
- **Simple Network Management Protocol (SNMP)**   Used to communicate with and manage network devices such as switches and routers.
- **Server Message Block (SMB)**   Used to transfer files over a network in a Microsoft network.
- **SSH**   Used to encrypt some types of traffic such as SFTP.
- **SFTP**   Used to transfer large files securely.

> **EXAM TIP** Know the basic purpose of the protocols in the list. All of these protocols have a lot more depth, but for the A+ exams, you need to be aware of only their primary purposes.

TCP vs. UDP

Most IP traffic transmitted over an Ethernet network uses either Transmission Control Protocol (TCP) or User Datagram Protocol (UDP). The characteristic differences determine which is the most suited for specific traffic, so you need to know the basic differences between them for the A+ exam.

True or false? TCP is known as a connectionless protocol, and UDP is known as a connection-oriented protocol.

Answer: *False*. The definitions are reversed. TCP is known as a connection-oriented protocol, and UDP is known as a connectionless protocol.

"Connection" in this context refers to how the protocols communicate. TCP exchanges three packets between two systems before sending data. These packets verify that the computers are able to connect. In contrast, UDP packets are just sent without checking to see whether the other system is operational.

Table 2-1 lists some of the common differences between TCP and UDP. TCP uses a three-way handshake to create a connection, but UDP does not. TCP provides guaranteed delivery by verifying that packets were received with receipt acknowledgements and resending them if necessary. In contrast, UDP makes a best effort to deliver the data but doesn't verify that it has been received. If a UDP packet isn't received, it's lost.

TABLE 2-1 TCP vs. UDP

TCP	UDP
Connection-oriented (uses three-way handshake before sending)	Connectionless (no handshake)
Guaranteed delivery	Best effort delivery
Receipt acknowledgements	No acknowledgments

NOTE Table 2-1 highlights some of the best characteristics of TCP, so the benefits of UDP might not be apparent. UDP is very effective when transmitting audio and video where occasional data loss is acceptable. It has less overhead because it doesn't verify delivery of each packet, resulting in faster transmissions and bandwidth utilizations.

You can think of TCP like a connection made with a phone call between two people. Imagine Bob wants to tell Susan that she was just announced as a winner of $1,000 on a local radio station but that she has to call in within ten minutes. The three-way handshake starts like this:

1. Bob calls Susan.
2. Susan answers the phone with "Hello."
3. Bob replies with "Hi, this is Bob" and then gives her the message.

If Susan doesn't hear or understand the message, she can ask Bob to repeat it. When the call is over, Bob knows that Susan did get the message.

UDP is similar to sending a text message. Bob might send messages to Susan all the time, so he could send a text message about Susan winning the prize and the need to call immediately. It will probably work, but any number of things might go wrong. There might be a problem with settings on Bob's system, Susan's system, or the network sending the traffic.

If the message is important and timely, the phone is the best option. If the message isn't important, a text message could be used.

Similarly, when you need guaranteed delivery of data over a network, TCP is used. If it's acceptable for some packets to be lost (such as when streaming audio or video), UDP is a good choice.

EXAM TIP TCP creates a connection with a three-way handshake and provides guaranteed delivery. UDP is connection-less and uses a best-effort to deliver the data.

Can you answer these questions?

You can find the answers to these questions at the end of this chapter.

1. What ports are used for email traffic?
2. What protocol is encrypted with SSH and is used to transfer large encrypted files?
3. When comparing TCP and UDP, which protocol provides guaranteed delivery of traffic?

Objective 2.5: Compare and contrast wireless networking standards and encryption types

Wireless networks are commonly used in home networks, small offices, and even large organizations. PC technicians are often asked to work on these networks and need to have a basic understanding of the various wireless standards that are available and their characteristics. Security is a primary consideration when configuring a wireless network, so you also need to know what encryption types are available, including which ones provide the best security.

Exam need to know...

- Standards
  For example: Which 802.11 standard is the fastest? Which 802.11 standard uses 5 GHz?
- Encryption types
  For example: What wireless encryption type is the least secure? Which wireless encryption type provides the best protection?

Standards

Wireless networks are known as 802.11 networks, and there are four primary standards you should know about. They are 802.11a, 802.11b, 802.11g, and 802.11n.

True or false? 802.11a networks broadcast on the 5-GHz frequency range.

Answer: *True.* 802.11a networks use only the 5-GHz frequency range. They have a maximum speed of 54 Mbps and have the shortest range when compared to the others.

The speed and range of wireless signals is affected by many variables. Physical obstructions such as walls and trees impede the signals. Also, other radio transmissions in the area can affect how far signals can travel. When wireless devices connect, they attempt to connect at the fastest possible speed of the standard without any errors. When devices are far from each other, they use a slower speed to eliminate errors.

True or false? 802.11g networks have the highest possible speed of each of the wireless standards.

Answer: *False.* 802.11n networks have the highest possible speed with throughputs of 150 Mbps, 300 Mbps, or 600 Mbps. 802.11g networks have a maximum throughput of 54 Mbps.

802.11n uses multiple input multiple output (MIMO) antennas, allowing it to transmit data on two different channels within the same frequency spectrum at the same time. The other standards use a single antenna. 802.11n is also backward compatible with 802.11g.

True or false? 802.11b networks have the lowest maximum speed of each of wireless the standards.

Answer: *True.* 802.11b networks have a maximum speed of 11 Mbps, which is the lowest throughput of all of the wireless standards.

Table 2-2 shows the characteristics of the four wireless standards.

TABLE 2-2 Wireless standards characteristics

STANDARD	FREQUENCY	MAXIMUM SPEED	RANGE
802.11a	5 GHz	54 Mbps	Shortest
802.11b	2.4 GHz	11 Mbps	Medium
802.11g	2.4 GHz	54 Mbps	Medium
802.11n	2.4 GHz and 5 GHz	Up to 600 Mbps	Longest

EXAM TIP Know the key points listed in Table 2-2. One way to memorize facts like this is to simply draw the table from scratch once a day for several days. You probably won't remember everything at first, but after a few days or so, you'll know the information without looking to check your answers. This information is also needed if you plan on taking the Network+ exam.

MORE INFO The Microsoft article titled "Wireless Networking: Frequently Asked Questions" provides more details about wireless networks: *http://windows.microsoft .com/en-US/windows7/Wireless-networking-frequently-asked-questions.*

Encryption types

Encryption types are used to provide security for wireless transmissions. The three wireless encryption types are Wired Equivalent Privacy (WEP), Wi-Fi Protected Access (WPA), and WPA2.

True or false? WPA is the least secure of the different encryption types.

Answer: *False.* WEP is the least secure of the different encryption types.

Attackers can easily discover the security key used for a WEP encrypted network. Because of this, WEP is not recommended for use.

WPA was created as an interim replacement for WEP. Later, WPA2 was standardized and is now recommended for use whenever possible. WEP, WPA, and WPA2 commonly use a passphrase or a pre-shared key. When joining a network, you need to know the name of the network, the type of security used, and the passphrase.

WPA and WPA2 both can use either Advanced Encryption Standard (AES) or Temporal Key Integrity Protocol (TKIP) to encrypt the data. AES is a widely used standard and recommended for use.

EXAM TIP WEP is the least secure wireless encryption type, and WPA2 is the most secure wireless encryption type. WPA2 with AES provides strong security for wireless networks.

MORE INFO Check out the following article for steps used to set up a wireless router: *http://windows.microsoft.com/en-US/windows7/set-up-a-wireless-router.* You can also watch the following video, which shows how to view and connect to available wireless networks: *http://windows.microsoft.com/en-US/windows7/View-and-connect -to-available-wireless-networks.*

Can you answer these questions?

You can find the answers to these questions at the end of this chapter.

1. Which 802.11 wireless standard uses the 5-GHz frequency range?
2. Which 802.11 wireless standard can transmit the most data at a time?
3. Which encryption type has been broken and should not be used?

Objective 2.6: Install, configure, and deploy a SOHO wireless/wired router using appropriate settings

It's very common for a small office home office (SOHO) to have a network with a wireless router used as the central networking device. Computers can connect to the wireless router to share resources on the network and for access to the Internet. Additionally, wireless routers commonly include wired connections and additional services for the network.

Exam need to know...

- MAC filtering
  For example: What is a MAC? What is the benefit of MAC filtering?

- Channels (1-11)
  For example: What is the default channel used for wireless? What channel(s) should you use instead for better performance?

- Port forwarding, port triggering
  For example: What is the difference between port forwarding and port triggering?

- Built-in networking services
  For example: What are the common services built into wireless routers? What should be enabled to automatically assign IP addresses?

- Wireless security
  For example: What is the SSID? What can be done to hide a wireless network from casual users?

- DMZ
  For example: What is a DMZ? What computers would be placed in a DMZ?

MAC filtering

Wired and wireless network interface cards (NICs) use media access control (MAC) addresses. MAC addresses are represented as six groups of two hexadecimal characters similar to this: 1A-2B-3C-4D-5E-6F. MAC addresses are burned into NICs and can be used to identify specific computers.

True or false? You can use MAC filtering on a wireless router to restrict access to only certain devices.

Answer: *True.* MAC filtering can be enabled on a wireless router by using only the MAC addresses of authorized devices.

You can also use MAC filtering with wired routers. The router will block access to the network to all systems except for ones with the specifically allowed MAC addresses.

> ***EXAM TIP*** MAC address filtering can be used to block access to a network based on the client's MAC address. It can be enabled on both wireless and wired routers. When enabled, it will block access to unidentified clients attempting to access the network.

MORE INFO   The MAC address is also known as the physical address or the hardware address. You can view the MAC address of a system with the **ipconfig /all** command from the command prompt. In this command, it's listed as the physical address. Chapter 14 of the CompTIA A+ Training Kit (Exam 220-801 and Exam 220-802), ISBN-10: 0735662681, shows how to use the command prompt and the **ipconfig /all** command.

Channels (1–11)

Wireless protocols are associated with specific frequency bands, such as 2.4 GHz or 5.0 GHz. However, each of these bands is divided into several channels. While a wireless router will automatically pick one of these channels, it is possible to manually select a specific channel.

True or false? If channel 6 has excessive interference, you should select channel 5 or 7 to improve performance.

Answer: *False*. Channel 6 is usually selected by default. However, channels 5, 6, and 7 all overlap with each other, so interference on channel 6 will also affect channels 5 and 7.

If channel 6 has excessive interference, it's recommended to select channel 1 or 11 instead. There isn't any overlap with the signals between these three channels.

Wireless networks in areas where multiple wireless networks are active frequently have performance problems due to interference from other networks. For example, an apartment complex might have several active wireless networks from different residents. You can eliminate interference with most networks by switching to channel 1 or 11.

EXAM TIP   Wireless networks include 11 channels. If channel 6 has interference, you can often get better performance by switching to channel 1 or 11.

MORE INFO   Microsoft At Home has a good article titled "10 Tips to Help Improve Your Wireless Network." One of these tips is to change the wireless channel. You can view the article here: *http://www.microsoft.com/athome/setup/wirelesstips.aspx*.

Port forwarding, port triggering

Many wireless routers and firewalls support port forwarding and port triggering. These are two methods used to allow specific types of traffic through a router or firewall.

True or false? Port forwarding opens a specific incoming port after traffic is sent out on a different port.

Answer: *False*. Port forwarding forwards all traffic from the Internet by using a specific port to a specific IP address.

Port forwarding can be used to provide access to a system within a private network from the Internet. For example, all traffic coming in port 80 can be forwarded to a web server on an internal network.

Port triggering uses one outgoing port as a trigger to open a specific incoming port. For example, an application might send traffic out on port 3456 and receive traffic in on port 5678. A port trigger on the router or firewall will automatically open incoming port 5678 only when traffic is sensed going out of port 3456.

EXAM TIP Port forwarding sends traffic coming in from the Internet on a specific port to an internal system with a specific IP address. Port triggering opens a specific incoming port only after traffic is sent out on a specific port.

MORE INFO Port Forward (*http://portforward.com/*) includes many free resources that can be used to understand port forwarding and to configure port forwarding on many different routers.

Built-in networking services

Hardware devices sold as wireless routers generally also include multiple services that are often enabled by default. This simplifies the setup of the internal network for users.

True or false? Wireless routers commonly include DHCP to assign IP addresses to internal devices.

Answer: *True.* Wireless routers include multiple services, including DHCP.

DHCP assigns a range of IP addresses to DHCP clients and also provides the IP address of the wireless router as each client's default gateway. If desired, you can disable DHCP and manually assign IP addresses to internal systems.

If DHCP has been disabled, DHCP clients will assign themselves an APIPA address starting with 169.254. However, you can manually assign IP addresses and other TCP/IP configuration information for all internal clients. It takes more time, but it is possible.

DHCP can be configured to assign IP addresses for a limited range in a network, and other IP addresses in the range can be manually assigned. For example, you can have DHCP assign IP addresses in the range of 192.168.1.100 through 192.168.1.254 with a subnet mask of 255.255.255.0. You can then manually assign other IP addresses from 192.168.1.1 through 192.168.1.99.

NOTE It's common to manually assign IP addresses to servers and printers so that each always has the same IP address, even after being turned off and back on.

It's also possible to have addresses assigned based on their MAC addresses. For example, you can have DHCP always assign the same IP address to a printer. When the printer requests an IP address, the request includes the printer's MAC address, and you can map this MAC address to a specific IP address in DHCP. This is known as a DHCP reservation.

Other services commonly included in a wireless router include the following:

- **Firewall**   The firewall filters traffic in and out of a network. Traffic can be filtered based on IP addresses, MAC addresses, logical ports, and protocols. Most firewalls are configured to block all traffic except for traffic that is specifically allowed.

- **Network Address Translation (NAT)**   NAT is a service that replaces private IP addresses used internally on a network with public IP addresses used on the Internet. The wireless router will have a single public IP address connected to the Internet, and all internal devices can share it when accessing the Internet.

- **Basic Quality of Service (QoS)**   QoS is a group of a technologies used to control traffic on a network by assigning different priorities to specific types of traffic. For example, it can give streaming video a lower priority than other types of traffic.

EXAM TIP   DHCP is included as a service on most wireless routers. When enabled, it automatically assigns IP addresses to DHCP clients in a network. It can be disabled if desired, but IP addresses need to be manually assigned if DHCP is disabled.

Wireless security

A primary step you need to take for wireless security is to select a secure encryption type such as WPA2, as described in Objective 2.4, "Explain common TCP and UDP ports, protocols, and their purpose," earlier in this chapter. A strong passphrase should be used, and the passphrase should be kept secret. In addition to using WPA2 with a strong passphrase, there are some additional steps you can take.

True or false? You can enable SSID broadcast to prevent users from connecting to a wireless network.

Answer: *False*. You can *disable* service set identifier (SSID) broadcasts to prevent users from easily seeing and connecting to a wireless network.

The SSID is the name of the network, and you need to know the SSID when connecting any device. When SSID broadcast is enabled, the network is visible to anyone in range of the network, making it easier for users to select the network. When SSID broadcast is disabled, users need to type in the name manually.

True or false? WPS allows users to configure security by pressing a button or entering a personal identification number (PIN).

Answer: *True*. Wi-Fi Protected Setup (WPS) is a feature on some wireless routers, designed to make security configuration almost as easy as pressing a button. Unfortunately, WPS is vulnerable to attacks and not recommended for use.

EXAM TIP   You can hide wireless networks from casual users by disabling SSID broadcast. When SSID broadcast is disabled, it is difficult for other users to see the network without using special tools.

MORE INFO   Wireless topics are also mentioned on 220-802 objectives such as Objective 2.5 covered in Chapter 7, "Security," of this book. Chapter 23 of the CompTIA A+ Training Kit (Exam 220-801 and Exam 220-802), ISBN-10: 0735662681, covers wireless networks in more depth, including the differences between wireless access points and wireless routers, the different wireless security types, and how to configure wireless routers.

DMZ

A demilitarized zone (DMZ) is a buffer network that provides a layer of protection for an internal network and a device that can be accessed from the Internet. DMZs are also known as screened subnets, perimeter networks, or buffer networks and are typically created with two firewalls. One firewall routes traffic between the Internet and the DMZ. The second firewall routes traffic between the internal network and the DMZ.

True or false? Internet-facing servers are placed in a DMZ to provide a level of protection.

Answer: *True.* Any server that can be accessed from the Internet has an added layer of protection when it is placed in a DMZ.

On home networks, users might place a gaming server in the DMZ to protect it while still making the server accessible to other users through the Internet. In larger networks, mail servers and web servers are commonly placed in a DMZ.

Without a DMZ, Internet-facing servers would need to be placed directly on the Internet with a public IP address or within an internal network. Note that you can place an Internet-facing server in one of the following three locations:

- **On the Internet**   It has a public IP address and minimal protection. It is susceptible to a wide variety of attacks.
- **Internal network**   If the system is successfully attacked, the attacker might be able to access other systems on the internal network. That is, this presents additional risks to internal systems.
- **DMZ**   The Internet-facing server has a layer of protection against Internet attacks from the firewall between it and the Internet. The internal network has an additional layer of protection against a successful attack against the Internet-facing server.

EXAM TIP   Internet-facing servers are often placed in a DMZ for extra security. This includes gaming servers in home networks, and mail or web servers in corporate networks.

MORE INFO   There are many different configurations for a DMZ. The Wikipedia article on DMZs includes good descriptions and diagrams of different DMZs. You can view it here: *http://en.wikipedia.org/wiki/DMZ_(computing)*.

Can you answer these questions?

You can find the answers to these questions at the end of this chapter.

1. What type of address can you use to block network access for specific computers?

2. What channel(s) should you use if your wireless network has excessive interference on channel 6?

3. Where should you place a gaming server that needs to be accessible from the Internet but also needs protection?

Objective 2.7: Compare and contrast Internet connection types and features

This objective requires you to know about the different ways that users can connect to the Internet. You should know when the connection types are available or most appropriate. You should also have a basic understanding of the relative speeds of the different connections.

Exam need to know...

- Cable and fiber
  For example: What is the relationship of the speed of cable and fiber broadband connections compared to other connections?

- Phone lines
  For example: What types of connectors are used for phone lines?

- Satellite
  For example: When is satellite Internet access most appropriate?

- Cellular (mobile hotspot)
  For example: What is a MiFi device?

- WiMAX and line of sight wireless Internet service
  For example: Where is WiMAX used?

Cable and fiber

Years ago, all television broadcasts were sent over the air as radio frequency RF transmissions. Anyone that wanted to watch TV used an antenna on their TV or rooftop and had access to a limited number of channels. Telecommunications companies began running cables to as many houses as they could and then charging users to connect to the cable, so most homes now have cable TV. Cable TV provides a clearer picture and delivers more channels, so it quickly became popular.

In time, these telecommunications companies realized that in addition to sending television signals over the cable, they could also provide Internet access over the same cable. These companies expanded their services and became Internet Service Providers (ISPs).

True or false? Broadband cable Internet connections are significantly faster than any dial-up or ISDN access.

Answer: *True*. Broadband cable has been the fastest Internet connection available to home users for many years.

Cable television originally used copper coaxial cable, and many cable connections still use coaxial cable. However, some telecommunications companies have started to run fiber to neighborhoods and homes as a faster alternative. Fiber cable connections typically provide faster connections than traditional cable TV connections.

> **EXAM TIP** Fiber and cable Internet connections are often referred to as broadband connections. They provide significantly faster Internet connections than any type of connection using phone lines.

> **MORE INFO** The Microsoft article titled "Set Up a Broadband (DSL or Cable) Connection" includes details and some diagrams showing how a single computer and a home network can be configured with a broadband Internet connection. You can view it here: *http://windows.microsoft.com/en-US/windows7/Set-up-a-broadband-DSL-or -cable-connection.*

Phone lines

In the early days of the Internet, the only way people could connect to the Internet was through the plain old telephone service (POTS). Phone lines are still used to provide Internet access to many people living in rural areas that do not have cable or fiber connections available at their homes.

True or false? Computers with a modem and a POTS line can connect to the Internet.

Answer: *True*. A dial-up connection to the Internet needs only a computer with a modem and simple phone line.

A modem is a modulator/demodulator that converts the signals between the formats needed by the computer and by the transmission line. The modem can be built into the computer or added as an external device.

The following three different types of connections use phone lines:

- Dial-up connections use a simple POTS phone line and a traditional modem.
- Integrated Services Digital Networks (ISDNs) use digital signals and terminal adapters in place of modems. A benefit is that a user can talk on the phone at the same time that the phone line is being used for the Internet connection.
- Digital subscriber lines (DSLs) also use digital signals and are available in large metropolitan areas. Technically, they use a transceiver instead of a modem, but the transceiver is commonly called a DSL modem.

True or false? In an ADSL line, the upload speed is faster than the download speed.

Answer: *False.* An asymmetric DSL (ADSL) does have different speeds for uploads and downloads. However, the download speed is faster than the upload speed.

Most users need faster downloads than uploads. For example, when users are browsing the Internet, they typically send very small requests to view a webpage in upload requests. However, the webpage can include a significant amount of data, such as text, graphics, audio, and video that is downloaded to the users.

> **EXAM TIP** Common methods of Internet access that use a phone line are dial-up, ISDN, and DSL. Simple dial-up connections can use POTS lines. ISDN and DSL use digital signals. ADSL lines have faster download speeds than upload speeds. Because they connect through phone lines, they use twisted-pair cable and RJ-11 connectors.

Satellite

Most rural areas do not have cable television, but they do have satellite television as an alternative. Users can subscribe with a satellite provider. They have satellite dishes that can receive television signals from an orbiting satellite. Additionally, many current satellite television systems can also transmit basic signals up to the satellite.

Just as telecommunications companies began using their cable and fiber connections for Internet access, many satellite providers began using their satellite connections for Internet access. Additionally, some companies specialize in only Internet access via satellite connections.

True or false? A major drawback with satellite signals is signal latency.

Answer: *True.* Signal latency refers to the amount of delay between when a user sends a request and receives a reply.

With broadband fiber and cable connections, users start to see a webpage download almost immediately when they send the request. In contrast, users with a satellite connection might see a significant delay between the time when they click a link and the webpage starts to load. This is because the signal must travel to the satellite in orbit, back down to Earth, back up to the satellite, and back to the user.

> **EXAM TIP** Satellite connections are used in rural areas and give users much faster connections than a dial-up connection. The primary drawback is the high degree of latency.

> **MORE INFO** Satellite Internet services have historically received inconsistent reviews. They are sometimes great in one area but poor in another area. The following page includes reviews of some popular satellite Internet providers: *http://satellite-internet-review.toptenreviews.com/.*

Cellular (mobile hotspot)

Smartphones use cellular access both for telephone calls and for Internet access. When users subscribe to the service, they can surf the Internet and access email with their smartphones. This same service is available for mobile hotspots. A mobile hotspot connects to the cellular service and acts as a wireless router for multiple wireless devices.

True or false? Cellular Internet access is the best choice for a user who frequently travels.

Answer: *True*. Devices with cellular Internet access can access the Internet from almost anywhere.

Mobile hotspots are also known as MiFi devices. A MiFi device is a small battery-powered device that users can take with them just about anywhere. After turning it on, it automatically connects to the cellular service. Users can configure mobile devices with the MiFi SSID and passphrase and connect to the Internet through the MiFi device. A single MiFi device typically supports five or more wireless devices.

> **EXAM TIP** Cellular hotspots are ideal for users who travel. They provide Internet access for users from anywhere cellular access is available.

WiMAX and line of sight wireless Internet service

Worldwide Interoperability for Microwave Access (WiMAX) is another wireless standard. It can deliver high-speed wireless Internet access for large geographical areas, such as a metropolitan area network (MAN).

True or false? When connecting to WiMAX networks, WiMAX towers need a clear line of sight between each other.

Answer: *True*. WiMAX towers use microwave links between each other, and these require a clear line of sight between each other.

Internet service providers (ISPs) have a wired connection to a WiMAX tower. The WiMAX towers connect to each other wirelessly, and end users can connect to the closest tower wirelessly.

> **EXAM TIP** WiMAX is used in metropolitan areas. When available, it provides fast wireless access over a large geographical area.

Can you answer these questions?

You can find the answers to these questions at the end of this chapter.

1. Which wired Internet connection provides the highest speeds?
2. What type of Internet connections use phone lines?

3. What type of Internet connection is most appropriate for a traveling salesman?

4. What type of Internet connection is mobile and can be used to provide Internet access for multiple users?

Objective 2.8: Identify various types of networks

When people are talking about a network they are usually talking about a local area network in a single location. However, there are several other types of networks. As a PC technician, you don't necessarily need to be an expert in all the different types of networks, but you should understand the terminology used. Most local area networks are configured in a star topology, but there are other types, and you're expected to know what differentiates each type.

Exam need to know...

- LAN
  For example: What is a LAN?

- WAN
  For example: What is the primary characteristic of a WAN?

- PAN
  For example: Where is a PAN located?

- MAN
  For example: What is the difference between a MAN and a WAN?

- Topologies
  For example: What are the different topologies? Which topology provides the best fault tolerance?

LAN

A local area network (LAN) is a network in a single location. Devices connected to the LAN can access network resources such as servers and printers.

True or false? A LAN is the primary type of network used in a SOHO.

Answer: *True.* A SOHO network would be in a single location and is a LAN.

A LAN can include multiple networks (sometimes called subnets). For example, an organization could have one network for servers, one network for people in the Sales department, and another network for all other employees. Within each network, all of the devices are connected with switches. Within the organization, one or more routers connect the different networks and provide a path to the Internet.

> **EXAM TIP** A LAN is in a single location. It can include multiple networks within the location, but if all the networks are located together, it is called a LAN.

WAN

A wide area network includes two or more LANs geographically separated. For example, a company might have a LAN in Virginia Beach and another LAN in New York. If they connect the two LANs, they are creating a WAN.

True or false? A WAN includes networks that can cover a large physical distance.

Answer: *True*. WANs can include networks in different cities, states, countries, or regions. The key is that they are geographically separated.

> **EXAM TIP** A WAN includes networks that are geographically separated. They typically cover large physical distances.

PAN

A personal area network (PAN) is a network of devices that are connected around a person. For example, a person might have a smartphone and a tablet device with wireless capabilities, and a mobile hotspot used to connect to a cellular network. After turning on the hotspot, they can use it to connect to the Internet with the smartphone and their tablet.

True or false? A PAN can include devices in a separate building within a single campus.

Answer: *False*. A PAN is centered around a single individual only. While the signals might travel farther than a few feet around a person, the PAN is still focused on the person.

> **EXAM TIP** A PAN is centered around a person. It might include just a smartphone and a Bluetooth-enabled headset, or it might include more advanced devices, such as a mobile hotspot and a tablet.

MAN

A metropolitan area network (MAN) is a group of networks in the same geographical location but spread across a wide area. For example, a university campus that has connected networks throughout several buildings is a MAN.

True or false? The MAN and WAN are essentially the same.

Answer: *False*. A WAN includes LANs that are separated by a large physical distance, but a MAN includes networks that are in the same general geographical location.

The difference between a LAN and a MAN is that a LAN is within a single building, while a MAN will span multiple buildings.

> **EXAM TIP** A MAN includes multiple networks spread throughout two or more buildings in the same geographical location. WiMAX is used for some MANs.

Topologies

Computers are organized within a network by using different network topologies. A *topology* refers to how the devices are logically connected, and the most common topology is the star topology.

True or false? A mesh topology provides redundancy for each network device.

Answer: *True.* A mesh topology includes multiple redundant connections for each device in the network. If any single connection fails, the device can tolerate the failure and continue to communicate with devices by using other connections.

True or false? A bus topology provides redundancy with a MAU.

Answer: *False.* A bus topology does not have any redundancy. If a single connection fails, the entire network fails. Token ring networks often use a multistation access unit (MAU) for redundancy. The four primary topologies are star, ring, mesh, and bus. Figure 2-2 shows diagrams of each, and they are defined as follows:

- In a star topology, devices connect to each other through a central network distribution device such as a hub or a switch.
- In a ring topology, devices are connected in a physical or logical ring. A logical token is passed to each device in turn, and devices can transmit only when they have the token. Some token rings use a central MAU to eliminate the possibility of a single device failing and breaking the ring.
- A mesh topology includes multiple connections. In a full mesh network, every single device has connections to every other device in the network.
- A bus network connects devices in a line. Each end of the bus must be terminated. If a terminator is removed, all devices stop communicating. Similarly, if the bus has a failed connection anywhere on the bus, it results in two separate segments that each have only a single terminator. That is, any break in the bus stops communication for all devices.

A hybrid network uses a combination of any two or more topologies.

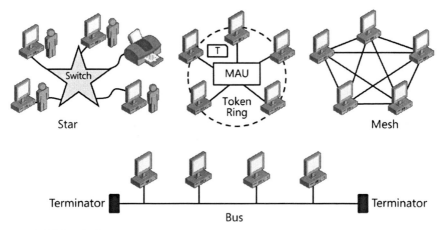

FIGURE 2-2 Topologies.

Can you answer these questions?

You can find the answers to these questions at the end of this chapter.

1. What type of network is centered around an individual?
2. What type of network connects multiple networks located in separate geographical locations?
3. What network topology provides the most redundancy?

Objective 2.9: Compare and contrast network devices and their functions and features

Computers and printers within a network are connected to various network devices such as hubs, switches, routers, access points, bridges, and modems. This objective expects you to know the functions and features of each of these network devices.

Exam need to know...

- Hub
  For example: What is the difference between a hub and a switch?
- Switch
  For example: What are benefits of switches over hubs?
- Router
  For example: What additional protocols are often included on routers used in SOHOs?
- Access point
  For example: What is the difference between a WAP and a wireless router?
- Bridge
  For example: What is the difference between a bridge and a switch?
- Modem
  For example: What type of connector does an internal modem use?
- NAS
  For example: What is the primary purpose of a NAS?

- Firewall

  For example: What is created on a firewall to allow traffic through?

- VoIP phones

  For example: What type of calls can be made with VoIP phones?

- Internet appliance

  For example: What is the purpose of an Internet appliance?

Hub

A hub is a simple network device used to connect multiple devices together in a network. Ethernet hubs were once very common. They have multiple RJ-45 ports, which were connected to computers or other network devices via twisted-pair cable.

True or false? A hub sends unicast traffic that it receives to all other devices that are connected to the hub.

Answer: *True.* A hub transmits all data that it receives on one port to all other ports.

When looking at the features of various network devices, it's valuable to know the difference between unicast, broadcast, and multicast traffic, as follows:

- Unicast traffic is sent from one device and addressed to one other device. Even though unicast traffic is addressed to only one device, the hub still forwards unicast traffic to all other devices connected to the hub.

- Broadcast traffic is sent from one device to all other devices on a network. Broadcast traffic is not sent through a router.

- Multicast traffic is sent from one device to multiple other devices.

True or false? A hub has the most security when compared to a switch.

Answer: *False.* A hub has less security than a switch.

If sensitive data is sent to one port on the hub, it is automatically sent to all other ports. Any computer connected to the hub will receive this data and can intercept it with the right tools. In contrast, a switch forwards unicast traffic to only one port.

> **NOTE** Both unicast and broadcast traffic sent to one port on a hub go to all physical ports on the hub.

> **EXAM TIP** A hub has no intelligence or selectivity. All data sent to one port of a hub goes to all other ports. It is less secure than a switch, and many organizations have replaced hubs with switches.

Switch

A switch includes circuitry that allows it to be selective when sending data through the switch. It can identify which device is connected to each physical port, based on the media access control (MAC) address.

True or false? A switch sends unicast traffic to a single physical port.

Answer: *True*. A switch transmits data that it receives to specific ports. It analyzes packets to determine the destination MAC address and sends the packet to the port where that MAC address is being used.

Switches learn which devices are connected to which physical port by analyzing traffic that comes into the port. They build an internal table mapping the physical port number with the MAC address. They then send unicast traffic only to the specific port where the MAC address is used.

In contrast, a hub forwards traffic to all other ports on the hub. The selectivity of the switch provides better performance for devices connected to the switch. Additionally, the switch adds some security by not sending unicast traffic to all ports.

> **NOTE** Broadcast traffic sent through a switch goes to all physical ports on the switch. However, unicast traffic is sent to only a single port on the switch. The switch uses the MAC address to determine which port to use when sending unicast traffic.

> **EXAM TIP** A switch sends unicast packets only to specific ports. This improves performance by segmenting the traffic and also improves security by restricting which ports receive traffic.

Router

Routers are used to connect networks or subnets together. In general, the networking devices are connected together with a switch or a hub in a network, and multiple networks are connected together with a router. Routers evaluate the IP address of traffic and determine the best path to send it to get it to its destination. Each router in a path is also referred to as a hop.

True or false? A router is placed between an internal network and the Internet.

Answer: *True*. Routers connect networks, and in this case, the internal network is one network and the Internet is a huge network of networks.

Routers placed between the Internet and an internal network commonly uses network address translation (NAT). NAT translates private IP addresses used internally, within a network, to public IP addresses used on the Internet.

A company could have multiple routers, with some used to connect internal networks and another one used to connect to the Internet. The internal routers would not use NAT.

> **NOTE** Broadcast traffic sent to a router is not passed through the router. Unicast traffic is sent through the router port that provides the best path to the destination network. The router uses the IP address to determine the best path.

> **EXAM TIP** Routers are used to connect networks together. Routers used in SOHOs often have additional capabilities, such as NAT and DHCP.

MORE INFO The Microsoft article "Start Here to Set Up a Home Network in Windows 7" includes details about six separate steps to set up a home network with Windows 7. It includes information about setting up a router, and it is available here: *http://windows.microsoft.com/en-US/windows7/start-here-to-set-up-a-home-network -in-windows-7.*

Access point

A wireless access point (WAP) is sometimes referred to as simply an access point. It provides access for wireless clients to a network.

True or false? Wireless access points provide the same services as a wireless router.

Answer: *False.* A router provides more services than a mere access point.

A wireless access point and a wireless router are not the same things. Specifically, an access point provides connectivity only for wireless clients to other wireless clients and to a wired network. However, a wireless router includes multiple other components.

Figure 2-3 shows the components of a typical wireless router. It has RJ-45 con- nections for wired clients and wireless capabilities for wireless clients. These wired and wireless clients are connected to each other using the switch component of the wireless router. The wireless router has a wide area network (WAN) connection used to connect to the Internet, and all of the clients can go through this router for Internet access.

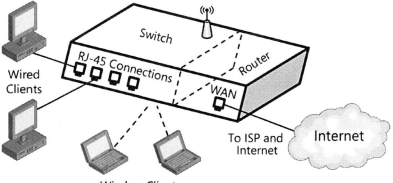

FIGURE 2-3 Wireless router.

NOTE An access point might look similar to Figure 2-3, with the following differ- ences. It would not have a router component or a WAN connection. Also, it would typically have only one RJ-45 connection to a wired network instead of multiple wired RJ-45 ports.

Bridge

A bridge is similar to a switch but instead of connecting individual devices, it's used to connect groups of devices. For example, two groups of computers might be connected to each other with two separate hubs. You can then use a bridge to connect the two groups together via the bridge. Even though the two groups are connected, the bridge is selective about what data is forwarded between the two groups of devices.

True or false? Bridges are used instead of switches in most networks today.

Answer: *False.* Bridges are rarely used. When the functionality of a bridge is needed, switches are typically used instead.

Modem

Modems are used for Internet access connections for a computer via a phone line. They use RJ-11 connections to connect to the phone line. Many modems are internal to a computer, but external modems are also available. An external modem typically connects to a computer with a USB connection.

True or false? A modem converts digital signals to analog signals.

Answer: *True.* A modem converts digital signals coming from a computer to analog signals that can be transmitted on a phone line.

The analog signals are modulated by the modem before being placed onto the phone line. The modem is also able to demodulate received data to convert the analog data into digital data needed by the computer.

NAS

Network attached storage (NAS) is a dedicated computer system used to provide disk storage on a network. A NAS device includes one or more disk drives, and storage sizes of 1 TB or greater are common. They have RJ-45 ports used to connect a twisted-pair cable to a switch or router on a network.

True or false? NAS devices do not have any security, so sensitive data should never be stored on the NAS.

Answer: *False.* NAS devices include an operating system that can be used to assign permissions and restrict access to folders.

Many NAS devices use Unix or Linux as the operating system and require very little configuration or management. They often include a web-based interface that you can use to create additional users, groups, and folders, and to assign permissions to the folders. In addition to using NAS devices to share data, many people use them to store backups.

EXAM TIP A NAS device includes an operating system and provides disk storage for any device on the network. Access can be restricted by assigning permissions.

Firewall

A firewall filters traffic in and out of a network or in and out of an individual computer. Firewalls are generally classified as either network-based or host-based. A network-based firewall is often used in conjunction with a router to filter traffic in and out of a network. A host-based firewall is additional software running on a computer for additional security protection.

True or false? Firewalls can block outgoing email by blocking traffic on port 25.

Answer: *True*. Firewalls can filter traffic based on ports. Port 25 is used for outgoing email, so if this port is not open on the firewall, it will block outgoing email.

Firewalls can also filter traffic based on IP addresses, network IDs, and protocols with simple packet filtering. Most firewalls also support more advanced filtering, allowing them to analyze traffic to determine whether the data should be allowed or blocked.

Most firewalls use an implicit deny philosophy with exceptions. That is, all traffic is blocked (denied) unless a rule or exception has been created to allow it. For example, if you wanted to allow outgoing email, the firewall needs to have a rule opening port 25 for outgoing traffic.

EXAM TIP Firewalls can filter traffic based on IP addresses, ports, and protocols. Wireless routers include firewall capabilities allowing them to allow or block traffic.

VoIP phones

A Voice over Internet Protocol (VoIP) phone is used to make telephone calls over an IP network. They resemble a regular phone, but instead of plugging into a telephone line with an RJ-11 connector, they plug into a network device like a switch or router with an RJ-45 connector.

True or false? VoIP phones can be used instead of traditional phones for long distance calls.

Answer: *True*. As long as you have Internet access, you can use the VoIP phone to make telephone calls.

EXAM TIP You can mimic the capabilities of a VoIP phone with a headset and microphone connected to your computer. You'll need specialized software to make the connections, but this is often available when you subscribe to a service.

MORE INFO Skype is a popular service that people use to make long distance calls. People subscribe with a flat fee and can make phone calls by using their computer. You can read more about it here: *http://skype.com*.

Internet appliance

Internet appliances are small devices used to access the Internet for web browsing or email access. Many of the features of an Internet appliance are included with mobile devices such as smartphones and tablets.

NOTE The term *Internet appliance* is rarely used today. Also, there are very few Internet appliances available that are dedicated only to surfing the Internet or accessing email. However, many security appliances are common. For example, a network security appliance might include a firewall, along with malware and spam filters. Similarly, some SOHOs subscribe to Internet security services, such as an online spam filtering service. These services use Internet security appliances.

Can you answer these questions?

You can find the answers to these questions at the end of this chapter.

1. What is a benefit of a switch over a hub?
2. What type of network device would include NAT?
3. What type of device is used to connect to a dial up ISP?
4. What type of device blocks all traffic unless a rule is created to allow the traffic?

Objective 2.10: Given a scenario, use appropriate networking tools

Network technicians use several different tools to create cables, wire networks, and troubleshoot problems. This objective expects you to know about many of these tools, including the scenarios when these tools are appropriate to use.

Exam need to know...

- Crimper
  For example: What is the primary purpose of a crimper?
- Multimeter
  For example: What setting on a multimeter is used to check for cable breaks?
- Toner probe
  For example: What is the primary purpose of a toner probe?

- Cable tester
  For example: What information is provided by a cable tester?
- Loopback plug
  For example: What is tested with a loopback plug?
- Punchdown tool
  For example: Where is a punchdown tool used?

Crimper

Network technicians are often tasked with creating cables. The job is much easier when technicians have the correct tools, such as wire crimpers.

True or false? A crimper is used to secure an RJ-45 connector onto a twisted-pair cable.

Answer: *True.* Crimpers are used to secure connectors onto cables. The wires are placed into the connector in the proper location, and the crimper squeezes the connector onto the cable.

There are many specific types of crimpers, including those used to crimp RJ-45 cables onto twisted-pair cables. Other crimpers are available for other types of cables, and some can crimp multiple types of connectors. For example, crimpers are available to secure RJ-11 connectors to phone cables and to secure RJ-45 connectors onto network cables.

EXAM TIP Crimpers are used to secure connectors onto cables, such as securing RJ-45 connectors to twisted-pair cables. In addition to knowing what a crimper is used for, you should also be able to identify a crimper in a group of different tools.

MORE INFO If you aren't familiar with the different hardware tools, check out *http://www.bing.com/images.* Enter search words, such as **crimper.** You can use the same technique to see pictures of any of the tools mentioned in this objective. Chapters 18 and 24 of the CompTIA A+ Training Kit (Exam 220-801 and Exam 220-802), ISBN-10: 0735662681, cover these tools in much more depth.

Multimeter

Multimeters include two probes and are used to measure voltage, amperage, and resistance. These are commonly used to measure voltages from power supplies but have a different use with networks.

True or false? Multimeters are commonly used to measure amperage going through network cables.

Answer: *False.* Multimeters are rarely used to measure amperage (or current) through network cables.

Most multimeters include a continuity checker that can be used to verify that a cable doesn't have any breaks. This setting measures when a cable has zero resistance or is continuous from end to end. When you select the continuity check function and touch both probes together, the multimeter beeps, indicating that there is a continuous connection. Similarly, when you touch both ends of a cable with each of the probes, it beeps if the cable is good. If you don't hear a beep, you know the cable has a break.

> **EXAM TIP**   Multimeters may be used to measure voltage, amperage, and resistance. A continuity check function measures near-zero resistance and can be used to verify that a cable doesn't have a break.

Toner probe

A toner probe includes two components. One component creates a tone, and the second component has a speaker to hear the tone.

True or false? A toner probe is used to verify that a NIC is operational.

Answer: *False*. A toner probe is used to trace network cables between two different locations.

For example, if you have 50 cables going from an office to a wiring closet, you sometimes need to identify both ends of the same cable. You can connect the component that creates the tone to one end of the wire in the office. Next, you go to the wiring closet and begin touching the speaker probe to different wires. When you hear the tone, you have found the wire.

> **EXAM TIP**   Toner probes are used to trace cables between rooms in a building. One part of the toner probe creates a tone that is placed onto a wire. The other part has a speaker to play the tone when touched to the other end of the wire.

Cable tester

Cable testers are used to verify that a cable is wired correctly and is operational. Many include LED displays to show exactly how the cable is wired. If the cable is wired incorrectly, the cable tester shows specifically which pins have the wrong wires.

True or false? A cable tester is used to trace cables going between two floors of a building.

Answer: *False*. The cable tester is used to test the operation of a cable but doesn't include the capabilities of a toner probe to trace cables.

Cable testers are often used with twisted-pair cables. They have RJ-45 ports where you connect the cable. The cable tester first verifies the wiring and then verifies that the cable meets operational characteristics. For example, a cable tester can verify that a CAT 6 cable can transmit data at a rate of 10 Gbps using a frequency of 250 MHz.

> **EXAM TIP**   Cable testers are used to test the wiring and operational characteristics of a cable.

Loopback plug

A loopback plug is a simple plug that loops transmit signals back into the receive signals. A simple loopback plug is an RJ-45 plug with send pins connected to the transmit pins.

True or false? A loopback plug is used to test the characteristics of a cable.

Answer: *False.* A loopback plug is used to check a NIC. Cable testers are used to check characteristics of a cable.

> **EXAM TIP** Loopback plugs are commonly used to check NICs. You can plug the loopback plug into the NIC and verify that signals can be sent and received with the plug.

Punchdown tool

A punchdown tool is used to attach twisted-pair cables to wall jacks or punchdown blocks in wiring closets. The tool has a spring that punches down on a wire when pressed. The technician places the wire in the correct location on the wall jack or punchdown block and presses down with the punchdown tool. When the spring releases, it pushes the wire into the connector.

True or false? You must remove the jacket covering before securing a wire with a punchdown tool.

Answer: *False.* The jacket covering and insulation of a wire is removed when the punchdown tool forces the wire into place.

There are normally several individual segments between a computer in an office and a switch in a wiring closet, as follows:

- One cable runs from the computer to the wall jack. It has RJ-45 connectors on each end, and a crimper is used to secure the RJ-45 connectors onto the cable.
- Another cable runs between the wall jack and the wiring closet. This cable runs through walls, ceilings, and/or plenum spaces. It is connected to the wall jack on one end and to the back of a punchdown block on the other end. The punchdown tool secures the wire to the wall jack and the punchdown block.
- The last segment is a short patch cable that runs from the front of the punchdown block to a port on a hub or a switch. The devices are mounted in a bay close to each other. RJ-45 connectors are attached both ends of the patch cable with a crimper.

> **EXAM TIP** Punchdown tools are used to speed the process of connecting twisted-pair cables to wall jacks and punchdown blocks.

Can you answer these questions?

You can find the answers to these questions at the end of this chapter.

1. What type of tool is used to connect RJ-45 connectors to twisted-pair cable?
2. What type of tool is used to trace wires between two rooms?
3. What computer component is a loopback plug commonly used to test?

Answers

This section contains the answers to the "Can you answer these questions?" sections in this chapter.

Objective 2.1: Identify types of network cables and connectors

1. Fiber cable uses LC, ST, and SC connectors.
2. RJ-11 connectors are used for phone lines, and RJ-45 connectors are used for networks. Both connectors use twisted-pair cable.
3. F-type screw-on connectors are used with coaxial cable.

Objective 2.2: Categorize characteristics of connectors and cabling

1. Fiber supports the longest cables without a repeater. SMF cable supports longer cable runs than MMF cable.
2. CAT 6 cable supports data transmissions up to 10 Gbps.
3. RG-6 cable supports both analog and digital transmissions.

Objective 2.3: Explain properties and characteristics of TCP/IP

1. The IP address 192.168.15.7 is a Class C address. The first number in the IP address 192.168.15.7 is 192, and addresses with the first number between 192 and 223 are Class C addresses.
2. The IP address FC00::42A:0:0:7F5 is an IPv6 address with leading zeros omitted and using zero compression.
3. Addresses starting with 169.254 are APIPA addresses, and they are assigned to DHCP clients when a DHCP server has not answered with an available IP address.
4. DNS provides a mapping for user friendly names (host names) to IP addresses. Clients send the name (such as bing.com) to the DNS server, and the DNS server responds with the IP address.
5. DHCP provides IP addresses and other TCP/IP configuration information to DHCP clients.

Objective 2.4: Explain common TCP and UDP ports, protocols, and their purpose

1. Email uses ports 25 (SMTP), 110 (POP3), and 143 (IMAP).
2. SFTP is encrypted with SSH, and it is used to transfer large encrypted files.
3. TCP uses a three-way handshake to establish a connection and provides guaranteed delivery.

Objective 2.5: Compare and contrast wireless networking standards and encryption types

1. Both 802.11a and 802.11n use the 5-GHz frequency range.
2. 802.11n can transmit up to 150 Mbps, 300 Mbps, or 600 Mbps at a time by using multiple antennas. In comparison, 802.11g has a maximum of 54 Mbps.
3. WEP has been broken and should not be used.

Objective 2.6: Install, configure, and deploy a SOHO wireless/wired router using appropriate settings

1. You use MAC addresses with MAC address filtering to block network access to specific computers.
2. Channels 1 and 11 are good alternative channels if channel 6 has excessive interference from other wireless networks.
3. Internet-facing servers (including gaming servers) should be placed in a DMZ to provide an extra layer of protection.

Objective 2.7: Compare and contrast Internet connection types and features

1. Fiber and cable broadband connections provide the highest speeds when compared with other wired connections.
2. Dial-up, DSL, and ISDN connections use phone lines.
3. Cellular Internet connections are appropriate for people who frequently travel.
4. Mobile hotspots (also called MiFi) connections are mobile and can be used to provide Internet access for multiple users.

Objective 2.8: Identify various types of networks

1. A network centered on an individual is a PAN.
2. A WAN connects two or more networks located in separate geographical locations.
3. A mesh topology provides the most redundancy.

Objective 2.9: Compare and contrast network devices and their functions and features

1. Switches provide performance improvements because each device connected to the switch uses a separate segment, resulting in less traffic for each segment. Also, switches provide some security because traffic is not sent to all devices connected to the switch.

2. Routers used to connect to the Internet commonly include NAT to translate public and private IP addresses. In many cases, the router also includes firewall capabilities.

3. Modems are used for dial-up Internet connections.

4. Firewalls block all traffic unless an exception or rule is created to allow the traffic.

Objective 2.10: Given a scenario, use appropriate networking tools

1. Crimpers are used to connect RJ-45 connectors to twisted-pair cable.

2. A toner probe is an effective tool used to trace cables.

3. Loopback plugs are commonly used to test NICs.

CHAPTER 3

Laptops

The Laptops domain covers approximately 11 percent of the A+ 220-801 exam. You'll need to have a good understanding of laptop hardware components, including basics of hardware installation and replacement. Laptops have unique components that you won't find in regular desktop computers, and you'll be expected to know what these are. It's especially important to understand the different types of displays used with laptops and some of the common components included within laptop displays. Lastly, this objective expects you to understand some common laptop features, such as the special function keys found on the keyboards.

This chapter covers the following objectives:

- Objective 3.1: Install and configure laptop hardware and components
- Objective 3.2: Compare and contrast the components within the display of a laptop
- Objective 3.3: Compare and contrast laptop features

Objective 3.1: Install and configure laptop hardware and components

When preparing for this objective, ensure that you understand common expansion options available on laptop computers that aren't available on typical desktop computers. You'll also need to have an understanding of what hardware devices can be replaced.

Exam need to know...

- Expansion options
  For example: What are the two types of ExpressCards available for laptop computers? What type of memory is used in a laptop computer?

- Hardware/device replacement
  For example: What hardware is often accessible by removing panels on the bottom of a laptop? What is the primary difference between hard drives used in laptop computers and desktop computers?

Expansion options

Laptop computers can be upgraded by adding additional hardware. Some hardware can be added internally to the computer, and almost all laptop computers also have external expansion slots that you can use to add additional components.

True or false? The /34 in an ExpressCard/34 indicates that it has 34 pins.

Answer: *False*. The /34 indicates the ExpressCard is 34 mm wide.

Both types of ExpressCards have 26 pins and are 5 mm thick, but are different in the following ways:

- ExpressCard/34 is rectangular and 34 mm wide.
- ExpressCard/54 is L-shaped; it is the same size as the ExpressCard/34 on the connector end, but it is 54 mm wide on the other side.

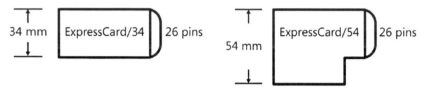

FIGURE 3-1 ExpressCard/34 and ExpressCard/54.

> **EXAM TIP** ExpressCard/34 and ExpressCard/54 both have 26 pins and can fit into any ExpressCard slot. The /54 card provides more space for components, such as a 1.8-inch disk drive platter. The larger card is also used for components that generate a lot of heat because the larger card dissipates heat better than the smaller card.

An older version of expansion card is called *PC Card*. PC Cards were previously known as Personal Computer Memory Card International Association (PCMCIA) cards. There are three types:

- Type I is the thinnest, at 3.3 mm and one row of pins.
- Type II is thicker, at 5.0 mm and two rows of pins.
- Type III is the thickest, at 10 mm and three rows of pins.

ExpressCard and PCMCIA cards are hot swappable, meaning that you can remove them when the power is on. However, if you want to ensure that you do not lose any data, you should click the Safely Remove Hardware icon on the taskbar and stop the device before removing it.

True or false? Small outline dual inline memory modules (SODIMMs) are used within laptop computers.

Answer: *True*. When upgrading memory in laptop computers, compatible SODIMMs should be used.

You can access the SODIMMs in most laptop computer systems by removing a panel on the bottom of the computer. After removing the panel, you release hold-down clips, which allow the SODIMM to pop up for easy removal. In some laptops, one SODIMM is accessible after removing the panel but you can't reach the second SODIMM unless you partially disassemble the computer.

Hardware/device replacement

There's an extensive list of hardware devices within a laptop computer that can be replaced or upgraded. Some components are relatively easy to replace or upgrade, such as RAM, a hard drive, or an optical drive. You can often access these components after removing panels from the back of the laptop computer. Others are much more difficult to replace and require dismantling the laptop before you can access them.

Some systems provide easy access to some of the components but not to all of them. For example, you might run across a laptop that has easy access to one RAM slot, while a second slot might be accessible only after disassembling the computer.

True or false? Drives used in laptop computers are 3.5 inches in size.

Answer: *False.* Many laptop computers have two drive bays, but 2.5 inch drives are used instead of the larger 3.5-inch drives used in desktop computers and servers.

Many solid state drives (SSDs) come in 2.5-inch versions and can be used in place of the original drive or as an additional drive. These use the standard Serial ATA (SATA) interface and use the same type of flash memory used with Universal Serial Bus (USB) flash drives. A great benefit of SSD drives is that they are less susceptible to damage if the drive is dropped.

True or false? If wireless capability in a laptop computer fails, you can replace the Peripheral Component Interconnect Express (PCIe) card.

Answer: *False.* Laptop computers use Mini-PCIe, not the full-sized PCIe cards found in desktop computers.

Most laptop computers include a Mini-PCIe wireless card that can be replaced if it fails. This is often accessible after removing a panel at the bottom of the laptop. It will have an antenna connected to it that must be disconnected before replacing it. This antenna is normally routed around the display's bezel.

True or false? A plastic wedge is an important tool to have when working on laptop computers.

Answer: *True.* A plastic wedge allows you to pry plastic laptop components apart without damaging them.

Laptop computers have a lot of hard plastic pieces that don't come off easily after just removing the screws. Instead, they need to be pried off. You can damage the plastic if you try to pry them off with a screwdriver or some other type of metal tool.

> **EXAM TIP** The primary tools you need when working with laptop computers are screwdrivers, a plastic wedge, and ESD protection equipment such as an ESD wrist strap.

True or false? A faulty DC jack can prevent the battery from charging.

Answer: *True.* If the DC jack is faulty, it can stop AC power from reaching the system and charging the battery.

Other reasons why the battery is not charging include a faulty alternating current (AC) adapter or loose connection with the AC adapter. The direct current (DC) jack will normally have a light emitting diode (LED) indicating that it's receiving power. If this LED is not lit, verify that the AC adapter is plugged in. Many AC adapters also have LEDs showing that they are operating. If the AC adapter is plugged in and operational, the DC jack is probably faulty.

> **EXAM TIP** Check the easy solutions first when troubleshooting. It is much easier to check for LEDs and verify that components are plugged in than it is to start disassembling a computer to replace components.

True or false? If you need to replace the system board on a laptop computer, you'll need to remove the keyboard.

Answer: *True.* The system board is not accessible without disassembling the laptop computer and removing many components, including the keyboard.

The system board is not accessible by removing access panels on laptop computers. Instead, the computer needs to be disassembled, and this almost always requires removal of the keyboard. The central processing unit (CPU) is located on the system board but is typically soldered into the board and not easily replaceable.

> **EXAM TIP** Before disassembling a laptop computer or upgrading any internal components, you should ensure that it is unplugged from power and the battery is removed. When disassembling a laptop computer, refer to the manufacturer documentation for specific steps. Often, components need to be taken apart in a specific order to prevent damage.

True or false? A DVD drive can usually be replaced from a laptop computer after removing just one or two screws.

Answer: *True.* Optical drives are typically held in place by one or two screws. They can be easily removed after removing the screws.

Not all laptop computers have built-in optical drives. However, when they do, they are typically easy to replace.

Many laptops include a touchpad that can be used instead of a mouse. You drag your finger over the touchpad to move the mouse and can tap it to simulate mouse clicks. If this fails, it can be replaced and is normally accessible after removing the keyboard. One thing to check before replacing it is to ensure the system has the most up-to-date driver for the touchpad. A corrupt driver can stop the touchpad from working properly and replacing the driver is much easier than replacing the touchpad.

The speakers within a laptop typically aren't the highest quality and some users want to replace them with better speakers. Speakers come in a wide variety of sizes so it's important to ensure that the replacement speakers are compatible with the laptop.

In some laptops, you can access the existing speakers after removing the keyboard but in other laptops, you'll need to remove the display screen before you can access the speakers. The speakers are often attached to the case with screws that you'll need to remove, and the speaker wires are connected to the motherboard. When installing the new speakers, ensure that the wires are routed to the same location so that the sounds for the right and left speakers aren't reversed.

> **EXAM TIP** When preparing for the A+ 220-801 exam, you should have a basic understanding of what components can be easily removed and what components require a lengthy disassembly process. For most systems, it's relatively easy to remove, replace, or upgrade memory, disk drives, optical drives, the battery, and the Mini-PCIe wireless card. Other components require much more time and effort.

> **MORE INFO** Chapter 8 of the CompTIA A+ Training Kit (Exam 220-801 and Exam 220-802), ISBN-10: 0735662681, discusses the removal of many hardware components. It includes several pictures of laptop computers with components partially removed.

If the system doesn't work after replacing a component, check the obvious things first. For example, if you replace RAM and now the RAM is not recognized, verify that the RAM is installed correctly. If you replace the keyboard and it's not working, verify that it's been connected.

Can you answer these questions?

You can find the answers to these questions at the end of this chapter.

1. How many pins are in an ExpressCard expansion slot used for an ExpressCard/34 card?

2. What types of disk drives are used in new laptop computers?

3. What tools are commonly used by a laptop hardware technician?

4. What components can be replaced or upgraded in most laptop computers without an extensive disassembly process?

Objective 3.2: Compare and contrast the components within the display of a laptop

This objective requires you to differentiate between common components used within a laptop computer. Technicians who understand these differences can troubleshoot laptop computers more quickly and more effectively. The most important difference is related to the type of displays used in laptops and the supporting hardware needed for different types of displays.

Exam need to know...

- Types
  For example: What is the difference between a liquid crystal display (LCD) and a light emitting diode (LED)–based display?

- Wi-Fi antenna connector/placement
  For example: Where is the Wi-Fi antenna located on most laptop computers? When should the antenna be disconnected from the Wi-Fi card?

- Inverter and its function
  For example: What type of laptop display requires an inverter? What is the purpose of an inverter?

- Backlight
  For example: What type of backlight is used with an LCD-based display? What is a symptom of a faulty backlight?

Types

Laptop computers have a built-in display. In addition to acting as a monitor for the laptop computer, most laptop displays have additional components built in. For example, laptops commonly have a web camera attached to the display.

True or false? The two most common types of displays used in laptop computers are plasma and Organic Light Emitting Diode (OLED).

Answer: *False.* The two most common types of displays used with laptop computers are LCD and LED-based displays.

Plasma and OLED displays aren't used as often in laptop computers. Plasma displays draw more power than LCD or LED displays. OLED displays are much more expensive and typically found only in smaller devices.

True or false? LED-based displays use the same type of crystals that are used in LCD-based displays.

Answer: *True.* The primary difference between an LED-based display and an LCD-based display is that an LED-based display uses LEDs for the backlight.

LCD-based displays use a cold cathode fluorescent lamp (CCFL) as a backlight. CCFLs require alternating current (AC) power, which cannot be supplied directly by battery power. An inverter is required in laptops that use LCD-based displays to convert direct current (DC) power from the battery to AC power needed by the CCFL.

NOTE In the context of the A+ exam and laptops, an LED-based display is more correctly known as an LED-backlit LCD display. That is, it uses LEDs for the backlight instead of a CCFL as the backlight. However, you'll rarely see this spelled out as an LED-backlit display. Instead you'll see it listed simply as an LED display. Some signs and billboards use only LEDs for the display, but these don't have the same resolution as a monitor that uses crystals.

EXAM TIP Most laptop computers use either LCD-based displays or the older LED-based displays. Both have crystals used for the display, but both have different types of backlights. Only LCD-based displays require a CCFL and the inverter to power it. While you can replace the display in a laptop, it is often a better choice to replace the entire laptop. Also, the video card is built into the motherboard, so you usually cannot upgrade or replace the video card.

Laptop computers commonly have additional video connections that can be used for external monitors or overhead projectors. These include Video Graphics Array (VGA), Digital Visual Interface (DVI), and/or High-Definition Multimedia Interface (HDMI) connectors.

Wi-Fi antenna connector/placement

Most contemporary laptop computers include built-in Wi-Fi capability supporting one or more of the 802.11 wireless versions. It's common for a laptop computer to have a Wi-Fi card and an antenna.

True or false? When replacing a faulty display within a laptop computer, the Wi-Fi card should also be replaced.

Answer: *False*. The antenna is often snaked through the laptop computer and hidden inside the display bezel, but the card is completely separate.

When removing or replacing the display, you need to disconnect the Wi-Fi cable at the Mini-PCIe card. The mini-PCIe card is often accessible after removing one of the panels on the bottom of the laptop computer. In some laptops, the system board has built-in wireless capabilities, so you might need to disconnect the antenna cable from the system board.

True or false? If the Wi-Fi antenna isn't reconnected, it will affect 802.11 performance.

Answer: *True*. Wireless capabilities follow the 802.11 standards, and the wireless card requires an antenna for best performance.

Different wireless standards (such as 802.11a, 802.11b, 802.11g, and 802.11n) have different bandwidth capabilities and transmission distances. However, each requires an antenna to provide the best performance. Without the antenna, the connection speed will be very slow, if it connects at all.

Inverter and its function

An inverter is used in laptop computers to convert DC power to AC power. Commercial AC power is available at surge suppressors connected to wall outlets. Batteries provide DC power within the laptop, allowing a laptop computer to operate even if it's not connected to a commercial power source.

True or false? An inverter is not needed in LED-based monitors.

Answer: *True*. An LED-based monitor uses LEDs for the backlight, which does not require AC power, so an inverter is not required.

The LEDs used in an LED-based monitor are powered by the battery's DC power. In contrast, LCD-based monitors use a CCFL as a backlight. CCFLs require AC power, and the inverter is required to convert the DC power from the battery to AC power for the backlight.

Backlight

Monitors that use crystals have a backlight that shines through the crystals. Electricity is applied to the crystals to orient them in different ways. Based on how the crystals are oriented, they can display different colors.

True or false? Backlights are required in LCD, LED, OLED, and plasma displays.

Answer: *False*. Backlights are required in LCD and LED displays but not in OLED or plasma displays.

The crystals used in LCD-based and LED-based displays cannot emit light on their own. Backlights are used to shine light through the crystals. In contrast, OLED-based and plasma-based displays can emit light and do not need a backlight.

True or false? A common indication of a faulty backlight in an LCD-based display is a dark or dim display.

Answer: *True.* The display is barely visible when a backlight fails.

Depending on how much light is in the room, you might not see anything displayed if the backlight has failed. One way to verify that the backlight has failed is by shining a flashlight into the display. If you can see some of the display, it verifies that the backlight is the problem.

> **EXAM TIP** If the display is dim or not visible on an LCD-based laptop display, the probable causes are the inverter, the CCFL, or the LCD display itself.

True or false? If the display is dim or dark on an LED-based display, the CCFL backlight should be replaced.

Answer: *False.* This is an indication of a faulty backlight or faulty display, but LED-based displays do not use CCFLs.

CCFLs are used in LCD-based displays but not in LED-based displays. With an LCD-based display, you should suspect the CCFL, the inverter, or the display itself. The problem could also be something as simple as the brightness control. Before replacing components, you should try to turn up the brightness.

> **EXAM TIP** LED-based and LCD-based displays require a backlight because crystals do not emit light on their own. A recent change in technology is that more laptop displays use LED-based displays instead of LCD-based displays. LCD backlights tend to fail less than CCFLs. Additionally, LEDs do not require inverters.

Can you answer these questions?

You can find the answers to these questions at the end of this chapter.

1. What are the four types of displays that can be used in laptop computers?
2. What is the purpose of an inverter?
3. What type of display requires a backlight?
4. What are likely components to check if an LCD-based display goes dim or dark?

Objective 3.3: Compare and contrast laptop features

There are several components and features that are common in laptop computers but are not used on most desktop computers. As a PC technician, you should be able to recognize and describe these features. This includes special function keys used on laptops, the differences between a docking station and a port replicator, and methods of physically locking a laptop computer.

Exam need to know...

- Special function keys
  For example: What key is used to modify the functionality of the F1 key on a laptop computer? What are common alternate purposes of function keys on a laptop computer?

- Docking station vs. port replicator
  For example: What are some benefits of using a docking station? What are the primary differences between a docking station and a port replicator?

- Physical laptop lock and cable lock
  For example: What is the purpose of a cable lock? What do users need to know about cable locks?

Special function keys

Laptop computers often have special function keys that can be used for a variety of purposes. They are designed as easy methods for users to change the laptop's behavior. However, users who don't understand the keys might accidentally press them and then think that their laptop is malfunctioning. With this in mind, it's important for technicians to understand what keys are commonly available and how they work.

True or false? Laptop computers commonly have standard function keys labeled F1 through F12, which have dual purposes.

Answer: *True.* These keys commonly have two purposes and can be used with or without a special Fn key.

Function keys have standard purposes and are found on any computer. For example, in many Windows-based applications, the F1 key brings up help and the F5 key will often refresh the display. On laptop computers, an extra key (often labeled Fn) is used with the function keys. The Fn key works similarly to how a Shift key works. If you press the A key by itself, the computer types a lowercase a, but if you press Shift+A, it types an uppercase A. Similarly, if you press the F1 key, it does one action, but if you press the Fn with the F1 key, it does something different.

> **EXAM TIP** The actual purpose of the Fn and function keys might be different on different laptop computers and even in different applications. However, the key point to remember is that the Fn key exists on laptop computers and can be used to modify the typical behavior of the function keys.

True or false? Many laptop computers include a key to disable the display.

Answer: *True.* The key is commonly referred to as a dual display key but, when pressed, it can disable the display.

Public speakers and trainers often connect an overhead projector to a laptop's secondary output. They can then select how they want the display to behave with one of the following four choices:

- **Primary display only** This is the normal operation.
- **Secondary display only** The primary display is not used, and instead all output is sent to the projector via the secondary output. This can also be used by a secondary monitor if the primary display fails.
- **Mirrored display** The same content is displayed on both the primary display and the overhead projector.
- **Extended display.** Users can drag items from one display to the other. Some speakers like this because they can control what the audience sees and be able to view their notes or other content on the laptop's display.

EXAM TIP If a laptop is not displaying data on the primary display, you might be able to return it to normal by toggling the dual display key. This key often has an icon of two screens and can be accidentally pressed by a user, disabling the display.

True or false? If a user's wireless connection suddenly stops on a laptop computer, you should check the wireless access point first

Answer: *False*. The easiest thing to check first is the user's system. The user might have accidentally toggled the wireless key.

Wireless systems commonly have a function key that can be toggled to enable and disable wireless capabilities. Users can accidentally toggle it, disabling the wireless connection. It's much easier to toggle this key to see whether the symptoms change than to start troubleshooting the wireless access point.

EXAM TIP Toggling the wireless key will enable or disable wireless capabilities. Most systems will provide a visual indication that the wireless key has been toggled, such as displaying a message at the lower-right corner of the screen. There isn't a standard key used for this function, but it will often be designated as an alternate use of one of the function keys (F1 through F12). On some systems, it is a separate key, button, or switch. For example, some systems have touch panels on the front of the system, with corresponding LEDs indicating when wireless is enabled or disabled.

True or false? If a user is unable to enter numbers when pressing the numbers keys in the numeric keypad, the Caps Lock key should be checked.

Answer: *False*. If numbers aren't typing when the user presses any of the number keys in the numeric keypad, the Num Lock key should be checked.

Most systems have alternate uses of number keys in the numeric keypad, such as moving the cursor. When the Num Lock key is toggled, the function of the number keys in the numeric keypad switches between typing a number and the alternate use.

Many smaller laptops omit the numeric keypad. Instead, alternate keys on the keyboard are used for both numbers and letters. On these systems, the Num Lock key toggles between letters and numbers.

True or false? Laptop computers often include alternate uses of function keys, including modifying the volume, modifying the brightness, and disabling Bluetooth capabilities.

Answer: *True*. These are common alternate uses of function keys.

If a function key is not working as you'd expect it to, you should ensure that the system has up-to-date drivers. For example, some keyboards have special keys that will launch an application such as an email program or Internet Explorer. If these keys aren't working, you might be able to resolve the program by updating a driver available from the laptop manufacturer's website.

Docking station vs. port replicator

Many organizations issue laptop computers that employees use while traveling and when working within the organization. However, when they bring the laptop back to the organization, they often want to connect the laptop to other hardware so that it's easier to use.

True or false? When users insert a laptop computer into a docking station, they can use a different mouse, keyboard, and monitor while still using the laptop's processor and disk drive.

Answer: *True*. When a laptop is plugged into a docking station, it provides access to other hardware but will still use the laptop's hard drive and CPU.

Docking stations support different hardware, and it is common to use a different mouse, keyboard, and monitor when a laptop is plugged into the docking station. These are typically full-sized components that users can't carry around with their laptop computers. Docking stations are also useful if the laptop computer doesn't have any external connections for multiple displays. For example, by plugging the laptop into a docking station, a user can have access to dual monitors.

True or false? If a laptop battery is not charging when it is in a docking station, it indicates that the laptop is not fully connected to the docking station.

Answer: *True*. A docking station should provide power to the laptop. If the battery is not charging, it indicates that the laptop is not connected.

Another possibility is that the docking station is not plugged in or turned on. Both items should be checked.

> **EXAM TIP** Docking stations are created for specific brands of laptop computers. The connectors on the laptop line up perfectly with the docking station. After the laptop is plugged into the docking station, it can use all of the components that are connected to the docking station.

True or false? When using a docking station with a Windows 7–based system, you need to configure different hardware profiles.

Answer: *False*. Hardware profiles are used with Windows XP and earlier operating systems but are not needed on Windows 7.

Windows XP systems needed separate hardware profiles. Users would boot into one hardware profile to recognize the hardware connected to the docking station. When not connected to the docking station, they would boot into a different hardware profile. In contrast, Windows 7–based systems automatically detect the available hardware when a system is started and neither need nor support hardware profiles.

True or false? Most port replicators can be used with different brands of laptop computers.

Answer: *True*. While docking stations are created for specific laptop models, port replicators can be used with different models.

Port replicators plug into a laptop computer and provide multiple ports. A common port replicator plugs into a single USB port.

> **EXAM TIP** Port replicators provide more flexibility than docking stations. They can be used with more brands and models of laptop computers and are typically cheaper.

Physical laptop lock and cable lock

Laptops are easily stolen when they aren't protected. For example, many laptops are stolen at conferences and training events when users leave them unattended during lunch or a break. Thieves can easily tuck laptops under their arm and walk away as if the laptop belongs to them.

True or false? Laptops can be protected with physical security by using a cable lock similar to a lock used to secure a bicycle.

Answer: *True.* Cable locks deter physical theft of laptop computers by securing the laptop computer to a desk or other piece of furniture.

Cable locks are strong cables that plug into the laptop and are secured with a combination lock. Users first wrap the cable around a desk or chair and then plug the end into the laptop computer. After spinning the combination lock, the cable cannot be removed without damaging the laptop computer.

> **EXAM TIP** Cable locks provide inexpensive physical security for laptop computers. Many users aren't aware of how often laptop computers are stolen, so when a company purchases cable locks for laptop computers, they need to also train users on the purpose and use of the locks. Training helps users understand the risks and recognize how simple it is to secure a laptop computer with a cable lock.

> **MORE INFO** Chapter 8 of the CompTIA A+ Training Kit (Exam 220-801 and Exam 220-802), ISBN-10: 0735662681, has a picture of a standard cable lock plugged into a laptop computer.

Can you answer these questions?

You can find the answers to these questions at the end of this chapter.

1. What is used to modify the purpose of function keys on a laptop computer?
2. What are common alternate purposes of function keys on laptop computers?
3. What is the difference between a docking station and a port replicator?
4. What can be used to provide physical security for a laptop computer?

Answers

This section contains the answers to the "Can you answer these questions?" sections in this chapter.

Objective 3.1: Install and configure laptop hardware and components

1. All ExpressCard slots have 26 pins. An ExpressCard/34 is 34 mm wide and an ExpressCard/54 is 54 mm wide.
2. New laptop computers use 2.5-inch Serial ATA (SATA) drives. Some include a solid state drive (SSD) with a SATA interface.
3. Tools used to maintain laptop computers are screwdrivers, plastic wedges, and ESD damage prevention equipment, such as ESD wrist straps.
4. Components that can be easily replaced in most laptop computers include memory, disk drives, optical drives, batteries, and wireless Mini-PCIe cards. Other components require an extensive disassembly and reassembly process.

Objective 3.2: Compare and contrast the components within the display of a laptop

1. CompTIA lists LCD, LED, OLED, and plasma as display types that can be used within a laptop. However, LCD and LED displays are the most common, with newer laptops using LED-based displays more often.

2. An inverter converts DC power provided by the battery to AC power in a laptop computer. It is needed only in laptops with traditional LCD-based displays. These displays use a CCFL as a backlight, and the CCFL requires AC power provided by the inverter.

3. Only LCD-based and LED-based displays require a backlight because they cannot emit light on their own. OLED-based and plasma-based displays do not require a backlight.

4. If an LCD-based goes dim or dark, it indicates a problem with the back-light. The two primary components to check are the CCFL backlight and the inverter that converts DC power to AC power needed by the CCFL.

Objective 3.3: Compare and contrast laptop features

1. Laptop computers have an extra Fn key used to modify the purpose of function keys. This key can be used with a normal function key (such as F1 through F12), or the function key can be used alone. This allows each of these keys to have dual purposes.

2. Most laptop computers support alternate purposes of the function keys. Common alternate uses are as follows: enable and disable dual displays, enable or disable wireless capabilities, modify the speaker volume, modify the display brightness, enable or disable Bluetooth capabilities, and enable or disable the keyboard backlight.

3. A docking station is designed for a specific brand and model of a laptop computer, and the laptop plugs directly into the docking station. Hardware devices attached to the docking station can then be used with the laptop computer. A port replicator typically plugs into one USB port on the laptop computer and provides access to multiple other ports. The port replicator provides access to additional hardware similar to the docking station, but it connects to the laptop computer differently.

4. Cable locks provide physical security for laptop computers. They are first wrapped around a desk or other piece of furniture and then plugged into the laptop. They include a combination lock and cannot be removed without the correct combination or damaging the laptop.

CHAPTER 4

Printers

The Printers domain covers approximately 11 percent of the A+ 220-801 exam. A PC technician will be expected to perform regular maintenance on printers and needs to be aware of common printers used in different organizations and how to install and maintain them. The corporate world uses laser printers extensively, so it's extremely important for PC technicians to have an in-depth understanding of laser printers. Because of this, you can expect the exam to have more questions related to laser printers than other types. However, the objectives also mention inkjet, thermal, and impact printers, so you'll need to understand the differences between these printers.

This chapter covers the following objectives:

- Objective 4.1: Explain the differences between the various printer types and summarize the associated imaging process
- Objective 4.2: Given a scenario, install, and configure printers
- Objective 4.3: Given a scenario, perform printer maintenance

Objective 4.1: Explain the differences between the various printer types and summarize the associated imaging process

For this objective, you need to understand each of the four basic printer types (laser, inkjet, thermal, and impact) and their differences. Laser printers have the most complex imaging process, but if you understand this process, you'll be better prepared to troubleshoot common laser printer problems. Inkjet printers are used within homes and small offices and provide superb printouts. They are often used in place of laser printers by home users and some small businesses. Thermal printers and impact printers are less common than laser printers and inkjet printers, but they do have specific abilities that make them useful in certain situations.

Exam need to know...

- Laser
  For example What is the purpose of a fuser assembly? What occurs during the cleaning process?

- Inkjet
For example: When should an inkjet printer be calibrated? What is needed to print two-sided copies with an inkjet printer?
- Thermal
For example: Where are thermal printers used? What are the components in a thermal printer?
- Impact
For example: What is the primary usage of impact printers? How is carbon paper used with an impact printer?

Laser

Laser printers provide high-quality output at a relatively low cost per printed page. They are commonly used in corporate environments, and their reasonable cost makes them economical for many small businesses too.

True or false? Laser printers can print two-sided output as long as they have a transfer belt.

Answer: *False.* A duplexing assembly (not a transfer belt) is required to print two-sided output on a laser printer. Many inkjet printers also use duplexing assemblies to print two-sided paper.

A transfer belt is used on some high-end color laser printers. Colors are applied to the transfer belt and then to the paper. This step is repeated for different colors.

> **EXAM TIP** Duplexing assemblies are needed for two-sided printing. They are typically mounted on the back of a laser or inkjet paper. After one side is printed, the paper is routed to the duplexing assembly, which turns the paper over and reroutes it through the printer a second time. Without a duplexing assembly, dual-sided printing must be done manually.

True or false? The primary purpose of the fuser assembly is to melt toner onto a piece of paper.

Answer: *True.* The fuser assembly generates heat, which melts the plastic particles in the toner and fuses them onto the paper.

Other components of a laser printer include the following:

- A raster image processor (RIP) accepts data to be printed and converts it to a raster image. The raster image is a group of dots organized as characters, words, and graphic images.
- An imaging drum is a round rotating cylinder covered with a photosensitive surface. Images are written onto the drum by shining a focused light from the laser onto the drum. Laser printers have a drum.
- A primary charge roller (or in some cases a corona wire) applies between -500 and -1,000 VDC to the imaging drum. This charge neutralizes the photosensitive surface of the drum and prepares it to receive an image.

- A highly focused laser shines light onto the imaging drum through one or more mirrors. The laser writes the raster image created by the RIP onto the drum by removing the negative charge wherever the light from the laser hits it.
- The toner is charged with a high negative charge and applied to the drum. Because of the electrical charge, the toner is only attracted to the drum where the laser wrote the image.
- Pickup rollers applied to the top of the paper are used to pick up paper from the paper tray and begin feeding it through the printer.
- Separator pads spin in the opposite direction from under the paper and push extra paper back. These pads help prevent more than one piece of paper from being sent through the printer at a time.
- The transfer roller charges the paper with a high voltage. As the drum turns and the paper is moved through the printer, the charged paper attracts the toner away from the drum. The result is that the toner is transferred from the drum onto the paper.
- A static eliminator or electrostatic discharger removes the charge from the paper as it passes the drum. This helps prevent the paper from sticking to the drum.
- A fuser assembly melts the toner onto the paper with a combination of friction and heat.
- An erase lamp shines light onto the drum to neutralize the voltage on the entire drum. This removes the previous image from the drum.
- Similar to a windshield wiper, a scraper removes residual or excess toner from the drum.

EXAM TIP When preparing for the CompTIA A+ 220-801 exam, ensure that you know what the common components are within a laser printer and their purposes. For example, you should know that the fuser assembly melts the toner onto the page, so if the toner smudges or wipes off the printed page, it's because of a faulty fuser assembly.

MORE INFO Laser printers are the primary printers used in many businesses, and the A+ exams focus heavily on it over the other printers. Ensure that you can identify all of its components and understand the laser printing process. For additional information, Chapter 7 of the CompTIA A+ Training Kit (Exam 220-801 and Exam 220-802), ISBN-10: 0735662681, provides more detailed information about printers. In addition to explaining the components, it covers many of the basics of printing including terminology, paper types, and many common tools. It also includes pictures of different printer components.

True or false? The order of the imaging process in a laser printer is processing, charging, exposing, developing, transferring, and fusing.

Answer: *True.* This is the proper order of the laser printer imaging process.

Figure 4-1 shows the seven steps of the laser imaging process. Each of the steps occurs as the imaging drum turns.

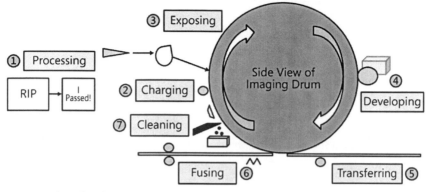

FIGURE 4-1 Laser imaging process.

NOTE You might see documentation that indicates that cleaning occurs first, and other documentation that indicates it occurs last. As long as remnants of the last job are cleaned at the end of a print job, the drum doesn't need to be cleaned again, so it could be argued that this happens last. However, cleaning the drum first ensures that it's ready to accept a new image. Regardless, CompTIA lists all the other processes in the correct order and lists cleaning as the last step in the imaging process. Some people might like to debate it, but when taking the exam, remember that CompTIA lists cleaning last.

The first two steps in the laser imaging process are processing and charging, which consist of the following operations:

- **Processing** The image is converted to a raster image by the RIP and stored in the printer's memory.

- **Charging** The imaging drum is charged with a high negative voltage (between -500 and -1,000 VDC) with a primary charge roller. In older laser printers, a corona wire applied the high negative voltage instead of a primary charge roller.

Figure 4-2 shows these two stages.

RIP **processes** the
raster image

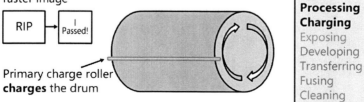

Primary charge roller
charges the drum

Processing
Charging
Exposing
Developing
Transferring
Fusing
Cleaning

FIGURE 4-2 Processing and charging stage in the laser imaging process.

True or false? The laser writes the image onto the imaging drum during the developing stage.

Answer: *False.* The image is written onto the drum during the exposing stage, not the developing stage.

The next two steps in the laser imaging process are exposing and developing, consisting of the following operations:

- **Exposing** During this stage, the laser writes the raster image onto the drum as shown in Figure 4-3.

- **Developing** The toner is applied to the drum during the developing stage, as shown in Figure 4-4.

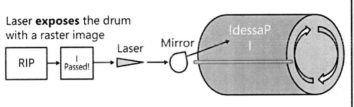

FIGURE 4-3 The exposing stage in the laser imaging process.

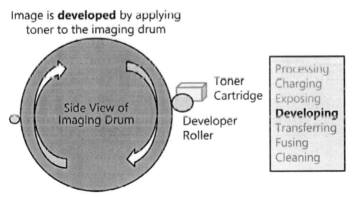

FIGURE 4-4 The exposing stage in the laser imaging process.

True or false? The toner is applied to the paper in the transferring stage of the laser imaging process.

Answer: *True.* During the transferring stage, toner is transferred from the imaging drum to the paper.

After the toner is transferred to the paper, it is melted onto the paper during the fusing stage. During the transferring stage, pickup rollers and separator pads pick up a single sheet of paper and start moving it through the printer. A transfer roller (or a transfer corona) applies a charge to the paper as it passes. The charged paper attracts the toner and the toner is transferred from the imaging drum to the paper.

At this point, the only thing holding the toner in place on the page is electrostatic charge. As the paper passes the drum, an electrostatic discharger removes the charge from the paper to prevent it from sticking to the drum, as shown in Figure 4-5. At this point, only gravity and friction hold the toner in place on the page.

Image is **transferred** to the paper

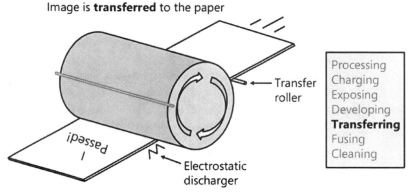

FIGURE 4-5 The transferring stage in the laser imaging process.

True or false? If toner falls off the printed pages, the most likely cause is a faulty fuser assembly.

Answer: *True*. The fuser assembly melts the toner, so if the toner is not sticking to the paper, the most likely cause is a faulty fuser assembly.

Figure 4-6 shows the fusing stage of the laser imaging process. The fusing assembly provides both friction and heat to the paper as it passes through, melting the toner onto the paper.

Image is **fused** to the paper

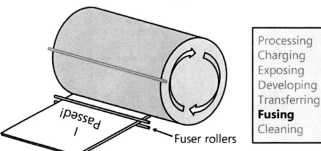

FIGURE 4-6 The fusing stage in the laser imaging process.

True or false? If print jobs show a ghost image of a previous printed page, the erase lamp or scraper might be the problem.

Answer: *True.* The erase lamp and scraper work together to remove remnants of the previous print job during the cleaning phase of the imaging process.

Figure 4-7 shows the cleaning process. A plastic or hard rubber scraper removes excess or residual toner. If the toner is not being removed, the scraper might need to be replaced. The lamp shines over the entire photosensitive surface of the drum, exposing it all and neutralizing the electrical charge. In contrast, the laser has a focused beam to expose only parts of the drum.

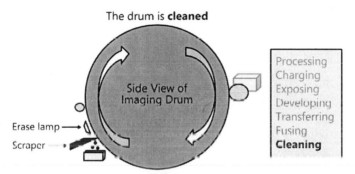

FIGURE 4-7 The cleaning stage in the laser imaging process.

Inkjet

Inkjet printers are popular with home users and small businesses. They provide excellent quality printouts and are relatively inexpensive to purchase. The biggest drawback is that the cost of the ink is exceptionally high, resulting in a high cost per printed page.

True or false? Inkjets use small pins to hammer the ink onto the page.

Answer: *False.* Impact printers (not inkjet printers) use small pins to hammer ink onto a page from a ribbon.

Inkjet printers have one or more print heads that move from side to side on a carriage and belt assembly. In some printers, each ink cartridge includes a disposable print head. In other printers, the ink is separate and is fed to a fixed print head when needed. Disposable print heads will last as long as the ink but aren't built to last for a long time. In contrast, fixed print heads are meant to last much longer.

Paper is fed though an inkjet printer with a roller and feeder assembly similar to how paper is fed through a laser printer. A pickup roller works with one or more separator pads to ensure that only one piece of paper is picked up at a time. Many inkjet printers include a duplexing assembly used to print on both sides. When used, the rollers feed the paper through the printer to print on one side. The paper is then routed to the duplexing assembly where it is turned over and then rerouted through the printer to print on the back.

Inkjet printers use one of the following two methods to print:

- **Thermal printing** This is also known as bubble jet printing. Small heaters within the print head heat the ink, creating small ink bubbles. These bubbles are then ejected onto the paper.

- **Piezoelectric printing** In this method, a crystal oscillator vibrates, causing the ink to break up into small droplets. These small droplets are given an electrical charge as they leave the print head, causing them to either stick to the paper or fall off. Ink that falls off is recaptured.

EXAM TIP In thermal inkjet (or bubble jet) printing, only the ink that is needed is sent through the print head. In piezoelectric printing, a steady stream of ink is sent through the print head, and unused ink is recaptured to be used again. Because of this, thermal inkjet printers are more prone to clogging up if they aren't used very often.

MORE INFO Jeff Tyson wrote an informative article, entitled "How Inkjet Printers work," available at *http://computer.howstuffworks.com/inkjet-printer3.htm*. Page 3 of the article compares heat and vibration methods.

True or false? Printouts with colors that aren't aligned on an inkjet printer indicate that the printer should be calibrated.

Answer: *True.* Inkjet printers commonly have calibration programs that can be used to align the print heads when colors are misaligned. A calibration program performs electronic adjustments to improve the print quality.

Inkjet printers include one or more test pages that you can print to check the quality of the printouts. These usually include specific patterns, with notes on what to do if the printout isn't perfect.

Thermal

Thermal printers are frequently used to create receipts at point of sale (POS) locations. After the sale is completed, the printer creates the receipt.

True or false? The print head in a thermal printer includes a heating element used to heat the paper.

Answer: *True.* Thermal printers use a special type of paper that responds to heat. The print head heats the paper to create the printout.

The paper on thermal printers is typically wound around a spindle. The spindle is attached to a sprocket type of feed assembly, and as the printer prints, the sprocket turns, feeding the paper through the printer.

Impact

Impact printers include pins within the print head. These pins strike an ink ribbon, and the ink ribbon leaves a dot on the paper.

True or false? Impact printers are also known as dot matrix printers.

Answer: *True.* Impact printers use pins to print dots within a matrix, and by printing different dots, they can print characters and images.

Figure 4-8 shows how a 9-pin print head can be used to print the capital *B* by printing specific dots in a dot matrix. Near letter-quality impact printers have print heads with 24 or 48 pins. The extra pins fill in the holes between the dots, providing a higher-quality printout.

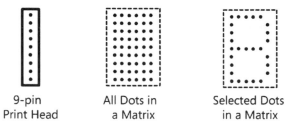

9-pin
Print Head

All Dots in
a Matrix

Selected Dots
in a Matrix

FIGURE 4-8 A dot matrix from an impact printer.

True or false? Businesses that need multiple copies of printouts commonly use impact printers.

Answer: *True.* Impact printers are ideal for printing multipart forms using carbon or carbonless paper to create multiple copies at a time.

Many businesses use multipart forms that have carbon paper between each copy. When the print head strikes the top paper, the force is felt through each page and presses the carbon paper onto the other copies.

> **EXAM TIP** Impact printers were the primary type of printers used for a long time. However, at this time, their use is limited. The most common usage is within business-es that require multipart forms separated with carbon paper. Only impact printers will print multipart forms with carbon paper. Some businesses have switched over to laser printers and just print multiple copies individually, but impact printers are still being used in some businesses.

True or false? It's common to use a tractor feed mechanism to feed paper through an impact printer.

Answer: *True.* Impact printers often use continuous feed paper with holes along the sides. The tractor feed mechanism has sprockets that fit into these holes to pull the paper through.

Impact paper used in impact printers can be continuous feed paper or individual sheets. When continuous feed paper is used, the paper is fed through the printer with the tractor feed mechanism. Single sheets of impact paper are fed through with friction from the platen, similar to how paper was fed through old typewriters. For best print quality, continuous feed paper and a tractor feed mechanism are used to ensure the paper is fed through at a consistent rate. Continuous feed paper is available with carbon paper to print multipart forms, or multiple copies at the same time.

Can you answer these questions?

You can find the answers to these questions at the end of this chapter.

1. What voltages are inside a laser printer that aren't in other printers?
2. Name two safety concerns related to laser printers.
3. What are two common types of inkjet printing?

4. Where are thermal printers used?

5. What can be easily printed by impact printers but not by laser printers?

Objective 4.2: Given a scenario, install, and configure printers

A common task with printers is to install and configure them. This objective expects you to know common methods used to connect printers to a computer or a network. Additionally, you should understand how printers are shared across a network and how to connect to a shared printer.

Exam need to know...

- Use appropriate printer drivers for a given operating system
  For example: When should you install a printer driver? What steps are required to install a USB printer?
- Print device sharing
  For example: What wired methods are used for printer connections? What wireless methods are supported for printer connections?
- Printer sharing
  For example: What comes after the "\\" in a Universal Naming Convention (UNC) name? What comes after the "\" in a UNC name?

Use appropriate printer drivers for a given operating system

All hardware devices require specific drivers so that the operating system can communicate with them. A software driver is one or more files that give the operating system the details it needs to send and receive information to and from the device.

True or false? When installing a USB printer, you should always install the print driver after inserting the USB cable.

Answer: *False.* When installing any device, you should follow the directions provided by the manufacturer, and manufacturers often indicate that the print driver should be installed before inserting the cable.

As a general guideline, it's usually best to install the provided driver before installing a device. Manufacturers include the drivers on a CD with directions for how to install the drivers and in what order.

When the device is installed, the operating system uses plug and play technology to automatically install the driver it identifies as the best choice. In many cases, this works fine even if the driver wasn't installed first. However, in some cases, the device won't work correctly or won't support all the features. It requires additional troubleshooting steps to uninstall the device, install the recommended drivers, and then reinstall the device.

True or false? You should install 64-bit print drivers on an x86-based system.

Answer: *False*. You should install 32-bit print drivers on x86-based systems and 64-bit drivers on x64 based systems.

Print drivers are specific to the operating system, such as Windows XP or Windows 7. Additionally, different print drivers are used for 32-bit and 64-bit Windows versions.

Print device sharing

It's common to share a printer among several users. There are multiple ways this can be done, depending on how the printer is connected.

True or false? A single printer with an Ethernet connection can be shared in a wired network.

Answer: *True*. If the printer has an Ethernet connection, it can be added to the network, and all users within the network can use it.

It's also possible to share a printer that is connected directly to a computer. For example, a printer connected to a computer with a USB or parallel connection can be shared on that computer, and other users in the network can print to it.

True or false? A printer can be connected directly to a computer by using a USB port as long as the printer has a USB connection.

Answer: *True*. USB connections are very common with printers.

The printer typically has a USB Type B port, and a USB cable goes from the printer to a common USB Type A port on a computer. Methods used to connect a printer directly to a computer include the following:

- **USB** This is the most common direct connection method used with printers today.
- **Parallel** This is an older method used before USB became popular. The cable connects to a DB-25 connection on the computer and to a Centronics or other type of parallel connection on the printer. Parallel ports are designated as LPT1 through LPT4.
- **Serial** A serial cable connects from the printer to a DB-9 or DB-25 connection on the computer. This is not common at all for current printers. Serial ports are designated as COM1 through COM4.

EXAM TIP Printers can be connected directly to a computer by using USB, parallel, or serial connections. USB connections are the most popular and the easiest to install. On Windows 7, you can often just plug in the printer and it will be available. Serial and parallel printers require additional steps to install.

True or false? Wireless printers can be shared by multiple computers within a wireless network.

Answer: *True*. Wireless printers are becoming very popular and most often use one of the 802.11x protocols (802.11a, 802.11b, 802.11g, or 802.11n).

A wireless printer connects to a wireless network just like any other wireless device. When connected, it is available to all other users on the network.

EXAM TIP Wireless printers are configured to connect to a wireless access point (WAP) or wireless router. You need to have the service set identifier (SSID) and password or passphrase used by the wireless network. Also, the printer should be assigned a specific IP address, just as a wired network printer should use a specific IP address.

MORE INFO Chapter 2 "Networking" of this book covers all of the 802.11x protocols in the context of Objective 2.5. This includes the speeds, distances, and frequencies used by these protocols, and the encryption types used to secure wireless networks. Chapter 2 also covers other networking topics, such as how IP addresses are assigned. By default, a network printer will typically be configured to receive an IP address using DHCP. However, it's recommended to statically assign an IP address to the printer or to configure DHCP to always assign the same IP address to the printer based on the printer's media access control (MAC) address.

True or false? Printers using infrared have a shorter wireless range than printers using 802.11g.

Answer: *True*. Infrared wireless ranges are very short, with a maximum distance of 5 meters (about 16 feet). Wireless printers using 802.11g have a range of about 38 meters (about 125 feet).

Some wireless printers can use Bluetooth or infrared technologies in the following scenarios:

- **Bluetooth** Printers that support Bluetooth connections typically use Class 2 Bluetooth, allowing the printer to be as far as 10 meters (33 feet) away.

- **Infrared (IR)**   If the printer has a clear line of sight from the computer, an IR connection can be used. This is the same type of IR used in TV remote controls. The drawback is that the connection is lost if the line of sight is broken. That is, if anything is placed between the computer and the printer, the printer will no longer print.

Printer sharing

After connecting a printer to a computer, it's possible to share it with other network users. A computer sharing a printer is referred to as a print server, although it could be running Windows XP, Windows 7, or some other desktop operating system. That is, a print server isn't necessarily running a server operating system.

Sharing a printer is similar in concept to sharing a folder on a computer. After a folder is shared, users with permissions can access the folder. Similarly, after sharing a printer, users with permissions can print to the printer.

True or false? Network printers are accessible by using a Universal Naming Convention (UNC) path similar to \\ShareName\ServerName.

Answer: *False*. Network printers are accessible by using a UNC path, but the UNC path has the format of \\ServerName\ShareName. The server name must be placed first in the UNC name, or the connection will fail.

For example, if you have a computer named Win7, sharing a printer named ClrLaser, other users can connect to it with the UNC path of \\Win7\ClrLaser. If users try to connect with \\ClrLaser\Win7, their systems will look for a computer named ClrLaser and the connections will fail.

> **EXAM TIP**   Printers can be connected directly to computers by using USB, parallel, or serial connections. When the printer is connected, it can be shared and other users can connect to it by using a UNC path name.

True or false? Printers can be shared from Devices and Printers in Windows 7.

Answer: *True*. This is accessible from the Start menu, and the Printers And Faxes section includes all of the printers installed on the computer.

You can share a printer in Windows 7 with the following steps:

1. Right-click the printer icon in Devices And Printers, and select Printer Properties.
2. Click the Sharing tab.
3. Select the Share This Printer check box. Optionally, change the name of the shared printer in the Share Name text box.

By default, the Everyone group can print to a printer when it is shared. You can modify this by using the Security tab of the Printer Properties dialog box.

If you are unable to share a printer, verify that print sharing is enabled on the computer. On Windows 7–based systems, this is accessed on the Networking tab of the network interface card's properties page and is called File And Printer Sharing For Microsoft Networks.

NOTE You can share a printer from Printers And Faxes in Windows XP. This is accessible from the Control Panel after changing the view to list the items individually. You can also find it in the Printers And Other Hardware category within the Control Panel.

MORE INFO The following video shows how to share a printer on Windows 7: *http:// windows.microsoft.com/en-US/windows7/help/videos/sharing-a-printer.*

True or false? You can add drivers for multiple operating systems when sharing a printer from a Windows-based system.

Answer: *True.* When sharing a printer, an Additional Drivers button is available on the Sharing tab. You can click this to add drivers for different operating systems.

When users connect to a shared printer by using the UNC path, the correct driver is automatically downloaded from the print server if it is available. If you need to update the driver, you need to update it only on the print server. The updated driver is automatically downloaded to clients the next time they connect.

True or false? Print jobs sent to a printer via a print server will not print if the print server loses network connectivity.

Answer: *True.* If the print server is not accessible on the network, users will not be able to send print jobs to it.

EXAM TIP A print server is any computer used to share printers. If a shared printer is powered on but users cannot print to it, verify that the print server is powered on and has network connectivity. Print drivers for multiple operating systems can be added to the print server and will automatically be downloaded to clients when they connect.

MORE INFO The following two videos show how you can change printing options or change the default printer on Windows 7: *http://windows.microsoft.com/en-US/windows7/ change-your-default-printer* and *http://windows.microsoft.com/en-US/windows7/help/ videos/printing-options.*

Can you answer these questions?

You can find the answers to these questions at the end of this chapter.

1. What is the most common method used to connect a printer directly to a computer?

2. What is a primary concern with networked printers to ensure that users can continue to access them even after the printer is turned off and back on?

3. What information do network users need for connecting to a shared network printer?

Objective 4.3: Given a scenario, perform printer maintenance

PC technicians are expected to perform basic maintenance on printers in the workplace. Laser printers require more maintenance than other printers, but they are also used more often. CompTIA doesn't include inkjet printers in this objective because there is very little maintenance required. You might need to replace inkjet cartridges, replace print heads, or run calibration programs on an inkjet printer, but those tasks are covered in Objective 4.1, "Explain the differences between the various printer types and summarize the associated imaging process."

Exam need to know...

- Laser
  For example: What determines when a maintenance kit should be applied to a laser printer? What is typically included in a laser printer maintenance kit?

- Thermal
  For example: How can the thermal head be cleaned? What should you use to clean a thermal printer?

- Impact
  For example: What are common maintenance tasks required with an impact printer? What can help prevent damage to the pins on a print head?

Laser

Many components within a laser printer will wear out and should be replaced periodically. Maintenance kits include key components that should be replaced and typically include the following items:

- Pickup rollers and separator pads
- Transfer rollers
- Fuser assemblies
- Toner

True or false? When a laser printer displays a message such as "Service Required," a maintenance kit should be applied to the printer.

Answer: *True.* "Service Required" or "Perform Printer Maintenance" are two common error messages indicating that a maintenance kit should be applied.

Laser printers often count how many pages have been printed and display maintenance messages when specific counts are reached. At other times, the laser printer might develop problems that can be resolved by applying a maintenance kit.

> **EXAM TIP** Laser printers track the count of printed pages and notify users when printer maintenance is required. These error messages sometimes alarm users, but they are normal. The manual for the printer provides clear directions about what to do.

True or false? If toner spills, it's best to vacuum it up with a regular vacuum cleaner.

Answer: *False*. If toner spills, it's best to consult the Material Safety Data Sheet (MSDS) to identify the best method of cleaning it. If a regular vacuum cleaner is used, the toner will pass through the vacuum cleaner and go back out into the air.

Vacuums with high-efficiency particulate arresting (HEPA) filters can be used to vacuum toner. The HEPA filter will capture the toner particles. If a vacuum cleaner with a HEPA filter isn't available, you can often clean the spill by dabbing with a paper or cloth towel soaked with cold water. Warm water or the heat of friction generated by scrubbing can melt the resin and can make the spilled toner more difficult, if not impossible, to remove.

> **EXAM TIP** Replacing toner in a laser printer is a task that many users can do themselves. The directions are generally clear and easy to follow. Some common problems that occur are that users don't shake the new toner cartridge prior to installing it or they forget to remove the cover before installing it. If the toner cartridge isn't shaken to redistribute the toner, it can all settle during shipping or storage to one end of the drum, and the other end might produce pale or blank output. When the toner cover is not removed, the printouts are blank.

True or false? If two or more pieces of paper are regularly being pulled into the laser printer, replacing the separator roller will likely solve the problem.

Answer: *True*. The pickup and separator rollers work together to pick up a single piece of paper, and if the separator roller is worn, the printer will often pick up more than one sheet of paper. Replacing the roller solves the problem.

Using the wrong type of paper or damp paper can cause the same problem. When paper is stored or used in areas with high humidity, it can absorb the water and start jamming within the printer. The solution is to use the correct paper and/or store it in an area with an acceptable level of humidity.

> **EXAM TIP** Clean or replace pickup rollers and separator pads if a printer is picking up more than one sheet of paper from a tray and you've verified that the paper is not the problem.

> **EXAM TIP** Color laser printers have calibration programs similar to inkjet calibration programs. If the printout isn't clear or the colors are misaligned, calibrate the printer by using the manufacturer-supplied calibration program, just as you would do for an inkjet printer.

Thermal

Thermal printers don't require a lot of attention or maintenance, but they can still benefit from some basic care. One of the primary concerns is a buildup of paper dust within the printer, which should be periodically removed.

True or false? An electrostatic discharge (ESD)–safe vacuum cleaner should be used when cleaning a thermal printer.

Answer: *True.* An ESD-safe vacuum cleaner helps prevent ESD damage to the printer while it is being cleaned.

Paper used in thermal printers is typically on a single continuous roll with the last part of the roll marked with a different color on one side. When the user sees the printouts with the different color paper, they know the printer is almost out of paper. For most thermal printers, replacing this paper is as simple as replacing a roll of paper towels. You simply open the printer, remove the empty roll of paper, and install the new roll of paper.

When removing dust from the printer, the heating element on the print head should also be cleaned. The heating element on the print head can be cleaned with isopropyl alcohol and a lint-free cloth or cotton swab.

EXAM TIP If thermal printers are not periodically cleaned, the print dust within the printer can shorten the life of the thermal print head. Cleaning it consists of cleaning the heating element on the print head and removing the print dust.

Impact

Impact printers have a lot of activity as paper is pulled through the printer and the print head pins hammer onto the ink ribbon to the paper. Because of this, it's highly recommended to regularly clean these with an ESD-safe vacuum to remove the paper dust. Alternatively, you can take the printer outside and use compressed air to blow the dust out.

True or false? The ink cartridge should be refilled when the printout on an impact printer is faded.

Answer: *False.* Impact printers use ink ribbons not ink cartridges. The ink ribbon should be replaced when the printout is faded.

It's sometimes possible to re-ink the ribbon to get more use out of it. However, this can be done only a limited number of times because, eventually, the repeated impacts to the print head will tear through the ribbon.

EXAM TIP The ink ribbon on an impact printer is held in place by two spindles. One spindle pulls the ribbon to it, and the other spindle releases the ribbon. When it gets to the end, the process is reversed so that the ribbon is pulled by the other spindle. This allows the ribbon to be continuously reused. However, if the printout is faded, the ribbon should be replaced.

True or false? Paper jams in impact printers can be caused by tractor feed problems.

Answer: *True.* Impact printers commonly use continuous feed paper, and problems with the tractor feed mechanism are the most common source of paper jams.

True or false? Keeping an impact printer clean can help prevent problems with the print head.

Answer: *True*. Impact printers generate a lot of paper dust, and this can cause pins in the print head to jam.

A jammed pin might rip the paper if it's jammed in the out position. If it's jammed in the in or out position, it will impact the print quality.

In addition to keeping the inside of the printer clean, the platen should be periodically cleaned also. The platen is the round cylinder that turns with the paper. The print head pins hammer through the ribbon and paper onto the platen. Over time, the platen can have multiple indentations, but you can renew the platen by rubbing it with isopropyl alcohol.

> **EXAM TIP** Keeping an impact printer clean is the primary maintenance required, besides replacing the paper and replacing the ink ribbon. The print heads are durable and normally last a long time if the printer is kept clean. If a pin jams, you'll need to replace the print head.

Can you answer these questions?

You can find the answers to these questions at the end of this chapter.

1. What is included in a laser printer maintenance kit?
2. What is the primary maintenance required for a thermal printer?
3. When would a print head on an impact printer need to be replaced?

Answers

This section contains the answers to the "Can you answer these questions?" sections in this chapter.

Objective 4.1: Explain the differences between the various printer types and summarize the associated imaging process

1. A laser printer has a high-voltage power supply, providing between -500 and -1,000 VDC. This voltage is used by the primary charge roller (or in older laser printers, a corona wire) to charge the imaging drum.
2. The two primary safety concerns related to laser printers are the high-voltage power supplies and the high-temperature fuser assemblies. The high-voltage power supply can deliver lethal electric shocks, and the fuser assembly can cause burns.
3. The two types of inkjet printing are thermal (or bubble jet) printing and piezoelectric printing. Thermal inkjets heat the ink, creating small bubbles that are sent out the heads. Piezoelectric printing uses a crystal to create small droplets, and these droplets are charged so that they stick to the paper or drop off.

4. Thermal printers are commonly used at point of sale locations to create receipts.

5. Impact printers are used to print multipart forms that have carbon paper within them. The impact of the pins on the head prints on each form. In contrast, a laser printer cannot print multipart forms, but it can print multiple individual copies.

Objective 4.2: Given a scenario, install, and configure printers

1. USB connections are the most common method used to connect printers directly to a computer. They are also the easiest, especially on Windows 7. If the driver is installed, the printer is automatically added when the USB connection is plugged in.

2. A primary concern with networked printers is ensuring that they are assigned the same IP address each time they are turned off and back on. This can be done by manually assigning an IP address or by configuring DHCP to assign the same IP address to the printer based on the printer's MAC address.

3. Users need to know the UNC path to a shared printer in order to connect to it. This is in the format of \\ServerName\ShareName, where the server name is the name of the computer sharing the printer and the ShareName is the share name of the printer.

Objective 4.3: Given a scenario, perform printer maintenance

1. A laser printer maintenance kit typically includes one or more pickup rollers, a separator pad, a transfer roller, a fuser assembly, and toner. Toner can be replaced at other times.

2. The primary maintenance required for a thermal printer is to periodically clean out the paper dust and the print head. An ESD-safe vacuum cleaner can be used to remove the dust, and isopropyl alcohol with a lint-free cloth can be used to clean the print head.

3. An impact printer print head needs to be replaced if one or more of the pins jam.

CHAPTER 5

Operational procedures

The Operational Procedures domain covers approximately 11 percent of the A+ 220-801 exam. It starts off with safety procedures that protect both personnel and equipment. Environmental controls are employed to maintain the proper temperature and humidity and also provide protection against power anomalies. Customer service skills are important for technicians to understand and practice, and this domain includes some basic communication and professionalism skills needed by technicians. Lastly, technicians might come across prohibited content or activity during a typical day and need to know how to respond. One of the most important responses is to report the incident to a supervisor or manager in accordance with the company policy. Additionally, if technicians collect anything that might be used as evidence, they must create a chain of custody log.

This chapter covers the following objectives:

- Objective 5.1: Given a scenario, use appropriate safety procedures
- Objective 5.2: Explain environmental impacts and the purpose of environmental controls
- Objective 5.3: Given a scenario, demonstrate proper communication and professionalism
- Objective 5.4: Explain the fundamentals of dealing with prohibited content/activity

Objective 5.1: Given a scenario, use appropriate safety procedures

Safety procedures are in place to protect personnel and equipment. Electrostatic discharge (ESD) damage can damage equipment, but it's relatively inexpensive and easy to implement ESD damage prevention practices. Beyond protecting the equipment, there are many basic steps PC technicians can take to ensure their personal safety. This includes disconnecting power before repairing PC components, removing jewelry, understanding basic lifting techniques, and knowing how to respond to electrical fires. There are also certain regulations that personnel within an organization need to understand.

Exam need to know...

- ESD straps
  For example: What is the purpose of an ESD strap? Where are ESD straps attached?
- ESD mats
  For example: Where are ESD mats used?
- Self-grounding
  For example: What does a technician touch for self-grounding?
- Equipment grounding
  For example: What is a benefit of ensuring that a system stays grounded? What does a diagram of ground look like?
- Personal safety
  For example: What is "soft power" in a typical PC? What should be done to fight an electrical fire?
- Compliance with local government regulations
  For example: What is a regulatory concern with cathode ray tube (CRT)–based monitors?

ESD strap

Electrostatic discharge (ESD) poses a significant damage risk to many electronic components. Because of this, technicians need to understand the ESD risks and how to prevent the damage.

True or false? An ESD wrist strap should be connected to a technician's wrist and an electrical ground.

Answer: *True*. A wrist strap wraps around the technician's wrist and provides metal-to-skin contact. It includes a wire with an alligator clip on the other end that is connected to an electrical ground. This prevents static buildup, which can cause ESD damage.

The connection created with the wrist strap ensures that the technician is at the same electrical potential as the equipment.

EXAM TIP ESD wrist straps should be worn by technicians when working on computers. This is especially true when handling CPUs and RAM because they are the most susceptible to damage. However, as a best practice, technicians should use a wrist strap when handling any type of computer.

MORE INFO You can see pictures of ESD straps by searching Bing.com images (*http://www.bing.com/images/*) using the search phrase "ESD wrist strap."

ESD mats

ESD mats are an additional method that can be used to prevent ESD damage. These mats are made of a special material that prevents static buildup.

True or false? An ESD mat is used beneath carpet to prevent static buildup.

Answer: *False*. ESD mats are used on floors and workbenches but not under a carpet.

Static easily builds up on carpet, so carpet is not recommended in locations where computers are maintained or in use. Additionally, computers should not be placed directly on carpet. Specially designed antistatic carpet is available and used in some situations, but this is more expensive than traditional carpet.

> **EXAM TIP** ESD mats are key components used to prevent ESD damage. They are often used in front of workbenches so that a technician is standing on the mat while working on the computer.

> **MORE INFO** In addition to ESD wrist straps and ESD mats, antistatic bags are used to store ESD-sensitive components. Chapter 1 of the CompTIA A+ Training Kit (Exam 220-801 and Exam 220-802), ISBN-10: 0735662681, provides more information about ESD and common methods used to protect against ESD damage.

Self-grounding

Self-grounding refers to a technician touching the metal part of a computer case or other metal that is connected to an electrical ground.

True or false? A technician can ensure that he is at the same electrical potential of a computer system by touching the case.

Answer: *True*. This is recommended as a method of preventing ESD damage.

By touching the computer case periodically, the technician ensures that static electricity is not building up between the technician and the computer. This isn't necessary if a technician is using an ESD wrist strap. It's common to connect the ESD wrist strap directly to the computer case so that the technician is always connected to the case.

> **EXAM TIP** Ideally, a technician will use an ESD wrist strap while working on a computer. If this is not possible, technicians should periodically touch the case to ensure that they are at the same electrical potential as the computer.

Equipment grounding

Ground in electronics refers to an electrical potential that is the same as Earth. It provides a return path for current and is used as a reference point when measuring voltages.

True or false? Ground can be Earth ground, chassis ground, or signal ground.

Answer: *True*. Depending on the context, ground can be Earth ground, chassis ground, or signal ground.

It's common for these three grounds to be connected together in a computer, but they are often identified by different symbols. Figure 5-1 shows the symbols for ground used in schematics and wiring diagrams. These ground types can be described as follows:

- The signal ground provides a return path for an electrical circuit. When measuring voltages, you would ensure that you are connected to a signal ground for the voltage.
- Chassis ground refers to the chassis or case of the computer or electronic system. The signal ground is connected to the chassis ground. For example, motherboards are secured onto cases with plastic standoffs and metal screws. The metal screws connect the signal ground on the motherboard to the computer case, which is the chassis ground.
- Earth ground provides a path to Earth. In buildings, one or more metal stakes are driven into the ground, and a wire is attached to provide the connection to Earth. This is connected to the ground connection used in electrical outlets. When a computer is plugged into an electrical outlet, the chassis ground is connected to the Earth ground.

Signal   Chassis   Earth
Ground   Ground   Ground

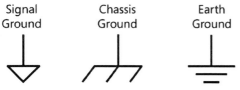

FIGURE 5-1 Common symbols for ground.

True or false? Ground connections are not always needed and can be removed if desired.

Answer: *False*. Ground connections provide electrical connections and provide important safety protections, so they should never be disconnected.

Electrical problems in any system using electricity can result in dangerous voltages being redirected to the case or chassis. As long as the chassis is grounded, these voltages will be sent to ground without risking danger to personnel. However, if grounds are removed, it can result in dangerous voltages being redirected to the case and shocking any user who touches the case.

> *EXAM TIP* Ensure that you know the differences between the three types of ground connections, including their symbols. Ground connections should never be removed from a system.

Personal safety

Computers are mass-produced things and can easily be replaced. In contrast, technicians are unique individual people and cannot be replaced. With this in mind, personal safety should always be at the forefront of any PC technician's mind.

True or false? Voltage is not sent to the computer when it is turned off by using the power switch on the front of the computer.

Answer: *False*. Voltage is still sent to the computer when it is turned off and plugged into an electrical outlet.

Computer power supplies use "soft power," which provides power to the motherboard even when the front panel power switch indicates that the computer is off. In some computers, the power supply has an on/off power switch that removes power from the system, but a safer step is to remove the electrical power cord.

EXAM TIP Technicians should remove all jewelry such as watches, rings, and bracelets prior to working on a computer, especially when measuring voltages from a powered-on system. The system should be powered off and unplugged prior to working on most internal components, but the power supply needs to be on to measure voltages.

Other safety considerations include using proper lifting techniques and being aware of weight limitations. It's best to lift using your legs, not your back. Get help when you need to lift more than 70 pounds.

True or false? An electrical fire should be extinguished with a water-based fire extinguisher.

Answer: *False*. Water conducts electricity, so an electrical fire should never be extinguished with a water-based extinguisher.

EXAM TIP When fighting an electrical fire, the first step should be to remove the power whenever possible. This might be accomplished by removing the power cord or by turning off the power at a circuit breaker. Under no circumstances should water be used on an electrical fire.

The four components of a fire are heat, fuel, oxygen, and a chemical reaction. Together, they are called a fire tetrahedron, and firefighting methods stop a fire by removing one or more of these components. Some fire classifications in the United States include the following:

- **Class A (ordinary combustibles)** This is the only type of fire that can be extinguished with water.
- **Class B (flammable liquids and gases)** Chemicals are used to extinguish these types of fires. In the European and Australian/Asian classification system, these are labeled as Class B and Class C fires.
- **Class C (electrical equipment)** The best way to stop an electrical fire is by removing the power source. Water should never be used on an electrical fire because it is conductive and can electrocute the person spraying the water. In the European classification system, electrical fires are labeled as Class F/D fires. In the Australian/Asian classification system, they are labeled as Class D fires.
- **Class D (combustible metals)** These metals burn at an extremely hot temperature but can be extinguished with special chemicals used to smother the fire. In the European and Australian/Asian classification system, combustible metals are also labeled as Class D fires.

True or false? Proper cable management is a safety concern and protects cables from damage.

Answer: *True*. Cable management refers to ensuring that cables are properly run from system to system without causing trip hazards or being susceptible to accidental damage.

Cables should be contained in conduit or cable runs. When connected from a computer to a wall outlet, they should follow a path that doesn't represent a risk for personnel or the equipment. Cable laid under a carpet might not be a significant trip hazard, but it can easily be damaged by people stepping on the cable or rolling chairs over it.

Compliance with local government regulations

Organizations have a responsibility to follow all government regulations, and this includes safety regulations.

True or false? When faced with protecting a computer or protecting a person, technicians should always value people first.

Answer: *True*. Technicians should always value the safety of individuals over the safety of equipment.

> **EXAM TIP** Safety regulations consistently reinforce the value of protecting people and the environment. If you keep this in mind when answering safety-related questions, they are usually easy to answer.

True or false? CRT displays use hazardous voltages that can kill a technician.

Answer: *True*. CRT monitors use high voltages that are lethal.

Only trained technicians should work on the inside of CRT monitors. The components within a CRT monitor can retain and build up electrical voltage even after they've been removed from power.

> **MORE INFO** Most organizations have replaced CRT monitors with other types of monitors. CRT monitors use more voltage and present more danger to personnel and the environment than other types. Chapter 6 of the CompTIA A+ Training Kit (Exam 220-801 and Exam 220-802), ISBN-10: 0735662681, covers monitors in depth, including specific safety concerns related to CRTs.

Can you answer these questions?

You can find the answers to these questions at the end of this chapter.

1. What are common components used to prevent ESD damage when working on PCs?
2. What are the three types of grounds used with electronics?
3. What should be done to extinguish an electrical fire?

Objective 5.2: Explain environmental impacts and the purpose of environmental controls

This objective addresses various issues in the computing environment, such as the temperature, humidity, ventilation, dust and debris, and power. If not adequately controlled, any of these environmental problems can affect the operation of a computer. In addition to understanding these issues, it's also important to know about some methods used to protect computers. This objective also includes Material Safety Data Sheets (MSDSs) and the data that they provide. Last, this objective addresses the importance of complying with local regulations.

Exam need to know...

- MSDS documentation for handling and disposal
  For example: What is the purpose of an MSDS?

- Temperature, humidity level awareness, and proper ventilation
  For example: What is the effect of high humidity?

- Power surges, brownouts, blackouts
  For example: What is the difference between a spike and a power surge?
  What protects a computer against a brownout or blackout?

- Protection from airborne particles
  For example: What is a symptom of a dirty computer? What is used to clean the inside of a computer?

- Component handling and protection
  For example: What components are the most susceptible to ESD damage?
  What should be used when transporting a circuit card?

- Compliance with local government regulations
  For example: What is a concern with CRT monitors when they reach the end of their life cycle?

MSDS documentation for handling and disposal

Material Safety Data Sheets (MSDSs) are available for many different products used within an organization, such as cleaning solvents. PC technicians should be aware of MSDS sheets and their purpose.

True or false? A user is complaining that his fingers are stinging after cleaning his monitor with a cleaning solvent. He should consult the MSDS for the solvent to determine what to do.

Answer: *True*. The MSDS provides information about potential hazards related to different chemicals and cleaning solvents. It also provides first-aid instructions and should be consulted if an individual has an adverse reaction after using the chemical or solvent.

The MSDS also indicates whether the material is considered hazardous or toxic waste. These sheets should be consulted when disposing of any excess cleaning solvents or supplies.

Temperature, humidity level awareness, and proper ventilation

Environmental controls are needed to ensure that the temperature, humidity levels, and ventilation are adequate for systems. If the room temperature is allowed to get too high, internal computer components can overheat and fail. It's important to ensure that the environment is controlled and that the system has adequate ventilation to move air through the computer.

True or false? Humidity levels should be kept as high as possible to prevent ESD damage.

Answer: *False.* Humidity levels should be maintained in a range between 40 and 60 percent.

If humidity is too low, it increases static electricity and the possibility of ESD damage. If it is too high, it causes condensation and the water buildup can damage the electronic components.

True or false? Grounding bars installed in equipment bays help reduce ESD damage.

Answer: *True.* Grounding bars are large copper bars that are attached to ground and ensure that all components have a clear path to ground. This helps prevent static buildup and ESD damage.

Power surges, brownouts, blackouts

Commercial power provided by power companies isn't always perfect. The voltage sometimes increases, causing power surges or power spikes, and sometimes decreases, causing brownouts or blackouts.

True or false? A surge protector protects against brownouts.

Answer: *False.* A surge protector protects against power surges and spikes but not brownouts or blackouts.

Power in North America and many other countries/regions is about 115 volts alternating current (VAC). In Europe and some other countries/regions, it is about 230 VAC. Minor deviations are common, but when the deviations become too great, it can cause problems. When discussing power problems, it's important to understand the basic terms. Typical problems are classified as either undervoltage or overvoltage and are then distinguished by their duration. Common power problems include the following:

- A power surge is a momentary increase in voltage. These are short in duration and can often be observed by a building's lights getting brighter.

- A power spike is a sharp increase in voltage but of shorter duration than a surge. A common cause is a lightning strike. Power spikes can cause significant damage to unprotected equipment.

- A brownout (sometimes called a *sag* if it lasts for less than a second) is a momentary decrease in voltage. Lights will flicker or become dimmer. Unprotected systems will often turn themselves off or restart.

- A blackout is a total loss of power. Unprotected systems will turn off.

True or false? An uninterruptible power supply (UPS) provides battery backup for a computer and keeps it running during short-term brownouts and blackouts.

Answer: *True.* A UPS system provides continuous power to a computer during sags, brownouts, and blackouts.

A UPS is intended to provide only short-term power. For example, a UPS system might provide a computer with continuous power after an outage for 15 or 30 minutes. The UPS can send a shutdown signal to the computer when the battery power is low. This gives the computer enough time to complete a logical shutdown if necessary.

EXAM TIP   A UPS system includes a battery and provides protection against sags, brownouts, and blackouts. The UPS is plugged into the wall power receptacle, and the computer is plugged into the UPS. If power drops below an acceptable level, the UPS still provides power to the computer by using the battery power, and the computer is unaffected.

True or false? Laser printers should be plugged into UPS systems.

Answer: *False.* Laser printers have high-voltage power supplies, which draw a significant amount of power, and they should not be plugged into UPS systems.

Protection from airborne particles

Computer cases have fans that draw air through them, over key components, and out through one or more vents. It's common for these fans to also draw dust and debris into the fan and into the case.

True or false? Computers used in industrial spaces can be kept in enclosures to protect them from airborne particles.

Answer: *True.* If the computer is used in an exceptionally dirty or dusty location, it can be protected within an enclosure.

Air filters are also useful to protect systems. They are installed before intake fans so that the filters capture dust and debris that would otherwise have been sucked into the system. These filters should be periodically cleaned.

True or false? Excessive dust and debris within a computer can cause it to be exceptionally loud and slow.

Answer: *True.* Excessive dust and debris restricts airflow, causing fans to work harder to keep the system cool, making them louder. When the fans can't keep the system cool, CPUs automatically slow down to avoid heat damage.

Many fans have thermistors that automatically sense increased heat and cause the fan to run faster. If the case is dirty, the fan cannot provide adequate ventilation, causing the temperature to rise and the fan to spin faster. Faster spinning fans can become quite loud. Similarly, CPUs and their fans have heat sensors. The fans spin faster as the CPU gets hotter, and if the fan can't keep the CPU cool, the CPU slows down.

True or false? Two common methods used to clean computer cases are with compressed air or with ESD-safe vacuum cleaners.

Answer: *True.* Computer cases can be cleaned with compressed air or ESD-safe vacuum cleaners.

Compressed air cans are commonly used to clean out computers, printers, and other components. Equipment should be taken outside first. When cleaning systems inside, they should be cleaned with ESD-safe vacuum cleaners.

> **EXAM TIP** A computer that has an excessive amount of dust and debris built up will be exceptionally loud and slower than normal. The solution is simple. It needs to be cleaned either by blowing out the dust with compressed air or by vacuuming it using an ESD-safe vacuum cleaner.

Component handling and protection

Components such as circuit cards, central processing units (CPUs), and memory should be protected when they are removed from computers. These can often be reused in a different computer but can easily be destroyed if not handled properly.

True or false? Electronic components should be stored in antistatic bags when not in use.

Answer: *True.* Antistatic bags prevent static from building up on electronic components and protect them from ESD damage.

In addition to using antistatic bags during storage of sensitive parts, they should be used when such parts are being transported between locations. For example, if memory needs to be replaced on a user's computer, the memory should be carried to the computer in an antistatic bag to prevent damage.

ESD damage is not visible to the naked eye, but it certainly exists. In extreme cases, ESD damage will prevent the component from working at all. More often, a component is weakened by ESD damage and it gives inconsistent results. For example, if memory is replaced without using ESD-safe practices, the computer will probably still recognize the memory. However, ESD damage will result in random reboots or system crashes.

Compliance to local government regulations

Organizations have a responsibility to follow all government regulations that apply to them. This includes country/regional regulations and local regulations.

True or false? CRT-based monitors have toxic substances and should be treated as hazardous waste.

Answer: *True.* CRT-based monitors include lead, cadmium, and phosphors and should not be mixed with regular trash.

Many laws govern how CRT-based monitors can be disposed of. In most countries/regions, they are considered hazardous waste and should be recycled rather than added to landfills.

Can you answer these questions?

You can find the answers to these questions at the end of this chapter.

1. What should be consulted if a technician is experiencing adverse reactions from a cleaning solvent?
2. What level of humidity causes increased risks of ESD damage?
3. What is an important consideration related to laser printers and UPS systems?
4. You need to replace a graphics card in a computer and decide to replace it at the user's location. What should be used when carrying the graphics card to the user's computer?

Objective 5.3: Given a scenario, demonstrate proper communication and professionalism

PC technicians must have technical skills, but that isn't enough to succeed as a PC technician. They also need basic customer skills so that they can communicate professionally and effectively with customers. These skills are simple to understand if you think of yourself as a customer. If you consider how you would want to be treated as a customer in any situation, you'll be able to answer the CompTIA questions in this objective.

Exam need to know...

- Use proper language—avoid jargon, acronyms, and slang when applicable
  For example: What acronyms are acceptable when talking to a customer?
- Maintain a positive attitude
  For example: When is it acceptable to complain about a job situation?
- Listen and do not interrupt the customer
  For example: When is it acceptable to interrupt the customer?
- Be culturally sensitive
  For example: What is meant by culturally sensitive?
- Avoid distractions
  For example: What distractions are acceptable when talking to a customer?
- Dealing with difficult customer or situation
  For example: What is an open-ended question?
- Be on time (if late, contact the customer), set and meet expectations/timeline, and communicate status with the customer
  For example: What should a technician do if a customer service is delayed due to a supplier issue?
- Deal appropriately with customer's confidential materials
  For example: When is it acceptable to pick up a customer's confidential materials?

Use proper language—avoid jargon, acronyms, slang when applicable

When technicians talk to other technicians, they often use technical jargon, acronyms, and slang. While this is common and acceptable, technicians need to avoid this language when talking to customers. Jargon, acronyms, and slang terms that are common to any PC technician are not necessarily common to customers. They can easily confuse a customer and should be avoided.

True or false? When talking to customers, technicians should simplify the terminology as though they are talking to someone in the first grade.

Answer: *False*. Technicians should simplify their language so that it is understood by non-technical people, but they should not be condescending and speak as though they are talking to a child.

Customers might not understand the inner workings of a computer, but that doesn't mean they aren't intelligent. They are often very knowledgeable in other areas. Technicians that talk down to customers often find themselves looking for other work.

EXAM TIP You can often get the answer for a user simply by reading the error message on a screen. Users are often inundated with messages that have technical details that they just don't get. Knowledgeable technicians understand these messages and can simplify the error message so that the user understands and can get back to work. Technicians should not attack the users with questions like, "Did you read the message?"

MORE INFO CompTIA lists several communication and professionalism topics that you should focus on for the exam. This is one of the objectives that is worthwhile to read again right before you take the test. If you don't have the objectives printed, you can download and print them from the CompTIA site: *http://certification.comptia.org/ getCertified/certifications/a.aspx*. Highlight the entire 5.3 objective list, and review the highlighted items just prior to taking the exam. Chapter 10 of the CompTIA A+ Training Kit (Exam 220-801 and Exam 220-802), ISBN-10: 0735662681, includes a full section on interacting with customers and covers all of these objectives in more depth.

Maintain a positive attitude

PC technicians should maintain a positive attitude at all times when working with customers. While this might not always be easy, it is a core element of customer service. No one wants to spend time with grumpy people, and this includes grumpy technicians.

True or false? Maintaining a positive attitude is required by a technician except when faced with a challenging situation.

Answer: *False*. Maintaining a positive attitude is always required, especially when faced with a challenging situation. There aren't any acceptable qualifiers when working with customers.

Most people don't have any problem maintaining a positive attitude when things are going well. The challenge is maintaining a positive attitude when things aren't going so well. However, employees that keep their cool in any situation and maintain a positive attitude focused on resolving problems often rise to the most senior positions within an organization.

Listen and do not interrupt the customer

Technicians need to listen to their customers and remain courteous. Interrupting someone else is considered rude by many people and can easily cause the customer to become dissatisfied with you and the service that you're providing.

True or false? If you recognize the problem right away, it's OK to interrupt the customer and tell them you can fix it.

Answer: *False*. It's not acceptable to interrupt the customer.

While you might recognize a problem and think you can fix it without hearing anything else from the customer, you still need to listen. Even if you quickly solve the problem, the customer might only remember that you are rude if you start by interrupting the customer.

EXAM TIP   Basic courtesy is important in all customer interactions. Even if you recognize the problem right away and know how to resolve it, you should take the time to listen to the customer.

Be culturally sensitive

Technicians will often interact with customers from just about anywhere in the world. Different cultures have different norms, and even if they aren't familiar or understood, technicians need to be sensitive to them.

True or false? When talking to a customer from another country, you recognize that he rarely looks directly at you. You should ignore this and continue the conversation.

Answer: *True*. People in some cultures do not make eye contact as a sign of respect. The technician should look beyond the cultural behavior and instead focus on assisting the customer.

Avoid distractions

When PC technicians are assisting a customer, they should avoid all outside distractions. A common guideline used by many professionals is to treat the person in front of you as the most important person in the world.

True or false? When talking to a customer, a PC technician should ignore all phone calls unless they are coming from coworkers.

Answer: *False*. PC technicians should avoid all phone calls when talking to a customer.

After completing a conversation with the customer, the technician can check the phone to determine who it was from. If it is work related, the technician might choose to return the call, but only after completing the conversation with the customer. Personal calls and personal interruptions should be avoided.

EXAM TIP   Technicians should avoid distractions while interacting with customers. This includes personal calls, personal interruptions, and interactions with coworkers.

Dealing with difficult customer or situation

Difficult customers and difficult situations often present the greatest challenges to technicians. It's not uncommon for a customer to be frustrated with a problem, and this frustration can easily be interpreted by the technician as anger.

True or false? Asking open-ended questions followed by restating the issue can defuse difficult situations.

Answer: *True.* Often, customers want only to be understood. When a technician asks open-ended questions and then restates the answer to verify understanding, it can defuse the situation.

An open-ended question is any question that can't be answered with a one-word answer. The customer must describe the issue. This allows the technician to narrow the scope of the problem and focus on the technical issue. An important point to remember is that the customer is rarely angry with the technician—at least at first. A customer might be frustrated with the situation, and if the technician doesn't handle the situation properly, this frustration can be redirected as anger toward the technician.

True or false? If a customer complains about waiting too long for service, empathize with the customer and focus on resolving the problem.

Answer: *True.* Many times customers think they've waited too long for assistance, and in some cases they actually have. The best response is to try to understand the customer and focus on fixing the problem.

> **EXAM TIP** In addition to asking open-ended questions to narrow the scope of the problem, technicians should also avoid arguing with customers and/or being defensive, should not minimize a customer's problems, and should avoid being judgmental. Additionally, you should not attempt to place blame elsewhere. Focus on resolving the problem because that is what the customer really needs.

Be on time / set and meet expectations

Customers expect promptness, and this includes promptness by technicians and technical services. Technicians who experience a delay should let the customer know as soon as possible. When repairs can't be completed immediately, it's also important to set expectations by giving the customer an expected time frame for when the repair can be completed. If this time frame can't be met, it's important to follow up with the customer to explain the situation.

True or false? As a PC technician, you should always communicate to the customer when repair parts are delayed.

Answer: *False.* You should communicate the delay to the customer if this delivery of the part affects the promised delivery date. However, if the delay doesn't change what you told the customer to expect, it isn't necessary to tell the customer.

For example, you might tell a customer that you can repair their computer within seven days. You order a part and expect to receive it in two days, but it takes four days. You can still meet your original promise of seven days to the customer. It is not necessary to bother the customer with the details of part deliveries.

Some other things to consider when working with customers include the following:

- Offer different repair/replacement options if applicable.
- Provide proper documentation on the services provided.
- Follow up with the customer/user at a later date to verify satisfaction.

EXAM TIP Professional PC technicians are on time whenever possible. This includes being on time for service calls and being on time with delivery promises. When an unavoidable delay occurs, they contact the customer to explain the situation and offer alternatives if available. They also follow up with customers to ensure that they are satisfied and that their needs are met.

True or false? If you need to take a server out of service for repair, you should communicate this to customers before you start.

Answer: *True*. This is true of any computers or devices you need to take out of service. Let users know before starting so that they can finish work that is in progress.

Deal appropriately with customer's confidential materials

While troubleshooting systems and assisting computers, it's easy for a PC technician to come across a customer's confidential materials. However, technicians need to respect the customer's privacy.

True or false? If a PC technician is asked to troubleshoot a printer and finds confidential documents in the paper tray, the technician should immediately give them to the customer.

Answer: *True*. If a customer's confidential materials are in the way of a technician, the technician should give the materials to the customer.

If the technician is working on the customer's computer and sees documents in the printer, the technician should leave these documents alone. That is, a technician should not be looking for confidential materials.

True or false? It is acceptable to copy the user's confidential data to create backups.

Answer: *True*. If a customer asks you to make backup copies, it is acceptable to do so. However, these backup copies should be created only with the user's permission and only for the user, not for the technician.

EXAM TIP Technicians should not keep any confidential materials belonging to the customer. If they come upon confidential materials, they should return them. If they use confidential materials for testing, such as printing out files to test a printer, the materials should be shredded or destroyed. It is acceptable to make backup copies of user data with the customer's permission.

Can you answer these questions?

You can find the answers to these questions at the end of this chapter.

1. What is the relationship between how a PC technician wants to be treated as a customer and how a PC technician treats customers?
2. What type of phone calls or interactions should be avoided when providing service to a customer?
3. What type of questions should be used to get information from a customer on a problem?
4. What should a technician do if a situation arises that will result in a delay?

Objective 5.4: Explain the fundamentals of dealing with prohibited content/activity

In the context of information technology, any prohibited content or activity is considered a security incident. While any unlawful activity is considered prohibited, organizations typically have security policies that outline specific content and activity that is prohibited. While the prohibited content and activity might differ slightly between organizations, the response is often the same. Technicians need to understand the concept of first response, the use of documentation, and the need to maintain a chain of custody for evidence.

Exam need to know...

- First response
  For example: Who should a technician notify if prohibited activity is suspected?

- Use of documentation/documentation changes
  For example: What is an acceptable usage policy?

- Chain of custody
  For example: When should a chain of custody be started?

First response

PC technicians are often the first technical person on the scene of a security incident. Depending on the organization and the type of incident, other security professionals might respond later. In the interim, the PC technician has a responsibility to take specific actions as the first responder.

True or false? An unauthorized application installed on a computer is an example of prohibited content or activity.

Answer: *True*. Anything that is not authorized is considered prohibited. This includes unauthorized applications or any type of files or other materials that are prohibited based on an organization's policies.

Other prohibited content or activity includes any type of attacks from outsiders, malicious insiders, or malicious software (malware) such as a virus. PC technicians who are the first to respond have the following responsibilities:

- **Identify** The first step is to verify that the content or activity is prohibited. Technicians might not know for sure if something is prohibited, but if they suspect it might be, their best response is to report it to a manager or supervisor.

- **Report through proper channels** Organizations typically have specific reporting requirements that should be followed. In most cases, the reporting is done within the organization, such as to a manager or supervisor.

- **Data/device preservation** When prohibited content or activity has been identified, all data or devices that might be evidence should be protected. If not protected, data or devices could be modified and they will no longer be acceptable as evidence.

EXAM TIP Key responsibilities of first responders are to identify the incident, report the incident, and preserve any data or devices that might be used as evidence. The importance of reporting incidents to management or a supervisor cannot be overemphasized. Technicians do not have a responsibility to confront anyone involved in an incident. They don't need to be an enforcer or to take any action against anyone involved in an incident. Technicians do have a responsibility to report the incident to comply with company policies.

True or false? A PC technician should turn off a computer immediately upon verifying that it is infected with a virus, to prevent it from spreading.

Answer: *False.* Containment or isolation of a virus is important, but so is the preservation of data. If the computer is turned off, it removes data in memory that might be useful to someone investigating the virus.

Organizations commonly have policies directing technicians to remove the network cable to isolate an infected system. This isolates the system without affecting any potential evidence.

NOTE IT security personnel consider containment or isolation of a security incident as the most important step after identifying an incident. The objectives from CompTIA do not include containment or isolation, but this should still be considered important, both on the job and if you see it on the exam.

Use of documentation/documentation changes

Organizations document their rules in security policies. Users typically read and acknowledge an acceptable usage policy when they are hired and periodically while they are employed. This policy identifies acceptable and authorized usage as well as what is prohibited.

True or false? Employees must be kept informed of any changes in the security policy if they are to be held accountable for violating it.

Answer: *True.* Changes in a security policy should be documented, and employees should be notified of the changes. There aren't any universal rules on how this must be done. However, if employees aren't informed of new rules, they cannot be held accountable to follow them.

Chain of custody

A chain of custody documents the location and control of evidence from the time it is first collected. It identifies who controlled it at any time since it was collected.

True or false? If a USB flash drive is seized from an employee and stored on a supervisor's desk overnight, data on the drive cannot be used as evidence against the original owner.

Answer: *True.* If the USB flash drive is stored on a desk overnight, it is not controlled and cannot be used as evidence in a court of law. Data on the drive could have been added, deleted, or modified.

The same rule applies to any evidence that is collected. For example, if a workstation or laptop computer is seized as evidence, it needs to be controlled after it is seized, and a chain of custody is used to document that it has been controlled. The chain of custody document is updated each time the evidence is transferred to another person or stored in a secure area. Information included in the chain of custody document includes date and time of the transfer and who accepted it.

EXAM TIP A chain of custody tracks the location and control of evidence and is required to maintain the integrity of the evidence. If the chain of custody is not maintained, the evidence can be challenged in a court of law and thrown out as inadmissible.

Can you answer these questions?

You can find the answers to these questions at the end of this chapter.

1. What are common steps a PC technician should take when prohibited activity is suspected?
2. What is a chain of custody?

Answers

This section contains the answers to the "Can you answer these questions?" sections in this chapter.

Objective 5.1: Given a scenario, use appropriate safety procedures

1. Common ESD prevention components are ESD wrist straps and ESD mats. Antistatic bags and humidity control are also important.

2. The three types of grounds are Earth ground, chassis ground, and signal ground.

3. An electrical fire should be extinguished by removing the power source first. If necessary, an approved extinguisher can be used to extinguish the fire, but under no circumstances should water be used to extinguish a fire.

Objective 5.2: Explain environmental impacts and the purpose of environmental controls

1. MSDS documents should be consulted if anyone experiences adverse reactions from a cleaning solvent or chemical.

2. Low humidity increases static and the risks of ESD damage. Humidity should be maintained between 40 and 60 percent.

3. Laser printers should never be plugged into a UPS. The high-voltage power supply of a UPS draws a significant amount of power, and manufacturers recommend against plugging them into a UPS.

4. Antistatic bags should be used to carry any type of electronic components between different locations. This helps prevent ESD damage.

Objective 5.3: Given a scenario, demonstrate proper communication and professionalism

1. PC technicians should treat customers as well as they would like to be treated when they are customers. Most exam questions in this objective can be answered correctly simply by assuming the role of the customer and what you would expect from someone helping you.

2. Personal phone calls and personal interactions should be avoided when working with a customer.

3. Open-ended questions are valuable to get information from a customer. An open-ended question cannot be answered with a simple yes or no. Open-ended questions can also be used when defusing difficult situations.

4. Delays should be communicated to customers as soon as possible.

Objective 5.4: Explain the fundamentals of dealing with prohibited content/activity

1. When prohibited activity is suspected, the first step is to verify that the activity is truly prohibited. The technician should then follow the organization's procedures, which will typically include the following steps: contain or isolate the incident, report the incident, and protect any data or devices involved with the incident.

2. A chain of custody is a document that records the location and control of evidence. It should be created when evidence is collected and maintained until the evidence is no longer needed.

Exam 220-802

CHAPTER 6

Operating systems

The Operating Systems domain covers approximately 33 percent of the A+ 220-802 exam. You are expected to be familiar with Windows XP, Windows Vista, and Windows 7 operating systems, although you'll find that the focus is on Windows XP and Windows 7. Windows 8 is not covered by the CompTIA objectives. You're expected to know the features and requirements of these operating systems and be able to install and configure them. This domain includes the command prompt, and you should be familiar with a wide variety of command-line tools. Beyond the command line, you need to be familiar with many of the tools and utilities used to administer, configure, and maintain Windows-based systems. You are also expected to understand client-side virtualization.

This chapter covers the following objectives:

- Objective 1.1: Compare and contrast the features and requirements of various Microsoft Operating Systems

- Objective 1.2: Given a scenario, install and configure the operating system using the most appropriate method

- Objective 1.3: Given a scenario, use appropriate command line tools

- Objective 1.4: Given a scenario, use appropriate operating system features and tools

- Objective 1.5: Given a scenario, use Control Panel utilities (the items are organized by "classic view/large icons" in Windows)

- Objective 1.6: Set up and configure Windows networking on a client/desktop

- Objective 1.7: Perform preventive maintenance procedures using appropriate tools

- Objective 1.8: Explain the differences among basic OS security settings

- Objective 1.9: Explain the basics of client-side virtualization

Objective 1.1: Compare and contrast the features and requirements of various Microsoft Operating Systems

The first objective in this domain expects you to understand the features and requirements of different editions of Windows XP, Windows Vista, and Windows 7. For example, you should understand the differences between Windows 7 Home Premium and Windows 7 Enterprise. It also expects you to know the features available in different versions of Windows, such as what features are available in Windows 7 that aren't available in Windows XP. Lastly, this objective includes upgrade paths and expects you to be familiar with tools that you can use to determine whether a system can be upgraded from one operating system to another.

Exam need to know...

- Windows XP Home, Windows XP Professional, Windows XP Media Center, Windows XP 64-bit Professional
  For example: What is the minimum amount of RAM needed for Windows XP? What is the maximum amount of RAM supported in Windows XP?

- Windows Vista Home Basic, Windows Vista Home Premium, Windows Vista Business, Windows Vista Ultimate, Windows Vista Enterprise
  For example: What Windows XP edition is similar to Windows Vista Home Premium?

- Windows 7 Starter, Windows 7 Home Premium, Windows 7 Professional, Windows 7 Ultimate, Windows 7 Enterprise
  For example: Which edition of Windows 7 supports Windows XP Mode? Which Windows 7 editions support 8 GB of RAM?

- Features
  For example: Which operating system version and editions include Aero? Which versions include Windows Firewall?

- Upgrade paths—differences between in-place upgrades, compatibility tools, Windows upgrade OS advisor
  For example: Can you upgrade Windows XP directly to Windows 7?

Windows XP Home, Windows XP Professional, Windows XP Media Center, Windows XP 64-bit Professional

Windows XP was introduced in 2001 and has been a popular Windows operating system. Sales of the Windows XP operating system discontinued in 2008, but new computers with Windows XP preinstalled continued to be sold by hardware vendors until October 2010. Microsoft will continue to provide support to Windows XP–based systems until April 2014 and there are still many Windows XP–based systems in use.

The following editions of Windows XP are mentioned in the objectives:

- Windows XP Home is targeted for home users. It provides basic capabilities.
- Windows XP Professional is targeted for business users and includes many more capabilities than the Home edition. For example, users can join a domain, encrypt files, and use remote desktop capabilities.

- Windows XP Media Center is an enhanced edition of Windows XP Home and gives users additional multimedia capabilities. For example, users can watch and record TV shows and listen to music.
- Windows XP 64-bit Professional is for users who want to use more than 4 GB of memory. It is also known as Windows XP Professional x64 Edition. It runs on Advanced Micro Devices (AMD) processors designated with "AMD64" and on Intel processors designated with "Intel 64."

Each edition of Windows XP requires a minimum of 64 MB of RAM to install it. However, it is recommended that Windows XP has at least 128 MB of RAM.

True or false? Windows XP Home supports a maximum of 2 GB of RAM.

Answer: *False*. Windows XP Home supports up to 4 GB of RAM.

Table 6-1 shows the maximum amount of RAM and the maximum number of processors supported in the different Windows XP versions.

TABLE 6-1 Windows XP system limits

	MAX RAM	MAX PROCESSORS
Home	4 GB	1
Professional	4 GB	2
Media Center	4 GB	2
XP 64-bit	128 GB	2
Professional x64	128 GB	2

If you install 4 GB of RAM on Windows XP–based systems, you'll find that the operating system seems to recognize only about 3.2 to 3.5 GB of RAM. A 32-bit system can address a total of 4 GB of address space, and some of this is reserved to address other devices such as graphics cards and other peripherals. The reserved space might be between 500 and 800 MB and isn't available to the user for applications.

EXAM TIP Windows XP 32-bit versions support a maximum of 4 GB of RAM. This is the same with any 32-bit version of Windows, including Windows Vista and Windows 7.

Windows Vista Home Basic, Windows Vista Home Premium, Windows Vista Business, Windows Vista Ultimate, Windows Vista Enterprise

Windows Vista was introduced in 2006 and was intended to replace Windows XP. Sales of the Windows Vista operating system discontinued in 2010, but new computers with Windows Vista preinstalled continued through 2011. Microsoft will continue to provide support to Windows Vista systems until April 2017. The following editions of Windows Vista are mentioned in the objectives:

- Windows Vista Home Basic is a basic edition for home users. It doesn't include Windows Aero or many of the other new features of Windows Vista.
- Windows Vista Home Premium includes more capabilities of Windows Vista and is comparable to the Windows XP Media Center Edition.
- Windows Vista Business is designed for businesses and enterprises and allows computers to join a domain and use encrypted files.
- Windows Vista Enterprise is available to businesses that subscribe to Microsoft's Software Assurance program. It includes BitLocker Drive Encryption.
- Windows Vista Ultimate includes all the features of the Enterprise edition with some extras and can be purchased through retail outlets without a Software Assurance subscription.

NOTE The Microsoft Software Assurance program provides customers with a wide range of services, such as 24/7 phone support, reduced costs for training, and access to additional software. Many medium-to-large organizations participate in this program, and it is also available to small businesses.

True or false? The 64-bit edition of Windows Vista Enterprise supports up to 128 GB of RAM.

Answer: *True.* The 64-bit editions of Windows Vista Enterprise, Business, and Ultimate all support up to 128 GB of RAM.

Windows Vista requires a minimum of 512 MB of RAM, but it is recommended that it not be installed without at least 1 GB of RAM. Table 6-2 shows the maximum amount of RAM and the maximum number of processors supported in the different versions.

TABLE 6-2 Windows Vista system limits

	MAX RAM 32-BIT	MAX RAM 64-BIT	MAX PROCESSORS
Home Basic	4 GB	8 GB	1
Home Premium	4 GB	16 GB	1
Business	4 GB	128 GB	2
Enterprise	4 GB	128 GB	2
Ultimate	4 GB	128 GB	2

EXAM TIP Windows Vista and Windows 7 operating systems are based on the same operating system kernel and have many similarities. You probably won't see many questions directly related to Windows Vista operating systems on the exam. If you do see questions on Windows Vista, you'll find that you can usually answer them if you have a good understanding of Windows 7.

Windows 7 Starter, Windows 7 Home Premium, Windows 7 Professional, Windows 7 Ultimate, Windows 7 Enterprise

Windows 7 was introduced in 2009 and has been a popular Windows operating system. It provided many changes to Windows Vista that customers were requesting and is viewed as an incremental upgrade including many of the popular features of Windows Vista. Windows 7 is still available through many channels at this writing, although Windows 8 has been released as its replacement.

NOTE CompTIA released the objectives to the A+ exams prior to the release of Windows 8, so Windows 8 is not in the objectives that are available as of this writing. Therefore, you will not be tested on Windows 8 in this revision of the A+ exams. It's worth noting that the previous version of the A+ exams (220-701 and 220-702) didn't originally include Windows 7 objectives, but CompTIA later modified the objectives to include Windows 7. It's impossible to know at this writing whether CompTIA will upgrade the objectives in the 800 series of exams to include Windows 8. However, if they do, you can read about the changes here: *http://blogs.getcertifiedgetahead.com/.*

True or false? The 32-bit version of Windows 7 Professional supports 8 GB of RAM.

Answer: *False.* None of the 32-bit editions of Windows 7 support more than 4 GB of RAM.

A 32-bit processor can directly address only 4 GB of RAM, and 32-bit versions of Windows 7 cannot use more than 4 GB of RAM. You'll often see 32-bit versions identified as x86 and 64-bit versions identified as x64.

Table 6-3 shows the minimum RAM required for each edition. It also shows the maximum RAM each edition can address and the maximum number of processors that they can use.

TABLE 6-3 Windows 7 system requirements and limits

	MIN RAM 32-BIT	MIN RAM 64-BIT	MAX RAM 32-BIT	MAX RAM 64-BIT	MAX PROCESSORS
Starter	1 GB	2 GB	2 GB	n/a	1
Home Premium	1 GB	2 GB	4 GB	16 GB	1
Professional	1 GB	2 GB	4 GB	192 GB	2
Enterprise	1 GB	2 GB	4 GB	192 GB	2
Ultimate	1 GB	2 GB	4 GB	192 GB	2

NOTE The maximum number of processors refers only to physical processors. If a single processor has multiple cores, Windows will be able to use all of the cores. For example, if you have a quad core processor in a Windows 7 Home Premium system, Windows will use all four cores. However, if you have two quad core processors in a Windows 7 Home Premium system, Windows will use only one of the processors.

True or false? You can use BitLocker drive encryption on Windows 7 Professional–based systems to encrypt partitions on hard drives.

Answer: *False.* BitLocker drive encryption is available on Windows 7 Ultimate and Enterprise editions but not on Windows 7 Professional.

True or false? Windows XP Mode is available in Windows 7 Home Premium.

Answer: *False.* Windows XP Mode is available in Windows 7 Professional, Ultimate, and Enterprise editions but not in Windows 7 Home Premium.

> **MORE INFO** If you'd like to see how Windows XP Mode works, check out these two videos: *http://windows.microsoft.com/en-US/windows7/products/features/windows-xp-mode* and *http://windows.microsoft.com/en-us/windows7/help/videos/using-windows-xp-mode.*

True or false? Users running Windows 7 Home Premium can join a domain.

Answer: *False.* Domains are used in work environments, and Windows 7 Home Premium cannot join a domain. Windows 7 Professional, Ultimate, and Enterprise editions can join a domain.

You should be aware of the different features available in different editions. Table 6-4 shows some of these differences for Windows 7–based systems.

TABLE 6-4 Windows 7 features

FEATURE	STARTER	HOME PREMIUM	PROFESSIONAL	ULTIMATE ENTERPRISE
Backup and Restore	Yes	Yes	Yes	Yes
Join homegroup	Yes	Yes	Yes	Yes
64-bit support	--	Yes	Yes	Yes
Aero	--	Yes	Yes	Yes
Join a domain	--	--	Yes	Yes
Back up to network	--	--	Yes	Yes
Offline Files	--	--	Yes	Yes
Encrypting File System (EFS)	--	--	Yes	Yes
Windows XP Mode	--	--	Yes	Yes
BitLocker Drive Encryption	--	--	--	Yes

> **EXAM TIP** Technicians are expected to help users pick an appropriate operating system, so they need to know what features are available in different editions. Table 6-4 includes important features that you should know.

Features

There are many different features in each Windows operating system. Some of these features are shared between versions and some features are available only in specific versions.

True or false? Aero is available in Windows Vista and Windows 7.

Answer: *True*. Aero is available in both Windows Vista–based and Windows 7–based systems. It is not available in Windows XP. Also, it is not available in the Windows 7 Starter edition.

Aero provides additional usability features, such as Aero peek, shake, and snap. It also includes additional graphics features, such as translucent effects and animations.

True or false? You can use the Program Compatibility tool in Windows 7 to run some older programs that aren't compatible with Windows 7.

Answer: *True*. The Program Compatibility tool allows you to configure legacy applications to run with different settings.

You can access this wizard by selecting Run Programs Made for Previous Versions of Windows in the Programs and Features category of the Control Panel on Windows 7–based systems. You can also right-click any executable program in Windows Explorer, select Properties, and select the Compatibility tab to manually configure the compatibility mode.

True or false? Homegroups are available on Windows Vista and Windows 7.

Answer: *False*. Homegroups are available only on Windows 7–based systems.

You can create homegroups on Windows 7–based systems, but Windows XP and Windows Vista systems cannot join a homegroup. Windows 7 Starter and Windows 7 Home Basic editions cannot create a homegroup, but they can join one if it is created by another edition of Windows 7.

Table 6-5 compares the different features available in Windows XP, Windows Vista, and Windows 7 editions.

TABLE 6-5 Comparison of Windows features in different editions

FEATURE	WINDOWS XP	WINDOWS VISTA	WINDOWS 7
Administrative Tools	Yes	Yes	Yes
Compatibility Mode	Yes	Yes	Yes
Event Viewer	Yes	Yes	Yes
System Restore	Yes	Yes	Yes
Windows Defender	Available as download	Yes	Yes
Windows Firewall	Yes	Yes	Yes

FEATURE	WINDOWS XP	WINDOWS VISTA	WINDOWS 7
Aero	--	Yes	Yes
BitLocker	--	Yes	Yes
Easy Transfer	--	Yes	Yes
Gadgets	--	Yes	Yes
ReadyBoost	--	Yes	Yes
Shadow Copy	--	Yes	Yes
User Account Control	--	Yes	Yes
HomeGroups	--	--	Yes
Windows Libraries	--	--	Yes
Windows XP Mode	--	--	Yes

Sidebar is a feature that was introduced in Windows Vista. It hosts gadgets such as the calendar, clock, and weather gadgets. These gadgets are mini-programs and are organized within the sidebar. The Sidebar is not available in Windows 7, but gadgets are available. Instead of using a Sidebar in Windows 7, gadgets are simply placed on the desktop.

Windows XP and Windows Vista include an applet called the Security Center. It monitors key security settings on a computer and notifies users if a security setting is not set to the recommended secure setting. This includes checks to ensure that the Windows Firewall is enabled, Automatic Updates are set to Automatic, and antivirus software is installed and running. The Security Center has been replaced with the Action Center in Windows 7.

The file structure between different Windows operating systems is largely the same but there are some paths that are different. The primary difference is related to where the user profiles are stored. On Windows XP systems, the user profiles are stored in C:\Documents and Settings. On Windows Vista and Windows 7, user profiles are stored in C:\Users.

Another difference is related to 32-bit and 64-bit operating systems. On 32-bit systems, the application or program files are located in the following path: C:\ Program Files. However, on 64-bit systems, the application or program files are organized differently and two separate directories are used:

- C:\Program Files (x86) is used for 32-bit applications. Most 32-bit applications can run on a 64-bit operating system.
- C:\Program Files is used for 64-bit applications.

EXAM TIP You should be aware of the features that are available in different versions of Windows, as shown in Table 6-5. It's also important to remember that some features are not available in each edition of any version of Windows. For example, BitLocker is available in Windows 7, but it's not available in the Windows Starter, Home Premium, or Professional editions. It is available only in the Ultimate and Enterprise editions, as shown in Table 6-4.

MORE INFO Wikipedia includes individual articles about most of these features. You can usually find them by searching from Bing.com, using the feature name followed by "wiki." For example, searching with "homegroups wiki" will show you the link to the Wikipedia article on homegroups. Chapters 11 through 17 of the CompTIA A+ Training Kit (Exam 220-801 and Exam 220-802), ISBN-10: 0735662681, explore features available in different operating systems in more depth.

Upgrade paths—differences between in-place upgrades, compatibility tools, Windows upgrade OS advisor

When installing a new operating system, you can either do an upgrade or a clean installation, and it's important to know the difference.

- An upgrade converts a system from one operating system to another one. It keeps all the supported programs and settings from the previous operating system so that users won't need to reinstall them. Depending on the existing and desired operating systems, not all programs and settings will be supported.

- A clean install does not include any applications or settings from previous installations. As long as the hardware supports a clean installation, you can perform a clean install on any system.

MORE INFO When you do a clean installation, you can still migrate data and settings from one operating system to another. Later in this chapter, Objective 1.4, "Given a scenario, use appropriate operating system features and tools," includes some of the tools that you can use to migrate data and settings. This includes the File And Settings Transfer Wizard, the Windows Easy Transfer tool, and the User State Migration tool (USMT).

The upgrade paths of many operating systems are limited. When users want to install a new operating system, they often want to upgrade their current system, but unfortunately, this isn't always possible. For example, a user might be running a 32-bit version of Windows XP and want to upgrade it to a 64-bit version of Windows 7, but this upgrade path isn't supported. It's important for technicians to know what upgrade paths are possible and what paths are not possible.

True or false? You can upgrade Windows XP directly to Windows 7.

Answer: *False.* You can upgrade Windows XP to Windows Vista and then to Windows 7, but you cannot upgrade Windows XP directly to Windows 7.

Table 6-6 shows the upgrade paths from various operating systems to Windows 7.

TABLE 6-6 Windows 7 upgrade paths

	UPGRADE TO HOME PREMIUM	UPGRADE TO PROFESSIONAL	UPGRADE TO ULTIMATE
From Windows XP	No	No	No
From Windows Vista Home Premium	Yes	Yes	Yes
From Windows Vista Business	No	Yes	Yes
From Windows Vista Ultimate	No	No	Yes
From 32-bit to 64-bit	No	No	No
From 64-bit to 32-bit	No	No	No

True or false? The Windows 7 Upgrade Advisor is a free tool that will identify hardware and software compatibility issues.

Answer: *True.* This tool can identify issues before an upgrade.

EXAM TIP You can upgrade Windows XP to Windows Vista and Windows Vista to Windows 7, but you cannot upgrade Windows XP to Windows 7 directly. You cannot upgrade any 32-bit operating system to a 64-bit operating system.

MORE INFO The upgrade advisor is available as part of the Windows 7 installation program and as a free download available by searching on "Windows Upgrade Advisor" on Microsoft's download site: *http://www.microsoft.com/download*. Microsoft also maintains the Windows Compatibility Center and the Windows Logo'd Product List (previously known as the hardware compatibility list) at *http://www.microsoft.com/windows/compatibility* and at *https://winqual.microsoft.com/HCL*, respectively.

Can you answer these questions?

You can find the answers to these questions at the end of this chapter.

1. What editions of Windows 7 support BitLocker Drive Encryption?
2. Will Windows 7 Home Premium support 8 GB of RAM?
3. A network has Windows XP–based, Windows Vista–based, and Windows 7–based computers. Which systems can join a homegroup?

Objective 1.2: Given a scenario, install and configure the operating system using the most appropriate method

This objective covers the various methods used to install Windows on systems, including some of the common issues related to installations. In addition to installing Windows, this objective also expects you to know about some of the basic steps that you should take immediately after the installation.

Exam need to know...

- Boot methods
  For example: What is the most common method of booting a system without an operating system during an installation?
- Type of installations
  For example: What is a PXE client? What is an image? How are different drivers loaded during an installation?
- Partitioning
  For example: How many partitions can you create on a FAT32 drive?
- File system types/formatting
  For example: What is the preferred file system for Windows-based systems?
- Load alternate third-party drivers when necessary
  For example: What is the most common reason you need to load alternate third-party drivers during an installation?
- Workgroup vs. domain setup
  For example: What additional hardware is required for a domain?
- Time/date/region/language settings
  For example: What changes when you modify the time, date, region and/or language settings?
- Driver installation, software and Windows updates
  For example: What is included with important Windows updates?
- Factory recovery partition
  For example: Is it possible to delete a factory recovery partition?

Boot methods

If you are doing an upgrade to a computer, it will already have an operating system. You can boot into the operating system, start the installation program, and complete the installation. However, if the computer doesn't have an existing operating system, you need to look for an alternative method of booting the computer.

The most common boot method for computers without an operating system is with a CD or DVD optical disc. When using this method, it's important to ensure that the BIOS is configured to boot to the optical disc.

True or false? While it is possible to boot to a USB drive on many computers, it is not possible to install Windows from a USB drive.

Answer: *False*. It is possible to configure a system to boot to a USB drive. If the USB drive is large enough, it can include all of the files necessary to install Windows.

A USB drive is an effective method of installing Windows on systems that do not have a DVD drive. The contents of the installation disc can be copied from the DVD to the USB and used to install Windows.

True or false? A PXE-enabled system can boot without an operating system installed on the computer.

Answer: *True*. A preboot execution environment (PXE, pronounced as *pixie*)-enabled computer can boot using the network interface card (NIC).

A PXE-enabled system includes a Basic Input/Output System (BIOS) and NIC that can be configured to boot using the NIC. The system will look for a compatible server on the network and download an operating system from this server. PXE-enabled computers do not need operating systems on their hard drives.

EXAM TIP A USB drive is an effective alternate for installing an operating system onto computers that do not have an optical drive. It is also possible to deploy an operating system over the network to PXE-enabled computers.

MORE INFO When doing a PXE boot, you might need to modify the boot order of the computer. Chapter 1, "PC hardware," of this book includes a topic and a screen shot of a BIOS used to modify the boot order. The BIOS can also be used to enable or disable different boot devices.

Type of installations

One way of installing an operating system is to insert a CD or DVD installation disc into the system, start the setup.exe program, and follow the installation wizard. However, there are several other methods used to install Windows onto a system.

Large enterprises often use images to automate installations. An image is pre-configured with specific settings and often includes additional applications needed by users in the organization. Figure 6-1 shows the overall process of using images for installations, and the following steps outline the process:

1. An operating system is installed and configured on a reference computer. Configuration includes installing desired applications and configuring security and other settings to match the needs of the organization.

2. The reference computer is tested to ensure that it works as expected. After testing, the computer is prepared to capture the image. This includes running the sysprep program on Windows-based systems.

3. The image is captured and stored on an imaging server. It's also possible to store the image on any portable media of sufficient size, such as a DVD or portable USB hard drive.

4. The image is deployed to target computers. The same image can be deployed to one computer or to multiple computers at the same time.

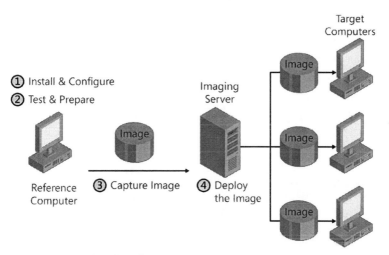

Target
Computers

① Install & Configure

② Test & Prepare

Imaging
Server

Reference
Computer

③ Capture Image

④ Deploy
the Image

Image

Image

Image

Image

Image

FIGURE 6-1 Image-based installations.

True or false? PXE clients simplify the process of performing remote network installations to multiple computers.

Answer: *True*. The remote installation process can be simplified with PXE-enabled computers.

A PXE client has the ability to boot through its NIC and connect to a server on the network. Administrators can set up servers to send images of full operating systems to clients after the PXE clients connect, requiring very little user interaction. If the computer isn't PXE-enabled, another method is required to boot the computer and connect it to a remote computer.

> **EXAM TIP** The primary reason for using a PXE-enabled client is so that you can install an operating system over the network. PXE clients are commonly used with image deployments.

True or false? Sysprep is used to prepare a Windows operating system image.

Answer: *True*. Sysprep removes unique information from a computer and is run on a reference computer before capturing an image.

Windows-based systems use a security identifier (SID) to uniquely identify the computer. Sysprep removes the SID (and other unique information) from the image before it is captured. A new SID is created after the image is deployed to target computers.

> **EXAM TIP** Images are commonly used to deploy Windows to multiple systems. To remove unique information, Sysprep is used prior to capturing the image.

True or false? An unattended installation can be used to reduce the total amount of time needed to install multiple computers.

Answer: *True.* Unattended installations use answer files and reduce the amount of hands-on time required by technicians when installing Windows.

Answer files can be used with an installation of individual computers from the installation media. Instead of a user or technician needing to answer all of the questions during the installation, the setup program reads the answer file to get these answers. Answer files can also be used with images to decrease the setup time after an image is deployed.

> **EXAM TIP** Unattended installations use answer files to automate the installation. An answer file is a text file that provides the answers, instead of requiring the user to answer the questions manually.

A repair installation is also known as a repair-in-place upgrade and it can be used to repair a corrupt Windows installation. A benefit of a repair installation is that it keeps existing user data files and only replaces system files. You can start a repair installation by booting from the installation CD or DVD and then selecting Repair.

Partitioning

Hard disk drives can be divided into separate sections called partitions. Most partitions are identified with a drive letter such as C, D, and so on, but some partitions can hold multiple logical drives identified with separate drive letters.

True or false? You can create up to four primary partitions on a disk drive.

Answer: *True.* Both File Allocation Table (FAT) and New Technology File System (NTFS) drives support up to four primary partitions.

It is also possible to create up to three primary partitions and one extended partition on these drives, but you are still limited to a total of four partitions. When working with partitions, you should be familiar with the following differences between primary and extended partitions:

- A primary partition is used for a single drive letter such as C, D, and so on.
- An extended partition can hold multiple drive letters. For example, if you wanted to have six drive letters on a basic disk, you could create three primary partitions (as C, D, and E) and one extended partition divided into three additional drives. Extended partitions aren't commonly used today.
- Logical drives are used on extended partitions. For example, an extended partition might be divided into three logical drives labeled as F, G, and H.

An important point to remember is that you should never install more than one operating system on any single partition. A dual boot (or multiboot) system includes more than one operating system. For example, you can have Windows XP installed on C and then install a clean installation of Windows 7 on D. However, if you install both operating systems on C, the later will corrupt the earlier of the installed operating systems. When you boot a dual-boot system, a menu appears giving you the choice of booting into Windows XP or Windows 7.

Microsoft systems support both basic disks and dynamic disks. Basic disks are used most often and give you the greatest flexibility. Dynamic disks provide some additional capabilities, such as the ability to have more than four partitions on a single disk. However, you cannot use a dynamic disk in a multiboot system.

NOTE The terms *partitions* and *volumes* are used interchangeably and typically mean the same thing when referring to disks on Windows-based systems. Partitions on a dynamic disk are always called volumes. However, partitions in a basic disk might be referred to as either partitions or volumes.

EXAM TIP Partitions divide a hard drive into separate sections, and you can have up to four primary partitions on a basic disk. After a drive is partitioned, each partition must be formatted before it can be used.

File system types/formatting

Before a hard disk can be used, it must be formatted with a specific file system. The file system creates a table used by the operating system to locate the files. This table is similar to an index in the back of a book and tells the operating system the exact location on the disk where the beginning of the file is located.

True or false? The FAT32 file system is compatible with more operating systems than NTFS.

Answer: *True*. NTFS provides the most benefits and capabilities and is the recommended file system with Windows-based systems, but it is not compatible with some non-Microsoft operating systems. FAT32 is compatible with both Microsoft and non-Microsoft operating systems.

True or false? NTFS is the primary file system used on optical media.

Answer: *False*. The Compact Disc File System (CDFS) is the primary file system used for optical media.

FAT disks include both FAT (also known as FAT16) and FAT32. FAT16 uses 16 bits to address locations on the drive, and FAT32 uses 32 bits to address locations. Table 6-7 shows the limitations for FAT16 and FAT32 on Windows-based systems.

TABLE 6-7 FAT versions

	FAT16	FAT32
Max partition size you can create	4 GB	32 GB
Maximum file size	2 GB	4 GB

Windows can recognize FAT32 partitions larger than 32 GB. However, Windows limits the size of new partitions to 32 GB.

If you try to copy a file larger than 4 GB to a FAT32 disk, you'll get an error indicating that you don't have enough space, even if the drive is empty. This is because

FAT32 can't handle these files. However, if you convert the drive to NTFS, you'll be able to copy files larger than 4 GB.

EXAM TIP FAT32 is a common file system supported by many different operating systems. Due to the extra capabilities, NTFS is recommended for all drives used by Windows XP, Windows Vista, and Windows 7. One of the biggest advantages of NTFS over FAT-based file systems is the ability to assign permissions to files and folders.

True or false? A quick format will overwrite data on a hard drive.

Answer: *False*. A quick format doesn't overwrite the data but instead overwrites only the table used to locate the files.

A quick format is similar to overwriting the index in the back of a book. It doesn't affect the data at all, but it does prevent an operating system from finding any of the data. Additionally, it doesn't perform any checks on the disk.

In contrast, a full format scans the disk for bad sectors. Sectors that fail the test are marked as bad, and the operating system will not write data to these bad sectors. Scanning the entire disk for bad sectors in a full format takes much longer than the time it takes to complete a quick format but is recommended for new disks.

If you did a quick format but later suspect the disk has faulty sectors, you can run the **chkdsk /r** command against the formatted partition or use the Check Disk tool. Both perform the same checks completed by a full format.

EXAM TIP The file system types supported by Windows-based systems for hard disk drives are FAT, FAT32, and NTFS. NTFS provides more capabilities, including better security. Partitions are formatted using one of the file systems, and a full format will check a disk for errors and mark faulty sectors as bad. CDFS is used on optical discs.

Load alternate third-party drivers when necessary

Hardware drivers are used by an operating system to communicate with hardware within the computer. The Windows installation program ships with a wide variety of different drivers, but there might be times when you need to load an alternate driver so that you can complete an installation.

True or false? If a RAID is not recognized by the Windows installation program, you should load the driver during the installation.

Answer: *True*. During the installation, you can select Load Driver if a disk drive or a redundant array of inexpensive disks (RAID) is not recognized.

It isn't common to need to load an extra driver during an installation for a desktop system, but it is sometimes required if the system is using a nonstandard disk or circuit card. This is sometimes required for RAID types or for disk drives using a Small Computer System Interface (SCSI) circuit card.

If the computer cannot recognize any hard drives, the installation program displays an error and directs the user to insert the media holding the driver. This is normally available with new hardware on a CD drive. If you download a driver, you can copy it to a CD or USB and browse to the location after selecting Load Driver.

Workgroup vs. domain setup

Computers used in an organization are commonly connected in a network, and networks can be configured as a workgroup or a domain. Both configurations allow users to share and access network resources after they log on to the network.

True or false? Domains are used in SOHOs when the owner wants to eliminate the cost of a central server.

Answer: *False.* Small office home offices (SOHOs) commonly use a workgroup to avoid the cost of a central server. A domain requires a server configured as a domain controller.

In a workgroup, users must have a user account on every computer that they use. These user accounts are stored in a local database known as a security accounts manager (SAM). If a user needs to log on to two computers, the user needs an account on each computer. This requires users to memorize multiple user names and passwords.

In a domain, most users have a single user account stored in a central database called Active Directory, or Active Directory Domain Services. This database is hosted on one or more central servers called domain controllers. One of the benefits is that users can access multiple resources in the domain with the single account. Domains also provide administrators with central administrative control over all resources in the domain.

Time/date/region/language settings

When installing Windows, you are given the option of selecting options used for displaying items such as time, date, region, and languages. These are primarily used by Windows to identify how data is displayed based on the selected custom. For example, in the United States, a number is separated by commas and periods like this: 1,234.56. In some other regions, the same number is displayed like this: 1.234,56.

True or false? You can modify how data is displayed by modifying settings in the Region and Language applet in the Windows 7 Control Panel.

Answer: *True.* The Region and Language applet is available when you set the Windows 7 Control Panel to the Large Icons or Small Icons views.

This applet is also available from the Clock, Language, and Region section in the Control Panel when using the Category view.

EXAM TIP **Windows-based systems support multiple languages, and they can be added and modified after Windows is installed. You can also modify the keyboard type to support different keyboard layouts.**

Driver installation, software and windows updates

After installing Windows, you should ensure that your system has the most up-to-date drivers and that all of the software is up to date. The easiest way to do so is with Windows Update.

True or false? The Windows Update Express setting should be selected if a user wants to install security updates as soon as possible.

Answer: *True*. The Express setting for Windows Update ensures that the computer periodically checks for updates and will automatically download and install security updates. This setting can be selected towards the end of a Windows installation and configures Windows with the default recommended settings for Windows Update.

Microsoft periodically releases updates to operating systems and applications. The three categories of updates are as follows:

- Important updates (or high-priority updates on Windows XP) improve security, privacy, and reliability of the system. They should be installed as soon as possible.
- Recommended updates target noncritical problems.
- Optional updates provide updates to drivers or new software. This is useful after installing the operating system. The installation media includes many drivers, but these drivers might have been updated after the media was released. Checking for optional updates after Windows was installed will help ensure that a system has the most up-to-date drivers.

Microsoft uses Windows Update to help users keep their systems up to date. You can configure Windows Update to automatically check Microsoft websites for updates, or you can do so manually. Microsoft recommends configuring updates to automatically install so that users do not miss important updates. The following settings are available for updates:

- **Install Updates Automatically (Recommended)** When this setting is selected, the system periodically checks for updates and automatically downloads them. It also includes a setting of when the updates should be installed, and the default is 3 AM daily.
- **Download Updates But Let Me Choose Whether To Install Them** This setting prevents the computer from installing an update without user interaction.
- **Check for Updates But Let Me Choose Whether to Install Them** This option is useful when systems have slow Internet connections.

- **Never Check for Updates (Not Recommended)** This might be used in a completely isolated system that doesn't have Internet access.

EXAM TIP Windows Update is used to download updates; selecting the Windows Update Express setting during the installation ensures that the recommended settings are used. Important updates will automatically be downloaded and installed on the system.

Factory recovery partition

Many computer resellers include a factory recovery partition on the disc drive. If the operating system becomes corrupt, users can use this to return the system to its original state. These partitions are often hidden and aren't assigned drive letters. That is, they aren't accessible during normal operation, but they can be used for recovery.

True or false? You can delete the factory recovery partition to gain hard disk space without losing any capabilities.

Answer: *False.* Deleting this partition will cause you to lose the ability to return the system to the state it was in when first received.

Many people see this partition and consider deleting it to gain disk space. If they delete it, they can use tools such as disk management to configure it as a usable partition. However, this option should be seriously considered only when the user has the ability to restore the computer through other means.

EXAM TIP The factory recovery partition is often hidden but is available to recover a system. It restores the system to the original state it was in when it was shipped from the factory. It does not recover user data.

Can you answer these questions?

You can find the answers to these questions at the end of this chapter.

1. How many primary partitions can be created on a basic NTFS disk?
2. What program is used to prepare a computer immediately before capturing the image?
3. What is the benefit of PXE?
4. What is the difference between a quick format and a full format?

Objective 1.3: Given a scenario, use appropriate command line tools

Windows-based systems include the command prompt, which is also called the command line. Instead of using the mouse, all commands are typed, and there are several tools available from the command line. Typical users often don't need to use these tools, but they can be very useful for PC technicians. Some of these commands are used specifically for networking, some are used for the operating system, and some are available only within the Windows recovery console.

Exam need to know...

- Networking
  For example: What is the command used to request a new DHCP lease?
- OS
  For example: What command is used to create a new directory? What command is used to change directories?
- Recovery console
  For example: What is the command to repair the MBR on Windows XP?

Networking

Networking commands are often used to check and troubleshoot connectivity issues for a computer on a network. Some of these commands give you information on the computer only, while others give you information about the network.

NOTE Mastering these commands will help you pass the A+ exam and be more effective on the job. If you plan to pursue the Network+ certification after the A+ certification, you'll find that many of these same commands are on that exam, too.

True or false? You can determine the MAC address of a computer with the **ipconfig /all** command.

Answer: *True.* The **ipconfig /all** command provides a wealth of information, including the media access control (MAC) address of the NIC.

You can enter the **ipconfig** command by itself to obtain basic information. It will show the system's IP address, subnet mask, and default gateway. When combined with the **/all** switch, it shows additional information, such as the server IP addresses used by the system for Domain Name System (DNS) and Dynamic Host Configuration Protocol (DHCP), when these services are being used.

Some other useful **ipconfig** commands with their switches include the following:

- **ipconfig /release**   Release a DHCP lease
- **ipconfig /renew**   Renew a DHCP lease, and get a new IP address
- **ipconfig /displaydns**   Show all host name to IP address mappings that are in the DNS cache
- **ipconfig /flushdns**   Remove host name to IP address mappings provided from DNS from cache

NOTE Most command prompt commands are not case sensitive. You can enter them as all uppercase, all lowercase, or any combination of uppercase and lowercase.

EXAM TIP The **ipconfig** command is useful to view the TCP/IP configuration information assigned to a computer. It can also be used to request a new IP address from a DHCP server, which is useful if there is an IP address conflict in the network.

True or false? You can get help for most commands with the **/?** switch.

Answer: *True.* The **/?** switch can be appended to most commands to get help with the command.

The help switch (**/?**) is an important tool to remember on the job for any command prompt commands. For example, you might remember that you can get the MAC address for a computer with the **ipconfig** command, but you might not remember what switch to use. After entering **ipconfig /?**, you'll see that you can use the **ipconfig /all** command.

> **NOTE** If you view the help for different commands, you'll see that some help files describe switches with the forward slash (/) and other help files describe the switches with a dash (-). Most commands support both characters. For example, **ipconfig /all** and **ipconfig -all** both give the same results.

True or false? You can use the **ping** command to test whether a computer is operational on a network.

Answer: *True.* The primary purpose of the **ping** command is to check connectivity with another system.

You can **ping** the host name or the IP address of a computer. For example, if server1 has an IP address of 192.168.1.10, you can use either **ping server1** or **ping 192.168.1.10**. If you **ping** the host name, **ping** will first try to resolve the host name to an IP address, typically by querying DNS. Some useful **ping** switches are:

- **-t (ping -t server1)** On Windows-based systems, **ping** sends out only four **ping** requests by default, but the -t switch causes **ping** to continue until you stop it by pressing CTRL+C. You can see how this works on your system by using **ping -t localhost**.

- **-a (ping -a 192.168.1.10)** This attempts to resolve the IP address to a host name before it sends out **ping** requests. This requires an available method to perform reverse lookups. DNS servers can do this, but they aren't always configured to do so. You can see how this works on your system by using **ping -a 127.0.0.1**.

- **-4 (ping server1 -4)** This forces **ping** to use IPv4. You can see how this works on your system by using **ping localhost -4**.

- **-6 (ping server1 -6)** This forces **ping** to use IPv6. You can see how this works on your system by using **ping localhost -6**.

> **EXAM TIP** The **ping** command is used to test connectivity with other systems. Technicians often use both the **ping** and **ipconfig** commands when troubleshooting network problems, and many of the switches are very familiar to them. Test takers should also be very familiar with these switches.

> **MORE INFO** Ping is an important tool that is used when troubleshooting connectivity problems and is mentioned in Chapter 9, "Troubleshooting," in the context of Objective 4.5 "Given a scenario, troubleshoot wired and wireless networks with appropriate tools." However, a firewall can block ping requests, so when you don't receive a ping reply, it doesn't necessarily mean that the other system isn't operational.

True or false? The **netstat** command can be used to view open ports on a computer.

Answer: *True*. The **netstat** command (short for network statistics) can show inbound and outbound TCP/IP connections.

Netstat can be useful for identifying a computer infection. For example, some malicious software (malware) directs the computer to connect to public IP addresses even without having a web browser open. The **netstat** command will show these connections and help verify the infection.

Some other useful networking commands include the following:

- **tracert**   Commonly pronounced as "trace route," this command will show all the routers between two systems. If you can't connect to another networked system, **tracert** can help you identify where the connection stops.

- **nslookup**   This command is used to look for specific records in a DNS server. For example, it can query DNS to determine whether DNS can accurately resolve a host name to an IP address.

- **nbtstat**   The NetBIOS over TCP/IP statistics (**nbtstat**) command is used to troubleshoot NetBIOS name resolution issues. The use of NetBIOS in networks is dwindling, and the need for the **nbtstat** command is significantly less than for other commands, such as the **nslookup** command.

> **MORE INFO**   If you want to dig into more commands, check out the A-Z list of commands used on Windows-based systems here: *http://technet.microsoft.com/library/cc772390.aspx*. Chapter 14 of the CompTIA A+ Training Kit (Exam 220-801 and Exam 220-802), ISBN-10: 0735662681, covers the basics about the command prompt, and Chapter 24 of that book covers the networking commands needed for the A+ exam.

OS

Many commands are used to manipulate files, folders, disks, and the operating system. You should have a good understanding of each of these commands and their purpose.

True or false? You can use the **chkdsk** command to resolve read/write errors on a disk drive.

Answer: *True*. The **chkdsk** command can be executed from the command prompt to locate bad sectors that cause read/write errors.

If you use the **chkdsk /r** command, it will locate faulty sectors on the disk, mark them as bad, and recover readable information. **Chkdsk** won't check a partition that is currently in use. For example, if you're booted into the C drive and try to run **chkdsk** on the C drive, it won't run. However, it will prompt you to schedule this to run the next time the system boots. If you select yes, you can reboot the system and **chkdsk** will run before Windows starts. You can also schedule **chkdsk** to run with the **chkntfs** command.

The system file checker (**sfc**) tool can be used to check the integrity of individual system files. Many viruses attempt to modify system files, and the **sfc** tool can repair them.

Some other commands that can be used with disks include the following:

- **format**   The **format** command prepares the disk with a file system such as FAT32 or NTFS.

- **fdisk**   The **fdisk** command is much older, and it was used to partition a disk before installing an operating system. Most operating system installation programs include disk partitioning tools, so **fdisk** is rarely needed anymore.

- **diskpart**   This is a much more advanced command that can be used to manipulate disks. It can do many of the same tasks that the Disk Managment graphical user interface (GUI) tool does.

True or false? The **md** command allows you to modify the command prompt context from one directory to another.

Answer: *False.* The make directory (**md**) command is used to create directories.

The change directory (**cd**) command is used to modify or change the context of the command prompt. For example, if the current prompt is C:\Windows, you can change directories to the C:\Data with the **cd \data** command. Another directory command is the remove directory (**rd**) command. This command is used to remove or delete a directory.

True or false? You can terminate a process on Linux-based systems with the **kill** command.

Answer: *True.* **Kill** is a command in Linux-based systems used to terminate processes.

The **kill** command isn't in Windows XP, Windows Vista, or Windows 7. However, a similar command is the **taskkill** command, which can be used to terminate processes. You can view a list of running processes on older Windows systems with the **tlist** command. This command was renamed to **tasklist** in Windows XP, Windows Vista, and Windows 7.

True or false? You can use the **copy** command to copy directories and subdirectories at the same time.

Answer: *False.* You can use the **copy** command to copy directories and files within a directory, but it cannot copy subdirectories.

The three primary commands used to copy files and directories are as follows:

- **copy**   The **copy** command is used to copy files, including all the files within a directory, but it cannot copy subdirectories.

- **xcopy**   This command does everything **copy** can do, but it can also copy subdirectories.

- **robocopy**   Short for robust copy, **robocopy** can do everything **copy** and **xcopy** can do. It can also copy many of the attributes of files and directories, such as their permissions or when they were first created.

The **del** command is used to delete files. Windows-based systems accept either **del** or **erase** as the command to delete files.

True or false? The **shutdown** command can be used to log off a computer.

Answer: *True.* The **shutdown** command can be used to turn off a computer (**shutdown /s**), restart the computer (**shutdown /r**), or log off the current user (**shutdown /l**).

Recovery console

The recovery console is a special tool used to troubleshoot Windows XP–based systems. It is not available in Windows Vista and Windows 7, but you can access similar commands from the Windows Recovery Environment (Windows RE). These tools are often used after a malware infection to restore a system to full functionality.

You can access the Recovery Console from the Windows XP installation CD by pressing R (for Repair) when the Welcome screen appears. You can also install it from the installation CD with the **winnt32.exe /cmdcons** command. If it is installed, it appears as another operating system choice when Windows XP is booted. The Windows RE is available from the Windows Vista or Windows 7 installation DVD and from a bootable system repair disc. You can also access it by pressing F8, as the system is booting, to access the Advanced Boot Options page, selecting Repair Your Computer, and then selecting Command Prompt from the System Recovery Options menu.

True or false? You can repair the master boot record by using the **fixboot** command from the Windows XP recovery console.

Answer: *False.* The **fixmbr** command is used to repair the master boot record. The **fixboot** command is used to repair the boot sector.

In Windows Vista and Windows 7, you can use the following commands from the Windows RE to repair similar problems:

- **bootrec /fixboot**   This will repair the boot sector.
- **bootrec /fixmbr**   This will repair the MBR.

EXAM TIP Malware often infects the boot sector, and after removing the virus from the boot sector, the computer might no longer boot. The **fixboot** command repairs the boot sector, and the **fixmbr** command repairs the MBR. Both are available in the Windows XP recovery console. Windows Vista and Windows 7 have similar commands: **bootrec /fixboot** and **bootrec /fixmbr**.

MORE INFO The following support article on Microsoft's website shows how to install the recovery console on a Windows XP system: *http://support.microsoft.com/kb/307654*. You can see a side-by-side comparison of some recovery console commands and the Windows RE equivalent here: *http://blogs.msdn.com/b/winre/archive/2006/10/20/where-are-recovery-console-commands.aspx*.

Can you answer these questions?

You can find the answers to these questions at the end of this chapter.

1. What ping switch is used to resolve an IP address to a host name?
2. What command can you use to identify open ports on a computer?
3. What command would you use to check the integrity of a disk that is experiencing read/write errors?
4. What command would you use to repair a faulty boot sector in Windows XP?
5. What command would you use to repair a faulty boot sector in Windows 7?

Objective 1.4: Given a scenario, use appropriate operating system features and tools

This objective covers a wide variety of operating system features and tools and expects you to know which tool to use for different situations. CompTIA calls out some of these tools, such as **msconfig**, Task Manager, and Disk Management, with their own headings in this objective. Others are simply mentioned in a list of other tools, but you can expect to be tested on any of them. PC technicians who know what tools are available and how to use them can quickly identify and resolve many common problems.

Exam need to know...

- Administrative
  For example: What tool is used to configure a password policy?
- MSCONFIG
  For example: What tab is used to manipulate which applications start when a user logs on?
- Task Manager
  For example: What tab is used to identify the PID of a process?
- Disk Management
  For example: What must be done in Disk Management before creating a RAID-1 within Disk Management on Windows 7?

- Other
  For example: What tools are available to migrate user settings?
- Run line utilities
  For example: What command is used to start the System Configuration tool?

Administrative

PC technicians commonly use administrative tools to configure and troubleshoot problems with Windows-based systems. Most of these tools are grouped in the Administrative Tools section of the Control Panel on Windows-based systems.

True or false? You can use the Local Security Policy tool to configure a password policy and force users to create strong passwords.

Answer: *True.* The Local Security Policy tool includes the Password Policy settings, which can be used to force users to create strong passwords.

The security settings in the Local Security Policy apply to the local computer only. The same settings are available in Group Policy. Domain administrators use Group Policy to manage multiple computers within a domain. For example, they can configure password policy settings one time and it will apply these settings to all the users in the domain.

> **MORE INFO** Chapter 7, "Security," discusses strong passwords in more depth. It also covers the various settings available in the Password Policy that can be configured to force users to create strong passwords and regularly change them.

True or false? You can use the Local Security Policy to lock an account if a user enters the wrong password too many times.

Answer: *True.* The Account Lockout Policy in the Local Security Policy can be configured to lock accounts.

The Account Lockout Policy has the following three settings:

- **Account Lockout Threshold**   This identifies how many times a user can enter the wrong password without locking the account. For example, if the threshold is five, the user can enter the wrong password four times without locking the account. The account is locked if the user enters the wrong password the fifth time.

- **Account Lockout Duration**   This identifies how long the account will remain locked. For example, if it is set to 30, the account is locked for 30 minutes when the user enters the wrong password too many times. If this is set to 0, the account remains locked until an administrator unlocks it.

- **Reset Account Lockout Counter After**   The system counts incorrect passwords, but it will lock an account only if the user enters the incorrect password repeatedly in a specific amount of time. For example, if this is set to 15 and the account lockout threshold is set to five, the account is locked only if the user enters the wrong password five times in 15 minutes.

True or false? You can configure the Local Security Policy to prevent a user from shutting down a computer.

Answer: *True*. The Local Security Policy incudes a User Rights Assignment node, which can be used to restrict rights on the computer, including the right to shut down a computer.

The User Rights Assignment Node is within the Local Policies group of the Local Security Policy. These rights can also be controlled with Group Policy.

EXAM TIP The Local Security Policy tool is a valuable tool to configure various security settings. You can use it to configure a password policy, an account lockout policy, and to restrict user rights on a system. In a domain, Group Policy is used to manage multiple systems by configuring the settings one time.

True or false? You can use Performance Monitor to send alerts when a computer's performance reaches a certain threshold.

Answer: *True*. You can configure alerts and notifications by using Performance Monitor.

Performance Monitor is valuable to measure the CPU, memory, disk, and network resources on a computer. Alerts are valuable to notify you of a potential problem. For example, you can configure Performance Monitor to send an alert if the CPU processing power exceeds 80% usage.

Table 6-8 shows a list of some additional administrative tools commonly used by PC technicians.

TABLE 6-8 Administrative tools

TOOL	COMMENTS
Computer Management	A group of several tools used to manage computers
Device Manager	Used to install, update, and roll back device drivers
Users and Groups	Used to create and manage users and groups
Services	Used to manipulate services
Task Scheduler	Used to schedule applications or other tasks to run at certain times
Windows Firewall	Used to enable/disable the Windows Firewall and create exceptions or rules
Windows Memory Diagnostics	Used to check the hardware memory
Component Services	Used to manually add Component Object Model (COM) reusable code. This is most commonly needed when an application is created by in-house developers.

TOOL	COMMENTS
Data Sources	Used to configure a connection to a database for an application. Many applications can configure the connection automatically, but some applications require technicians to follow specific directions and configure them manually.
Print Management	Used to manage multiple shared printers. You can add print drivers for different operating systems for each shared printer with this tool.

msconfig

The system configuration tool is used to view and manipulate the configuration of Windows-based systems. It can be started with the **msconfig** command, and it is commonly called **msconfig**. It is also accessible from the Administrative Tools group in the Control Panel in some Windows-based systems.

True or false? You can use the **msconfig** tool to identify and manipulate which programs start when a user logs on.

Answer: *True.* The Startup tab of the **msconfig** tool can be used to show what applications are configured to start when a user logs on, and it can also be used to prevent applications from starting.

Figure 6-2 shows the Startup tab of the **msconfig** tool. You can clear a check box to prevent an application from starting.

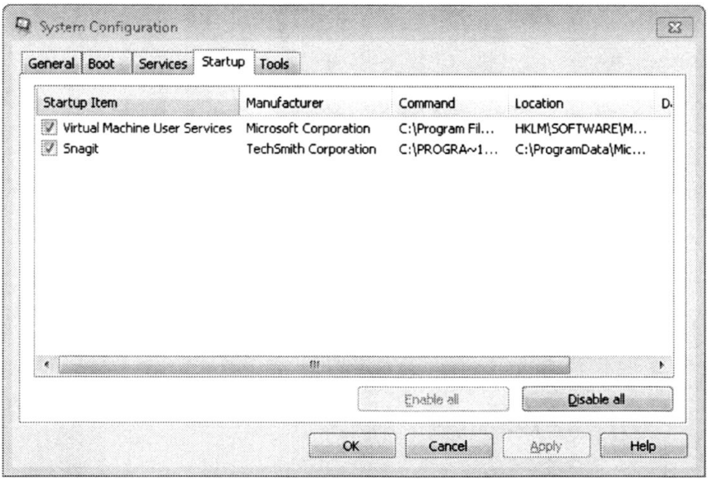

FIGURE 6-2 Startup tab of **msconfig** tool.

In addition to the Startup tab, **msconfig** also has the following tabs:

- **General**   You can use this tab to select a normal start, a diagnostic start, or a selective start using changes you've made on the Services and Startup tab.
- **Boot**   This tab is used to force the system to reboot into one of the different safe modes.
- **Services**   You can clear check boxes for services in the Services tab, similar to how you can clear check boxes in the Startup tab. The difference is that, on this tab, this affects services instead of applications.
- **Tools**   This tab lists many of the administrative tools, and you can start them from here.

NOTE   Services are used primarily by the operating system and can be configured to start when the computer is started. Applications are used primarily by users and can be configured to start when a user logs on. If a computer takes too long to start, you might be able to shorten the time by reducing the number of services configured to start when the computer starts. If it takes too long for a user to log on after entering a user name and password, you might be able to shorten the time by reducing the number of applications configured to start automatically.

EXAM TIP   The msconfig tool is used to view and manipulate which services start when Window starts from the Services tab. You can also view and manipulate which applications start when a user logs on from the Startup tab.

Task Manager

The Task Manager is a valuable tool that technicians often use when troubleshooting systems. It is commonly used to end misbehaving applications. One way to start it is by pressing the Ctrl+Shift+Esc keys at the same time.

True or false? The Task Manager can be used to identify what is causing a computer to run slower than normal.

Answer: *True.* The Task Manager allows you to determine how much processing power any individual process is taking.

A misbehaving application could be consuming most of a system's processing power, causing the rest of the system to run slow. Applications start processes, and by selecting the Processes tab, you can identify the amount of CPU power each process is consuming. You can end the corresponding application from the Applications tab or end the process from the Processes tab.

True or false? You can use the Task Manager tool to identify which users are currently logged on to a computer.

Answer: *True.* The Users tab of Task Manager shows which users are logged on to a computer.

Task Manager in Windows 7 has the following tabs:

- **Applications** This tab shows all of the applications that are running, including their current status. An application that shows a status of Not Responding can be terminated by selecting it and clicking the End Task button.

- **Processes** This tab shows all of the processes running on the system, along with the process ID (PID) and the percent of CPU processing power it is using.

- **Services** This tab lists the services on the computer, along with the status. If the service is running, it will also show the PID of the service.

- **Performance** This tab provides a graphical display of the system's processor and memory performance. Figure 6-3 shows a snapshot of the Task Manager with this tab selected.

- **Networking** This tab shows the usage of network interface cards with a graphical display.

- **Users** This tab shows which users are logged on to the system. From this tab, you can also disconnect or log off users.

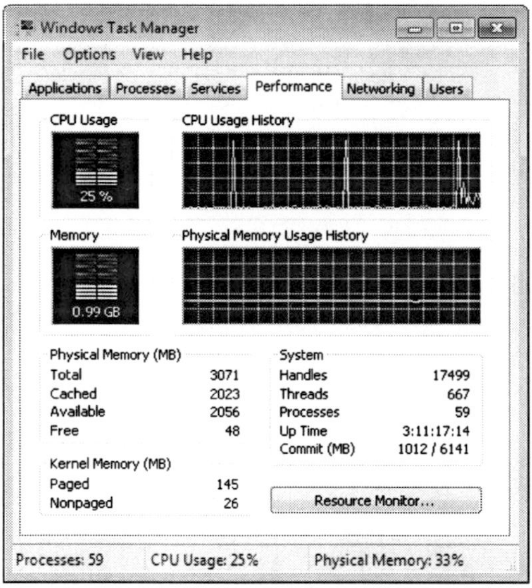

FIGURE 6-3 Performance tab of the Task Manager.

EXAM TIP You can use the Task Manager to determine what is causing a system to run slow, to end misbehaving applications, and to identify users that are currently logged on.

Disk Management

Disk Management is the primary tool used within Windows to manage disks and partitions. You can use it to view the statuses of volumes, manipulate partitions and drives, and create RAID volumes.

True or false? You can shrink a volume in Windows 7 and use the space to create a different volume.

Answer: *True.* The Disk Management tool in Windows 7 allows you to shrink a volume to create unallocated space.

You can use the Shrink tool as the first step to split a single volume into multiple volumes. After shrinking a volume, you can format the unallocated space as a separate volume.

Extending a volume works the opposite way. If a disk has unallocated space, you can extend the volume to include the unallocated space.

You can mount disks from within Disk Management. For example, if you want to add an additional drive to a system, but you want the user to access the drive as a folder, you can create an empty folder on an existing drive and then mount the new drive to this empty folder. Normally when you add an additional drive it is assigned a different drive letter such as D, E, and so on. If you mounted a new drive to an empty folder named Extra on the C drive, users would access the new mounted drive as C:\Extra.

Drive letters are automatically assigned by Windows but you can use Disk Management to manually assign a specific drive letter. For example, if you have an optical drive that is normally assigned the drive letter E but you want to assign it as letter M, you can use Disk Management to do so.

New disk drives are normally recognized automatically by Windows but there are some times when a disk isn't recognized. If you have installed a disk in a system but notice that it doesn't appear in Windows Explorer, you can start Disk Management to add the new disk. When you start Disk Management, you'll be prompted to initialize the disk and after the disk is initialized, it will be recognized in Windows Explorer.

True or false? You can use Disk Management to create a mirrored volume on Windows 7–based systems.

Answer: *True.* Disk Management can be used to create a RAID-1, which is also known as a mirror.

You must first convert the disks to dynamic disks before you can create a RAID. After converting the disks to dynamic, you can create a RAID-1. While computers support multiple types of RAIDs, Windows-based desktop systems support only the following two types of RAIDs created with Disk Management:

- **RAID-0** This is also known as a striped array. It includes two or more disks in an array and can be used to improve read and write access. It does not provide any fault tolerance. You can create a software-based RAID-0 on Windows XP–based, Windows Vista–based, and Windows 7–based systems after converting basic disks to dynamic disks.

- **RAID-1** This is also known as a mirror. It includes two disks in an array and provides fault tolerance. If one disk fails, a complete copy of the data is still available on the second disk. You can create a software-based RAID-1 on Windows 7 after converting basic disks to dynamic disks. However, you cannot create software-based RAID-1 on Windows XP–based and Windows Vista–based systems.

NOTE Disk Management can be used to create software-based RAID disks. That is, if you have two or more disks, you can create a RAID with Disk Management. A hardware-based RAID appears to Disk Management as a single disk, and Windows-based systems support any type of RAID that is hardware-based as long as there are compatible device drivers available.

EXAM TIP You can create RAID-1 mirrors on Windows 7–based systems after converting the disks to dynamic disks. Windows XP and Windows Vista support dynamic disks, but you cannot create a RAID-1 on Windows XP or Windows Vista. You can create a RAID-0 on each of these Windows operating systems.

Figure 6-4 shows the Disk Management tool on a Windows 7–based system. You can see that Disk 0 is configured as a basic disk and that Disk 1 is configured as a dynamic disk. If this system had two dynamic disks, you could use disk management to create a RAID-1 (mirror).

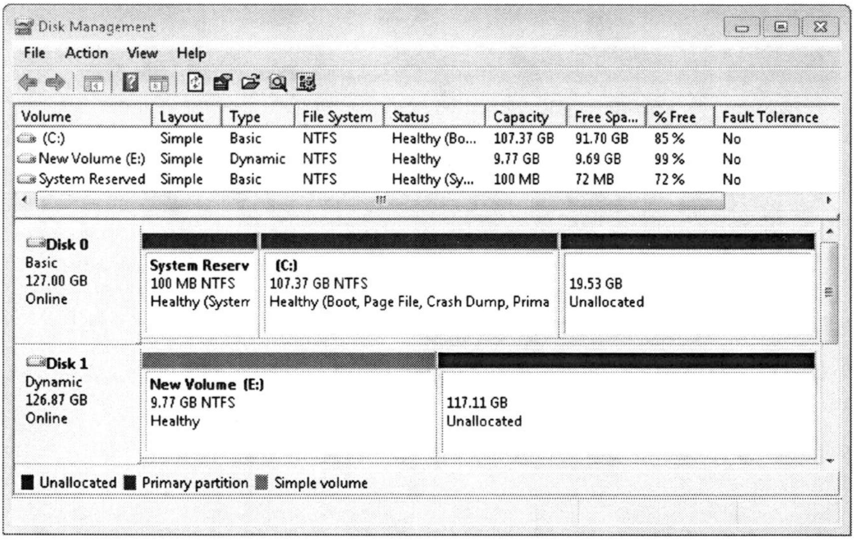

FIGURE 6-4 The Disk Management tool.

Disk Management includes a column to show the status of volumes. Additionally, the status of a disk is indicated under the size of the disk. Some of the indicators you might see include the following:

- **Healthy**   Indicates that the volume does not have any problems.
- **Failed**   This indicates a hardware problem or that the file system is corrupt. You might be able to use **chkdsk** to repair the disk or reformat it.
- **Foreign**   When you move a dynamic disk from one system to another, the new system identifies it as a foreign disk. You can right-click the disk and select Import Foreign Disk so that the new system recognizes it.

- **Missing** This is displayed if one of the disks for a volume is not accessible. It often indicates a hardware problem. For example, this would appear if one of the disks in a mirrored volume is not accessible. You might be able to reactivate the disk to get the system to recognize the missing disk.

- **Online** Online disks are available for read/write access.

- **Online (Errors)** This appears if input/output errors are detected on a dynamic volume. You can right-click the disk and select Reactivate to return it to Online status. This indicates that the disk might be failing.

- **Offline** The operating system might take a volume offline if it has detected a problem. The disk needs to be brought online to use it, and you can do so by right-clicking the disk and selecting Reactivate. If this doesn't work, it indicates a hardware problem.

- **Unreadable** This often indicates a hardware failure.

Other

When users switch from one operating system to another, they frequently want to migrate their user data and settings to the new system. For example, users running Windows XP who buy a new Windows 7–based system might want to migrate their data and settings from their Windows XP system to Windows 7. There are several tools that simplify this process.

True or false? The FAST wizard is used to transfer data and settings between Windows XP and Windows 7.

Answer: *False.* The File and Settings Transfer (FAST) wizard is used to migrate data to Windows XP–based systems but cannot migrate data to Windows 7.

The following are three primary tools used to transfer data and settings:

- The FAST wizard is available in Windows XP and can be used to transfer files and settings to Windows XP from Widows 2000, Windows ME, or other Windows XP–based systems.

- Windows Easy Transfer is available in Windows Vista and Windows 7 and is used to transfer data from older systems to Windows Vista or Windows 7. Data can be transferred over a special Easy Transfer cable using USB ports on two computers, over a network, or to an external hard disk or USB drive.

- User State Migration Tool (USMT) is a more sophisticated set of tools used in larger enterprises and uses command prompt tools. You can use **scanstate** to capture data from an older computer, and **loadstate** to load this data onto the new computer.

EXAM TIP FAST is used to migrate data to Windows XP–based systems, and Windows Easy Transfer is used to migrate data to Windows Vista and Windows 7. USMT is used in larger environments, and different versions are available to migrate data to Windows XP–based, Windows Vista–based, and Windows 7–based systems.

Run line utilities

Many Windows tools are started by entering the appropriate command at the command line or the run line. In Windows XP, you can access the Run line by clicking Start, Run. In Windows Vista and Windows 7, you can access the same run line by pressing the Windows+R keys.

True or false? You start the system configuration tool with the **mstsc** command from the run line.

Answer: *False.* The system configuration tool is started with the **msconfig** command.

Mstsc is short for Microsoft Terminal Services Connection, and it is used to start the Remote Desktop Connection (RDC) tool. You can connect to remote computers over a network with RDC.

True or false? You can access the local security policy settings with the **gpedit.msc** command on a Windows 7–based computer.

Answer: *True.* Entering the **gpedit.msc** command from the command prompt or from the Start, Search Programs And Files text box will start the Local Group Policy Editor. The Security settings are in the Computer Configuration, Windows Settings, Security Settings node. These are the same security settings in the Local Security Policy that can be started with the **secpol.msc** command.

Table 6-9 shows a list of common commands and the tools they start. None of these commands are case sensitive. They can be entered as uppercase, lowercase, or any combination.

TABLE 6-9 Run line utilities

COMMAND	TOOL
Cmd	Command Prompt
Dxdiag	DirectX Diagnostic Tool
Explorer	Windows Explorer
Gpedit.msc	Group Policy Editor
MMC	Microsoft Management Console
Mstsc	Remote Desktop Connection
Notepad	Simple text editor
Msconfig	System Configuration
Msinfo32	System Information
Secpol.msc	Local Security Policy
Services.msc	Services applet

Can you answer these questions?

You can find the answers to these questions at the end of this chapter.

1. What tool can you use to modify which applications are starting when a user logs on?
2. What tool is used to identify performance bottlenecks?
3. What command would you use to start the Group Policy editor?

Objective 1.5: Given a scenario, use Control Panel utilities (the items are organized by "classic view/large icons" in Windows)

The Control Panel includes multiple utilities, commonly called applets, and it's important for a PC technician to know what utilities are available and how to get to them. These can be organized in categories or list views, and the CompTIA objectives specifically mention the list views. You can change the view to Classic View in Windows XP and Windows Vista instead of Category View to list them individually. In Windows 7, you can select Large Icons or Small Icons instead of Category to view them as a list.

Exam need to know...

- Common to all Microsoft operating systems
  For example: What settings are modified by Internet Options?
- Unique to Windows XP
  For example: What applet is used to manipulate printers in Windows XP?
- Unique to Windows Vista and Windows 7
  For example: What tool would you use to remove an application in Windows 7?

Common to all Microsoft operating systems

There are several Control Panel applets that are common to all Windows operating systems, and CompTIA lists several of these applets in the objectives in this section. Other applets are unique to individual operating systems and are listed in the following sections.

True or false? You can use the Internet Options applet to modify the settings for Windows Explorer.

Answer: *False.* The Internet Options applet is used to modify the Internet Explorer web browser settings.

These settings can also be accessed from Internet Explorer. The method to get to the settings varies based on the version of Internet Explorer, but you can usually get to it by selecting Internet Options from the Tools menu within Internet Explorer.

The Internet Options applet has multiple tabs you can use to manipulate different Internet Explorer options:

- **Connections tab** If your organization uses a proxy server, you can configure Internet Explorer to always go through the proxy server by configuring the Proxy settings (via LAN Settings) from this tab. This tab also includes other ways to connect to the Internet such as through a Virtual Private Network, or a dial-up connection.

- **Security tab** Four security zones are preconfigured and can be manipulated from this tab. The security zones are Trusted Sites, Local Intranet, Internet, and Restricted Sites. Restricted Sites have the most security and Trusted Sites have the least security. Trusted web site addresses can be added into the Trusted Sites zone to relax security so that they operate correctly.

- **General tab** This tab includes miscellaneous settings such as the home page. Users can also access this tab to configure what data is temporarily kept on a system (such as passwords and form entry data), and delete all browsing history data.

- **Privacy tab** You can enable the Pop-Up Blocker from this tab and also configure how cookies are used. Cookies are text files that can store information related to a user's browsing activities. They are frequently used for marketing and advertising, and even referred to as spyware by some people.

- **Programs tab** The Programs tab can be used to set Internet Explorer as the default browser. It can also be used to manage add-ons used to extend the capabilities of Internet Explorer.

- **Advanced tab** Many detailed settings are available on the Advanced tab. For example, you can manipulate how animations or sounds are handled within webpages when you visit.

The Folder Options applet is used to modify the views and settings for Windows Explorer. For example, you can modify the Folder Options so that system files and/or file extensions are hidden. You can also access Folder Options from the Tools menu in Windows Explorer when the menus are showing. Folder Options has two common tabs:

- **General** Basic settings affecting how Windows Explorer works are set here. For example, you can configure it to open an item with a single click or a double click.

- **View** This tab is used to modify the views shown in Windows Explorer. For example, you normally cannot see hidden files but you can modify the view so that Windows Explorer shows hidden files, folders, and drives. Similarly, Windows Explorer normally doesn't show extensions for known file types or show protected operating system files, but you can change the view options so that these are shown in Windows Explorer.

True or false? You can modify the virtual memory settings by modifying the advanced settings in the System applet.

Answer: *True.* The advanced settings in the System applet give you access to various performance settings, including the virtual memory settings.

The System applet is used to modify many of the system settings in a computer. The Advanced tab of the System applet includes a Performance section. You can use this to modify how much virtual memory is assigned to a system. Virtual memory is created by using a paging file stored on the hard disk.

You can enable Remote Assistance and Remote Desktop by clicking on the Remote tab of the System Properties applet. Remote assistance is used to remotely help a user while the user is logged on. Remote Desktop is used to remotely connect to a computer over a network. In addition to enabling the remote settings, you also need to ensure that port 3389 is open on firewalls between the two systems to allow Remote Desktop Protocol traffic.

System Protection features are configured by clicking on the System Protection tab of the System applet on Windows Vista and Windows 7. On Windows XP, this is called System Restore and used only for restore points. When you enable System Restore on Windows Vista and Windows 7, you can also configure System Protection to save copies of previous versions of files.

True or false? You can modify the resolution of a monitor by using the Display applet.

Answer: *True.* The Display applet includes several settings, including the resolution setting.

If the resolution is set too low, the text on the screen will appear very large and the entire screen might not be viewable. The most common reason why you'll modify the resolution is when adding a new video card, a new monitor, or updating the display driver.

> **EXAM TIP** If you haven't done so before, it is worth your time to change the Control Panel view to list the applets individually and then start each applet. If the applet isn't familiar to you, take the time to explore it to remind yourself about what it does.

The User Accounts applet is used to create and manipulate user accounts. You can use it to modify passwords and account types. For example, regular users should use a standard account and only personnel that need administrative access should be given an administrative account. If you realize users have administrative access but don't need it, you can use the User Accounts applet to change the account from an administrator account to a standard account.

Each version of Windows includes the Windows Firewall applet in the Control Panel. Microsoft recommends keeping the firewall enabled. You can manipulate the Windows Firewall settings to allow specific types of traffic. For example, if you want to allow Remote Desktop traffic, you would open port 3389 on the firewall.

True or false? The Windows XP Presentation Power Scheme will prevent a computer from going into standby mode during a presentation.

Answer: *True.* Windows XP includes several Power Schemes in the Power Options applet, and the Presentation Power Scheme prevents the system from using any power saving modes.

The Power Options applet is in the Control Panel in Windows XP. Other Power Schemes in Windows XP include Home/Office Desk, Portable/Laptop, Always On, Minimal Power Management, and Max Battery. Each of the schemes is preconfigured with different power saving options.

On Windows Vista and Windows 7–based systems, the Power Schemes have been replaced with three Power Plans in the Power Options applet. The High Performance power plan favors performance over saving energy. The Power Saver power plan saves energy when possible by reducing the computer's performance. The Balanced power plan is recommended and balances performance and energy consumption.

The Advanced Configuration and Power Interface (ACPI) specification is an open standard that defines different power states for systems and devices. Power states range from having no power at all to running at maximum performance. While you don't need to know all of the different power states, you should understand the following terms related to power options:

- **Sleep/suspend** This is a low power state formally identified as G1, S3 by ACPI. G1 indicates it is a global low power state applied to multiple devices in the computer, and S3 is the sleep or suspend state. It maintains power to the RAM, provides low power to the CPU, and other devices such as disk drives and the display monitor are turned off. When users interact with the system, the system returns to full power. A system can wake up from a sleep mode very quickly, and while in sleep state it is still consuming some power.

- **Standby** The ACPI G1, S3 state is commonly referred to as standby and sometimes called sleep or suspend. When used to refer to the computer, it is a global state. Some devices such as display monitors use standby to refer to low power states. Devices in standby mode consume very little energy but can return to full power very quickly.

- **Hibernate** This is also known as suspend to disk. All the data in memory is written to the disk in a hibernate file, and the system is turned off completely. When the system is turned back on, the hibernate file is written back to memory and the system returns to the same state it was in when it hibernated. Hibernate mode doesn't consume any power after a system hibernates, but it takes longer for a system to return to full operation.

EXAM TIP The Power Options applet is available in each operating system, but it was changed significantly between Windows XP and Windows 7. In Windows XP, you select Power Schemes based on the purpose of the system, such as a presentation computer or office desktop computer. In Windows 7, three power plans are used instead: Balanced (recommended), High Performance, and Power Saver.

Unique to Windows XP

Each operating system has changes from the previous operating system, and many of these changes are in the Control Panel. Some applets used in Windows XP were either removed or renamed in later versions of Windows.

True or false? You can remove applications by using the Add/Remove Programs applet in Windows XP.

Answer: *True*. This applet can be used to install or uninstall applications.

Some other applets that are unique to Windows XP are:

- **Network Connections** You can use this applet to manipulate network interface cards (NICs). For example, if you need to configure a NIC with a manual IP address, you can configure the settings through here. This applet also has access to several wizards to set up different network connections such as a connection to the Internet through an Internet service provider or to a work network through a virtual private network (VPN). Windows Vista and Windows 7 include the Network And Sharing Center, which includes many similar tools and wizards.

- **Network Setup Wizard** This wizard is available from the Network Connections applet in the Network Tasks list on the left pane. You can use it to share an Internet connection, set up the Windows Firewall, share files and folders, and share a printer. You can start it by clicking on Set Up A Home or Small Office Network, or by selecting Network Setup Wizard from the File drop down menu.

- **Printers And Faxes** You use this applet to manually add printers or manipulate existing printers and their drivers. It is replaced with the Printers applet in Windows Vista and with the Devices And Printers applet in Windows 7.

- **Automatic Updates** This is used to enable, configure, or disable Automatic Updates. Microsoft recommends keeping this set to Automatic (recommended) so that a computer will automatically check for updates, download them when they're available, and install them. By default, downloaded updates are scheduled for installation at 3:00 a.m., but you can use this applet to change the time when they are installed. The Automatic Updates applet is replaced with Windows Update in Windows Vista and Windows 7.

Unique to Windows Vista

The following Control Panel items are only available in Windows Vista and not in either Windows XP or Windows 7:

- **Tablet PC Settings** Use this applet to configure Windows Vista when it is installed on a tablet device. This includes configuring which side of the display that menus appear, handwriting recognition settings, and the orientation of the device (such as portrait or landscape).

- **Pen and Input Devices** If a Windows Vista system has a touch device or supports the use of a stylus, you can configure different actions with this applet. For example, a double-tap is normally recognized as a double-click of the mouse and you can simulate a right-click of the mouse with a press and hold action, but you can modify these default actions if desired.

- **Offline Files** The offline files feature is useful for mobile computers that are sometimes disconnected from a network. For example, a sales person might regularly access files on a networked server while at work. When offline files are enabled, the sales person will also have access to these files while traveling and disconnected from the work network. Use this applet to enable offline files, configure how much space is used for offline files, and to set encryption for the files.

- **Problem Reports and Solutions** When enabled, this applet sends a description of problems experienced by Windows Vista to Microsoft, and checks to see if known solutions are available. For example, a system might be intermittently crashing with a specific error. If Problem Reports and Solutions is enabled, the system reports the error and when a solution is known, it is recorded in the applet. If a system has been experiencing problems and you're not sure how to resolve them, check this applet to see if a solution has been found.

- **Printers** Just as you'd expect, the Printers applet is used to configure printers. You can use it to add printers, set a printer as the default printer, share a printer, update printer drivers, configure permissions for a printer, and print test pages. Some print drivers add extra capabilities to the properties of printers that are also accessible here. For example, calibration and head cleaning tools for some inkjet printers are available through here.

Unique to Windows 7

Some Control Panel items are new in Windows 7, and the Control Panel also includes a search feature making it easy to find applets. Windows 7 includes Large Icons and Small Icons views, which are similar to the Classic View available in Windows XP and Windows Vista.

True or false? You can use the Programs And Features applet in Windows 7 to remove a Windows 7–based application.

Answer: *True.* The Programs And Features applet in the Windows 7 Control Panel is used to remove installed applications.

Windows Vista also includes the Programs And Features applet. In Windows XP, the Add Or Remove Programs applet is used instead.

True or false? Windows Vista and Windows 7 include the Homegroup applet.

Answer: *False.* Homegroups are available in Windows 7, and there is a Homegroup applet in Windows 7. Homegroups are not available in Windows Vista.

> *EXAM TIP* Homegroups can be created in Windows 7 Professional, Enterprise, and Ultimate editions, and any Windows 7–based system can join a homegroup. Windows XP and Windows Vista systems can join a workgroup, but they cannot join a homegroup.

Some additional applets that are unique in Windows 7 are:

- **Action Center** The Action Center in Windows 7 combines the features of the Security Center applet from Windows XP and Windows Vista with the features of the Problems Reports and Solutions applet in Windows Vista. It includes two primary sections: Security and Maintenance. You can access it directly from the Control Panel to check for issues and it will also notify the user with a small white flag just to the left of the clock in the task bar.

- **Remote applications and desktop applications** This applet is called RemoteApp and Desktop Connections. When administrators have published RemoteApp programs or virtual desktop computers in a network, you can use this app to configure them on individual computers.

- **Troubleshooting** The Troubleshooting applet includes several wizards you can use to troubleshoot different types of problems. This includes problems with programs, hardware and sound, network and Internet connectivity, appearance and personalization settings, and system and security problems.

Can you answer these questions?

You can find the answers to these questions at the end of this chapter.

1. What is used to modify Windows Explorer to show file extensions?
2. What applet is used to modify virtual memory for a system?
3. What is used to remove an application in Windows 7?

Objective 1.6: Set up and configure Windows networking on a client/desktop

Desktop computers are commonly configured within a network, and PC technicians are expected to know how to configure and set up networking on Windows-based systems. This objective builds on the networking knowledge from the Networking domain of the 220-801 exam and also overlaps with other objectives in the 220-802 exam. The Networking domain in 220-802 comprises approximately 27 percent of the 220-801 exam, and it's expected that you have that knowledge prior to taking the 220-802 exam. The Troubleshooting domain in the 220-802 exam includes an objective specifically related to troubleshooting network issues, and that objective expects you to have knowledge from this objective also.

Exam need to know...

- Homegroup, file/print sharing
  For example: What operating systems support homegroups? What operating systems can join a homegroup but not create a homegroup?
- Workgroup vs. domain setup
  For example: What hardware is needed for a domain?
- Network shares/mapping drives
  For example: What command is used to map a drive to a UNC path?

- Establish networking connections
  For example: What is a VPN?
- Firewall settings
  For example: What is configured on a firewall to allow traffic?
- Proxy settings
  For example: Where are proxy settings configured?
- Remote desktop
  For example: What port does Remote Desktop Connection use?
- Home vs. Work vs. Public network settings
  For example: What network setting should be selected when a user connects to a wireless network in a coffee shop?
- Configuring an alternative IP address in Windows
  For example: When is an alternative IP address assigned?
- Network card properties
  For example: What is WoL?

Homegroup, file/print sharing

Homegroups are available in Windows 7–based systems and are intended to provide small office and home office users with a simpler way of sharing resources in a network. After a homegroup is created, users can join it to share files from their libraries and share printers if desired.

True or false? Homegroups allow you to stream music and video between Windows 7–based computers in the Homegroup.

Answer: *True.* Windows 7–based systems joined to a homegroup can share files within their libraries. When one user shares music and video from a system, these files can be streamed to other users in the homegroup.

Homegroups require File And Printer Sharing For Microsoft Networks to be enabled. This is enabled by default on the properties of the networking interface card.

> **EXAM TIP** Homegroups allow users to share files in their libraries. Windows 7–based computers can join a homegroup, but Windows XP–based and Windows Vista–based systems cannot join a homegroup. You cannot create a homegroup on Starter or Home Basic editions of Windows 7–based systems, but these editions can join an existing homegroup.

> **MORE INFO** The Microsoft article "Get To Know Home Networking in Windows 7" includes a video on homegroups and other details about how to configure a network with Windows 7. You can access it here: *http://windows.microsoft.com/en-US/windows/ explore/get-to-know-home-networking*. The Microsoft article "Homegroup From Start To Finish" includes all the steps to create homegroups, join homegroups, share files, and share printers. You can access it here: *http://windows.microsoft.com/en-US/ windows7/help/homegroup-from-start-to-finish*.

Workgroup vs. domain setup

Small networks of up to 10 users are commonly configured as a workgroup. When the network gets larger than 10 to 20 users, an organization typically converts it over to a domain so that it is easier to manage.

True or false? Windows 7–based systems support a maximum of 20 concurrent connections.

Answer: *True.* Windows XP–based and Windows Vista–based systems support a maximum of 10 concurrent connections but Windows 7 supports up to 20.

A concurrent connection refers to how many other users are connected at the same time. For example, if a Windows 7–based system is sharing a folder named data, up to 20 other systems can connect to that folder at the same time to access files in the folder.

True or false? Domains provide centralized security through Group Policy.

Answer: *True.* Domains have one or more domain controllers, and Group Policy can be configured on the domain controller to manage all the computer and user accounts in the domain.

Security in a workgroup must be managed individually on each computer. This isn't too difficult in a workgroup with two or three systems but can become challenging in an organization with more than 10 computers. A domain provides centralized management through the domain controller and streamlines administration. Also, workgroups require users to have separate user accounts for every computer they use. In a domain, users typically have a single account that they can use to log on to multiple computers.

> **EXAM TIP** Windows XP and Windows Vista support up to 10 concurrent connections. Windows 7–based systems support up to 20 concurrent connections. Domains provide better security than workgroups by allowing administrators to manage the domains through centralized servers.

Network shares/mapping drives

One of the benefits of a network is the ability to share resources. Files and folders can be shared on one system, and users of other systems can access these files and folders by connecting to a network share.

True or false? The path to a shared folder is in the format of \\sharename \servername.

Answer: *False.* The path to a shared folder is in the format of \\servername \sharename. This is known as the Universal Naming Convention (UNC) format.

The order of server first and share second in the UNC path is sometimes hard for people to remember until they've done it several times. One way to remember it is that you must connect to the server first before you can connect to shares hosted on the server, and the server is first in the UNC path.

True or false? You can map a drive to a UNC path by using the net command.

Answer: *True*. The net command can be used to map a drive letter to a shared folder on another networked computer.

For example, you can map the M drive on a local computer to a shared folder named videos on another computer named Win7 with this command: **net use m: \\win7\videos**.

> *EXAM TIP* UNC paths have the format \\servername\sharename. You can map drives using either Windows Explorer or the **Net Use** command.

Establish networking connections

Computers within an enterprise are typically connected to a network with a wired connection. For example, many desktop computers have a wired NIC and are connected to a network through a switch with a twisted-pair cable. However, several other types of connections can be used.

True or false? Users can connect to an organization's internal network through a VPN connection from their home and through the Internet.

Answer: *True*. A virtual private network (VPN) connection provides access to a private network over a public network such as the Internet.

If an organization configures a remote access server for either dial-up access or VPN access, users can access the internal network even while they are away from work. Users can connect to a dial-up remote access server through a regular phone line as long as their computer has a modem. They can connect to a VPN server as long as they have access to the Internet. Administrators implement a variety of different security methods to prevent unauthorized personnel from accessing the internal network through these connections.

True or false? Cellular Internet connections are useful for users who travel often but need regular access to the Internet.

Answer: *True*. Several wireless wide area networks (WWANs) are maintained by communication companies and provide access to the Internet for mobile users.

Smartphones and many tablet devices include hardware to access the cellular WWANs. Users subscribe to the service and can then access the Internet through the cellular WWAN.

> *EXAM TIP* VPNs provide users with access to an internal network through a public network. The Internet is commonly used with VPNs, but organizations can also lease semi-private lines for VPNs.

Firewall settings

Windows-based systems include a built-in firewall that provides added protection to the computer. Windows XP was the first Windows operating system to include the Windows Firewall, and it has been improved in Windows Vista–based and Windows 7–based systems. As a best practice, systems should have a firewall enabled even when they are within a protected network. This helps prevent malware from spreading if they somehow breach a network firewall.

True or false? Firewalls typically block all traffic unless there is an exception to allow it.

Answer: *True*. Firewalls often use a *deny all* philosophy with exceptions or rules to identify traffic that is allowed.

A *deny all* philosophy is sometimes referred to as *implicit deny*. If a rule doesn't explicitly allow traffic, it is implicitly denied or blocked.

> **EXAM TIP** The Windows Firewall should be enabled unless a third-party firewall is in use. This provides protection to the Windows-based system from various threats, such as malware and direct attacks.

Firewalls can be configured with different types of exceptions or rules. A basic packet filtering firewall allows you to create exceptions based on IP addresses, protocols, logical ports, protocol identifiers, or a combination of any of these. As an example, the Windows Firewall in Windows Vista and Windows 7 includes several predefined exceptions that you can enable or disable with just a couple of clicks.

After starting the Windows Firewall from the Control Panel, click on Allow a Program or Feature Through Windows Firewall. You can browse through the existing exceptions to view what is available. Changes are disabled by default to prevent you from making accidental changes but you can enable changes by clicking on the Change Settings button. Once changes are enabled, you can enable an exception by selecting the checkbox for the exception in a Home/Work (Private) Network and/or a Public network.

If you can't find a predefined exception that meets your needs, you can click on the Allow Another Program button and follow the wizard to create an exception for a specific application. An advanced tool is Windows Firewall with Advanced Security, available in the Administrative Tools group. It includes many predefined exceptions listed as rules that you can enable or disable and it also allows you to manipulate settings at the granular level.

You can use the Windows Firewall applet to enable or disable the Windows Firewall. After starting the Windows Firewall applet, click on the Turn Windows Firewall On or Off. You can select the Turn Off Windows Firewall (Not Recommended) link for the Home or Work (Private) network and/or the Public network. The primary reason why you would disable the Windows Firewall is when you are using a third-party firewall on the system. It is not recommended to disable the firewall without another firewall in place.

Proxy settings

Many organizations use a proxy server to manage and optimize access to the Internet by internal users. For example, web browsers are configured to send all web requests to the proxy server, and the proxy server then retrieves the data and sends it back to the requestor.

True or false? Viruses are unable to modify proxy settings in a web browser.

Answer: *False.* Many viruses can and do modify the proxy settings in a web browser.

When a virus modifies the proxy settings, the user's system is typically configured to bypass the proxy and access Internet resources directly. This prevents the proxy server from tracking and controlling a user's Internet access.

In some organizations, firewalls are configured to block most Internet access that isn't going through the proxy server. The effect for users whose proxy settings have been changed is that they no longer have Internet access because it is blocked by the firewall.

EXAM TIP Viruses can modify the proxy settings for a web browser. In some situations, this blocks all Internet access for the user, and in other situations, it allows a computer to access malicious websites.

MORE INFO Larger organizations often use Group Policy to configure proxy settings. One benefit is that it is much more difficult for malware to modify the settings when they are configured with Group Policy. Even if the malware succeeds, Group Policy periodically checks the settings and resets them on target computers to match the Group Policy settings. Chapter 22 of the CompTIA A+ Training Kit (Exam 220-801 and Exam 220-802), ISBN-10: 0735662681, covers proxy servers in more depth, including their benefits, and provides steps to configure the Proxy settings for Internet Explorer by using the Internet Options applet.

Remote desktop

Remote desktop is used by Windows-based systems, giving users the ability to access Windows systems remotely. When technicians talk about remote desktop, they might be referring to one of the following:

- **Remote Desktop Connection (RDC)** This is a client-side application used to connect to a remote system. It can be started by entering **mstsc** at the run line.
- **Remote Assistance** This is a feature that allows one person to provide assistance to someone else by using a remote connection.
- **Remote Desktop Protocol (RDP)** This is the underlying protocol used by remote desktop applications. RDC and Remote Assistance both use RDP.

True or false? Remote desktop uses port 389 by default.

Answer: *False.* Remote desktop connections use port 3389 by default. The Lightweight Directory Access Protocol (LDAP) uses port 389 by default.

If a remote desktop connection is not working, one of the first things to check is firewall settings. An exception needs to be created to allow traffic over port 3389.

EXAM TIP Remote desktop technologies include RDC (started with the *mstsc* command), RDP, and remote assistance. RDP uses port 3389, and the most common reason why a remote desktop connection is not working is because the traffic is blocked on a firewall. An exception opening port 3389 usually resolves the problem.

MORE INFO You can view a short video on how remote desktop is used to access another computer here: *http://windows.microsoft.com/en-US/windows7/help/videos/remote-desktop-connection*. The following page answers some frequently asked questions about remote desktop: *http://windows.microsoft.com/en-US/windows7/Remote-Desktop-Connection-frequently-asked-questions*. The following page describes the steps to configure it: *http://windows.microsoft.com/en-US/windows7/allow-remote-desktop-connections-from-outside-your-home-network*.

Home vs. Work vs. Public network settings

The Windows Firewall on Windows Vista and Windows 7 uses special network location settings. These settings are designed to make it simple for a user to use the safest firewall settings based on the user's location. Each location has preconfigured firewall settings.

True or false? When users connect to the Internet directly through their ISPs from home and are assigned a public IP address, they should select the Home location.

Answer: *False*. The Public location should be selected any time the user is connected with a public IP address in a public location.

The three primary network locations are as follows:

- **Home Network** This is used when a computer is connected to a network in a home. A home network with Internet access will have a router connected directly to the Internet with a public IP address, but internal computers have private IP addresses. The router provides a layer of protection against Internet threats and typically includes a firewall.

- **Work Network** Select this when connected to a network within a work environment. Work networks typically have Internet access but are protected by firewalls.

- **Public Network** Select this when connected to a network in a public place, such as to a wireless network in a coffee shop. This should also be used when a single home computer connects directly to the Internet without using network router and firewall. For example, if a computer connects directly to an ISP without going through a router in a home network, this is the best choice. This setting configures the Windows Firewall with the highest level of restrictions to protect the user's computer.

EXAM TIP Mobile users who connect to wireless networks in public places should select the Public Network location. Public should also be selected anytime the user is assigned a public IP address.

MORE INFO The Microsoft article "Choosing a Network Location" provides more details about the different network locations and when each should be selected. You can access it here: *http://windows.microsoft.com/en-us/windows7/Choosing-a-network-location.*

Configuring an alternative IP address in Windows

If a computer is configured to use DHCP, you can configure it with an alternative IP address. If a DHCP server doesn't respond with an IP address and lease, the alternative IP address is used instead.

True or false? To use APIPA, an alternative IP address must be assigned.

Answer: *False.* An alternative IP address is assigned instead of using Automatic Private IP Addressing (APIPA).

APIPA addresses start with 169.254 and are self-assigned if a DHCP client doesn't receive a lease from a DHCP server. An alternative IP address is a manually assigned IP address that is used instead of an APIPA address when a DHCP client doesn't receive a lease from DHCP. When assigning an alternative IP address, you can assign the IP address, subnet mask, default gateway, and an address of a DNS server.

The most common reason to use alternative IP addresses is when a user has a mobile computer that connects to one network with DHCP and to another network that needs a manually assigned IP address. When the user connects to the DHCP-enabled network, DHCP assigns the IP address and other TCP/IP information. When the user connects to the network without DHCP, the system first tries to get an IP address from DHCP. When it fails to get a lease from DHCP, the system uses the alternative IP address.

EXAM TIP An alternative IP address can be manually configured for a system along with DHCP. If DHCP doesn't respond, the alternative IP address is assigned.

Network card properties

Network interface cards (NICs) have several properties that can be manipulated. You rarely need to manipulate these properties, but you should be aware of them in case you do need to make changes.

True or false? PoE is used to provide power to some IP telephony devices.

Answer: *True.* Power over Ethernet (PoE) is used with some telephony devices. It provides power to the devices over the Ethernet connection.

NOTE A typical NIC installed in a desktop system won't have a PoE property. However, the network interface used on some telephony devices can be configured to use power from a PoE device, such as a PoE switch, or to use power from another source.

Some other NIC properties include the following:

- **Duplex mode**   Most NICs can automatically sense the duplex mode used by the connection. However, you might need to manually configure for half duplex or full duplex mode on some older NICs. Full duplex mode supports both transmit and receive signals at the same time. Half duplex mode supports both transmit and receive signals, but only one can occur at a time.

- **Speed**   Most NICs can also automatically sense the speed of the connection. However, some older NICs might need you to manually configure them to match the connection.

- **Wake-on-LAN (WoL)**   Administrators often schedule system updates and other maintenance to occur during non-work hours, such as in the middle of the night. Systems are often in lower power states such as sleep or standby mode at this time, but systems that support WoL will wake up when they receive a special "magic packet." After returning to full power, updates and other maintenance occurs normally. WoL might need to be enabled on a NIC or in the BIOS.

EXAM TIP   You can access the network card properties of a NIC through the Device Manager or through the Advanced properties of the NIC.

MORE INFO   NIC manufacturers often have different properties that you can manipulate, and they aren't named the same way from one NIC to another. Chapter 19 of the CompTIA A+ Training Kit (Exam 220-801 and Exam 220-802), ISBN-10: 0735662681, covers the different settings of a NIC and includes an exercise to view and modify these settings.

Can you answer these questions?

You can find the answers to these questions at the end of this chapter.

1. What is the proper format of a UNC path?
2. What command can you use to map a drive to a UNC path?
3. What port should be open on firewalls to allow remote desktop?
4. What network location should be selected when a user connects to a wireless network at their home?

Objective 1.7: Perform preventive maintenance procedures using appropriate tools

You keep automobiles in their best running condition and help them have a longer useful life by performing preventive maintenance regularly. Similarly, there are many preventive maintenance procedures that technicians should know related to PCs. These procedures help keep systems running as efficiently as possible and also protect user data.

Exam need to know...

- Best practices
  For example: What are common backup types? What can be used to check a disk for fragmentation?
- Tools
  For example: What is the GUI equivalent of the **chkdsk** command?

Best practices

There are many best practices that should be used for any Windows-based system. Topics in this objective expect you to know the common best practices that are designed to protect user data, keep the system running efficiently, and keep all software elements up to date.

True or false? Patch management refers to the process of ensuring that Windows-based systems are kept up to date.

Answer: *True.* Microsoft regularly provides updates, and organizations implement patch management programs to keep systems up to date.

Microsoft regularly releases updates on the second Tuesday of each month. Technicians and administrators commonly refer to this as patch Tuesday and plan their patch management program around this release date. Microsoft occasionally releases updates outside of this schedule.

In smaller organizations, systems are configured to automatically download and install the updates. In larger organizations, updates are tested before they are deployed and systems are regularly checked with automated tools to ensure that they are kept up to date.

Updates commonly refer to operating systems and applications. However, it's also important to keep antivirus software up to date with current signature files. Signature files are used to identify malware, and because criminals release new malware regularly, these signature files must be regularly updated. Many antivirus applications can automatically check for updates and install them without any user interaction.

> **EXAM TIP** A common preventative maintenance practice is to ensure that operating systems and applications are kept up to date. Small organizations often do this by configuring systems to automatically download and install updates. Larger organizations use a patch management process to review and test updates before deploying them to target systems. Signature files for antivirus software should also be kept up to date.

True or false? You should always install firmware updates as soon as they are available.

Answer: *False.* Firmware updates aren't always needed.

You would install firmware updates if they correct a problem you are having or they add a feature that you need. However, if you aren't having a problem or don't need the feature, it isn't necessary to update the firmware. Flashing the BIOS is an example of a firmware update. It isn't critical to constantly check for BIOS updates and install them as soon as they are released. One reason is that flashing the BIOS is a risky operation. If a system loses power in the middle of a BIOS update, it could corrupt the BIOS, making the system unusable until you resolve the problem.

MORE INFO In Chapter 1, "PC hardware," of this book, Objective 1.1, "Configure and apply BIOS settings," covers flashing the BIOS. You can use an uninterruptible power supply to avoid problems due to power loss while flashing the BIOS. This is true for any firmware updates.

True or false? A differential backup will back up all data.

Answer: *False*. A full backup will back up all data, but a differential backup backs up only data that changed since the last full backup.

The following three types of backups are commonly used with systems:

- **Full** A full backup will back up all target data.
- **Differential** A differential backup is combined with a full backup. It will back up all data that has changed since the last full backup.
- **Incremental** An incremental backup is combined with a full backup. It will back up all data that has changed since the last full backup or the last incremental backup.

True or false? Disks should be regularly checked for fragmentation and defragmented when necessary.

Answer: *True*. Fragmentation of a disk can slow down the performance of a system, and you can prevent performance problems by reducing disk fragmentation.

The Disk Defragmenter GUI can be used to analyze a disk for fragmentation and to defragment a fragmented disk. Windows Vista and Windows 7 both include schedules that automatically check a drive for fragmentation once a week and defragment it when necessary. You can view these schedules in the Task Scheduler's Library of scheduled tasks.

NOTE Defrag is the command-line equivalent of the Disk Defragmenter GUI. It can be used in batch files to automate the process of checking and defragmenting disks.

EXAM TIP Scheduled tasks can be used to automate many preventative maintenance procedures. This includes scheduling backups, checking and defragmenting disks, and checking the integrity of disks with **chkdsk**.

Tools

Many tools are available to help you implement best practices related to preventative maintenance. Some of these tools are available as Windows-based applications, and some are available from the command prompt.

True or false? The Check Disk tool available from Windows Explorer works the same as the **chkdsk** command.

Answer: *True*. Check Disk is the GUI alternative to **chkdsk**.

You can access this tool from Windows Explorer in Windows 7. Right-click the disk, and select Properties. Select the Tools tab, and click Check Now. You can select Automatically Fix File System Errors, which works the same as **chkdsk /f**, or Scan For And Attempt Recovery of Bad Sectors, which works the same as **chkdsk /r**.

True or false? The System Restore tool is primarily used to restore previous versions of data files for users.

Answer: *False*. System Restore is used to undo system changes, but it does not undo changes to data files.

System Restore is a Windows feature that allows you to restore your system to a previous state. For example, if you installed an application or an update and find that the change is causing problems with your system, you can use System Restore to undo the changes. You undo changes by applying a previously created restore point. When System Restore is enabled, restore points are automatically created prior to system events such as installing an application or an update.

System Protection is available in Windows Vista and Windows 7. System Protection includes both System Restore and Previous Versions. When Previous Versions is enabled on a disk, it automatically creates copies of previous versions of files that can be restored by the user.

True or false? Windows Vista and Windows 7 include tools to back up an image of the entire computer, including the operating system, applications, and all data.

Answer: *True*. These are referred to as full image backups. The capability is not available in Windows XP.

> **EXAM TIP** Preventative maintenance tools include backup applications, System Restore, the Disk Defragmenter, the **defrag** command prompt tool, Check Disk, and the **chkdsk** command prompt tool.

Can you answer these questions?

You can find the answers to these questions at the end of this chapter.

1. What does patch management entail?
2. What type of backup will back up only target data that has changed since the last full backup?
3. What two tools are available to defragment a hard drive?

Objective 1.8: Explain the differences among basic OS security settings

Security is an important concern with any computer today, and PC technicians need to understand basic operating system security settings. This section covers some common users and groups used in Windows-based systems, with a focus on what type of user accounts should be used in different situations. It also covers NTFS and share permissions, along with topics on shared and system files and folders. User authentication is included in this objective, with a focus on single sign-on capabilities.

Exam need to know...

- Users and groups
  For example: What type of account should a regular user be given?
- Shared files and folders
  For example: What is an administrative share?
- NTFS vs. share permissions
  For example: When do share permissions apply to a user? When do share permissions not apply to a user?
- System files and folders
  For example: What is the system partition? What is the boot partition?
- User authentication
  For example: What is single sign-on?

User and groups

Windows systems have several default users and groups. These different users and groups have varied levels of privileges granted to them, and it's important to understand the differences.

True or false? Users in the Power Users group are granted privileges to install applications on Windows XP.

Answer: *False.* Users in the Power Users group in Windows XP cannot install applications. Users in the Administrators group can install applications.

The Power Users group is a step below Administrators group. Users in this group can install printers or add drivers in Windows XP. This group is included for backward compatibility in Windows Vista and Windows 7, but Microsoft recommends not using it in these operating systems.

True or false? Most users should be given a standard user account.

Answer: *True.* A standard user account gives users appropriate access for most purposes.

Users with a standard user account do not have permissions to make most system changes or install applications. This helps maintain the integrity of the system and also prevents the user from being tricked into installing malware.

MORE INFO Chapter 7, "Security," discusses the principle of least privilege, where users should be given only the access they need. Giving users an administrative account instead of a standard user account violates this principle.

The following types of accounts are used on Windows-based systems:

- **Administrator** The Administrator account has full privileges on a system. Use of this account should be restricted to personnel who need this level of access. When you add any user account into the Administrators group, it grants that account full administrative privileges.

- **Power user** A power user account is an account that has been placed into the Power Users group. It has more privileges than a standard user account and can install printers and drivers, but it doesn't have as many privileges as an Administrator account.

- **Standard user** Most user accounts are standard user accounts. They have enough permissions to operate a system but not make any changes.

- **Guest** This account has the least amount of privileges. The Guest account is disabled by default. It can be enabled to grant someone limited access to a system without creating a new account. The Guest account is in the Guests group.

EXAM TIP Administrators are granted the most privileges, and this account should be used sparingly. A power user account grants the user fewer privileges than an Administrator account but more than a standard user account. A standard user account is appropriate for most users, and if you want to prevent users from installing applications, you should use a standard user account. The Guest account has the least amount of privileges and is disabled by default.

MORE INFO User Account Control was introduced in Windows Vista and is used in Windows 7. It allows users with administrative privileges to do most of their work as a standard user. When administrative privileges are needed, the user is prompted by UAC to approve the action. Chapter 25 of the CompTIA A+ Training Kit (Exam 220-801 and Exam 220-802), ISBN-10: 0735662681, explains UAC and access tokens in greater depth.

Shared files and folders

You share files and folders on a networked computer by creating a share. A share is simply a folder that has been shared. All files and folders within the share are accessible to any user who can access the share.

True or false? The C volume is automatically shared on Windows as C$.

Answer: *True*. This is one of the administrative shares created by default, and it allows administrators to connect to a user's C drive remotely.

Several administrative shares are created by default on Windows-based systems. These can be used by administrators to access files and folders on the user's system remotely. They are appended with a dollar sign ($), which hides them. Some common administrative shares include the following:

- **Volumes**   Each volume (or partition) is shared with the drive name and a dollar sign, such as C$, D$, and so on.
- **Admin$**   This is the Windows folder, which is C:\Windows by default.
- **Print$**   This is the location where print drivers are stored. It points to the \Windows\System32\Spool\Drivers folder.

True or false? Permissions assigned to a folder are automatically inherited by all files in the folder.

Answer: *True*. Permissions propagate from the parent folder to the child files and folders. This is also known as permission inheritance.

It is possible to disable permission inheritance on folders, although it is generally discouraged. Permission inheritance makes it easy to manage permissions, but when it is disabled, managing permissions becomes much more difficult and complex.

> **EXAM TIP**   Administrative shares are automatically created on Windows-based systems and are appended with a dollar sign to hide them. Any folder can be shared on a computer, with or without the dollar sign. If a share is created with the dollar sign, it is hidden from casual users but can still be accessed if the full UNC path name is known.

NTFS vs. share permissions

One of the primary benefits of NTFS is the security features, including the ability to assign permissions to files and folders. NTFS permissions apply to users if they access files on a local system and also if they access files over a network.

The basic types of NTFS permissions are as follows:

- **Read**   Users can open files and read the contents. This does not give permission to save changes to a file.
- **Write**   Write allows a user to modify the contents of a file. It is normally assigned with the Read permission.
- **Read & Execute**   Programs require a user to have this permission to run an executable file. It is not needed for typical documents opened by a user.
- **Modify**   This is similar to Read, Write, and Read & Execute, with a significant addition. Users can also delete files.
- **Full Control**   Full Control allows the user to do anything and everything to the file. This includes the ability to take ownership of files and change permissions on the files.

Permissions can be assigned either directly to user accounts or to groups of which users are members. If more than one permission is assigned to a user, directly or via group membership, they accumulate and all permissions apply.

For example, if a user is directly assigned Read permission and is a member of the Administrators group, which is assigned Full Control, the user has a combination of both Read and Full Control. In this example, Full Control includes Read, so you could say that the effective NTFS permission is Full Control. However, the important point here is that if you allow one permission, it doesn't cancel another allowed permission.

True or false? If you assign Deny Full Control NTFS permissions to a folder and assign Allow Full Control permissions to specific files in the folder for a specific user, the user will be able to access the files.

Answer: *False*. Deny takes precedence over Allow, and the Deny permission assigned to the folder is inherited by all files in the folder.

If a user cannot access a folder and needs this access for job purposes, the appropriate step is to give the user the appropriate permissions. If the user still cannot access the files, you should check to see whether the user has been denied access.

> **EXAM TIP** NTFS permissions are cumulative when multiple permissions are assigned to a user. However, if a user is ever assigned a Deny permission in addition to an Allow permission, Deny takes precedence.

Share permissions are assigned to folders that are shared on a computer. Share permissions apply to a user only when the user accesses the share over a network. They do not apply if the user accesses the folder on the local computer. Also, if the share is located on an NTFS drive, both the share and the NTFS permissions apply.

The basic types of share permissions are as follows:

- **Read**   This is the default permission when a share is created.
- **Change**   This is similar to the NTFS Modify permission. It allows users to read and modify files.
- **Full Control**   This is the same as the NTFS Full Control permission. Users with full control permission can do anything with files within the share.

Just as NTFS permissions are cumulative, share permissions are also cumulative. For example, if a user is assigned Read permission directly and assigned Change permission as a member of a group, the user has both Read and Change permissions. In this example, Change includes Read, so you could say that the resulting share permission for the user is Change. However, the important point is that if you allow one permission it doesn't cancel another allowed permission. This works the same way for both NTFS and share permissions, with the only exception related to Deny. If a user is assigned both Allow and Deny for the same share permission, Deny takes precedence.

The cumulative NTFS permissions are not combined with the cumulative share permissions. Instead, the user is granted only the least restrictive permission between the accumulated NTFS permission and accumulated share permission.

For example, imagine that a user is granted Full Control NTFS permissions and Change share permissions. What is the user's permission when accessing the share over the network? Because Change permission is more restrictive than Full Control, the user's permission is limited to Change.

You can simplify this into the following three steps:

1. Determine the cumulative NTFS permissions, such as Full Control in the previous example.
2. Determine the cumulative share permissions, such as Change in the previous example.
3. Determine which one of these two is the most restrictive. In the previous example, Change is more restrictive than Full Control, so the user is granted Change permission to the share.

NOTE There is a potential for share and NTFS permissions to become confusing and difficult to manage. Many administrators simply assign Full Control share permission to the Everyone or Authenticated Users group for all the shares they create. They then control access by modifying NTFS permissions. This is effective because the NTFS permissions apply regardless of whether the files are accessed locally or over the network.

True or false? If a user can modify a file locally but cannot modify the file when accessing it via a share, the most likely problem is related to share permissions.

Answer: *True*. Share permissions don't apply locally but do apply when a user accesses the file via the network share.

EXAM TIP Share permissions apply only when the shared resource is accessed over the network. The default permission when creating a share is Read, and if this isn't changed, the user can read the file but will not be able to save any changes.

As another example, consider this scenario. Sally has files in the C:\Data folder on a system called Win7. She can modify these files when she is logged on to the Win7 computer. This indicates that she has the appropriate NTFS permissions. The folder is shared as Data, and Sally can connect to the folder by using the \\Win7\Data UNC path name from another computer. However, when she connects to the share, she can view the files but she can't save any changes to the files in the share. This indicates that she has Read share permission for the share, and Read permission isn't enough to modify the files.

Therefore, Sally's cumulative NTFS permissions are Read and Write. Her cumulative share permission is only Read. Read gives her the least access and is the permission that is applied.

EXAM TIP NTFS permissions are cumulative, and share permissions are cumulative. Cumulative permissions are sometimes referred to as the least restrictive permissions. When a user accesses a share over the network, the user is granted only the most restrictive permissions. This might be the cumulative NTFS permissions if they are more restrictive than the cumulative share permissions. It could also be the cumulative share permissions if they are more restrictive than the cumulative NTFS permissions.

True or false? The original directly assigned permissions for a file stay the same when a file is moved to a different location on the same volume.

Answer: *True.* When a file is moved on the same volume the permissions stay the same.

Any other instance of moving or copying a file causes the file to inherit the permissions of the folder where it is moved, as follows:

- Copying the file to a different location on the same volume.
- Copying the file to a different volume.
- Moving the file to a different volume.

EXAM TIP Directly assigned permissions for a file remain unchanged when a file is moved on the same volume. If the file is moved to a different volume or if the file is copied anywhere, it will inherit the permissions from the new location.

System files and folders

Windows operating systems have several system files and folders that are rarely manipulated directly. As a PC technician, you should be familiar with these files and folders and their locations.

True or false? The boot partition is the location where the Windows files are located.

Answer: *True.* The boot partition is the partition that includes the operating system, which is typically C:\Windows. The system partition is the partition that has the boot files used to start the computer. It is typically the C drive.

Table 6-10 lists some common files and their default locations on Windows-based systems.

TABLE 6-10 Common file locations

	DEFAULT LOCATION	COMMENTS
Root drive	C:\	Also called system partition.
Windows files	C:\Windows	The drive holding this folder is the boot partition.
System files	C:\Windows\System32	Includes Windows system files.
Temporary files	C:\Windows\Temp	Used by operating system for temporary file storage.
Offline files	C:\Windows\CSC	Also called Client Side Cache.
Fonts	C:\Windows\Fonts	Font files used for different typefaces.
Program files	C:\Program Files	Includes application files.

EXAM TIP The boot partition is the drive holding the \Windows folder (typically C:\Windows). The system partition is the drive holding the boot files and is typically C.

User authentication

User authentication is the process of a user claiming an identity and then proving it. For example, a user commonly claims an identity with a user name and then proves the identity with a password. When the user enters the proper password, the user is authenticated.

Authentication uses one more factor of authentication. The three primary factors of authentication are as follows:

- Something you know, such as a password.
- Something you have, such as a badge or a smart card.
- Something you are, proven with biometrics such as a fingerprint.

It is also possible to use multifactor authentication by using two or more of these factors. For example, a user might be required to enter a password (from the something-you-know factor) and also use a fingerprint reader (from the something-you-are factor).

True or false? A network configured as a workgroup with ten computers uses single sign-on.

Answer: *False.* Single sign-on technologies allow users to log on once and access multiple systems without authenticating again, but a workgroup requires users to have separate accounts for each computer.

A domain uses a central server and centralized accounts and provides single sign-on capabilities. Users can log on once and access multiple network resources without authenticating again.

> **EXAM TIP** A domain provides centralized authentication and single sign-on capabilities. A workgroup does not provide single sign-on capabilities.

Can you answer these questions?

You can find the answers to these questions at the end of this chapter.

1. On a Windows 7–based system, what type of account should you use for a regular user who should not install applications?
2. If permissions are configured to allow a user full access to a file and also configured to deny full access to the file, what is the effect for this user?
3. What is single sign-on?

Objective 1.9: Explain the basics of client-side virtualization

Client side virtualization refers to using virtualization capabilities on a client system. For example, Windows Virtual PC allows users to run multiple operating systems while booted into Windows 7. You should understand common reasons why virtual machines are used and the requirements to create and use them.

Exam need to know...

- Purpose of virtual machines
  For example: What are common reasons why people use virtual machines on client systems?

- Resource and network requirements
  For example: What are the most important hardware requirements when considering client-side virtualization?

- Hypervisor and emulator requirements
  For example: How does AMD indicate that a processor supports HAV?

- Security requirements
  For example: Do guest operating systems need updates if the host is kept up to date?

Purpose of virtual machines

A virtual machine (VM) is an instance of an operating system that runs within another operating system. There are many different types of virtualization software, including Windows Virtual PC, which runs on Windows-based systems and is available for free.

When using VMs, the computer running the virtualization software is known as the host. The VMs running within the host are known as guests. A single host can run multiple guests as long as the host has enough hardware to support them.

True or false? You can use a VM to run older applications that aren't compatible with the current operating system.

Answer: *True.* One of the reasons to use a VM is to run legacy applications.

For example, you can use Windows XP Mode in Windows 7 to run applications that will run in Windows XP but will not run in Windows 7.

True or false? A benefit of using VMs on a PC is that it reduces the amount of physical hardware required.

Answer: *True.* You can run multiple operating systems on one single computer. The single PC might need more CPU power and RAM, but it won't need a completely separate PC case, power supply, motherboard, and so on.

In contrast, if you wanted to run an instance of Windows XP and Windows 7 at the same time without virtualization, you'd need two separate computers.

Some other reasons to use virtualization include the following:

- **Learning** You can install operating systems and applications in a VM and then experiment with them to learn. Even if you make mistakes in the VM, your actions affect only the VM.

- **Testing** You can test new operating systems, new applications, and updates in a VM. If there are any problems, they affect only the VM.

Resource and network requirements

When considering the use of VMs, you'll need to ensure that your computer supports the hardware requirements. Most CPUs include hardware assisted virtualization (HAV) features, so this is rarely a problem today. However, you might need to enable virtualization in the BIOS.

True or false? The primary hardware consideration when using VMs is ensuring that you have enough CPU power and RAM.

Answer: *True.* Each VM needs enough memory to meet the operating system minimum requirements, and the system needs enough overall CPU power to run the host and guests.

RAM needed by the VM is in addition to the minimum amount of RAM needed for the core operating system. For example, you need a minimum of 2 GB of RAM for Windows 7 Ultimate (64-bit). If you wanted to run two VMs running the 64-bit edition of Windows 7 Ultimate in each, you'll need at least 2 GB for each of them, requiring a total minimum of 6 GB of RAM. Of course, each operating system will operate faster with more RAM.

Windows Virtual PC supports 32-bit VMs, but you cannot run 64-bit VMs using Windows Virtual PC. Other virtualization products such as Oracle's Virtual Box or VMware's free VM Player support 64-bit VMs. Also, Windows 8 includes Hyper-V in the Windows 8 Pro and Windows 8 Enterprise editions, and Hyper-V supports 64-bit VMs.

True or false? Network bandwidth and speed is an important consideration if you plan on allowing the VMs to access the physical network.

Answer: *True*. If you plan on allowing the VMs to access the network, they will share the NIC used by the host computer.

When running client-side VMs, this is rarely a problem. However, when a single physical host server is used to host multiple guest VMs, with each guest running a server operating system, the network usage can increase significantly. In these cases, high speed NICs and/or multiple NICs are used on the host system.

NOTE Most virtualization software includes options allowing you to choose how VMs are connected. These options often use a virtual switch. You can configure the virtual switch so that the VMs can communicate with each other as if they are connected in a network. You can configure it so that each VM is completely isolated from any other, without any type of connectivity. You can also configure connectivity so that VMs share the host's physical NIC and can access network resources just like the host system.

EXAM TIP RAM and CPU are the two most important resource requirements for a virtual host. You need 64-bit versions of Windows to be able to access more than 4 GB of RAM, so if multiple VMs will be used at the same time, you need a 64-bit version of Windows and plenty of RAM to support the VMs. If a single server is used to host multiple guest server operating systems, network bandwidth should also be addressed.

Hypervisor and emulator requirements

The software running on the physical host is called the hypervisor. It provides access to the host hardware and ensures that the VM runs in its own space without affecting other VMs or the host system. It also allows each VM to emulate the behavior of a physical system.

True or false? An AMD processor that supports HAV is annotated as VT-x.

Answer: *False*. Intel uses VT-x to indicate that a CPU supports HAV. AMD uses AMD-V to indicate that it supports HAV.

You need to enable virtualization in the BIOS with systems using an Intel CPU processor. This is often enabled without any BIOS settings on systems using an AMD processor.

EXAM TIP The hypervisor is the software that runs the virtualization software. The hypervisor software runs on the host system and ensures that each guest does not interfere with other guests.

Security requirements

The security requirements of an individual guest machine do not differ from the security requirements of a physical system. That is, you use the same security requirements to protect guest systems as you would use for the host.

True or false? When you install updates on a host system, these updates are automatically applied to the guest VMs.

Answer: *False.* Updates need to be applied individually to each guest VM just as if the VMs were physical systems.

A common mistake people make is that they do not keep the guest VMs up to date, but it is as important to keep guests VMs up to date as it is for the host. This includes keeping the operating system, applications, and antivirus software up to date.

EXAM TIP VMs should be kept up to date. This includes keeping the operating system, applications, and any antivirus software up to date.

MORE INFO Chapter 7, "Security," of this book includes some common security practices in Objective 2.3, "Implement security best practices to secure a workstation." These same practices should be applied to any workstation created as a VM.

Can you answer these questions?

You can find the answers to these questions at the end of this chapter.

1. What are common reasons people use client-side virtualization?
2. Which Windows 7 editions support Windows XP Mode?
3. A user plans on running at least four Windows 7 VMs in a virtual environment for testing and learning purposes. What is the most important operating system requirement, and what are the most important hardware requirements?

Answers

This section contains the answers to the "Can you answer these questions?" sections in this chapter.

Objective 1.1: Compare and contrast the features and requirements of various Microsoft Operating Systems

1. BitLocker Drive Encryption is included in Windows 7 Enterprise and Windows 7 Ultimate editions.
2. The 64-bit editions of Windows 7 (including Windows 7 Home Premium) will support more than 4 GB of RAM, and Windows 7 Home Premium 64-bit supports up to 16 GB of RAM.
3. Only Windows 7 systems can join a homegroup. Windows 7 Starter and Windows 7 Home Basic editions can join an existing homegroup, but they cannot create a homegroup.

Objective 1.2: Given a scenario, install and configure the operating system using the most appropriate method

1. Both FAT32 and NTFS support a maximum of four primary partitions on basic disks. If the disk is converted from a basic disk to a dynamic disk, you can create more than four partitions.

2. The **sysprep** program is run on a computer immediately before capturing the image. It removes unique information, such as the SID.

3. PXE-enabled computers can boot via the BIOS and a NIC. If an imaging server is available on the network, the PXE client can download an image from the server with minimal user interaction.

4. A quick format does not check the integrity of the disk. A full format checks the disk for faulty sectors and marks them as bad.

Objective 1.3: Given a scenario, use appropriate command line tools

1. The **-a** switch is used to resolve an IP address to a host name. This might not work if DNS is not configured to do reverse lookups.

2. The **netstat** command can be used to view open TCP and UDP ports on a computer.

3. The **chkdsk** command is used to check the integrity of a disk. It can identify faulty sectors, mark them as bad, and recover readable information from the disk.

4. The **fixboot** command is available in the recovery console in Windows XP and will repair a faulty boot sector.

5. The **bootrec /fixboot** command is used in the Windows RE in Windows 7 to repair faulty boot sectors.

Objective 1.4: Given a scenario, use appropriate operating system features and tools

1. The System Configuration (**msconfig**) tool can be used to modify which applications start when a user logs on. It can also be used to modify which services start when Windows starts.

2. When the overall performance of a system is degraded, it is typically due to a performance bottleneck from one component, and the Task Manager is one of the first tools you'd use to identify it. The Performance Monitor tool can also be used for advanced problems.

3. The **gpedit.msc** command is used to start the Group Policy editor.

Objective 1.5: Given a scenario, use Control Panel utilities (the items are organized by "classic view/large icons" in Windows)

1. The Folder Options applet is used to modify Windows Explorer settings. It can be used to modify the view to show file extensions.
2. The System applet is used to modify virtual memory. You can access Virtual Memory from the Advanced tab of the System Properties menu in Windows systems.
3. The Programs And Features applet is used in Windows 7 to remove applets.

Objective 1.6 Set up and configure Windows networking on a client/desktop

1. A UNC path has the format of \\servername\sharename.
2. The **net use** command is used to map drives to a UNC path. You can also map drives with Windows Explorer.
3. Remote desktop uses port 3389 by default, so this port should be open on firewalls to allow remote desktop connections.
4. The Home Network location should be selected when a user connects to a network at home.

Objective 1.7: Perform preventive maintenance procedures using appropriate tools

1. Patch management is the process of ensuring that systems are kept up to date. This includes Windows updates, application updates, and antivirus signature updates.
2. Differential backups will back up target data that has changed since the last full backup.
3. The Disk Defragmenter GUI and defrag command prompt tool can both be used to defragment hard drives.

Objective 1.8: Explain the differences among basic OS security settings

1. You should use a standard user account on Windows 7 if you do not want the user to install applications. A power user account is not recommended on Windows 7, and an administrator account allows users to install applications.
2. Deny takes precedence when both Allow and Deny permissions are assigned.
3. Single sign-on is an authentication strategy that allows a user to access multiple resources after signing on once. Domain environments with a domain controller support single sign-on, allowing users to access multiple resources after signing on once.

Objective 1.9: Explain the basics of client-side virtualization

1. Some common reasons why people use client-side virtualization are to run legacy applications and to test and learn new operating systems and applications.

2. Windows 7 Professional, Ultimate, and Enterprise editions support Windows XP Mode.

3. The operating system must be a 64-bit version, and the computer must include more than 4 GB of RAM. If a user plans on running four or more Windows 7–based VMs, these VMs require a minimum of 1 GB each for a total of 4 GB. This is in addition to the RAM required for the host. If a 32-bit version is used, it is unable to use more than 4 GB of RAM.

CHAPTER 7

Security

The Security domain covers approximately 22 percent of the A+ 220-802 exam. As a PC technician, you're expected to be aware of common prevention methods used to protect IT resources against security threats. This objective includes security best practices to secure a workstation and proper methods of destroying or disposing of resources in such a way that unauthorized individuals cannot access them. You're also expected to know how to secure both wireless and wired networks used in small offices and home offices.

This chapter covers the following objectives:

- Objective 2.1: Apply and use common prevention methods
- Objective 2.2: Compare and contrast common security threats
- Objective 2.3: Implement security best practices to secure a workstation
- Objective 2.4: Given a scenario, use the appropriate data destruction /disposal method
- Objective 2.5: Given a scenario, secure a SOHO wireless network
- Objective 2.6: Given a scenario, secure a SOHO wired network

Objective 2.1: Apply and use common prevention methods

Organizations commonly implement security in multiple areas as part of a defense-in-depth solution to protect IT resources. For example, they use physical security methods such as locks to restrict access to secure areas. They combine this with digital security methods such as antivirus software and firewalls to protect resources on a network. Users are educated about the need for the security methods and their responsibilities to help maintain security.

Exam need to know...

- Physical security
  For example: What is tailgating? What are some common methods used to restrict physical access?

- Digital security
  For example: What periodic maintenance is required with antivirus software?
- User education
  For example: What is a benefit of user education?
- Principle of least privilege
  For example: What type of account should regular users have?

Physical security

Physical security includes any security components that you can touch. Most physical security methods are used to restrict access to specific areas, but it is also possible to use physical security methods to restrict access to a computer system. For example, a locked door to a server room restricts access to the server room, and a fingerprint reader on a laptop can restrict access to the laptop's operating system.

True or false? Badges and locked doors are examples of physical security.

Answer: *True.* Physical security includes any security components that you can touch such as a lock on door or badges that users wear for identification.

Cipher locks are often used with locked doors. Instead of using a physical key, users are required to enter a code into the cipher lock to unlock it. Some door locks use radio frequency identification (RFID) or proximity readers. Users can unlock a door by waving their badge in front of the RFID or proximity card reader.

> **NOTE** Most IT security programs are focused on three core security goals—confidentiality, integrity, and availability. The goal of confidentiality is to ensure that unauthorized individuals do not have access to data or systems. The goal of integrity is to ensure that unauthorized individuals are unable to modify or delete data or change system configurations. The goal of availability is to ensure that systems and data are available to authorized individuals when needed. Defense-in-depth solutions combine multiple types of security methods to support these goals, and it's common for some physical security methods to be combined with digital security systems.

> **EXAM TIP** A basic physical security practice is to lock doors to prevent unauthorized access. Cipher locks require users to enter a code to unlock the door. Some electronic locks require users to wave a badge in front of a reader to open the door.

True or false? Man traps are used to prevent tailgating.

Answer: *True.* Man traps and turnstiles are effective methods of preventing tailgating.

Tailgating is the practice of a second person following closely behind someone else without using proper access procedures. For example, if one user opens a locked door after entering the proper code, the second person can follow right behind them without entering the code. A man trap or a turnstile ensures that only one person can pass through at a time. This requires each person to use proper access procedures.

Tailgating allows unauthorized individuals into a secured area. Man traps and turnstiles are effective preventive measures against tailgating. It is also useful to educate users about the social engineering practice of tailgating and encourage them to prevent anyone from following behind them.

True or false? A fingerprint reader can be used to track access into a secured area.

Answer: *True.* Any biometric authentication device, including a fingerprint reader, can be used for authentication and to track access into a room.

For example, a fingerprint reader can be used for access to a server room. Users might be required to place their finger into the reader each time they want to enter the room. The door opens after the user is authenticated. In addition to authenticating the user, the system can also record when the user authenticated, logging when the user entered the server room.

Biometric authentication devices have two phases. In the first phase, users are registered with the system. For example, each user's fingerprints are captured and associated with the respective user's identity. In the second phase, users are able to authenticate using their biometric information. For example, users can place their fingers in a fingerprint reader. If the system recognizes them, they are authenticated.

True or false? Biometrics can be used to restrict who can use a computer.

Answer: *True.* Many laptops include fingerprint readers, and only users with previously registered fingerprints can use the laptop.

Multiple biometric methods are available to verify user identity and authenticate the user. Another example is a retinal scanner, which scans the retina of the user's eye.

EXAM TIP Biometric methods of authentication such as fingerprint readers and retinal scans can be used for physical security. In addition to authenticating the user, they can also be combined with security logs to record when a user enters a secure area.

True or false? Key fobs and RSA tokens can be used for authentication.

Answer: *True.* These are small handheld devices that display a number that changes every 60 seconds. Each number displayed is generated by a complex algorithm known to the authentication server. Users must correctly enter the number currently displayed to prove that they have the device. They are generically known as *key fobs* or *tokens*, and they can usually be attached to a key chain. RSA is one company that sells them.

Figure 7-1 shows a common way that a key fob is used to authenticate over the Internet. The key fob is synchronized with a server, so at any given time, the server knows what number is displayed on the key fob. A user authenticates by entering a user name, password, and the number currently displayed on the key fob.

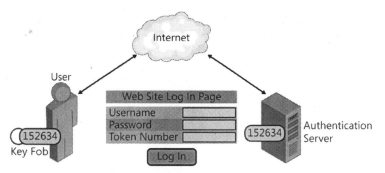

FIGURE 7-1 Using a key fob to authenticate.

MORE INFO Chapter 6, "Operating systems," describes the following three factors of authentication: something you know, something you have, and something you are. Passwords or cipher lock combos are in the something-you-know factor. Key fobs and RSA tokens are in the something-you-have factor. Biometrics methods are in the something-you-are factor.

Other elements of physical security include educating users about protecting physical documents, not writing down passwords, and shredding documents. Valuable documents can be secured by locking them in a safe. Shredding documents instead of throwing them away prevents "dumpster diving" attacks.

Digital security

Digital security includes all of the electronic or digital methods used to secure a computer system or network. Some basic digital security components include antivirus software and firewalls to protect against different types of attacks.

True or false? Antivirus signature definition files should be updated regularly.

Answer: *True*. Antivirus software uses signature definition files to identify viruses and other malicious software (malware). As new malware appears, the antivirus vendors update their signature definition files, and these updates need to be downloaded and installed on user systems.

Antivirus software often provides protection against all types of malware, including spyware. However, dedicated antispyware software is available that focuses only on spyware. Both antivirus and antispyware software need to be kept up-to-date.

MORE INFO Microsoft Security Essentials protects against malware, including viruses and spyware. It is available for free for home users and small businesses with up to 10 PCs. You can read about it and download a free copy from here: *http:// windows.microsoft.com/mse.*

True or false? Firewalls should be implemented on a network but are not needed on individual systems.

Answer: *False.* As part of a defense-in-depth solution, both host-based firewalls and network-based firewalls are used.

Network-based firewalls help protect the network from attacks, and host-based firewalls help protect individual systems. While most attacks come through the Internet and can be thwarted by a network firewall, other attacks can be launched from within a network. For example, if someone unknowingly brings a virus on a USB device, they can release the virus inside the network.

True or false? All users should be required to authenticate with the same user account.

Answer: *False.* Users should be required to authenticate with individual unique accounts. If users logged in with the same account, they couldn't be identified.

Users are assigned unique user accounts that they use for their online identity. Users prove their identity by entering a password associated with this account or by using some other form of authentication. When passwords are used, users should be required to use strong passwords and to change their passwords regularly.

True or false? You can restrict access to files and folders by assigning permissions.

Answer: *True.* Permissions are granted to users and groups to give them specified degrees of access to files and folders.

On Microsoft systems, disk drives are formatted with the New Technology File System (NTFS). NTFS permissions are assigned to files and folders to grant users appropriate access.

It's worth noting that identification and authentication are required first before you can start assigning permissions. That is, all users must have unique accounts that they use when accessing a computer or network. If all users had the same account, you could grant or block access to this account to files and folders and it would apply to all users equally. Without separate accounts, you couldn't be selective about what access you granted.

> **EXAM TIP** Digital security includes multiple elements, including keeping up-to-date antivirus and antispyware software. Firewalls provide protection for networks and individual computers. Users authenticate with strong passwords and can be granted access to files and folders based on their proven identity.

> **MORE INFO** Strong passwords are covered in greater depth in Objective 2.3, "Implement security best practices to secure a workstation," later in this chapter.

User education

User education is one of the best methods an organization can use to prevent a wide variety of security problems. When users don't understand common risks to IT resources, they don't recognize the value of security practices and they don't follow them. In contrast, when users understand how security practices prevent attackers from succeeding, they are more likely to follow them.

True or false? Teaching users about phishing can prevent users from revealing their passwords.

Answer: *True*. Many users are unaware of how attackers use phishing emails to trick them into giving up information, but if they are informed, they are less likely to be tricked.

Educating users is effective against many attacks. Social engineering (covered in the next objective) is thwarted by simply educating users in techniques that attackers use. This includes educating users about in-person social engineering attacks as well as attacks over the phone and through email.

> **EXAM TIP** Users should be educated about the various risks and the common methods used to protect against those risks. For example, users who understand how attackers use tailgating to enter secure areas are less likely to allow unauthorized personnel to tailgate. In some cases, an organization might be able to educate users instead of adding a man trap or turnstile to prevent tailgating. All social engineering attacks are reduced through user training.

Principle of least privilege

The principle of least privilege states that users are granted only the rights and permissions needed to perform their jobs. This principle is typically applied to both physical and digital security. For example, a limited number of employees perform maintenance on servers located in a server room. Physical security is used to restrict physical access to these servers to a limited number of employees. Additionally, digital security is used to restrict who can access these servers either locally or over the network.

True or false? When creating accounts for users, it's best to give all users an account with administrative privileges.

Answer: *False*. It's best to give them only the access they need.

Most users do not need administrative privileges, and giving all users administrative access is a direct violation of the principle of least privilege. Instead, a standard user account is more appropriate for regular users.

For example, it would be appropriate to give children using a shared computer standard user accounts. They would be able to use the computer but wouldn't have access to modify settings for their siblings.

This principle helps prevent both malicious and accidental damage. For example, a user who doesn't have permissions to access a file cannot delete it, either purposely or accidentally.

EXAM TIP The principle of least privilege states that users are given access only to resources that they need to perform their jobs. This includes granting them only the permissions to files and folders they need, and granting them only the rights needed. This principle can be applied to both physical security and digital security.

MORE INFO Chapter 6 presents information about the different types of user accounts, such as an administrative account and a standard user account. Any user in the Administrators group is an administrative account.

Can you answer these questions?

You can find the answers to these questions at the end of this chapter.

1. How can an organization prevent tailgating?
2. What type of accounts should users have for routine file access?
3. What principle states that users should be given the minimum access they require?

Objective 2.2: Compare and contrast common security threats

Risk is defined as the likelihood that a threat will exploit a weakness or vulnerability. With this in mind, it's important to be aware of the common threats against IT resources. Some criminals simply try to trick people with social engineering tactics. Other criminals write different types of malicious software to infect computers. This objective covers common social engineering tactics and different types of malicious software.

Exam need to know...

- Social engineering
  For example: What is the best way to prevent social engineering?
- Malware
  For example: What is malware? What are some different types of malware?
- Rootkits
  For example: What is a rootkit? What type of access is granted through a rootkit?
- Phishing
  For example: What is phishing? What is commonly obtained through successful phishing attacks?
- Shoulder surfing
  For example: What is shoulder surfing? How can shoulder surfing be prevented?
- Spyware
  For example: What is spyware? What does spyware modify?

- Viruses

  For example: What is a Trojan? What is the difference between a virus and a worm?

Social engineering

Social engineering is the practice of tricking people into revealing sensitive information that they normally wouldn't share or into taking risky actions that they normally wouldn't take. If a criminal calls people on the phone and demands that they reveal their user names and passwords, most people won't comply. However, conniving criminals use a variety of different tactics to trick people into revealing sensitive information such as their user names and passwords.

True or false? Impersonation is a social engineering tactic where an attacker assumes the role of someone else, such as a repairman or pest exterminator.

Answer: *True*. Attackers often can try to gain access to organizations by wearing the uniform of a known company and claiming to be there for a service call.

Attackers often try to trick users with social engineering attacks over the phone. A common attack occurs from people claiming to be from technical support. For example, the "Microsoft Imposter" scam involves criminals pretending to be Microsoft employees who call and tell users that their computer is infected with malware. They then attempt to get the user to pay to clean their computer, or they try to convince the user to install software that gives the criminals remote access to their computer. In simpler cases, the criminal simply tries to trick the user into revealing a password or some other information.

> *EXAM TIP* Social engineering includes different types of trickery by an attacker. The attacker might try to impersonate a legitimate vendor or try to trick a user over the phone or in person. User education is the best protection against social engineering.

> *MORE INFO* The Microsoft Malware Protection Center is a great source of up-to-date information about current threats. You can access it here: *http://www.microsoft.com/Security/portal/.* The following link discusses various tech support phone scams and how you can avoid them: *http://www.microsoft.com/security/online-privacy/avoid-phone-scams.aspx.*

Malware

Malicious software (malware) is software that has a malicious or harmful intent. Malware comes in many different forms and has different purposes or goals. Some malware damages operating systems or data. Some malware provides criminals complete control over one or more computers from remote locations via the Internet. Some malware attempts to collect personal information without the user's knowledge and send this information to a criminal. When criminals have access to a user's computer or their personal information, they can steal the user's identity, damage the user's reputation, and steal money from the user's bank or financial accounts.

True or false? A virus is one type of malware.

Answer: *True.* Malware includes any type of malicious software, such as viruses, rootkits, spyware, Trojans, and worms.

> **EXAM TIP**   Malware is any type of malicious software. People often use the term *virus* to refer to any type of malware, but that isn't technically accurate. All viruses are malware, but malware includes many other types of malicious software.

> **MORE INFO**   The Microsoft Malware Protection Center portal includes a comprehensive glossary of different types of malware and other threats. You can access it here: *http://www.microsoft.com/security/portal/threat/encyclopedia/glossary.aspx.*

Rootkits

Rootkits are a special type of malware that gives an attacker root access (also known as administrative access) to a computer. When successfully installed, a rootkit is often able to hide itself from antivirus software.

True or false? A rootkit will always block Internet access.

Answer: *False.* Criminals often use rootkits to remotely control computers. Internet access is needed for the criminal to remotely control the computer, so it would be rare for a rootkit to block Internet access.

Most malware in use today attempts to stay hidden and active as long as possible. If a user's computer can no longer access the Internet, it becomes obvious to the user that something is wrong, and the user will either stop using the computer or aggressively pursue a solution.

In contrast, consider a rootkit that quietly collects users' personal information and forwards it to a criminal. The users won't be aware of the problem until their identity is stolen or their bank accounts are emptied. Even after the theft, the user might not realize it was due to a computer infection.

> **EXAM TIP**   Rootkits are difficult to detect and remove. In addition to taking over a user's computer, they often provide criminals with back doors to the user's computer for remote access. The best protection is up-to-date antivirus software to prevent the initial installation of a rootkit.

Phishing

Phishing emails are used to trick users into giving up sensitive information or clicking links that will take them to malicious websites. A common phishing email will attempt to get users to give up sensitive information, such as a user name and password. There are many variations on phishing attacks. They usually describe some type of problem and urge the user to take immediate action to resolve the problem. If the user responds, they are often tricked into revealing sensitive information.

True or false? An email from an unknown person from another country proposing a business partnership is typically a phishing attempt.

Answer: *True*. Criminals send out phishing emails in bulk to people they don't know, hoping to get someone to reply.

The classic Nigerian scam has taken many forms. The scammer typically sends out phishing emails describing how a huge sum of money is locked up in an account. The email requests assistance in releasing the money, and in return, the recipient is promised a substantial share of the fortune. If the recipient replies, they are tricked into paying more and more money but never get anything in return. In some cases, people are tricked into revealing their banking details, with the promise that money will be transferred to their accounts. Instead, money is transferred out of their accounts.

Another common phishing attempt informs users that their account has experienced suspicious activity. This can be a bank account, an email account, or any type of account that requires a user name and password. Users are informed that they need to verify their credentials or their account will be locked. The phishing email includes a link that looks like it will take them to a legitimate website. However, the link instead takes them to a malicious website that looks legitimate. If they enter their user name and password, the attacker now has their credentials.

In some cases, the email merely encourages the user to click a link or open an attachment. Attackers can manipulate websites so that they automatically download malware when the user visits, so if the user clicks the link, they can inadvertently infect their computer. Similarly, infected attachments will infect the user's computer if the user opens those attachments.

For example, attackers have been known to embed malicious code in an Adobe Portable Document Format (PDF) file and then label the file as an official legal summons. They sent the file as an attachment with a short introduction message about a lawsuit and prompted the reader to open the file for more information. When users opened the PDF file, the text indicated that it didn't apply to them, so they would usually close the file without giving it another thought. However, the damage was done. When they opened the file, it infected their computer and gave the attacker remote access to their computer.

> **EXAM TIP** Phishing is a security threat delivered through email that attempts to trick users into giving up information or clicking a malicious link.

> **MORE INFO** Wikipedia has a good article about the Nigerian scam and how it has morphed over the years. You can access it here: *http://en.wikipedia.org/wiki/ Nigerian_scam*.

Shoulder surfing

Shoulder surfing is the practice of one person looking over the shoulder of another person to get information. In some cases, the shoulder surfer attempts to read data on a display monitor. In other cases, the shoulder surfer attempts to watch what a user is typing. For example, if a user types a password slowly, a shoulder surfer can learn the password just by watching.

True or false? The best way to prevent other users from viewing the content on a user's screen is with a password-protected screensaver.

Answer: *False.* A privacy filter is an effective method of preventing shoulder surfing, where someone observes the contents of a display. A password-protected screensaver is an effective method of automatically locking the computer when the user walks away.

> **EXAM TIP** Social engineers use shoulder surfing to gather information through casual observation. It does not require any technical methods, such as using malicious code, to gather information. Privacy filters defend against shoulder surfing. A privacy filter is placed over a display monitor and restricts the viewing angle so that only the user directly in front of the monitor can view it.

Spyware

Spyware is software that installs itself on the user's system or modifies the user's system, without the user's knowledge or consent. It might change the way an application behaves or simply collect information and periodically send data to a criminal via the Internet.

True or false? A program that modifies the user's home page without the user's consent is spyware.

Answer: *True.* Some spyware changes web browser settings, such as the home page.

Spyware might also install browser add-ins, such as a different search engine or a toolbar helper. When this is installed without the user's consent, it is spyware. Legitimate software that makes these types of changes with the user's consent isn't spyware.

Some types of spyware include key loggers that can record key strokes and screen captures. For example, one known spyware program waits for a user to visit specific banking and financial websites. When the user visits the site, the spyware captures keystrokes to get the user name and password. It then sends this information to the criminal monitoring the spyware.

Cookies are text files that are written to user's systems when they visit websites. These track the activity of the user, and many websites use these to provide targeted ads. For example, if you do web searches with Google on Las Vegas hotels and then later visit unrelated webpages hosting Google ads, these ads might be for Las Vegas hotels.

Some people consider cookies spyware, and some antivirus software reports the existence of cookies on a system as spyware. However, it's difficult to surf the Internet without using cookies. Some people insist that cookies are just part of the web browsing experience and that as long as web developers don't misuse them, they are benign.

Viruses

A virus is malicious code embedded into an application. When the application is started, the malicious code is also executed. Viruses have a replication component that allows the virus to find and infect other files and systems.

True or false? Viruses are most commonly found in text files.

Answer: *False.* Viruses must be executed, so they need to be in a file that supports executing the code. Malicious code cannot run from within a text file.

Viruses are most often embedded in programs or applications. These file types commonly have .exe, .com, or .dll file extensions. Some file types support dynamic content. For example, it's possible to include useful code within a Microsoft Word document or an Adobe PDF file. Criminals can insert malicious code into these types of files, and the code executes when the user opens the file.

It's also possible for viruses to be installed in other locations. For example, a boot sector virus infects the boot sector and runs when the computer boots. Similarly, some viruses are installed on removable media such as optical discs or USB flash drives. These execute when the media is installed, if autorun capabilities have not been disabled.

True or false? A worm is a virus that must be executed by a user to run.

Answer: *False.* A worm does not need any user interaction.

Worms travel over the network infecting other systems without any user interaction. This is a primary distinguishing characteristic between a virus and a worm.

True or false? A Trojan is a program that appears to be doing something useful while it also installs malicious software.

Answer: *True.* A Trojan (or Trojan horse) is malware that appears to be doing something innocent or useful while it also is performing malicious actions.

A common way that Trojans are installed is with free downloads. Users are enticed to download a free game, utility, or other program. The download includes the free software, but it also includes a malicious payload. When users install the desired software, they also install the malicious component.

EXAM TIP Viruses are embedded in an executable program and run when the program is started. They require user interaction to run. Worms infect systems over a network and do not require any user interaction. Trojans appear to be something useful but also include a malicious payload.

Can you answer these questions?

You can find the answers to these questions at the end of this chapter.

1. A criminal tries to enter a building by impersonating a pest exterminator. What type of attack is this?

2. Malicious software has installed a back door on a computer, which grants an attacker full administrative access to the computer from a remote location. When antivirus software is run on the computer, the malicious software hides itself so that it is not detected. What type of malware is being described?

3. A user receives an email that is trying to trick him. What is this called?

4. What can be used to prevent unauthorized individuals from viewing information on a display monitor?

5. A user has installed an application on a computer. During this installation, malicious software was also installed. What is this called?

Objective 2.3: Implement security best practices to secure a workstation

There are several best practices you can implement to secure a workstation. A core requirement is to ensure that users are required to have a user account, that they use strong passwords, and that their systems are configured to automatically lock with a password-protected screensaver. You can then assign permissions to users to give them the access they need. Windows-based systems have preconfigured Administrator and Guest accounts. The Administrator name should be changed, and the Guest account should be disabled. You can also prevent malware infections by disabling the autorun feature on the workstation.

Exam need to know...

- Setting strong passwords
  For example: What are the elements of a strong password?
- Requiring passwords
  For example: What can be used to force users to create strong passwords?
- Restricting user permissions
  For example: What principle should be followed when assigning user permissions?

- Changing default user names
  For example: What account name should be changed to a different name on Windows-based systems?
- Disabling Guest account
  For example: What permissions are granted to the Guest account?
- Screensaver required password
  For example: What is a benefit of a screensaver requiring a password?
- Disable autorun
  For example: Why should autorun be disabled for USB drives?

Setting strong passwords

A strong password has sufficient complexity that it is difficult to guess. In contrast, simple passwords are very easy to guess. Users sometimes use simple passwords (such as *123456* or *password*) because they are easy to remember, but accounts protected by such weak passwords are easier for attackers to break into and compromise.

True or false? A strong password must be at least eight characters long and use at least one character type.

Answer: *False.* Strong passwords must use multiple character types.

A strong password typically includes at least three of the following four character types:

- Uppercase letters such as A, B, C, and so on.
- Lowercase letters such as a, b, c, and so on.
- Numbers from 0 through 9.
- Special characters such as !, @, #, and so on.

Strong passwords include at least eight characters. When multiple character types are used and the password is sufficiently long, it makes it much more difficult for an attacker to guess the password.

True or false? Users should authenticate themselves before they are allowed to change a password.

Answer: *True.* Users should prove their identity before they are allowed to change the password on an account.

If the user knows the current password, this provides authentication. However, if users have forgotten their password, an alternate form of authentication is required. For example, online systems often use a series of security questions, such as the name of the user's first dog, their mother's maiden name, and so on. Users register their answers to these questions after they create the account. If they've forgotten their password, they can authenticate by correctly answering these questions.

> **EXAM TIP** A strong password includes multiple character types and is at least eight characters long. Users should prove their identity through some type of authentication mechanism before they are permitted to change a password.

MORE INFO The Microsoft article "Create Strong Passwords" provides more detailed information about how to create strong passwords: *http://www.microsoft. com/security/online-privacy/passwords-create.aspx*. You can check the strength of a password on the following page: *https://www.microsoft.com/security/pc-security/ password-checker.aspx*.

Requiring passwords

Passwords should be required for all user accounts. If a password isn't used, anyone can log on to the account and impersonate the user's online identity. This includes accessing any of the user's data. In contrast, when passwords are used for each account, users can keep their data private.

True or false? You can force users to set strong complex passwords with the Local Security Policy or Group Policy.

Answer: *True.* You can configure a password policy to force users to create strong complex passwords.

Figure 7-2 shows a screen shot of the Password Policy settings from within the Local Security Policy tool on a Windows 7–based computer. The Password Policy settings are identical in Group Policy. The difference is that the Local Security Policy applies only to the local computer, while Group Policy is configured by a domain administrator and applies to multiple computers within a domain.

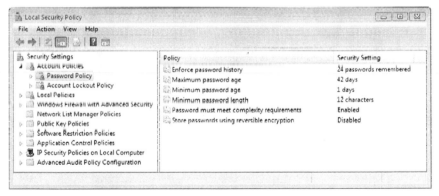

FIGURE 7-2 Password Policy settings in Local Security Policy.

Settings that make up a strong complex password include the following:

- **Enforce Password History** This requires users to use different passwords. In the settings shown in Figure 7-2, users cannot reuse a previous password until they have used 24 different passwords.

- **Maximum Password Age** This setting forces users to regularly change their password. The setting of 42 days shown in the figure requires users to change their password at least every 42 days.

- **Minimum Password Age**   This setting prevents users from changing their password right away. When used with the Enforce Password History setting, it helps prevent users from changing their password multiple times to get back to their original password.
- **Minimum Password Length**   This specifies the minimum number of characters used in a password.
- **Password Must Meet Complexity Requirements**   This includes several elements to ensure that the password is strong and complex. The user cannot create a password using the user's account name or full name. It also requires the password to include at least three of the four character types: uppercase letters, lowercase letters, numbers, and special characters.

The Store Passwords Using Reversible Encryption setting affects how the passwords are stored, not how a password is created. This setting should be disabled for best security.

True or false? When a password policy is set, users are prevented from creating a new password that doesn't meet the requirements.

Answer: *True*. This is the purpose of the password policy. It doesn't affect existing passwords, but when the user changes a password, the new password must meet the policy requirements.

If a user tries to create a password that doesn't meet the password policy, they will see an error message similar to this: "Password does not meet the complexity requirements." If the user's password has expired, they will not be able to log on to the system until they have created a password that meets the requirements.

> **NOTE**   Local Security Policy can be configured on any single computer. It can be started from the Administrative Tools section in the Control Panel. Within a domain, administrators use Group Policy to set the password policy for all computers in the domain. The Group Policy editor (started by typing **gpedit.msc** at the command prompt) includes the Password Policy in the Computer Configuration, Windows Settings, Security Settings, Account Policies node.

> **EXAM TIP**   You can use Local Security Policy or Group Policy to force users to create strong passwords and to change their passwords regularly.

Restricting user permissions

The principle of least privilege described earlier in this chapter states that users should have only the privileges they need to perform their jobs. With this in mind, users' access to files and folders are restricted by using permissions.

True or false? You can use the Local Security Policy to prevent users from shutting down a computer.

Answer: *True*. In addition to setting permissions on files and folders, you can restrict what users can do on a system, including preventing a user from shutting down or rebooting a computer.

The Local Security Policy includes a User Rights Assignment node that can be used to restrict what a user can do on a computer. The Shut Down The System setting is typically assigned to Administrators and regular users. However, if you have a computer that needs to stay on, you can take this ability away from regular users. For example, you might want to prevent someone from shutting down a computer if it is being used to share a printer or files used by other people on the network.

EXAM TIP Users should be restricted to only the privileges they need to comply with the principle of least privilege. This includes restricting their access to files and folders and restricting their ability to perform certain actions on some systems.

Changing default user names

As a security best practice, default user names should be changed. The reasoning is that if a default user name is not changed, it makes it easier for someone to guess the password and use the account.

True or false? The administrator account should be renamed to prevent unauthorized personnel from using it.

Answer: *True.* The administrator account is one of the primary accounts that should be renamed on any system.

If the administrator account name stays as administrator, an attacker can attempt to guess passwords for the account to use it. In contrast, if the administrator account is renamed to something like "Newadmin77", it's highly unlikely that an attacker will be able to guess the name of the account and the password.

EXAM TIP A security best practice is to change the default user names on any system. Administrator accounts on Windows-based systems should be changed to a name other than Administrator to comply with this best practice. Additionally, when any system ships with a default user name and password, the password should be changed as soon as possible.

Disabling the Guest account

The Guest account is a default account in Windows-based systems. It provides users with basic access to a system. It can be useful if you want to give someone temporary access to a system without creating a separate account and or giving them access to your account.

True or false? The Guest account has the least rights and permissions of any account.

Answer: *True.* The Guest account is the most restrictive when compared to other types of accounts on Windows-based systems.

The Guest account is in the Guests group by default and is granted only minimal rights and permissions. The Guest account is disabled by default in Windows-based systems. If you enable it, you should ensure that it is disabled when it is no longer needed.

Screensaver required password

Screensavers aren't needed anymore, but they are still commonly used. After a computer is idle for a period of time, a screensaver replaces the display with a slide show or some other random data that the user selects. Older-technology monitors were susceptible to screen burn-in if a screensaver wasn't used, but new monitors don't have this problem.

True or false? A password-protected screensaver can reduce the chances of unauthorized personnel using unattended computers.

Answer: *True*. When the screensaver is password-protected, unauthorized personnel cannot access the computer.

A password-protected screensaver requires a user to enter a password to access the computer after the screensaver activates. Users can also manually invoke this by locking their system. For example, users can press the Ctrl+Alt+Delete keys on Windows-based systems and select the option to lock the computer. When the password-protected screensaver is enabled, it will automatically lock the system. In either case, a user will have to enter a password to access the system again.

Many organizations implement security policies requiring the use of password-protected screensavers. These can be implemented locally or with Group Policy settings.

Disable autorun

Autorun is a feature on Windows-based systems that is designed to automatically run an application when a user inserts media. For example, when a user inserts a CD or DVD into a system, Windows looks for an autorun file. This is a text file that identifies the location of a file to run. A Windows installation DVD includes an autorun file that points to the Setup.exe file, which starts the installation program. That is, the installation program starts automatically when a user inserts the DVD.

True or false? The autorun feature should be disabled for all USB drives.

Answer: *True*. As a best practice, the autorun feature should be disabled for all USB drives to prevent the automatic installation of malware.

Legitimate software vendors often use the autorun feature to make it easy for users to install software. However, criminals have discovered this feature and modified it to automatically install malware when a user inserts the media.

The autorun feature is modified by configuring AutoPlay settings on Windows 7–based systems. AutoPlay is an applet in the Control Panel, and it can be used to modify the default action for different media.

EXAM TIP Autorun should be disabled on media by default to prevent the automatic installation of malware on systems. The autorun features are modified by manipulating AutoPlay settings.

MORE INFO Microsoft has released a Security Advisory (967940) discussing autorun that you can access here: *http://technet.microsoft.com/en-us/security/advisory/967940*.

Can you answer these questions?

You can find the answers to these questions at the end of this chapter.

1. What types of characters are used for a strong password?
2. What tool can be used to force users to create a strong password on a single Windows-based computer?
3. Which account has the least permission on a Windows 7–based computer?
4. What can be enabled to automatically lock a user computer after a short time?

Objective 2.4: Given a scenario, use the appropriate data destruction/disposal method

When systems reach the end of their life cycle they can be sold, given away, or thrown away. However, an important step when disposing of systems is ensuring that they do not have any usable data on them. For example, if a computer with sensitive information is thrown away, a dumpster diver could sift through trash in a dumpster, retrieve it, and use this information against the original owner. Systems are sanitized prior to disposal by removing all usable data or destroying the systems. PC technicians should understand the differences between a low-level format and a standard format, the different types of sanitization used for hard drives, and methods used to physically destroy a drive.

Exam need to know...

- Low-level format vs. standard format
  For example: What is written on a drive with a low-level format? Will a standard format remove data?

- Hard drive sanitation and sanitation methods
  For example: What are common methods used to sanitize a hard drive?
- Physical destruction
  For example: Name three methods used to destroy data.

Low-level format vs. standard format

Hard drives need to be formatted before they can be used by an operating system, and there are different types of formats that you should understand. The most common type of format performed by technicians is a standard format, which configures the hard drive with a specific file system such as NTFS used by Windows-based systems.

True or false? Formatting a hard drive will prevent access to any data on the hard drive.

Answer: *False.* Unformat programs are available that can recover data from a drive after it has been formatted.

While formatting a hard drive does make it difficult to retrieve data that was on the hard drive, it doesn't actually remove the data. Similarly, when you delete a file on a disk, it doesn't actually delete the file. Instead, the file is marked for deletion.

There are several tools available that can retrieve files that are still available on a formatted disk and files that have been marked for deletion. With this in mind, you shouldn't use a standard format or delete process to remove data. Instead, data should be removed with more advanced tools to completely remove all the data.

> **MORE INFO**   Chapter 6 of this book provides differences between a quick format and a full format. In the context of security, neither one is an acceptable method of adequately removing data from a hard drive. A quick format overwrites the file table used to locate the files, but the data can easily be retrieved with the right software tools. A full format overwrites some of the data as it checks file sectors but does not zero out the drive, and software tools can still retrieve files from the drive.

True or false? A low-level format will erase all data on a drive.

Answer: *True.* A low-level format writes bits over the entire drive, effectively erasing all data on the drive.

Many drive manufacturers provide utilities that you can use to perform a low-level format of their drive. These are available for free and are referred to as zero-fill utilities because they overwrite the entire hard drive with 0s. Additionally, there are many software programs that can be used to overwrite files to remove any remnants of the original data. These are sometimes referred to as file shredders because they effectively remove all readable data, similar to how a paper shredder can remove all readable information on paper.

NOTE Many years ago, the term *low-level format* referred to the initial formatting of a hard drive performed at the factory. Users or technicians then performed a standard format on the hard drive so that it could be used. In some cases, these older hard drives developed problems and technicians could perform a low-level format to restore the drive's usability. However, this type of low-level format is no longer required by technicians and can only be performed at the factory. Today, the term *low-level format* refers to a zero-fill utility, which writes 0s over the entire hard drive to sanitize it.

EXAM TIP A standard format does not erase data but instead prepares a hard drive with a file system. After a standard format is completed, usable data remains on the drive and can be retrieved with the right tools. A low-level format completely erases all usable data on the hard drive.

MORE INFO For more detailed information about how you can perform a low-level format on a Western Digital hard drive, check out the following page: *http://wdc.custhelp.com/app/answers/detail/a_id/1211*. It includes a link to download the Windows Data Lifeguard Diagnostics that can be used to perform a low-level format of a Western Digital hard drive.

Hard drive sanitation and sanitation methods

Within the context of IT security, sanitization refers to the process of removing all remnants of data. A hard drive that has been sanitized will not have any usable data on it. If a criminal found a sanitized hard drive, the criminal would not be able to retrieve any meaningful data from the drive.

True or false? Overwriting a disk drive with 1s and 0s can sanitize the drive.

Answer: *True*. Many programs are available that will write 1s and 0s throughout the drive, effectively removing any meaningful data from the drive.

These programs are also known as overwrite and drive wipe programs. Some overwrite programs will overwrite single files, and some will overwrite the entire hard drive. They can remove all remnants of the target data so that it cannot be recovered.

Most sanitization tools make several passes when overwriting the data. For example, a drive wipe program might first write all 0s onto the drive, then write all 1s onto the drive, and finish by writing a pattern of 1s and 0s. Many drive wipe programs also add an additional pass using an opposite pattern of 1s and 0s. For example, if it writes bytes using the pattern of 1010 1010, it would finish with a pattern of 0101 0101.

EXAM TIP Sanitizing a drive removes all remnants of data on a drive. Overwriting a drive with 1s and 0s is the most effective method of sanitizing it. Overwrite programs are available that are specifically designed to sanitize drives by using different patterns of 1s and 0s.

Physical destruction

An extreme sanitation method is the physical destruction of the media holding the data. When the media is destroyed, the data is no longer accessible.

True or false? Degaussing a hard drive will destroy the drive and remove access to all the data.

Answer: *True*. Degaussing is an effective method of destroying data on a hard drive, and it will also destroy the hard drive.

Hard drives and magnetic tapes store data by magnetizing ferromagnetic material on the media to represent individual bits. A degausser is a powerful magnet, and when it is used with hard drives and tapes, it changes these magnetic fields, effectively erasing the data.

When a tape is degaussed, it erases the data but the tape is still usable. However, degaussing a modern hard drive also destroys factory-embedded servo control data, making the drive unusable.

True or false? You can destroy a hard drive with an electrical drill.

Answer: *True*. Drilling holes into a hard disk drive platter will destroy the platter and make the data unreadable.

NOTE While drilling is listed as a method of destroying a hard disk drive in the CompTIA A+ objectives, it is rarely used as the only method of destruction by organizations with sensitive data. Instead, the drive would typically be sanitized first with a drive overwrite program and then destroyed.

True or false? Shredding papers is an effective method of preventing successful dumpster diving attacks.

Answer: *True*. Dumpster diving is the practice of going through trash to find valuable data on paper, and shredding prevents a dumpster diver from getting any useful information.

Paper can be shredded by using small office shredders or collected and turned over to a professional shredding company. Some companies, such as Iron Mountain (*http://www.ironmountain.com*), provide onsite shredding services where they bring a shredding truck to the customer's location. Many mobile shredding companies also have the ability to destroy media such as CDs, DVDs, and even physical hard drives.

Can you answer these questions?

You can find the answers to these questions at the end of this chapter.

1. What is the difference between a standard format and a low-level format?
2. What are common methods used to sanitize a hard drive?
3. What is the purpose of using a degausser on a hard drive?

Objective 2.5: Given a scenario, secure a SOHO wireless network

Wireless networks are very common in small offices and home offices (SOHOs). PC technicians are often asked to assist in configuring these networks and should ensure that they are configured with security in mind. Chapter 2, "Networking," of this book covers Objective 2 of the 220-801 exam. Objectives 2.5 and 2.6 cover the wireless standards, encryption types, and configuration information for wireless networks. You will probably notice that there is some crossover between those topics and this objective. This objective is focused more on securing the wireless networks than the basic configuration, but you do need to have an understanding of configuration settings for a wireless network.

Exam need to know...

- Change default user names and passwords
  For example: Why should default user names and passwords be changed as soon as possible?
- Changing SSID and disabling SSID broadcast
  For example: Why should you change the SSID? Why should you disable the SSID?
- Setting encryption
  For example: What is the best encryption to use for wireless networks?
- Enable MAC filtering
  For example: What does the MAC address look like? Why would you use MAC filtering in a wireless network?
- Antenna and access point placement
  For example: Where should you place an access point when the environment has other transmitting devices?
- Radio power levels
  For example: What is the effect of reducing power levels on usability of a wireless network?
- Assign static IP addresses
  For example: If you statically assign IP addresses, what else needs to be statically assigned?

Change default user names and passwords

Wireless routers are shipped with default user names and passwords. These are used by the new owner to access and modify the settings. For example, many Linksys routers come with a default administrator name of *Admin* and a default password of *admin*.

True or false? The default password should be changed as soon as possible when installing a new wireless router.

Answer: *True*. The password should be one of the first items that is changed when installing a wireless router.

Most routers host webpages that can be accessed using their factory-configured IP address. For example, many Linksys routers have an initial IP address of 192.168.1.1, and you can enter this IP address into a web browser to access the router's webpages. If the admin password is not changed, anyone who can access the webpage can log in and modify the wireless routers settings.

> **EXAM TIP** The password for the admin account should be changed as soon as possible for a wireless router. On systems that support changing the name of the administrator account, the name should also be changed.

> **MORE INFO** Default user names and passwords are easy to find by anyone who takes a little time to do so. For example, this site lists the common passwords for just about any wireless router: *http://www.routerpasswords.com/*.

Changing SSID and disabling SSID broadcast

The service set identifier (SSID) is the name of the wireless network. This is configured on a wireless router, and to connect to the network, users need to know the SSID.

True or false? The default SSID should not be changed on new wireless routers.

Answer: *False*. As a security best practice, the default SSID should be changed on new wireless routers. The goal with this security practice is to limit the information available to potential attackers.

Wireless routers typically ship with a default SSID assigned. This SSID often includes the name of the manufacturer and sometimes includes additional indicators to identify the model. When it isn't changed, an attacker can see it and know what type of router is in use. If this router has any known weaknesses or vulnerabilities, the attacker can easily exploit them.

In contrast, if the default SSID is changed, an attacker will not have any details on the router. Imagine these two SSIDs: linksys and MyWiFi. The first one is very likely a Linksys router while the second one can be any brand.

True or false? You can disable SSID broadcast to hide the wireless network from casual users.

Answer: *True*. Disabling SSID broadcast hides the wireless network from most users. They will need to know the SSID and enter it manually to connect to the network.

> **NOTE** Disabling SSID broadcast hides the wireless network from some users, but it isn't an effective method of hiding the wireless network from criminals. Criminals have tools that allow them to easily discover the SSID even when SSID broadcast is disabled.

> **EXAM TIP** The SSID should be changed from the default to prevent attackers from knowing what model it is. SSID broadcast is enabled by default, but this can be disabled to hide the wireless network from casual users.

> **MORE INFO** Chapter 2 of this book covers topics related to the SSID in Objective 2.6. Even though Chapter 2 is focused on the 220-801 exam, topics in that section cross over into this objective. Chapter 23 of the CompTIA A+ Training Kit (Exam 220-801 and Exam 220-802), ISBN-10: 0735662681, covers wireless networking in depth, including security concepts covered in this objective on the 220-802 exam.

Setting encryption

Wireless networks transmit data similarly to how a radio station transmits data. Anyone in range of the signal can receive it. Radio stations aren't encrypted, so you can tune in and listen to the transmissions whenever you want to. However, wireless networks are typically encrypted to prevent anyone from connecting to the network or from gathering information from intercepted transmissions.

> **NOTE** One of the basic goals of IT security is to ensure the confidentiality of data. In general, confidentiality can be ensured through encryption. Plain text data is encrypted, converting it into ciphertext data. When strong encryption methods are used, it is extremely difficult for unauthorized individuals to decrypt ciphertext data. In contrast, when encryption methods are not used, unauthorized individuals can easily view plain text data, reducing the likelihood that the data will remain confidential.

True or false? WEP should be used whenever possible to secure wireless networks.

Answer: *False*. Wired Equivalent Privacy (WEP) is not secure and should not be used.

Strong security types such as Wi-Fi Protected Access (WPA) or Wi-Fi Protected Access version 2 (WPA2) should be used instead of WEP. Attackers can easily break into a wireless network protected with WEP, using software they can download from the Internet. In contrast, WPA2 using Advanced Encryption Standard (AES) has not been cracked. WPA and WPA2 can also use Temporal Key Integrity Protocol (TKIP), but AES is recognized as a stronger encryption standard.

EXAM TIP WEP is not secure and should not be used for wireless networks. Whenever possible, WPA2 with AES should be used instead. Securing the wireless router with WPA2 and AES prevents unauthorized access to the router and the wireless network.

MORE INFO Chapter 2 of this book covers topics related to the wireless encryption standards in Objective 2.5. Even though Chapter 2 is focused on the 220-801 exam, topics in that section cross over into this objective.

Enable MAC filtering

Media access control (MAC) filtering is a security technique used to restrict access to a network to systems based on their MAC address. MAC addresses are 48 bits long and are typically displayed as a string of six pairs of hexadecimal characters, similar to this: 1A-2B-3C-4D-5E-6F.

True or false? MAC address filtering can be used to prevent unknown systems from connecting to a network.

Answer: *True.* Network interface cards (NICs) are assigned MAC addresses, and you can enable MAC address filtering to allow known systems based on their MAC addresses. Unknown systems will be blocked.

There are two ways you can enable MAC filtering. The most common way is to identify specific MAC addresses that are authorized and block all others. Another way is to authorize all devices except for specific devices that you want to block, using their MAC address.

The following steps outline the process of enabling MAC address filtering on a wireless router:

1. Identify the MAC address of known systems. You can identify the MAC address of Windows-based systems using the **ipconfig /all** command. You can identify the MAC address of wireless printers from the printer menu or with a test printout from the printer.

2. Enable MAC filtering on the wireless router. You can typically access a wireless router's web interface by using the IP address of the router as the URL like this: *http://192.168.1.1/.* Most wireless routers used in SOHOs have a default IP address of 192.168.1.1 or 192.168.0.1.

3. Enter the MAC addresses of known devices into the wireless router, and select the setting that blocks all other devices. The wireless router will then block access to all systems that have different MAC addresses.

EXAM TIP You can access the web interface of many routers by using a web browser such as Internet Explorer and the router's private IP address. This is often *http://192.168.1.1/ or http://192.168.0.1/.*

Figure 7-3 shows a screen shot of the web interface for a Cisco router. You can see that the setting is set to Enabled and that the Permit PCs Listed Below To Access The Wireless Network setting is selected. Also, there are four MAC addresses, listed as MAC 01 through MAC 04. Systems with these MAC addresses are allowed access to the wireless network, but the router will block access to the wireless network for any other systems.

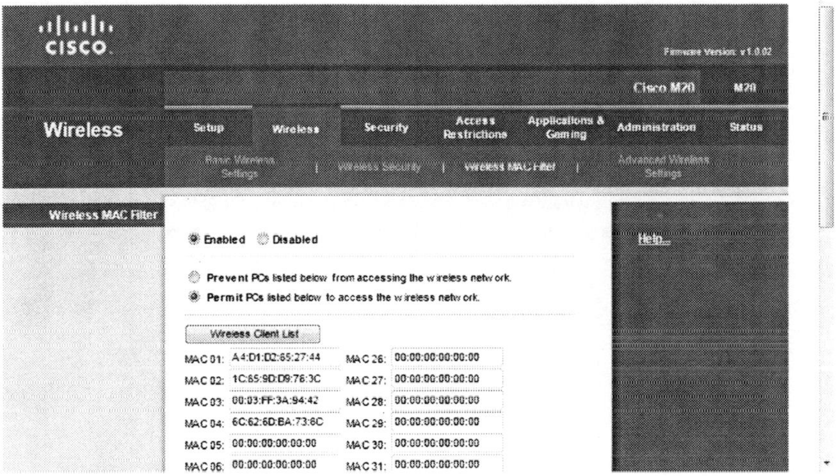

FIGURE 7-3 Enabling MAC filtering.

NOTE When taking the A+ exam, you should know that MAC filtering can be used to restrict access. However, in practice, you should know that it is relatively easy to change the MAC address of a system to get around this restriction. That is, it isn't a reliable method of ensuring that unauthorized clients cannot connect to a wireless network.

EXAM TIP Use MAC address filtering to restrict access to a wireless network to only known clients. MAC filtering provides an added layer of security to a wireless network and helps ensure that only authorized clients can access the network.

MORE INFO Chapter 2 of this book covers topics related to MAC filtering in Objective 2.6. Even though Chapter 2 is focused on the 220-801 exam, topics in that section cross over into this objective.

Antenna and access point placement

Wireless network transmissions are affected by the location of the access point and the orientation of the antenna. Depending on the owner's goals, you can manipulate these to limit or maximize the transmission distances.

True or false? Physical objects, including walls and furniture, can limit wireless transmissions.

Answer: *True.* Physical objects, including walls, floors, ceilings, and furniture, can absorb the signal, limiting the transmission distance.

Wireless transmissions are also susceptible to interference from many sources. Electromagnetic interference (EMI) can come from equipment using magnets and from fluorescent lights. Radio frequency interference (RFI) can come from other transmitters, such as cordless phones, baby monitors, and microwaves. Access points should be located at least three feet away from any of these devices.

NOTE The primary security goal that you're trying to achieve by modifying the placement of the antenna or access point is availability. By minimizing interference, you can increase the quality of the wireless signal.

EXAM TIP Ensure that wireless access points are located at least three feet away from other transmitting devices, such as cordless phones, baby monitors, and microwaves.

Radio power levels

Many wireless access points (WAPs) and wireless routers include settings to adjust the radio power levels. The area where wireless devices can receive and connect to a WAP is known as its footprint.

True or false? You can increase the radio power level of a WAP to prevent unauthorized individuals from connecting to a wireless network.

Answer: *False.* Increasing the radio power level increases the footprint and allows systems to connect from farther away. It doesn't prevent unauthorized individuals from connecting.

You can decrease the footprint by decreasing the radio power levels, and systems outside the footprint will not be able to connect as easily. The tradeoff is poorer performance for systems that are able to connect. As a reminder, a wireless device and an access point will negotiate the fastest speed that they can connect to each other without errors. With an 802.11g network, this can be up to 54 Mbps. However, with lower power levels, the speed can be significantly slower.

NOTE Most WAPs and wireless devices use omni-directional antennas, transmitting and receiving from all directions at the same time. However, attackers have been known to use uni-directional antennas to eavesdrop on wireless network from far away. By pointing a uni-directional antenna directly at a wireless transmitter, they can connect to it even if they are outside of the omni-directional footprint.

EXAM TIP You can decrease the footprint of a WAP by decreasing the radio power levels. With lower power levels, the signal doesn't transmit as far, making it more difficult for unauthorized individuals to connect.

Assign static IP addresses

Most wireless routers include Dynamic Host Configuration Protocol (DHCP) service, which is enabled by default. Any clients that can connect to the router are automatically given an IP address and other TCP/IP configuration, such as a subnet mask and the default gateway address. However, it is also possible to disable DHCP and statically assign IP addresses.

True or false? You can decrease the ability of other users to connect to your wireless network by disabling DHCP and changing the network ID.

Answer: *True*. With DHCP disabled, attackers would have to manually assign an IP address.

Many wireless routers use the IP address of 192.168.1.1 with a subnet mask of 255.255.255.0. DHCP then issues IP addresses somewhere in the range of 192.168.1.2 through 192.168.1.254 with the same subnet mask and provides clients with the default gateway address of 192.168.1.1. If you want to assign static IP addresses for security, you can take the following steps:

1. Disable DHCP on the wireless router.

2. Manually assign an IP address to the router. When manually assigning IP addresses this way, it's common to use a different network ID, so you might assign IP address of 192.168.55.1 with a subnet mask of 255.255.255.0.

3. Manually assign static IP addresses to wireless clients in the range of 192.168.55.2 through 192.168.55.254, with a subnet mask of 255.255.255.0

4. Manually assign the default gateway of 192.168.55.1 to the wireless clients.

5. If Internet connectivity is needed or DNS is used on the internal network, an address of a DNS server must also be manually assigned.

NOTE While this method is possible, it is labor-intensive and a knowledgeable attacker can still beat it. Attackers can capture and analyze transmissions going over the air to determine what IP addresses are used and can then manually configure a system with an IP address in the appropriate range.

EXAM TIP You can disable DHCP and assign IP addresses statically to reduce the ability of unauthorized individuals from connecting to your wireless network.

Another option related to IP addresses is to continue to use DHCP to automate the assignment of IP addresses and other TCP/IP configuration. However, you can restrict the range of IP addresses that DHCP assigns to exactly the number of devices you have in your network. For example, if the network has five devices, you can configure DHCP to assign only five IP addresses, such as the addresses 192.168.1.51 through 192.168.1.55. You can also use DHCP reservations to assign specific IP addresses to each client, based on their MAC addresses.

Can you answer these questions?

You can find the answers to these questions at the end of this chapter.

1. What can be done with an SSID to support security?

2. What type of security should be avoided with wireless networks?

3. What can be configured on a wireless router to authorize specific wireless clients?

Objective 2.6: Given a scenario, secure a SOHO wired network

While many SOHOs use wireless networks combined with a wired network, there are also many that use only a wired network. This objective covers some specific methods used to secure a wired network. You'll notice that there is a lot of crossover between the topics in this objective and the previous objective. For example, in both types of networks you should change default user names and passwords, you can enable MAC filtering, and you can use static IP addresses.

Exam need to know...

- Common security steps
  For example: What are common security steps you should take with both a wired and a wireless router?
- Disabling ports
  For example: Why would you disable a physical port on a switch?
- Physical security
  For example: Where should you locate routers and switches in a SOHO?

Common security steps

There are several common security steps that you should take with both wired and wireless networks. It's worth noting that the primary difference between a wireless network and a wired network is that a wireless network has a wireless router and/or a wireless access point but a network using only wired devices doesn't have these components. A wired network has a wired router and includes physical cables connected to every device in the network.

True or false? Changing default user names and/or passwords should be one of the first steps you take to secure a wired router.

Answer: *True.* This ensures that only authorized personnel can access it and change the configuration.

Some of the common steps you can take for both wireless and wired networks include the following:

- **Change default user names and passwords**   Just as default user names and passwords should be changed on wireless routers, they should also be changed on wired routers. This prevents unauthorized individuals from accessing the router and changing the configuration.
- **Enable MAC filtering**   MAC filtering can be used to restrict access to a network based on the MAC address of the device.
- **Assign static IP addresses**   This includes disabling DHCP and prevents someone from automatically getting an IP address and gaining access to network resources.

Disabling ports

Most routers and switches include the ability to disable a physical port on the device. When the port is disabled, traffic is no longer sent to or from the port even if a device is connected to it.

True or false? You can prevent users from connecting to a network from an office or cubicle by disabling a port at a switch.

Answer: *True.* If ports aren't being used by legitimate employees, you can disable the port at the switch to prevent anyone else from using the port to connect to the network.

This is commonly referred to as port security. When ports are not disabled, any user can plug a laptop or other computer into an RJ-45 port in the wall and connect to the network. When DHCP is enabled, the client can be given an IP address and other TCP/IP configuration automatically. The same practice can be used on both switches and routers for security.

True or false? Webcam transmissions can be blocked at the router to prevent them from leaving the network.

Answer: *True.* Any transmission can be stopped by blocking the port that it uses.

For example, a webcam used with a baby monitor can be connected to a network via a switch so that parents can monitor the baby from another room. Imagine that this webcam and its software uses logical port 5100. The parents can then block logical port 5100 at the router to prevent the transmissions from leaving their home.

From a different perspective, if users cannot perform certain activities, it could be because a logical port is blocked. For example, web browser traffic over the Internet with Hypertext Transfer Protocol (HTTP) uses port 80. If users can access internal network resources but they cannot browse the Internet, the problem might be because port 80 is blocked at the firewall.

Physical security

Physical security of a wired network is the simple practice of ensuring that network devices are not easily accessible by unauthorized individuals. This is commonly done by locating these devices in a locked area.

True or false? Servers should be physically secured, but it is not necessary to use physical security with routers.

Answer: *False.* Physical security is important with any device that has value to an organization.

Organizations often locate routers and switches together with their servers. However, you might also see routers and switches located in a wiring closet while servers are located in another secure area. Either way, it is still important to provide physical security to both.

In some small offices or home offices, it isn't feasible to physically locate a network device in a separate locked room. In these cases, you can still use port security to disable unused ports and limit the ability of someone to connect to the device.

Can you answer these questions?

You can find the answers to these questions at the end of this chapter.

1. What does MAC filtering provide in a wired network?
2. What is the difference between a physical port and a logical port, and how can you provide security for each?
3. What is port security in relation to physical ports?

Answers

This section contains the answers to the "Can you answer these questions?" sections in this chapter.

Objective 2.1: Apply and use common prevention methods

1. A man trap or turnstile is commonly used to prevent tailgating. It ensures that each user follows the appropriate access procedures and cannot just follow closely behind someone else. It's also possible to prevent tailgating by educating users, although this isn't generally as reliable as using a man trap or turnstile.

2. Users should be given unique standard user accounts, and they should be granted permissions to access files through these accounts. Regular users should not be given administrative accounts.

3. The principle of least privilege states that users should be given minimum access to resources.

Objective 2.2: Compare and contrast common security threats

1. Impersonation is one type of social engineering attack. Criminals can impersonate any type of vendor or service person. They can also try to impersonate technical support personnel and can do so in person, over the phone, or via email. The best protection against social engineering is educated personnel.

2. A rootkit provides full administrative access to a computer and can usually hide itself from antivirus software. A rootkit can include a back door that provides a criminal access to the computer from a remote location over the Internet.

3. Email designed to trick users is called phishing. It might attempt to trick the user into giving up information by entering data into a bogus website, or it might trick the user into giving up information by answering an email to help someone from another country.

4. A privacy filter can be used to prevent unauthorized individuals from reading data on a display monitor by shoulder surfing.

5. A Trojan (or Trojan horse) is software that appears to be something useful but includes additional software that is malicious.

Objective 2.3: Implement security best practices to secure a workstation

1. Strong passwords include at least three of the four character types: uppercase letters, lowercase letters, numbers, and special characters.

2. The Local Security Policy tool can be used on a Windows-based computer to configure a Password Policy. The password policy requires users to create passwords of a specific length and complexity and to change the passwords regularly. Group Policy is used in domains and sets a password policy for multiple computers in the domain at the same time.

3. The Guest account has the least permission on a Windows 7–based computer. This account should be disabled by default.

4. Password-protected screensavers can be enabled to automatically lock a computer after a period of time.

Objective 2.4: Given a scenario, use the appropriate data destruction/disposal method

1. It is possible to retrieve data from a drive formatted with a standard format. It is not possible to retrieve data from a drive formatted with a low-level format or a zero-fill program.

2. Sanitizing a hard drive refers to removing all remnants of data, and this can be done with a drive wipe or overwrite program. Destroying the hard drive also sanitizes it.

3. A degausser will destroy all the data on a hard drive. It also destroys the hard drive components, making it unusable.

Objective 2.5: Given a scenario, secure a SOHO wireless network

1. The default SSID should be changed. It's also possible to disable SSID broadcast to hide a wireless network from casual users.

2. WEP is not secure and should be avoided. WPA2 with AES is preferred over WEP.

3. MAC address filtering can be configured on a wireless router to authorize specific wireless clients, based on their MAC address.

Objective 2.6: Given a scenario, secure a SOHO wired network

1. You can use MAC filtering to restrict access to a network, based on MAC addresses assigned to devices.

2. A physical port is a port on a switch or router into which a cable can be plugged. It can be secured by disabling the physical port. A logical port is a number used to identify a protocol or the type of traffic. Routers can be configured to block traffic based on the port number.

3. Port security refers to disabling unused physical ports on switches and routers. This prevents unauthorized personnel from using the port to connect to a network.

CHAPTER 8

Mobile devices

The Mobile Devices domain covers approximately 9 percent of the A+ 220-802 exam. It includes various mobile devices that are commonly used today, such as smartphones and tablets. As a PC technician, you need to be aware of the different types of operating systems used by these devices, how they can connect to a wireless network and the Internet, methods used to secure them, and how they can be synchronized. You also need to be aware of the hardware differences between tablets and laptops, such as what can be serviced or upgraded on each.

This chapter covers the following objectives:

- Objective 3.1: Explain the basic features of mobile operating systems
- Objective 3.2: Establish basic network connectivity and configure email
- Objective 3.3: Compare and contrast methods for securing mobile devices
- Objective 3.4: Compare and contrast hardware differences in regards to tablets and laptops
- Objective 3.5: Execute and configure mobile device synchronization

Objective 3.1: Explain the basic features of mobile operating systems

The CompTIA exam focuses on the Android and iOS operating systems used on many mobile devices. You need to know which operating system is used on which devices, and where users can purchase apps for these devices. This objective specifically mentions the accelerometer and gyroscope used in many devices and how they are used by different apps. Touch devices can sometimes require screen calibration, and you should understand what this is and when it is needed. Last, you need to know what is meant by terms *global positioning system* (GPS) and *geotracking*, and how they can be used with location services.

Exam need to know...

- Android vs. iOS
  For example: Which operating system is open source? Where can apps be purchased for devices using the iOS operating system?

- Screen orientation and calibration
  For example: What determines whether a tablet is moving and how quick it is moving? What hardware is required to maintain screen orientation?
- GPS and geotracking
  For example: What is geotracking? What is a benefit of location services?

Android vs. iOS

Mobile devices created and sold by Apple use the iOS operating system. Many other mobile devices use the Android operating system, which is closely associated with Google.

NOTE While the Windows 8 phone and Windows 8 tablets are in use, they aren't currently included in the objectives for the CompTIA exams.

True or false? The Android operating system is an open source operating system.

Answer: *True.* The Android operating system is a Linux-based operating system, which is open source.

Many different hardware companies use the Android operating system on devices they create and sell. They don't have to pay Google or anyone else to use the operating system. In contrast, only Apple makes hardware devices using the iOS operating system. No other company is authorized to use it on non-Apple devices. The difference between open source and closed source software is defined as follows:

- Open source software is freely available to anyone. Developers can modify and redistribute the code without paying anyone else for the license to use it.
- Closed source software (also called vendor-specific software) is proprietary to a company and not available without a license to use it.

EXAM TIP Ensure that you know the difference between open source and closed source software. Android is open source software, and iOS is closed source or vendor-specific software.

True or false? You can purchase iOS-based applications only from Apple's App Store.

Answer: *True.* Apple tightly controls all software used on Apple devices, and this software can be purchased only from Apple's App Store.

A benefit of the App Store is that the applications are free from viruses. Apple screens all applications before making them available for purchase. If a virus is discovered, it can be immediately removed from the store. Additionally, if a developer does upload a virus, Apple knows the developer's identity and can take immediate action against the developer.

Android-based apps are available through Google Play (previously called Android Marketplace), and Google controls the apps available here. However, there are additional locations where users can purchase Android apps. For example, Amazon includes a section where you can buy Android-based apps.

Screen orientation and calibration

Mobile devices such as tablets and smartphones can automatically sense their orientation. They can modify the display for the user, such as change from portrait mode to landscape mode based on how the user is holding the display.

True or false? Tablets use an accelerometer and a gyroscope to determine the position of the device.

Answer: *True.* Many devices have a single chip with an accelerometer and a gyroscope used to determine the position of the device.

The accelerometer/gyroscope chip sends an output to the operating system and applications. If the feature is enabled in the operating system and supported by the app, the display is automatically adjusted when the user changes the orientation of the device. For example, a user can be reading an eBook in an app using portrait mode, with the device held so that the height is greater than the width. If the user repositions the device so that the width is greater than the height, the device automatically switches to landscape mode.

Optionally, you can disable the feature so that the display remains constant no matter how the device is held. For example, you can enable Rotation Lock on an iPad to lock the display.

True or false? An accelerometer can measure how fast a tablet is moving in a given direction.

Answer: *True.* The accelerometer measures velocity or speed of the tablet in a given direction. This is often used with games on tablet devices.

True or false? If the device cannot determine its position, you can sometimes recalibrate it by moving the entire device in a figure 8 pattern.

Answer: *True.* In some cases, the device can no longer determine its position. You can hold the device with both hands in front of you and move it in a figure 8 pattern to recalibrate it.

> **EXAM TIP** Not all mobile devices include a gyroscope. If you find that a device is not automatically switching between landscape and portrait mode, it could be because the device doesn't have a gyroscope or because the feature is disabled.

GPS and geotracking

Mobile devices have the ability to determine their location by communicating with global positioning system (GPS) devices. This is used by many applications to give users location-specific information. For example, maps can show the user's location, and weather applications can show the local weather.

True or false? GPS can be used to show a user's location and their movements as they travel.

Answer: *True.* Most mobile devices are tied into a GPS system and can automatically show the location.

Some families use apps that allow them to keep track of each other. For example, Life360 allows you to invite family members, and your location will automatically appear on their devices no matter where you are. In the event of an emergency, you can easily send messages through the app to verify that family members are OK.

True or false? A gyroscope is used to determine the location of a device.

Answer: *False.* A gyroscope works with an accelerometer to determine the position of a device, not the location.

GPS services can be turned off. For example, on an iPad you can disable Location Services as a privacy setting. Many mobile devices create a log identifying recent locations. This log can be accessed by others to show someone's location (commonly called geotracking). If GPS services are turned off, the device will normally not store this log, but smartphones sometimes still use the log to locate cell towers.

> **EXAM TIP** GPS services are used by applications to identify the user's location. They can also be used to locate a missing or stolen phone.

Can you answer these questions?

You can find the answers to these questions at the end of this chapter.

1. Is the Android operating system closed source or open source?
2. Where are apps for devices running iOS purchased?
3. What is the purpose of the gyroscope and accelerometer in a mobile device?

Objective 3.2: Establish basic network connectivity and configure email

Smartphones and tablets can use either wireless or cellular connections to connect to the Internet. This allows users to browse the Internet and also to send and receive email. This connectivity can be disabled to save power or when traveling on a plane to comply with regulations. Additionally, some devices support Bluetooth. A challenge for many users is the initial configuration for email, so you should have an understanding of the basic information needed to configure a device for email.

Exam need to know...

- Wireless/cellular data network (enable/disable)
  For example: What is an easy way to disable both wireless and cellular access on a mobile device?
- Bluetooth
  For example: What is discovery mode?
- Email configuration
  For example: What is needed when configuring an email account for a corporate Microsoft Exchange server?

Wireless/cellular data network (enable/disable)

To use a smartphone, you need to have access to a cellular network. Many communication services also provide access to a cellular data network (when the user subscribes) so that users can access Internet services with their smartphones. These devices also commonly include wireless capabilities so that users can connect to a wireless network and avoid charges with the cellular network.

Similarly, mobile devices such as tablets will commonly include wireless capabilities but not necessarily include cellular access. For example, you can purchase an iPad with wireless and cellular access, or you can buy one with only wireless access.

True or false? Disabling the wireless and cellular access will conserve battery power.

Answer: *True.* If a user wants to conserve battery power, the wireless and cellular access should be disabled.

True or false? Placing a tablet into airplane mode disables cellular and wireless access.

Answer: *True.* This prevents the tablet from broadcasting by using either cellular or wireless signals, assuming both are available on the device.

A device that can connect to both a wireless network and a cellular network will typically default to the wireless network for data access first. Cellular data subscription plans will usually have a limit, and if users exceed the limit, they are charged additional fees. Using the wireless network first saves bandwidth for the user.

EXAM TIP When cellular and wireless access is enabled, a device transmits and receives signals. Disabling the cellular and wireless access on a smartphone or mobile device will conserve power, and one way to do so is to place it in airplane mode. It can be enabled for a short time, such as to download email, and then disabled again to conserve battery power.

Devices connected to a wireless network are assigned an IP address and other TCP/IP configuration information. There are different paths to view this information, depending on the device and the current version of software running on it, but you can almost always get to it through the Settings page. For example, on an iPhone, you can view the IP address by selecting Settings, Wi-Fi, and then selecting the connection. A previous version required you to select Settings, General, Network before you could get to the Wi-Fi settings, but you still started with Settings.

Bluetooth

Bluetooth is a type of wireless protocol most commonly used for personal area networks (PANs). A common example is a Bluetooth-enabled headset, which includes an earpiece and microphone. The Bluetooth headset can be wirelessly connected with a Bluetooth-enabled smartphone. Users wear the headset and can talk on the phone, leaving their hands free.

True or false? Two Bluetooth devices can be paired with each other while in discovery mode.

Answer: *True*. Discovery mode is used to allow two devices to connect and pair with each other.

The basic steps used to pair two devices are as follows:

1. **Enable Bluetooth** The process is different for different devices, but it must be enabled for wireless Bluetooth transmissions to operate.

2. **Enable pairing** This can be done by enabling discovery mode on devices that use older Bluetooth protocols. It is automated on devices that use the newer Secure Simple Pairing (SSP), also referred to as the "Just Works" Bluetooth method.

3. **Find device for pairing** The device looks for other devices in pairing mode or in close proximity, depending on the underlying Bluetooth protocol.

4. **Enter appropriate PIN code** As a security precaution, you sometimes need to enter a personal identification number (PIN) code for one of the devices. Sometimes the PIN is configurable, or if you can't find the PIN, you can often use either the last four digits of the device's serial number or 0000.

5. **Test connectivity** The last step verifies that the two devices can communicate with each other.

If you needed to enable discovery mode for the devices, you should disable it after verifying that connectivity is working. This prevents someone else from pairing with the device without your knowledge.

EXAM TIP Discovery mode is often used when pairing Bluetooth devices. If you need to enable discovery mode, you should disable it after the devices have been paired. If you can't locate the PIN, you can often use 0000 or the last four digits of the device's serial number.

MORE INFO You can watch the following short video to learn how to connect Bluetooth and other wireless or network devices to your computer: *http://windows .microsoft.com/en-US/windows7/Connect-to-Bluetooth-and-other-wireless-or-network-devices*.

Email configuration

A benefit of smartphones and other mobile devices is the availability of email while users roam. When the mobile device is configured correctly, users have access to their email anywhere that they have access to the Internet.

True or false? When configuring a smartphone to access email from a corporate network, all you need is the user's user name and password.

Answer: *False.* When configuring an email account for a corporate network, you'll also need the name of the server and the domain.

The domain is implied in the email address. For example, an email account named darril@getcertifiedgetahead.com implies a domain name of getcertifiedgetahead.com. The address doesn't give the server name, but you are also required to enter the server name. When configuring some accounts, such as a Google Gmail account, only the email address and password is needed with some email applications. The email application is programmed with the Google server name and domain name so that it doesn't need to be entered manually.

True or false? A smartphone using a Microsoft Exchange account can synchronize email, calendar, and contact information.

Answer: *True.* A Microsoft Exchange account is used for email, and it also includes calendar and contact information, such as an address book.

Microsoft Exchange email servers are commonly used in corporate networks for email. When configured for mobile users, the organization will have at least one email server that is accessible on the Internet.

In some cases, you need to enter ports used for different email protocols. The following ports are the most relevant:

- 25—Simple Mail Transport Protocol (SMTP)
- 110—Post Office Protocol v3 (POP3)
- 143—Internet Message Access Protocol (IMAP)
- 465—Secure SMTP (SMTP over SSL)
- 995—Secure POP3 (POP3 over SSL)
- 993—Secure IMAP (IMAP over SSL)

True or false? Restarting a smartphone is often a good troubleshooting step if it stopped receiving email.

Answer: *True*. Restarting the smartphone is a common troubleshooting step for any application that stops working.

> **EXAM TIP** When configuring mobile devices for corporate email accounts, you'll need to know the server name and its domain. Most use Microsoft Exchange with common port numbers, so you don't have to configure the ports separately. In some cases, the mobile device will know the server name and domain information, such as with Gmail, so this information doesn't need to be entered separately.

Can you answer these questions?

You can find the answers to these questions at the end of this chapter.

1. What is disabled with airplane mode?
2. What mode is used for a Bluetooth device when pairing two devices?
3. What ports are used for basic email configuration?

Objective 3.3: Compare and contrast methods for securing mobile devices

There are several different methods available to secure mobile devices against various threats. The primary threats related to mobile devices are loss of the device, loss of data on the device, and compromised data on the device. There are several basic protections you can take against these losses if a device is lost or stolen. Additionally, viruses present a risk to some mobile devices, but antivirus software and keeping devices up to date helps protect them.

Exam need to know...

- Passcode locks
  For example: When should users enable a passcode?
- Remote wipes
  For example: When should you enable remote wipe on a device?
- Locator applications
  For example: What is the primary purpose of a locator application?
- Remote backup applications
  For example: When backing up data from a mobile device, where can you store it?
- Failed login attempts restrictions
  For example: What happens if a user enters the wrong passcode too many times and failed login attempts restrictions have been enabled?
- Antivirus
  For example: What operating system is least susceptible to viruses?

- Patching/OS updates

  For example: How are patches and updates related to security?

Passcode locks

A passcode lock on a mobile device is similar to a password screensaver on a Windows-based PC. When users start to use a device after a period of inactivity, they must enter the proper passcode, which is typically a four-digit number.

True or false? Passcodes should be used only if GPS is disabled.

Answer: *False*. Entering a password is a good first security precaution that a user can take with a new mobile device, but it is unrelated to GPS.

If a user loses a mobile device and the passcode lock is enabled, it is much more difficult for someone else to use the device.

> **EXAM TIP** Passcode locks provide a basic protection against someone using a lost or stolen device. It can be enabled only while the user has the phone, so entering a passcode lock should be one of the first actions a new user takes if security is important. It can be combined with failed login attempts restrictions for better security.

Remote wipes

A remote wipe capability allows you to send a signal to a remote device to erase everything on it. This effectively wipes out everything on the device, making it unusable.

True or false? Remote wipe is an effective data security method as long as it is enabled after the device is lost.

Answer: *False*. To provide data security, remote wipe must be enabled before a device is lost. If remote wipe is enabled, the remote wipe signal can be sent to the device after it is lost. If remote wipe hasn't been enabled before the device is lost, you cannot send a remote wipe signal to the device.

Knowledgeable thieves have been known to immediately turn off a phone after it is stolen to prevent it from receiving a remote wipe signal. If they turn it on in an area that cannot receive a signal (such as in a shielded room), they can prevent the device from receiving the signal.

> **EXAM TIP** Remote wipe is an effective method of providing data security as long as it is enabled before the device is lost. When enabled, it allows a signal to be sent to a lost or stolen device to delete all data.

Locator applications

Locator applications are used to pinpoint the exact location of a mobile device. They can be useful for identifying the current location of a lost or stolen device.

True or false? One of the biggest security threats related to mobile devices is theft.

Answer: *True.* Mobile devices are easy to steal. If a user sets a mobile device down for just a moment, it's easy for a thief to pick it up and slip it into a pocket undetected.

Locator applications use the built-in GPS capabilities of a mobile device. When enabled, users can locate their device with a web browser.

EXAM TIP Locator applications use GPS within a mobile device and help to locate devices that have been stolen. To use it, you normally have to enable the locator application on the device before it is lost.

Remote backup applications

A challenge all users have is keeping reliable backups of their data, and this includes data stored on mobile devices. If data is corrupted, it can be restored, but only if a reliable backup is available. One way many users resolve this is by using remote backup applications. These applications allow the users to back up their data over an Internet connection to a remote location.

True or false? Users with Apple devices can use iCloud to back up their devices to a remote location.

Answer: *True.* iCloud is an Apple service that allows users to back up their data to a remote location on the Internet.

EXAM TIP Windows SkyDrive offers 7 GB of free storage, and it can be used with Windows-based, Android, and Apple devices for remote storage and backups. Google Drive offers 5 GB of free storage, which can be used for a wide variety of devices, including Android, Apple, and Windows-based devices. Apple's iCloud service gives users approximately 5 GB of free storage that they can use for remote backups.

MORE INFO You can read more about Microsoft's Skydrive here: *http://windows. microsoft.com/en-US/skydrive/download.* Google Drive details are available here: *http://www.google.com/intl/en_US/drive/start/.* Apple's iCloud information is available here: *http://www.apple.com/icloud/features/.*

Failed login attempts restrictions

Passcodes are normally only four digits, resulting in 10,000 possible combinations. A persistent thief could enter each combination (0000 through 9999) into the phone until the correct passcode is found. To prevent this, you can enable failed login attempts restrictions. When enabled, it tracks how many times the login is entered incorrectly.

True or false? You can configure iOS devices to automatically erase all data on a device after 10 failed passcode attempts.

Answer: *True*. When you enable a passcode on an iOS device, you can also enable the Erase Data feature, which will track the failed passcode attempts. If a user enters the wrong password 10 times in a row, the feature will erase all data on the system.

> **EXAM TIP** Failed login attempts restrictions prevent a thief from guessing a passcode. Most mobile devices can be configured to erase all data on the device if the wrong passcode is entered too many times.

Antivirus

A common security step for regular PCs and laptop computers is to install antivirus software. Antivirus software protects against viruses and other malicious software (malware).

True or false? Viruses are considered a security threat for mobile devices.

Answer: *True*. While some devices are more vulnerable than others to viruses, viruses do represent a threat to mobile devices.

Viruses and other malware aren't as big a threat to mobile devices as they are to regular computers, but they are a threat. The Apple iOS has had relatively few problems with malware because Apple vigorously screens apps before they are offered for sale on the Apple app store, and apps for iOS aren't easily available anywhere else. It's difficult for an attacker to create an infected app and get it onto the store. Also, it is difficult for a user to install apps from any other source.

In contrast, Android apps are available from multiple sources, so it is easier for attackers to infect apps and make them available to users. Still, the incidence of malware on any type of mobile device is minimal when compared to typical desktop PCs.

Patching/OS updates

Just as patches and updates are used to keep regular PCs up-to-date, they are also used to keep mobile devices up-to-date. Some patches are simple updates, and some are major updates to the operating system.

True or false? Patches and updates for mobile devices are issued to resolve security issues and to address bugs.

Answer: *True*. Patches and updates are issued to fix security vulnerabilities and usability issues.

In some cases, operating system updates add additional capabilities for the device. This is similar to how service packs sometimes add additional updates to operating systems on regular PCs.

> **EXAM TIP** Just as it is best to keep regular PCs up-to-date with current patches and updates, it is important to keep mobile devices up-to-date.

Can you answer these questions?

You can find the answers to these questions at the end of this chapter.

1. What is the purpose of a passcode lock?
2. What can be used to delete data on a lost mobile device?
3. What can you implement on a mobile device to prevent a thief from guessing the passcode?

Objective 3.4: Compare and contrast hardware differences in regards to tablets and laptops

There some significant hardware differences you should be aware of when comparing tablets and laptops. This objective expects you to know differences related to serviceability, upgradability, and common components found in typical tablets and laptops.

Exam need to know...

- No field serviceable parts
  For example: Are there any serviceable parts in a laptop? Are there any serviceable parts in a tablet?
- Typically not upgradable
  For example: What are some components that can be upgraded in a laptop? What are some components that can be upgraded in a tablet?
- Touch interface
  For example: What is a pinch gesture? What technology in a touch interface supports a gesture to zoom out?
- Solid state drives
  For example: What are benefits of solid state drives besides speed?

No field serviceable parts

One of the primary differences between a tablet and a laptop is that a tablet is a single unit without any serviceable parts. It cannot easily be taken apart to replace components. In contrast, laptops are serviceable, and you can replace the RAM, disk drives, optical drives, the wireless mini-PCIe card, and other components if they fail.

True or false? If a tablet fails, the only way it can be repaired is by returning it to the manufacturer.

Answer: *True.* Many people consider tablets disposable after the warranty expires. If something stops working after the warranty, the cost to repair is typically so high that users would rather purchase a new one.

> **EXAM TIP** Tablets are sealed units and are not serviceable by PC technicians. They can be returned to the manufacturer when they are under warranty, but if the warranty has expired, the cost to repair the item is typically not worth it. Instead, customers purchase a newer tablet.

Typically not upgradable

Just as tablets are not serviceable, they are typically not very upgradable. In contrast, you can easily upgrade many items in a laptop. For example, it's common to upgrade the RAM in a laptop with higher-capacity small outline dual inline modules (SODIMMS).

True or false? The only item that is upgradable in a tablet is an SSD.

Answer: *False*. None of the internal items are upgradable in a tablet device, including the solid state drive (SSD). Because of this, it's often recommended to get the biggest drive that a user can afford.

It is possible to add some capabilities to a tablet if it has external ports. For example, if the tablet has an external USB port, you can plug in USB devices.

> **EXAM TIP** Tablets rarely have any internal upgradable components. Instead, the capacity and features of the unit when it is new are all that it will ever have. For example, if a tablet device doesn't have internal cellular access when it is purchased, you cannot add this internally later.

Touch interface

Mobile devices have a touch interface with a minimum of mechanical buttons. This allows users to do most of their interaction with the device with gestures on the touch screen.

True or false? Multitouch is the capability that allows a mobile device to detect a pinch gesture to zoom in.

Answer: *True*. Touch screens support multitouch so that they can detect when two fingers (or a finger and a thumb) touch the screen at the same time. A pinch gesture causes the screen to zoom in. A spread gesture reverses the action of a pinch and zooms out.

> **NOTE** *Touch flow* refers to the ability of the screen to recognize users dragging a finger across the screen. This is important when a user is doing flick gestures and when doing pinch and spread gestures. It is mentioned in the objectives specifically as "touch flow," but this term is not commonly used.

Multitouch is combined with touch flow capabilities, which can detect when a user is moving one or more fingers across the screen. This is useful for pinch and spread gestures and simple flick gestures. All mobile devices, including Android and iOS devices, include multitouch and touch flow capabilities.

> **EXAM TIP** The touch interface depends on multitouch and touch flow capabilities. Multitouch senses when you touch the screen in more than one place at the same time. Touch flow senses when you drag one or more fingers across the screen. Combined, these two technologies support a wide range of gestures, such as pinch to zoom in, and spread to zoom out.

MORE INFO If you aren't familiar with standard gestures used on mobile devices, check out the following article on gestures: *http://msdn.microsoft.com/library/ windows/apps/hh761498.aspx.* It's written for Windows-based devices but provides outstanding descriptions and graphics so that the gestures are easy to understand. You can also watch the following video, which shows how to use Windows Touch: *http://windows.microsoft.com/en-US/windows7/help/videos/using-windows-touch.*

Solid state drive

Solid state drives (SSDs) don't have any moving parts but instead are integrated circuit (IC) chips. They typically use the same type of flash memory as USB flash drives. They are more expensive per GB than traditional hard disk drives, but they have several benefits over hard disk drives.

True or false? Tablet devices start quicker than a regular PC because they use SSD drives.

Answer: *True.* Regular PCs typically use serial ATA (SATA) drives, which are faster than parallel ATA (PATA) drives, but SSDs are much faster than either SATA or PATA hard drives.

SSDs are also less susceptible to damage if they are dropped, because they don't have any moving parts. In contrast, traditional hard drives can be easily damaged if they are dropped but will often have additional protection against shock damage. SSDs also consume less power than hard drives, which is valuable for tablets that run on batteries.

EXAM TIP Tablets use SSDs because they are faster, lighter, consume less power, and are more durable than traditional hard drives. SSDs can also be used in laptops, and they have the same benefits when used in laptops as they have when used in tablets. However, laptops will usually have traditional hard drives because they can hold more data and are cheaper than SSDs.

MORE INFO Network World published a good article comparing hard drives and SSDs, which you can view here: *http://www.networkworld.com/reviews/2010/041910- ssd-hard-drives-test.html.* It explains some of the reasoning about why SSDs are more expensive than hard drives.

Can you answer these questions?

You can find the answers to these questions at the end of this chapter.

1. What is typically true about serviceability and upgradability with a laptop that is not true with a tablet?
2. What is needed in a touch interface to support pinch gestures?
3. What type of drive is commonly used in tablet devices?

Objective 3.5: Execute and configure mobile device synchronization

Synchronization ensures that mobile devices have the same data as another device. For example, users might want to have their contacts synchronized between a PC and a smartphone so that if they add or update a contact in one device, the change is added to the other device. Just about any mobile device supports synchronization, but there are different methods used depending on the device and the operating system it uses. There are even differences between operating system versions, such as between iOS 5 and iOS 6. You should also know how devices are connected for synchronization.

Exam need to know...

- Types of data to synchronize
  For example: What types of data can be synchronized?
- Software requirements to install the application on the PC
  For example: What application is used to synchronize data between an iOS device and a Windows operating system?
- Connection types to enable synchronization
  For example: What are the two primary connection methods used for synchronization?

Types of data to synchronize

Data synchronization ensures that data on one device is the same as data on another device. Without synchronization capabilities, you'd have to enter the same information on every mobile device you own.

True or false? Creating an email account on a mobile phone will also enable contact synchronization to update contact information.

Answer: *True.* When an email account is created, it typically includes contact information, and when synchronization is enabled, the contacts are automatically synchronized too.

You can synchronize the following types of data:

- **Contacts**   This includes names, phone numbers, email addresses, birthdays, and more. When other apps are installed, they often interact with the contacts information. For example, if a user is using Facebook on a mobile device, pictures from their friends Facebook pages are automatically added into the contacts.
- **Programs or apps**   These are often configured within the app itself to automatically update when changes are identified.
- **Email**   Many devices support either fetch or push features for email. This allows you to always have email pushed to your device when it's available, or alternatively, you can configure it to periodically query an email server to fetch new email.

- **Pictures** This allows you to take pictures on a mobile phone and have them synchronized to other devices. When cloud services are used, this can be done automatically so that you can take a picture with a phone and have it automatically copied to your tablet. The picture is actually copied from the first device to a "cloud" location on the Internet and then copied to the second device from the Internet location.
- **Music** Music files can be synced between devices. On Apple devices, the primary way this is done is through iTunes.
- **Videos** When a mobile device supports videos, you can sometimes have them synched to the device.

EXAM TIP All of the major mobile operating systems support synchronization. The primary tool used by Apple devices is iTunes, and it can be used to synchronize iOS devices.

Software requirements to install the application on the PC

Different devices use different applications for synchronization. Apple devices use the iTunes app to synchronize with a PC, and it is available as a free download.

True or false? A single version of iTunes is available for most 32-bit versions of Windows.

Answer: *True.* Both 32-bit and 64-bit versions of iTunes are available, and versions are available for Windows XP, Windows Vista, and Windows 7.

The basic requirements to install iTunes on a PC are as follows:

- 400 MB of available disk space
- Internet connection to use iTunes

EXAM TIP Mobile devices can be synchronized with PCs when the appropriate application is installed on the PC. iTunes is used for most Apple mobile devices, and versions are available that can be installed on most commonly used operating systems, including all currently supported versions of Windows.

MORE INFO You can download and install iTunes on your PC even if you don't have an Apple mobile device. The free download is available here: *http://www.apple.com/ itunes/download/.*

Connection types to enable synchronization

After installing the appropriate application on a PC, the next step is to connect the mobile device. If you can't connect the mobile device, you will not be able to synchronize it.

True or false? You can synchronize iOS devices using either a USB or a wireless connection.

Answer: *True*. The two primary methods of synchronizing a mobile device are by connecting it to a computer running iTunes or by connecting it directly to another mobile device with a USB cable or over a wireless network.

Another common method used to synchronize devices that have Internet access is via the Internet. For example, Apple devices use iCloud, and if you enable it on multiple devices, you can synchronize data between the devices with iCloud. For example, if someone owns an iPad and an iPhone, they can configure iCloud on both devices to have pictures automatically synchronized between the devices.

EXAM TIP The most common way mobile devices are connected for synchronization is via a wireless network or with a USB cable.

Can you answer these questions?

You can find the answers to these questions at the end of this chapter.

1. What types of data can be synchronized by a typical synchronization program?
2. What is the most common tool used to synchronize Apple devices?
3. What can be used to synchronize a mobile device that doesn't have a wireless connection?

Answers

This section contains the answers to the "Can you answer these questions?" sections in this chapter.

Objective 3.1: Explain the basic features of mobile operating systems

1. The Android operating system is an open source operating system based on the Linux operating system.
2. iOS is the Apple operating system, and apps can be purchased at Apple's App store.
3. The gyroscope determines the screen orientation and can be used to modify the display when the user changes the orientation of the device. The accelerometer determines how fast a device is moving.

Objective 3.2: Establish basic network connectivity and configure email

1. Airplane mode disables cellular and wireless transmissions. This can be useful to conserve battery power.

2. Bluetooth devices use discovery mode when pairing two devices. In older Bluetooth devices, you need to manually configure discovery mode, but some newer Bluetooth devices can be paired automatically.

3. SMTP uses port 25, POP3 uses port 110, and IMAP uses port 143.

Objective 3.3: Compare and contrast methods for securing mobile devices

1. It prevents people from easily using mobile devices that aren't theirs.

2. Remote wipe is a security feature available in many mobile devices that sends a signal to the device to delete all the data.

3. You can implement failed login attempts restrictions on a mobile device to prevent passcode guessing. When enabled, the device can be configured to delete all data if the incorrect passcode is entered too many times.

Objective 3.4: Compare and contrast hardware differences in regards to tablets and laptops

1. You can replace and upgrade hardware components in a laptop, but you cannot replace or upgrade hardware components in a tablet.

2. Touch interfaces include multitouch and touch flow technologies to support gestures such as pinch to zoom in or spread to zoom out.

3. Solid state drives are commonly used in tablet devices because they are faster, lighter, consume less power, and are more durable than traditional hard drives.

Objective 3.5: Execute and configure mobile device synchronization

1. Almost any type of data can be synchronized, including the following: email, contacts, calendars, reminders, notes, photos, documents, programs or apps, music, and videos.

2. iTunes is the most common tool used to synchronize Apple devices, and it is available as a free download for common operating systems.

3. USB connections can be used to synchronize mobile devices if a wireless connection isn't available.

CHAPTER 9

Troubleshooting

The Troubleshooting domain covers approximately 36 percent of the A+ 220-802 exam. It expands on many of the topics from the 220-801 exam, but instead of merely understanding the hardware components, it expects you to have knowledge of how to troubleshoot and maintain these components. The goal within this domain is for you to be able to put together all the knowledge related to PC hardware and operating systems and apply it to real-world scenarios. Most of these objectives expect you to be able to evaluate a scenario based on common symptoms, recognize the problem, and identify the best solution. Additionally, many of these objectives expect you to be aware of common tools used to resolve problems and when to use these tools.

This chapter covers the following objectives:

- Objective 4.1: Given a scenario, explain the troubleshooting theory

- Objective 4.2: Given a scenario, troubleshoot common problems related to motherboards, RAM, CPU and power with appropriate tools

- Objective 4.3: Given a scenario, troubleshoot hard drives and RAID arrays with appropriate tools

- Objective 4.4: Given a scenario, troubleshoot common video and display issues

- Objective 4.5: Given a scenario, troubleshoot wired and wireless networks with appropriate tools

- Objective 4.6: Given a scenario, troubleshoot operating system problems with appropriate tools

- Objective 4.7: Given a scenario, troubleshoot common security issues with appropriate tools and best practices

- Objective 4.8: Given a scenario, troubleshoot, and repair common laptop issues while adhering to the appropriate procedures

- Objective 4.9: Given a scenario, troubleshoot printers with appropriate tools

Objective 4.1: Given a scenario, explain the troubleshooting theory

CompTIA provides specific steps that they expect technicians to use to troubleshoot systems. These steps are identified as troubleshooting theory, and you should understand each of the steps, what to do during each step, and the specific order of these steps. This objective builds on knowledge from Objective 5.3, "Given a scenario, demonstrate proper communication and professionalism," from Exam 220-801, covered in Chapter 5, "Operational procedures."

Exam need to know...

- Identify the problem
  For example: What types of questions should a technician use when trying to get information from users?

- Establish a theory of probable cause
  For example: What types of problems should a technician look for first?

- Test the theory to determine cause
  For example: What should a technician do if a theory cannot be confirmed?

- Establish a plan of action to resolve the problem and implement the solution
  For example: What must be done before establishing a plan of action?

- Verify full system functionality and, if applicable, implement preventive measures
  For example: What is prevented by verifying full system functionality?

- Document findings, actions, and outcomes
  For example: When should technicians document their findings?

Identify the problem

The first step in the CompTIA troubleshooting theory process is to identify the problem. This is often done by questioning the user in addition to observing the behavior of the system.

> **EXAM TIP** CompTIA is including performance-based questions in the 220-801 and 220-802 exams. Instead of simple multiple choice questions, you can expect to see some different types of questions. One question type might require you to organize steps in a specific order, and the CompTIA troubleshooting theory is a perfect candidate for this type of question. If you see a list of items, you should be able to identify which items are in the CompTIA troubleshooting theory and their proper order.

True or false? The primary goal when questioning a user during the troubleshooting process is to identify the problem.

Answer: *True.* A direct question, such as "Can you tell me what isn't working?", allows the customer to describe the problem.

Open-ended questions are more useful than closed-ended questions when gathering information from a user. An open-ended question cannot be answered with a simple yes or no. Questions such as "Can you turn the computer on?", "Can you log on to the computer?", or "Can you browse the Internet?" are all closed-ended questions and won't necessarily give you as much information as an open-ended question.

> **MORE INFO** Chapter 5 of this book includes methods of interacting with customers in Objective 5.3. One of the topics in that section included the use of open-ended questions to get useful information from a user.

True or false? A computer manual is often the best source of information to determine the meaning of lights and other indicators.

Answer: *True.* Computers have a variety of different indicators used to indicate their current state, and a computer manual will describe their purpose.

A computer manual can be a key tool used to identify problems. For example, if a computer is not booting but you see light emitting diodes (LEDs) or other lights on the computer, you might be able to use the computer manual to interpret the meaning of the lights.

In addition to gathering information about the problem, CompTIA lists "perform backups before making changes" in this step. If you expect that any action you take might risk user data, ensure that you take steps to protect it. This might be as simple as ensuring that user data is saved before doing a reboot or backing up the data to another location.

> **EXAM TIP** The first step in the CompTIA troubleshooting theory is to identify the problem. Use open-ended questions when asking the user about the problem, and use the computer manual to interpret different indicators. If your actions present any risk to user data, ensure that the data is saved or backed up first.

> **MORE INFO** CompTIA lists troubleshooting theory topics that you should focus on for the exam. This is one of the objectives that are worthwhile to read again right before you take the test. If you don't have the objectives printed, go to the CompTIA site (*http://certification.comptia.org/getcertified/certifications/a.aspx*) and print them now. Highlight the entire Objective 4.1 list. As one of your final reviews, read the highlighted items. Chapter 10 of the CompTIA A+ Training Kit (Exam 220-801 and Exam 220-802), ISBN-10: 0735662681, includes a full section on troubleshooting theory.

Establish a theory of probable cause

After verifying a problem, you should establish a theory of the likely or probable cause. In this step, it's useful to look for the simplest and most obvious causes first.

True or false? If a display monitor is dark, one of the first things you should check is the graphics card.

Answer: *False.* If a display monitor is dark, one of the first things you should check is power.

If a display monitor is not plugged in and turned on, it won't work. This certainly seems obvious when you say it or read it. However, there are many trouble calls where a user overlooks the obvious. For example, a display monitor might have worked yesterday but it is not working today because a cleaning person accidentally bumped the power cord last night. Ideally, end users would check the power before calling a technician for help, but you can't count on end users to check for the obvious cause. In contrast, it would be embarrassing if a technician spent an hour troubleshooting a display monitor that simply wasn't plugged in.

EXAM TIP When establishing a theory of probable cause, it's important to check for the obvious problems. Another way of thinking about this is to look for the simplest problems first. After verifying that the problem isn't caused by an obvious issue, you move on to the less obvious problems.

Test the theory to determine cause

The next step after establishing a theory is to test the theory to determine whether it is the cause of the problem. If you can confirm the theory, you can then move onto the next steps to resolve the problem. If you can't confirm your theory, you'll need to establish a new theory and try again.

True or false? Technicians should escalate problems if they cannot come up with any other theories that they can confirm.

Answer: *True.* When technicians exhaust their knowledge about a problem, they should escalate it using established procedures within the organization.

Escalation means that a technician either consults with a supervisor or sends the problem to the next level of the organization's help desk. However, it is important for technicians to attempt to do everything they can to resolve the problem before escalating it.

Testing the theory is often repeated with the previous step of establishing a theory while troubleshooting. For example, imagine that you are asked to trouble-shoot a display monitor and you see that the power LED isn't lit. You might repeat the two steps of establishing a theory and testing the theory multiple times until you can resolve the problem. This process might look like this:

- Establish a theory: You suspect it isn't turned on.
  - Test the theory: You toggle the on/off switch, but the symptom doesn't change.
- Establish a theory: You suspect it isn't plugged in.
  - Test the theory: You reseat the plug on the monitor and the power strip, but the symptom doesn't change.
- Establish a theory: You suspect the power strip is turned off.
  - Test the theory: You see that the power switch on the power strip is off, confirming your theory.

It's worth noting that experienced technicians go through this process very quickly. They don't necessarily slow their thoughts down by thinking "I need to establish a theory" and "I need to test the theory." Even though they go through the process quickly, successful technicians still go through this process.

EXAM TIP If a theory is confirmed, a technician begins the next step to resolve the problem. If a theory is not confirmed, a technician either re-establishes a new theory or escalates the problem.

Establish a plan of action to resolve the problem and implement the solution

After testing a theory and verifying a problem, technicians should establish a plan of action to resolve the problem. The goal is to implement their plan to restore the system to full functionality.

True or false? Technicians should establish a plan of action immediately after identifying a theory of probable cause.

Answer: *False*. Technicians should test their theory before establishing a plan. After verifying that the theory is accurate, technicians should establish a plan.

EXAM TIP Technicians should establish a plan of action to resolve a problem after successfully testing a theory and determining the cause of the problem.

Verify full system functionality and, if applicable, implement preventive measures

Technicians should verify that a system is fully functional before returning it to service or returning it to the user. The system might have multiple problems that need to be addressed. Additionally, it is possible for technicians to inadvertently introduce problems during the repair, and these will be discovered and resolved while checking it out. For example, if you replace toner in a laser printer, you'll want to ensure that it prints successfully after replacing the toner. If you don't check it out, users can end up with systems that aren't operational and they submit another trouble call.

True or false? If another problem is identified after fixing one problem and resolving it, you should establish another theory to continue the troubleshooting process.

Answer: *True*. If you fix one issue but the system still has additional problems, you should repeat the troubleshooting process.

As you verify full system functionality, you might identify another problem, which returns you to the first step in the troubleshooting process. You then go to the next step to establish a theory of probable cause. For example, you might run antivirus software and remove a virus from a system. While checking out the system, you might then discover that some system files have become corrupt. You'll want to fix all the problems before returning the system to the user.

EXAM TIP After resolving a problem, technicians should check out a system to verify that it is fully functional.

Document findings, actions, and outcomes

The last step in the CompTIA troubleshooting theory process is to document your findings, actions, and outcomes. Many organizations have a specific method of documenting activity, and it's important to understand what the organization's expectations are and to follow the established procedures.

True or false? Technicians should document their findings before verifying that the system is fully functional.

Answer: *False.* The CompTIA troubleshooting theory process specifies that technicians should document their findings after verifying that the system is fully functional. That is, documentation is the last step in the process.

> **EXAM TIP** The last step in the CompTIA troubleshooting process is "Document findings, actions, and outcomes."

Can you answer these questions?

You can find the answers to these questions at the end of this chapter.

1. List the six CompTIA troubleshooting steps in their proper order.
2. What should a technician do after confirming a theory of probable cause?
3. What should a technician do if a theory cannot be confirmed?
4. What is the last step in the CompTIA troubleshooting theory process?

Objective 4.2: Given a scenario, troubleshoot common problems related to motherboards, RAM, CPU and power with appropriate tools

Many common problems are related to core hardware components such as the motherboard, random access memory (RAM), central processing unit (CPU), and the power supply. Technicians should be able to evaluate a scenario and identify likely causes. There are many common symptoms that point to specific issues that technicians should know. Additionally, there are some common tools that help technicians troubleshoot these types of hardware problems. This objective builds on knowledge from several objectives from the PC Hardware domain from Exam 220-801. This includes Objective 1.2, "Differentiate between motherboard components, their purposes, and properties"; Objective 1.3, "Compare and contrast RAM types and features"; and Objective 1.6, "Differentiate among various CPU types and features and select the appropriate cooling method." These objectives were covered in Chapter 1, "PC hardware," of this book.

Exam need to know...

- Common symptoms
  For example: What does a "non-bootable drive" error typically indicate?

- Tools
  For example: What two tools are used to measure voltages for a power supply?

Common symptoms

There are many common symptoms resulting from computer hardware problems that technicians will encounter. Some of these problems point to a single hardware component, but other symptoms might be due to one or more possible hardware problems. Some symptoms can also be caused by configuration errors.

True or false? A computer that cannot boot but emits only a beep code might have faulty memory.

Answer: *True.* The power on self-test (POST) checks key components, including the memory, and emits a beep code if one of the components fails the test.

Some of the hardware that is verified by a successful POST includes RAM, CPU, system timer, keyboard, and video components. Components that aren't needed for a system to boot aren't checked by POST and won't cause POST errors. For example, a modem is used only after booting into the operating system and is not checked by POST.

The POST beep codes vary from one BIOS to another. System manuals have details on the beep codes, and these manuals are usually available online.

A buzz or a quickly repeating beep often indicates a problem with random access memory (RAM). You can sometimes resolve the problem by reseating the RAM.

True or false? A blank screen accompanied by a series of beeps after turning on a computer indicates a faulty hard drive.

Answer: *False.* The beeps indicate a POST error, which, accompanied by a blank screen, likely indicates a video card problem. If the hard drive has a problem, it will not prevent the POST from displaying data on the monitor.

> **EXAM TIP** The POST checks out key hardware components such as memory, video, the motherboard, the keyboard, and the power supply. If one of these components fails the test, the POST emits a beep code. A single beep typically indicates that the system has passed the POST.

True or false? Dust buildup within a computer can cause a system to overheat and turn off after a period of time.

Answer: *True.* Excessive dust buildup restricts airflow and can result in problems related to overheating.

A computer can fail from overheating, causing it to shut down. Many systems have internal sensors that cause the system to automatically shut down before heat can damage the computer.

If a system is shutting down by itself after running for a while, it's worth your time to open it up and clean it out. You can take it outside and blow it out with compressed air or vacuum it out with an electrostatic discharge (ESD)–safe vacuum cleaner. This problem could also be due to failing or disconnected fans.

Two components that help keep the CPU cool are the heat sink and the CPU fan. The heat sink is clamped to the CPU with thermal paste between the two, and a fan is typically placed on top of the heat sink. If the heat sink isn't secured to the CPU or if the CPU fan isn't working properly, the CPU can overheat. This can also result in unexpected shutdowns or system lockups.

EXAM TIP Systems that overheat will shut down after a short period of time. They might overheat due to faulty fans or due to excessive dust preventing adequate airflow. In some cases, a system will have internal temperature sensors and turn itself off before it is damaged. In other cases, the overheating results in random errors, such as the system locking or giving a stop error, also known as a Blue Screen of Death, or BSOD.

Several objectives refer to BSOD, which is short for Blue Screen of Death. This is actually a stop error that causes Windows to stop, but it doesn't actually indicate that Windows is dead.

Stop errors are displayed on a blue screen, and they provide valuable information about the problem. In some cases, the plain text information shown on the blue screen gives you a clear idea of what caused the problem. In other cases, the text includes a hexadecimal code that you need to look up.

For example, you might see a stop error with the following code: 0x0000007B. The 0x indicates that the number is hexadecimal (often read as "hex"), and the number includes leading zeros. In this case, it's often referred to as a hex 7B stop error. If you search Bing.com with "7B stop error," you'll find that it is typically caused by a problem with the hard drive, such as an incorrect driver being used with the hard drive.

MORE INFO The following site includes a list of many stop error codes, with short explanations of the code and links to get more information: *http://pcsupport.about.com/od/findbyerrormessage/tp/stop_error_list.htm*.

True or false? A strong burning odor coming from a PC indicates a failed CMOS battery.

Answer: *False.* A strong burning odor typically indicates a faulty power supply unit (PSU) or possibly a burnt electronic component on the motherboard or one of the circuit boards.

PSUs have many electronic components. When some of them fail, they emit an odor and sometimes emit smoke but they usually don't catch on fire. If the power supply fails, it should be replaced.

When a complementary metal oxide semiconductor (CMOS) battery fails, it affects the settings in the BIOS. In some cases, a failing battery results in checksum or battery errors reported by the BIOS when the system is booted, errors with the system time and date settings, or a slow boot as all the BIOS hardware settings are rebuilt each time that the computer is turned on. A failing battery won't emit a burning odor.

> **EXAM TIP** A strong burning odor coming from a PC typically indicates a failed power supply. You should inspect the system, and if you don't see components on the motherboard or circuit boards that are obviously damaged from heat, the power supply is the most obvious choice. You won't necessarily see damage on the outside of the power supply, but you can often detect the burning smell as being strongest from the power supply vents. The system should be powered down prior to replacing a power supply.

> **MORE INFO** Chapter 1 of the CompTIA A+ Training Kit (Exam 220-801 and Exam 220-802), ISBN-10: 0735662681, includes more detailed information about power supplies, including steps to replace them.

True or false? Faulty RAM can cause random reboots on a system.

Answer: *True*. Faulty RAM can cause a system to randomly reboot. This typically occurs anytime the faulty RAM is accessed. However, this isn't predictable, so it appears random.

Random reboots can be caused by many problems, including the following:

- **Faulty RAM** The RAM could have a specific address that is faulty or have addresses that are slightly damaged by ESD and intermittently fail. This type of problem often results in a stop error indicating a memory error. You can run the Windows Memory Diagnostic on RAM to check its integrity.

- **Faulty PSU** PSUs normally provide consistent voltages to systems, but if these voltages are out of tolerance, it can cause random reboots. For example, a 12-VDC rail should not waver more than 5 percent (from 11.2 VDC to 12.6 VDC). A faulty power supply can waver, and when it is too far out of tolerance, it can cause system problems.

- **Overheating** System problems from overheating typically occur soon after a system is started but can also appear to be random. For example, a system might operate without any problems when a user opens a single application but overheat when the user opens multiple applications, stressing the CPU.

- **Malicious software (malware)** Malware will sometimes cause random reboots. If the problem isn't hardware-related, antivirus software should be run to check the system.

Some additional symptoms you might encounter are:

- **Intermittent device failure** Intermittent failures are difficult to trouble-shoot because sometimes they work and sometimes they don't, and you have to see it when it's not working to troubleshoot it effectively. One of the first things to check is signs of overheating due to failing fans or excessive dust clogging the airflow through the system. Another thing to check is the PSU. A failing PSU with voltages that fall out of tolerance periodically can cause intermittent failures. You can check the voltages with a multimeter or a power supply tester. If you see the voltages varying at all, replace the PSU.

- **Fans spin—no power to other devices** This symptom indicates that the CPU is not receiving power. Motherboards have a special 4-pin or 8-pin power connector used to provide power to the CPU. You'll find it located close to the CPU. Check to ensure this connector is plugged in and verify that it is receiving the proper voltage from the PSU. You might need to replace the PSU if the motherboard isn't receiving the correct voltage. If this connec-tor is receiving power but you still have this symptom, it indicates the voltage regulator on the motherboard has failed. You'll probably need to replace the motherboard.

- **Indicator lights** Computers have LED indicators used to show when a system is powered on. If the power LED is not lit and the system has no power even after pressing the power button, you should ensure that the system is plugged into a power outlet such as a surge protector or uninter-ruptible power supply (UPS) that is turned on. Some PSUs have separate power switches on the rear of the computer and you should ensure this is turned on. Additionally, you should ensure the voltage selection switch is set to the proper input voltage. For example, if the computer is located in North America, you should ensure the voltage selection switch is set to 115. The power supply will not work if it is set to 230. If you've checked all of these items, the next step is to replace the PSU.

Tools

Some hardware problems are very easy to diagnose, but others require that PC technicians use specific tools. For example, if you smell a burning odor coming from the power supply, it's very likely that the power supply is faulty. You don't need any tools other than your sense of smell. However, subtle failures with a power supply require special tools to diagnose and resolve. Successful PC technicians are aware of common hardware tools, when they should be used, and how to use them.

True or false? A power supply tester can check a power supply that is removed from a computer.

Answer: *True*. Power supply testers provide the necessary load for a power supply so that they can be checked without being installed in a computer.

Multimeters are often used to measure the voltage coming from a power supply, but the power supply must be connected to a load. For example, if you want to measure the power going to the 20 pin or 24 pin connector for the motherboard, the power supply needs to be connected to the motherboard. If you try to measure the voltage with the connector disconnected, the measurements aren't accurate.

A power supply tester provides a load and allows you to check a power supply even if it isn't installed in a computer. You hook up the power cables to the power supply tester, connect the power supply to AC power, and turn it on. Power supply testers typically provide a visual indication of exact voltages, and some even point out specific problems.

> **EXAM TIP** Use a multimeter to check voltages from a power supply that is connected to a computer. Use a power supply tester to measure voltages from a power supply that isn't connected.

True or false? A POST card can be used to diagnose some hardware problems on a computer that cannot boot into Windows.

Answer: *True*. If a system cannot boot, you can use a POST card to identify the failure.

POST often gives beep codes that you can interpret with the manual, but a POST card can provide much more detailed information than just a series of beeps. Some motherboards include POST decoders built into them. They typically have an LED that can display two digit codes, and the motherboard manual provides detailed information about each of the codes. If the motherboard doesn't include a POST decoder, you can use a POST card that plugs into an expansion slot.

> **EXAM TIP** POST cards and built-in POST decoders provide detailed information about the power on self-test after a system starts. These are effective when the simple beep code doesn't give you enough information to diagnose and resolve the problem.

> **MORE INFO** You can see pictures of multimeters, power supply testers, and POST cards by searching on *http://bing.com/images* using the appropriate search phrase. Chapter 2 of the CompTIA A+ Training Kit (Exam 220-801 and Exam 220-802), ISBN-10: 0735662681, includes more detailed information about POST and POST cards. It also includes a picture of a motherboard with an onboard POST decoder.

Can you answer these questions?

You can find the answers to these questions at the end of this chapter.

1. What is the most likely result if a heat sink clamp breaks and is not repaired?
2. What are some common hardware issues that can result in unexpected shutdowns or system lockups?
3. What is used to measure voltages on a power supply that isn't installed in a computer?

Objective 4.3: Given a scenario, troubleshoot hard drives and RAID arrays with appropriate tools

Hard drives are an important component within computers, but because they are among the few components within a computer that have moving parts, they are highly susceptible to failure. PC technicians need to be able to recognize common symptoms related to hard drives and be familiar with tools they can use to diagnose, repair, and/or replace them. Many systems support RAID (redundant array of inexpensive disks) configurations, which include two or more disk drives. Individual disks within a RAID work the same internally as other hard disk drives. However, technicians need to be aware of the different types of RAID configurations, especially which ones provide fault tolerance. This objective builds on knowledge from Objective 1.5, "Install and configure storage devices and use appropriate media," from Exam 220-801, covered in Chapter 1 of this book.

Exam need to know...

- Common symptoms
  For example: What does a loud clicking noise indicate?

- Tools
  For example: What can you use to read data from a functioning hard drive removed from a failed laptop?

Common symptoms

There are many common symptoms that PC technicians see when working with hard drives. Some symptoms indicate that a drive has failed or is failing. Other symptoms indicate that a drive isn't recognized by the computer because it hasn't been configured properly.

True or false? Two PATA drives will function in the same IDE channel as long as one is configured as master and the other is configured as anything else, such as slave or cable select.

Answer: *False.* Parallel ATA (PATA) drives will not function in the same integrated drive electronics (IDE) channel if one is configured as master and the other is not configured as slave.

A single IDE channel supports up to two drives. If one is configured as the master, the second drive should be configured as the slave. If both drives are configured with cable select (CS), they will be assigned as master or slave, depending on their position on the cable. Special cables are used, and one connector is labeled master and another connector is labeled slave, as shown in Figure 9-1.

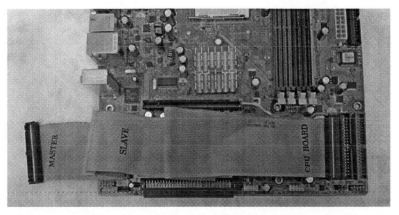

FIGURE 9-1 Master/Slave cable used with cable select.

If the drives are not jumpered as master and slave or if both drives are not configured with cable select, it causes errors. Some errors that you might see from incorrectly configured PATA jumpers include the following:

- Primary drive 0 not found
- No boot device found
- Drive not recognized
- OS not found

NOTE Even though PATA drives have been widely replaced with serial ATA (SATA) drives in newer computers, there are still many PATA drives in use. Also, the exam objectives specifically mention PATA drives, so you should be familiar with common errors related to jumpers.

EXAM TIP PATA drives have jumpers that need to be properly configured. You can use master/slave jumpers to set one drive as the master and the second drive as the slave. You can also use a special cable and configure both drives with cable select.

True or false? A loud clicking noise from a computer often indicates a failing hard drive.

Answer: *True.* A classic symptom of a failing hard drive is a clicking noise.

Hard drives have platters that spin at high speeds, such as 5,400 revolutions per minute (RPM) or higher. If something gets out of alignment just a little, it can cause the platter to make contact with other components inside the drive and you'll hear a clicking noise. When you hear a drive clicking, you should assume that it is failing and replace it as soon as possible before it fails completely.

If a drive is failing for any reason, you should attempt to back up the data from the drive as soon as possible. If it is the primary drive in a computer, it might not be able to boot the system successfully, but it might still have data that you can retrieve. You can install the drive in another computer as a secondary drive long enough to back up data from the drive.

EXAM TIP A loud clicking noise coming from a computer typically indicates a failed or failing hard drive. You should attempt to back up data from the hard drive as soon as possible and take the hard drive out of service.

True or false? If one drive in a RAID-0 fails, you can still retrieve data from the RAID.

Answer: *False.* A RAID-0 does not provide data redundancy, and if one drive fails, you need to replace the drive and restore the data from a backup.

Some RAID configurations provide fault tolerance. This means that the RAID can suffer a fault but tolerate the failure and continue to operate. Some of the common RAID configurations and their fault tolerance characteristics include the following:

- **RAID-0 (striped array)** This uses two or more disks and provides enhanced performance over a single disk. It cannot tolerate a failure of any disk in the array. If any disk fails, all data is lost.

- **RAID-1 (mirror)** This uses two disks. It writes the same data on each of the disks, and it can tolerate a failure in either drive without losing any data.

- **RAID-5 (striping with parity)** This uses three or more disks and uses the equivalent of one drive for parity. The parity provides fault tolerance, and a RAID-5 can tolerate a failure in any single drive in the array without losing data.

- **RAID-10 (a stripe of mirrors)** This uses an even number of disks, such as four, six, eight, and so on. Disks are paired and configured as mirrors similar to RAID-1. These mirrors are then combined into a stripe similar to a RAID-0. A RAID-10 combines the performance enhancements of a RAID-0 with the fault tolerance of a RAID-1 and tolerates the failure of multiple drives as long as two drives in any mirror do not fail.

EXAM TIP If a drive in a RAID array fails, you'll need to replace it. If it is a RAID-0, you'll need to restore data from backups. If it is a RAID-1, RAID-5, or RAID-10, you need to follow the procedures to restore the RAID after replacing a failed drive, but the data should still be available without requiring you to restore it.

MORE INFO Chapter 6, "Operating systems," of this book included information about software-based RAID configurations supported by Windows. As a reminder, Windows XP and Windows Vista operating systems support RAID-0 on dynamic disks. Windows 7 supports RAID-0 and RAID-1 on dynamic disks. All three operating systems support hardware-based RAID-0, RAID-1, and RAID-5 disk subsystems. A hardware-based RAID is treated as a single disk by the operating system.

Other symptoms or errors that you might see related to a failed or failing hard drive include the following:

- Read/write failures
- Slow performance
- Failure to boot
- RAID not found
- RAID stops working
- Stop error (BSOD) indicating a drive problem

Tools

When a drive fails, you'll often replace it. One of the primary hardware tools that you'll use when replacing a hard drive is a screwdriver, although many systems are designed to permit drive replacement without needing any tools. There are several other tools you might also use when troubleshooting and repairing issues with hard drives.

True or false? A USB hard drive enclosure is useful for accessing data from a failed laptop computer.

Answer: *True*. You can remove the hard drive from a failed laptop, install it in a USB hard drive enclosure, and access the data by plugging it into the USB port of another computer.

External hard drive enclosures are available for both SATA and PATA drives. They are typically designed to accept the smaller 2.5-inch hard drives used in laptop computers. After installing the drive in the enclosure, you can plug it into a USB port of another computer and use it as an external hard drive.

> **EXAM TIP** External enclosures are useful tools for accessing data from laptop drives. If a laptop fails, you can usually remove the hard drive rather easily, install it in an external enclosure, and have instant access to the data.

> **MORE INFO** Hard drive enclosures are relatively inexpensive and available for a wide variety of hard drives. Chapter 8 of the CompTIA A+ Training Kit (Exam 220-801 and Exam 220-802), ISBN-10: 0735662681, includes detailed information about laptops and has a picture of an open laptop with one drive partially removed.

True or false? Screwdrivers can become magnetized and should be used with caution around magnetic media.

Answer: *True*. Any type of magnet, including magnetized screwdrivers, can corrupt data on magnetic media.

Screwdrivers are sometimes magnetized on purpose so that screws stick to them or to easily pick up dropped screws in tight places. They can be useful in many situations but should be used with caution around magnetic media.

Besides physical tools, there are also software tools that can be used with disks, including the following:

- **chkdsk**   This command prompt tool is useful for checking the integrity of disks. It can also be used to repair problems and recover data in certain situations. The GUI equivalent is the Check Disk tool available in Windows Explorer.
- **format**   You use the format command to configure a disk with specific file systems, such as FAT32 or NTFS.

- **fdisk**   This is used to partition a disk when you have only older command prompt tools available. It is not needed in Windows operating systems or when installing current operating systems.
- **File recovery software**   This includes backup programs to restore data and specialty software designed to recover software from a failing disk.

MORE INFO   The chkdsk, format, and fdisk command line tools were covered in different objectives in Chapter 6 within Objective 1.2, "Given a scenario, install, and configure the operating system using the most appropriate method"; Objective 1.3, "Given a scenario, use appropriate command line tools"; Objective 1.4, "Given a scenario, use appropriate operating system features and tools"; and Objective 1.7, "Perform preventive maintenance procedures using appropriate tools."

EXAM TIP   Chkdsk is a very useful tool when troubleshooting problems with hard drives. If you are getting read errors from a disk, you can use the chkdsk command to recover information from the disk, check the entire disk for bad sectors, and mark bad sectors so that they aren't used again.

Can you answer these questions?

You can find the answers to these questions at the end of this chapter.

1. How should you configure two PATA drives used in the same IDE channel?
2. What type(s) of RAID cannot tolerate a single failed drive and require you to restore data after rebuilding the RAID?
3. What tool would you use to check the integrity of a disk?

Objective 4.4: Given a scenario, troubleshoot common video and display issues

The quality of video coming out of computers and the quality of display monitors have become progressively better and better over the years. When everything is working, the video can be dazzling. However, just like any other computer component, PC technicians are likely to be called upon to diagnose and resolve systems experiencing problems with video cards or display monitors. This objective expects you to be aware of common symptoms and their likely cause. This objective builds on knowledge from Objective 1.10, "Given a scenario, evaluate types and features of display devices," from Exam 220-801 covered in Chapter 1 of this book.

Exam need to know...

- Common symptoms
  For example: What will you see if a video cable is loose? Why would a display monitor go to sleep?

Common symptoms

There are several symptoms that point to problems related to the graphics of a computer. The primary components that can cause problems related to video are as follows:

- The motherboard, if the system is using onboard graphics
- The video card, if the system is using a dedicated graphics card
- Device drivers for the system's graphics
- The cable between the computer and the monitor
- The monitor itself
- The monitor's power connection

True or false? A monitor will go to sleep instead of displaying video if it is configured for the wrong input mode.

Answer: *True.* Most monitors will go to a lower power mode known as sleep if they are not receiving any input from the computer.

Some monitors can be configured for a specific input mode such as Video Graphics Array (VGA), Digital Visual Interface (DVI), and High-Definition Multimedia Interface (HDMI). If the monitor is manually configured to receive a DVI input, it will use data only from the DVI port. If you connect an HDMI cable to the HDMI port but don't connect anything to the DVI port, the display will behave as if the computer is turned off. Given enough time, it will go into a low power state. Many newer monitors automatically scan all the ports, looking for one that is connected instead of using a single port.

True or false? Computers with a dedicated video card have another video port available on the back of a computer and either one can be used.

Answer: *False.* When a dedicated video card is added, the onboard video port from the motherboard is disabled in the BIOS but it is still available at the back of the computer.

If you plug a monitor into an onboard video port that has been disabled, it will not display any data and will go to sleep after a while. When manufacturers sell computers with a dedicated video card, they will typically add a label indicating that the port is disabled and should not be used. However, when people plug in the video connection from the monitor, they often reach around to the back of the computer and don't see the label. Because the port is disabled, the monitor will go to sleep after a short time.

True or false? Dedicated video cards often require additional power connections.

Answer: *True.* Many video cards are Peripheral Component Interconnect Express (PCIe) cards, and they require extra power connections, typically provided by either a 6-pin or 8-pin power connector.

Power supplies commonly have a PCIe power connector, and when the motherboard's onboard video is used, this connector is plugged into the motherboard. When you add a dedicated video card that you'll use instead of the onboard video, you often need to move this power connection from the motherboard to the video card.

True or false? A loose connection to a monitor can result in video problems with the display when the monitor is swiveled on its base.

Answer: *True.* A loose connection can result in a wide assortment of display problems, and these will be apparent when the monitor is moved.

If the quality of a display is inconsistent on a monitor, one of the first things to do is to check that the cable is securely attached to both the monitor and the computer. Many video cable types have screws, allowing you to ensure that it is securely attached.

True or false? A screen with stuck or dead pixels will have white, black, or colored dots that never change.

Answer: *True.* Dead pixels and stuck pixels are small dots on the monitor that don't change.

A monitor uses picture elements (pixels) typically composed of three separate sub-pixels representing red, green, and blue. When none of these sub-pixels can turn on, the pixel is dead and stays as only white (or only black, depending on the type of display). While some methods claim to fix a dead pixel, you'll find that most dead pixels cannot be repaired. If the dead pixels on a monitor are too distracting, the only clear resolution is to replace the monitor.

When one or two of these sub-pixels cannot turn on, the pixel is stuck in a color. In some cases, stuck pixels can be repaired by massaging the monitor around the stuck pixel. There are also programs available that try to quickly cycle the pixels through different colors to shock the pixels into working.

MORE INFO The following WikiHow article describes some methods that can be used to fix a stuck pixel on an LCD monitor: *http://www.wikihow.com/Fix-a-Stuck-Pixel-on-an-LCD-Monitor.*

True or false? An incompatible video driver can cause random loss of video displayed on a monitor.

Answer: *True.* Incompatible video drivers can cause a wide assortment of problems, including random loss of video.

Windows will usually prevent you from installing an incompatible driver. However, it is sometimes possible to install a similar driver that is not compatible with the device. If a similar but incorrect driver is installed, you'll see problems with the displayed video, affecting its quality. In some cases, a similar but incorrect driver will cause Windows to stop with a fatal stop error. If Windows doesn't have a compatible driver, it will often default to VGA mode.

Random video problems can also be caused by a failing video graphics processing unit (GPU) or video card. GPUs can generate as much heat as a CPU and often have additional fans used to keep them cool. If they overheat they can send corrupted video to the monitor with random artifacts or other problems.

> **EXAM TIP** Using the incorrect video driver will cause random problems, such as random artifacts or random loss of video. If these problems persist with the valid driver, the video card might be overheating or failing.

True or false? If a specific area of an LCD monitor is discolored, you can degauss it to resolve the problem.

Answer: *False.* You can degauss a cathode ray tube (CRT) monitor, but you cannot degauss a liquid crystal display (LCD) monitor.

CRT monitors can become magnetized, causing a specific area of the screen to be discolored. CRT monitors typically have a degaussing button, and when you press it, it removes the problem. Other monitor types are not degaussed.

Some additional symptoms you might encounter are:

- **Flickering image** You are most likely to see a flickering image on a CRT monitor. The flickering is caused by the refresh rate being set too low and it can cause headaches. If you increase the refresh rate to 72 Hz or higher, it eliminates the flicker. Other types of monitors such as LED and LCD monitors are not susceptible to flicker from a low refresh rate. However, if the cable is loose, you might notice random flickering on any type of monitor. You can resolve this by reseating the cables.

- **Distorted image** A distorted image can be caused by many different things. First, ensure that the cable is not too long and it is plugged in securely. If the size of the image is distorted on LED or LCD monitors, ensure that the resolution is set to the native resolution of the monitor. This symptom can be caused by incorrect drivers so you should you have the most up-to-date drivers for the video card. The problem can also be due to a failing video card, or a failing video chip on the motherboard.

Can you answer these questions?

You can find the answers to these questions at the end of this chapter.

1. You are asked to troubleshoot a monitor that is not displaying video. You've verified that the monitor has power and that the computer is turned on. What else should you check?

2. What is the most likely cause of a few white dots in specific locations on a monitor?

3. What is a possible result of using the incorrect driver for a video card?

Objective 4.5: Given a scenario, troubleshoot wired and wireless networks with appropriate tools

In this objective, you'll need to be able to recognize common symptoms related to both wired and wireless networks, and the likely cause of these symptoms. Networking problems result either in a total loss of connectivity for one or more clients or in limited or reduced connectivity. In addition to knowing the symptoms, you also need to be aware of tools that you can use to troubleshoot and resolve problems. Some tools are hardware tools, such as a cable tester, and other tools are software tools, such as the ping command. This objective builds on knowledge from the Networking domain of the 220-801 exam covered in Chapter 2, "Networking," of this book. It also builds on Objective 1.6, "Set up and configure Windows networking on a client/desktop"; Objective 2.5, "Given a scenario, secure a SOHO wireless network"; and Objective 2.6, "Given a scenario, secure a SOHO wired network," covered in Chapter 6 and Chapter 7, "Security," of this book.

Exam need to know...

- Common symptoms
  For example: What can cause intermittent connectivity on a wireless network?

- Tools
  For example: What hardware tools are used to create and test cables? What software tools are used to test connectivity?

Common symptoms

When working with networks, you need to have a good understanding of how things work normally before you can understand and recognize the common symptoms indicating problems. As a reminder, the Networking domain makes up 27 percent of the 220-801 exam. If you have mastered that material, it is much easier to recognize symptoms when things aren't working.

True or false? You should check the RJ-45 connection if a modem gives an error of "no dial tone."

Answer: *False.* A modem uses a phone line with an RJ-11 connection, so the RJ-11 phone connection should be checked instead of an RJ-45 connection.

RJ-45 connections are used with twisted-pair cables to connect networking devices. If the RJ-45 connector is removed, a system won't have network connectivity, but it won't affect its ability to connect with a modem.

True or false? You can often resolve IP conflicts in a network using DHCP by rebooting a system.

Answer: *True.* If you reboot a system using Dynamic Host Configuration Protocol (DHCP), it will usually eliminate an IP address conflict.

An IP address conflict is caused by two systems having the same IP address. This is typically caused by someone manually configuring an IP address on a device or system with the same IP address previously issued by DHCP. If you reboot a system using DHCP, it will normally get an IP address that doesn't cause a conflict.

For example, imagine that a computer named Win7 receives an IP address of 192.168.1.151 from DHCP. Later, a technician manually assigns a printer with an IP address of 192.168.1.151, causing a conflict. If you reboot the Win7 computer, it will get a different IP address and resolve the conflict.

Windows-based systems check for conflicts before accepting a lease from DHCP. If DHCP offers an IP address that is assigned on the network, the Windows-based system will reject the lease and request a new one with a different IP address. Administrators can also configure DHCP to check for conflicts before issuing an IP address.

This is a good example of how you can often resolve many computer ills by rebooting a system. There are many technical details underlying all the reasons why a reboot helps, but you don't always have to know or understand them all. If a system has problems, reboot it and see whether the problem remains. You will need to dig deeper if you see the same problem repeating.

EXAM TIP You can often eliminate an IP address conflict by rebooting a DHCP client. When the client is rebooted, it will get a new IP address removing the conflict.

MORE INFO DHCP topics are covered in Chapter 2 of this book within Objective 2.3, "Explain properties and characteristics of TCP/IP." Also, Chapter 21 of the CompTIA A+ Training Kit (Exam 220-801 and Exam 220-802), ISBN-10: 0735662681, provides more detailed information on DHCP.

True or false? You can often resolve intermittent connectivity issues by reducing the power levels of the WAP.

Answer: *False.* Increasing the power levels of a wireless access point (WAP) improves connectivity for wireless devices and helps prevent intermittent connectivity issues.

You can reduce the power levels to reduce the overall footprint of the wireless network. This is sometimes done to prevent unauthorized individuals from connecting to the network. The drawback is reduced performance for the clients that are connected. Other methods used to prevent unauthorized connections include media access control (MAC) address filtering and securing the wireless network with encryption, such as with Wi-Fi Protected Access version 2 (WPA2).

When unauthorized individuals can connect to a network, it presents a potential security issue, which is addressed in Chapter 7. From a simpler perspective, unauthorized individuals connected to a network can result in slower transfer speeds. For example, if a user sets up a wireless network in an apartment building, unauthorized users in other apartments could potentially tap into the network. If they succeed, they sap network performance, resulting in slower transfer speeds for the owner.

EXAM TIP Some methods used to prevent unauthorized individuals from connecting to a wireless network include using encryption (such as WPA2), MAC address filtering, and reducing the power levels of the WAP. The most secure method is WPA2.

True or false? A user cannot connect to a wireless network without using the proper SSID.

Answer: *True.* The service set identifier (SSID) is the name of the wireless network, and it is needed to connect to the wireless network.

The SSID is often set to broadcast by default, which makes it easy to identify the wireless network. However, if the SSID broadcast is disabled, users need to enter the SSID manually.

True or false? Out-of-date drivers for a wireless card can result in intermittent connectivity.

Answer: *True.* Drivers are updated by manufacturers to resolve problems, and if a wireless card has intermittent connectivity, it might be resolved by updating the drivers.

This issue might appear when purchasing a new laptop or when installing a new wireless card. The driver for a new system or included with a new wireless card might be an early version. If a newer driver is available, it should be installed, especially if the card is not performing properly. In contrast, if a wireless card has been working and suddenly started having intermittent connectivity issues, the problem is most likely external to the laptop.

EXAM TIP This philosophy extends for any new systems or new devices. It's best to ensure that the system is using the most up-to-date drivers for the installed hardware.

Another symptom you might see is a low RF signal. This indicates that the WAP is not sending out a strong enough signal, interference is reducing the strength of the signal, the wireless device is too far away from the WAP, or the wireless device has a problem with its wireless antenna. As mentioned previously, you can check the power levels of the WAP and increase them.

Interference can come from electromagnetic or radio frequency (RF) sources. Electromagnetic interference comes from devices close to the WAP such as fluorescent lights and you can reduce this problem by moving the WAP. If there are several other wireless networks, it's very possible they are interfering with each other. Most wireless networks use channel 6 so you can change the WAP to use channel 1 or 11. There is enough separation between channels 1, 6, and 11 that they do not interfere with each other.

Last, the problem might be in the wireless device itself. Most laptops use a PCIe card for wireless connections. This wireless card has two antenna cables connected to it which are typically routed around the display panel. Verify that the antenna cables are attached securely to the wireless card.

Tools

Both hardware and software tools are used to maintain and troubleshoot networks. Test takers are expected to understand the purpose of these tools and how they are used.

True or false? A crimper is used to fasten an RJ-45 connector onto twisted-pair cables.

Answer: *True*. Crimpers are used to secure connectors onto cables, and this includes securing RJ-45 connectors onto twisted-pair cables.

Wire strippers are also used when attaching connectors to cables. You cut the cable to length, remove the cable jacket from the cable, and position the individual wires in the connector. The crimper then creates the electrical and mechanical connections between the cable and connector. Many crimpers have wire stripping tools built into them.

True or false? Punch down tools are used to secure twisted-pair cables to patch panels, and crimpers are used to secure twisted-pair cables to wall jacks.

Answer: *False*. Punch down tools are used to secure twisted-pair cables to both patch panels and wall jacks.

The typical paths of a twisted-pair connection (such as a CAT 5E or CAT 6 cable) from a computer to a switch in a wiring closet are as follows:

- **From computer to wall jack** This cable has RJ-45 connectors on both ends, secured with a crimper.
- **From back of wall jack to rear of patch panel in wiring closet** This cable is secured to both the wall jack and the patch panel with a punch down tool.
- **From front of patch panel to switch** This is a short jumper cable with RJ-45 connectors on both ends, secured with a crimper.

EXAM TIP Wire strippers are used to remove cable jackets and wire insulation. Crimpers are used to secure RJ-45 connectors onto twisted-pair cables. Punch down tools are used to secure twisted-pair cables onto wall jacks and punch down blocks.

True or false? You can use a toner probe to ensure that a cable is plugged into the correct port on a patch panel.

Answer: *True*. Toner probes are used to trace cables between rooms and can be used to verify that they are plugged into the correct port.

For example, imagine that you are connecting cables for a room that has six RJ-45 wall jacks labeled as WJ-1 through WJ-6. The cables from these jacks go to a punch down block in a wiring closet, and you want to ensure that the connections from the punch down block go to ports 1 through 6 on the network switch. That is, WJ-1 should go to port 1 on the switch, WJ-2 should go to port 2 on the switch, and so on.

A toner probe has two components. One component generates a tone that can be connected to one end of a cable, and the other component has a speaker used to hear the tone on the other end. You can connect the tone to a wire at WJ-1. You can then go to the wiring closet and connect the speaker to different wires on the punch down block until you hear the tone. When you find the wire on the back of the punch down plug, you know what port it is connected to on the front of the punch down block. You can then ensure that this port is connected to port 1 of the switch.

Two other hardware tools that can assist with troubleshooting networks are cable testers and loopback plugs:

- Cable testers are used to verify that a cable is wired properly and performing up to specifications. For example, it can verify that a CAT 6 cable meets the specifications of a CAT 6 cable.

- Loopback plugs are used to test individual systems. For example, you can plug a loopback plug into a network interface card (NIC) to verify that the NIC is functioning properly.

EXAM TIP Toner probes are used to trace cables and can be used to ensure that you are plugging a cable into the correct ports. Cable testers verify that a cable is wired correctly and meets specifications. Loopback plugs are used when testing NICs.

MORE INFO You should be able to identify the various hardware tools by sight. If you aren't familiar with them, go to *http://www.bing.com/images* and enter the name of the tool to see pictures. For example, if you enter "crimper," you'll see several pictures of different types of crimpers.

True or false? Ipconfig is useful when troubleshooting to verify that a system has a valid IP address.

Answer: *True.* When a system has connectivity problems, the **ipconfig** command can help you quickly verify that a system has an IP address.

When a system has connectivity problems, both **ipconfig** and **ping** are often used to check out the system. **Ipconfig** verifies the IP address and other TCP/IP configuration information. It can be followed with one or more **ping** commands to check connectivity with other systems on the network.

True or false? A firewall can block pings even when a system is operational.

Answer: *True.* **Ping** requests can be blocked by a firewall.

If a **ping** succeeds, you know that a system is operational on the network. However, if it fails, it doesn't necessarily confirm that the system is not operational. Many firewalls block ping requests to protect systems from known attack methods.

Some other tools that can assist with troubleshooting networks include the following:

- **tracert**   This command shows all the routers between two systems. It can help identify a connectivity problem between two systems.
- **netstat**   This command is useful for viewing open ports on a computer.
- **nbtstat**   This command is used to troubleshoot NetBIOS name resolution issues.
- **Wireless locator**   Administrators use this to identify the footprint of a wireless network and locate unauthorized WAPs.

Can you answer these questions?

You can find the answers to these questions at the end of this chapter.

1. What is a potential performance impact of lowering power levels on a WAP?
2. What hardware tools would you use to create and test a twisted-pair cable?
3. What can cause intermittent connectivity on a wireless network?

Objective 4.6: Given a scenario, troubleshoot operating system problems with appropriate tools

In this objective, you're expected to be able to recognize common symptoms related to Windows operating system problems and resolve them with available tools. This objective builds on knowledge from many of the objectives covered in the Operating Systems domain of Exam 220-802 covered in Chapter 6 of this book.

Exam need to know...

- Common symptoms
  For example: What can you use to repair a system that no longer boots after installing new device drivers? What does the error "NTLDR is missing" indicate?
- Tools
  For example: What tool would you use to repair system files? What tool is used to read system log files?

Common symptoms

Many of the common symptoms in this section refer to problems that prevent the computer from starting at all. Other symptoms refer to problems where you can still boot into Windows but indicate that Windows isn't operating properly.

In some cases, a system will fail to boot properly. It might go directly into a blue screen stop error. If it does, you need to read the messages on the screen to get some insight into the error. Occasionally, a fault will cause Windows to go into a spontaneous shutdown/restart cycle. It tries to boot, fails, and then restarts itself. It repeats this cycle until you either turn it off or resolve the problem. These symptoms are often referred to as problems related to a missing graphical interface, or a problem where the graphical interface fails to load. Windows is the graphical interface but when you see these symptoms, you are not able to start Windows.

True or false? The "NTLDR is missing" error can occur if the boot sector of a hard drive has a problem.

Answer: *True*. Some common reasons why you might see this error include a corrupt boot sector, a corrupt master boot record (MBR), a corrupt NTLDR file, or the incorrect boot order configured in BIOS.

You can repair boot sector and MBR problems by using the recovery console in Windows XP and the Windows Recovery Environment (RE) in Windows Vista and Windows 7. Some of the commands from the Windows XP recovery console include the following:

- **fixboot**   This will repair the boot sector.
- **fixmbr**   This will repair the MBR.
- **bootcfg /rebuild**   This re-creates the boot.ini file.

The Recovery Console is a valuable tool used in Windows XP, but it isn't available from the Windows installation by default. You can access it from the installation CD by pressing R when the Welcome screen appears, or you can install it on the Windows XP system so that it is readily available.

You install the Recovery Console from the installation CD with the following command (replacing the *x* with the drive letter assigned to your CD): **x:\i386\ winnt32.exe /cmdcons**.

After it is installed, your system will show a multiboot menu with Microsoft Windows Recovery Console as one of the options.

In Windows Vista and Windows 7, you can use the following commands from the Windows RE to repair some problems:

- **bootrec /fixboot**   This will repair the boot sector.
- **bootrec /fixmbr**   This will repair the MBR.
- **bootrec /rebuildbcd**   This will rebuild the boot configuration data (BCD) store used on Windows Vista and Windows 7. The BCD store replaces the boot.ini file used on Windows XP systems.

EXAM TIP   You can repair common problems with the boot sector and master boot record by using **fixboot** and **fixmbr** commands from the Windows XP recovery console. Similar commands in Windows Vista and Windows 7 are **bootrec /fixboot** and **bootrec /fixmbr**.

MORE INFO   The next section, "Tools," in this objective includes information about how you can access the Windows RE in Windows Vista and Windows 7.

True or false? An error indicating that a drive is not bootable might be because of the incorrect boot order selected in the BIOS.

Answer: *True*. This error can be caused if the system BIOS is configured to boot to a USB drive first and a non-bootable USB drive is plugged into the computer.

The error might indicate that the device is not bootable, that it is an invalid boot disk, that the operating system is not found, or that a boot drive cannot be found. There are several possible solutions in this case. You can reconfigure the BIOS boot order to not boot to the USB drive first or simply remove the USB drive and reboot the system. You can also remove the USB drive from the boot order.

> **NOTE** From a security perspective, it's common to configure systems so that they do not boot to a USB device first. If a USB drive is infected and a user accidentally boots from it, it can infect the user's system. When booting this way, the normal operating system and antivirus software isn't running.

When a computer starts, it typically gives visual indications about what it is doing, which can be useful when troubleshooting. For example, if you're asked to troubleshoot a computer that has an error message of no boot drive found, you can use this information to check each optical drive for removable discs and remove them. Similarly, you can disconnect all the USB drives. Next, you'd reboot the system and observe it to see whether the symptoms have changed.

> **EXAM TIP** Errors indicating that a device is not bootable, the system has an invalid boot disk, the operating system is not found, or a boot drive is not found usually indicate that the system is trying to boot to a different device than normal. Ensure that all removable disks are removed, or check the BIOS boot order to resolve the problem.

Some of the other symptoms you might encounter related to disk problems include messages related to a missing boot.ini, missing operating system, or an invalid boot disk. Some common steps you can take to resolve these problems include the following:

- **Verify the boot order in BIOS** Ensure that the system is not trying to boot to a non-bootable device, such as a non-bootable USB disk or optical disc. You can also remove the device to resolve the problem.

- **Repair or replace the Boot.ini file** Boot.ini is used on Windows XP–based systems, and you can see some of these errors if it is missing or corrupt. The **bootcfg /rebuild** command can be executed in the recovery console to rebuild it.

- **Repair or replace the BCD** The BCD is used instead of the boot.ini file on Windows Vista and Windows 7, and some of these errors can be caused if the BCD is missing or corrupt. The **bootrec /rebuildbcd** command can be executed in the Windows RE to rebuild the BCD store.

- **Fix the boot sector** If the active partition has a corrupted boot sector, it might not be able to locate the NTLDR file. Fix it with the **fixboot** command in the recovery console or the **bootrec /fixboot** command in the Windows RE.

- **Fix the MBR** The MBR might be corrupt, causing this error. Fix it with the **fixmbr** command in the recovery console or the **bootrec /fixmbr** command in the Windows RE.

- **Manually copy the file** If a file is actually missing, you can simply copy it from another computer or from the installation media.

True or false? An error indicating that the trust relationship to a domain has been broken can be fixed by rejoining the domain.

Answer: *True*. You rejoin a domain by first disjoining it (joining a workgroup) and then joining the domain again.

This error indicates that the computer account's password is out of sync with the domain controller in a domain. When you rejoin the domain, it resets the password and resolves the problem.

Some other symptoms that you might run across include:

- **Service fails to start** Services are used by the operating system and different applications. The most obvious reason why a service fails to start is if it is disabled in the Services applet, so this is a good place to start looking. If it's disabled and you need it to run, enable it. Some services are dependent on other services running. You can check the Dependencies tab of the failing service to identify dependent services and then verify they are running. When a service fails to start, you'll often see an error appear in a dialog box indicating the failure. You can get details from this message or view the System log in Event Viewer to get more details. If the service is related to a specific application, you can look at the Application log in Event Viewer.

- **Compatibility error** While many applications will run in newer operating systems, some applications are not compatible. For example, some Windows XP applications will not run in Windows 7 but instead fail to start. Sometimes you'll see an error indicating a compatibility problem, and other times the application just doesn't start. The Application log in Event Viewer will usually include errors you can view to get more details of what caused the problem.

- **File fails to open** Normally, you can open a file by double-clicking it. For example, if you double-click a text file, it opens Notepad and shows the text file. This is because text files have a .txt extension and are associated with Notepad. If you run across a file that is not opening when you double-click it, check the associations. On Windows XP, you can view and modify associations from the File Types tab of Folder Options applet. On Windows Vista and Windows 7, you can use the Default Programs applet to view and manipulate associations.

Tools

Tools used to troubleshoot operating system problems include Windows-based applications and applets as well as commands executed from the command prompt. You also need to know about some tools outside of Windows, such as safe mode and the Startup Repair tool in Windows 7. When you know which tool to use for different problems, you can repair the system quicker.

True or false? You can use the **sfc** command to resolve problems with system files.

Answer: *True.* The **sfc** command (short for System File Checker) is used to check and repair system files.

Malware often tries to corrupt or replace system files. The **sfc** tool can be used to scan a specific system file or all of the system files used in a Windows-based system. Some common ways **sfc** is used include the following:

- **sfc /scannow**   This will scan all protected system files and attempt to repair any problems it finds.

- **sfc /verifyonly**   This scans all protected system files and reports its findings, but it doesn't attempt any repairs.

You can also use the **sfc** command on a specific file with the **/scanfile** and **/verifyfile** switches. You need to include the path to the file that you want to check.

EXAM TIP   The sfc command is used to check and repair system files. It is useful when repairing a system after a malware infection.

True or false? The Services applet will give you detailed information about why a service is not starting.

Answer: *False.* You can use the Services applet to configure services, but it does not include logged information related to the starting or stopping of a service.

The Event Viewer tool includes multiple logs that you can view to get information about the system, and it is available from the Administrative Tools group in the Control Panel. The three primary Windows logs are as follows:

- **System log**   The Windows operating system sends events to this log. It includes events about when a service is started or stopped, or when a driver fails to load. It often includes errors that appear to users in pop-up windows, so if a user remembers that an error appeared but doesn't remember what it said, you can look here to get information about the error.

- **Application log**   Applications send events to this log. For example, a third-party antivirus application can log when a virus is discovered or when a virus scan is started or stopped.

- **Security log**   Security-related events are sent to this log, and most events must be configured by an administrator before they are logged. It can include events such as when someone fails to log on due to an incorrect password or when someone accesses or deletes a file.

Figure 9-2 shows the Event Viewer with a specific event selected in the System log. The selected event is an error that was logged when the Microsoft Antimalware Service failed to start. It lists a code that provides more detail about the error. In this case, the system also gave a pop-up message indicating that Microsoft Security Essentials was unable to start because the system wasn't activated. Additionally, events were logged into the application log at about the same time, giving more information about the error.

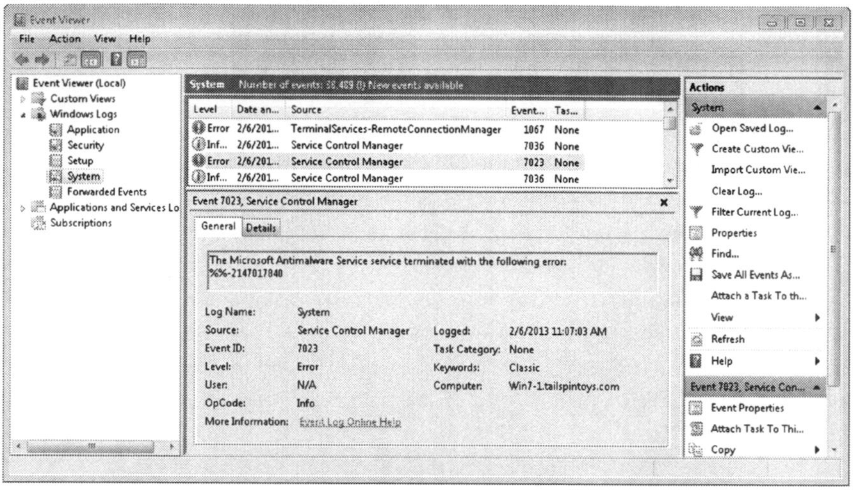

FIGURE 9-2 Event Viewer with error from the System log.

EXAM TIP The Event Viewer includes several logs that you can use to troubleshoot a system. If an application or a service is not starting, you can often gain insight into the problem by looking at the System log by using the Event Viewer. Additionally, some applications maintain their own logs that you can review if a specific application is not starting.

True or false? If a system can no longer start Windows normally after installing a new video driver, you can resolve the problem in safe mode.

Answer: *True.* Safe mode uses only basic drivers, so you will be able to boot into safe mode without using the new driver.

This scenario is the same for just about any type of driver that causes problems preventing Windows from booting normally. For example, if you update a driver for a NIC and your system stops with a blue screen error after rebooting, you can resolve the problem by booting into safe mode.

You would reboot the system and press F8 to access the Windows Advanced Options menu (also known as the Windows Advanced Boot Options menu and the Advanced Startup Options menu). You can then select Safe Mode from this menu. After the system boots into safe mode, you can use Device Manager to remove or roll back the faulty driver. Figure 9-3 shows the Windows Advanced Options page on a Windows XP-based system.

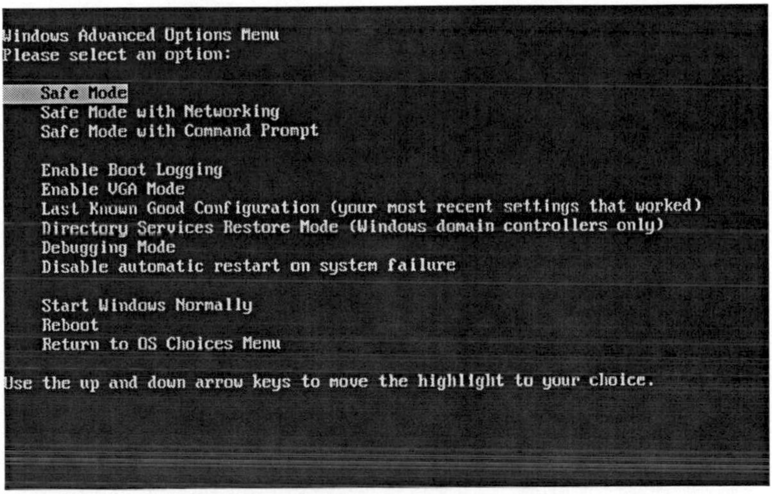

```
Windows Advanced Options Menu
Please select an option:

  Safe Mode
  Safe Mode with Networking
  Safe Mode with Command Prompt

  Enable Boot Logging
  Enable VGA Mode
  Last Known Good Configuration (your most recent settings that worked)
  Directory Services Restore Mode (Windows domain controllers only)
  Debugging Mode
  Disable automatic restart on system failure

  Start Windows Normally
  Reboot
  Return to OS Choices Menu

Use the up and down arrow keys to move the highlight to your choice.
```

FIGURE 9-3 Windows Advanced Options on Windows XP.

True or false? You can use the Startup Repair tool in Windows XP to resolve many problems preventing Windows XP from starting normally.

Answer: *False*. Startup Repair is available in Windows 7 but not in Windows XP.

The Startup Repair tool runs through a series of checks and can repair a variety of different problems that prevent your computer from booting normally. In some cases, Windows will sense that it has a problem and will automatically start the Startup Repair tool. In other cases, you need to start it manually.

You can access the Startup Repair tool through the System Recovery Options menu in Windows 7–based systems. Use the following steps to access the Startup Repair tool:

1. Reboot the system and press F8. This will start the Advanced Boot Options menu.

2. Select Repair Your Computer. This is the first option on the Advanced Boot Options menu in Windows 7, but it is not available on Windows XP.

3. When prompted, select a keyboard language.

4. When prompted, log on with an administrative account. You'll see a screen similar to Figure 9-4. Select the Startup Repair tool.

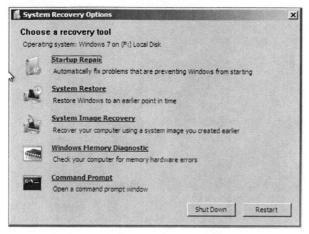

FIGURE 9-4 System Recovery Options menu on Windows 7.

Note that the System Recovery Options menu includes several other choices, including the following:

- **System Restore** You can use this to undo system changes by reverting your computer to a previous restore point. This works the same way as System Restore works within the operating system, but you can use it if a recent change prevents you from booting into the system normally.

- **System Image Recovery** If you've previously captured an image of your system, you can use this option to restore the image.

- **Windows Memory Diagnostic** This is used to run diagnostics on memory within the system. It is the same diagnostic tool that you can start from the Administrative Tools menu in Windows 7.

- **Command Prompt** This is not a normal command prompt but instead is the Windows Recovery Environment (Windows RE) prompt. You have access to the bootrec commands mentioned in the previous section from the Windows RE.

EXAM TIP Be familiar with each of the tools available from the System Recovery Options menu. Each of these tools can be used to resolve different types of problems.

Some of the other tools available to resolve operating system problems include the following:

- **msconfig** This can be used to modify what services start when the operating system starts and what applications start when the user logs on. Objective 1.4, "Given a scenario, use appropriate operating system features and tools," in Chapter 6 covers **msconfig** in depth.

- **defrag** If a system is running slow, it could be due to a fragmented disk. **Defrag** is the command line equivalent of the Disk Defragmenter, and both are mentioned in Objective 1.7, "Perform preventive maintenance procedures using appropriate tools," of Chapter 6.

- **regedit** The registry editor is used to view, modify, and back up the registry. It is rarely needed in day-to-day maintenance but is sometimes used to make advanced changes to a system.

- **regsvr32** This is used to register dynamic link libraries (DLLs). If you see a message indicating that your system is missing a DLL needed by an application, you can use this command to register the DLL and make it available to the operating system.

- **Repair disks** You can create system repair disks in Windows Vista and Windows 7. A system repair disk is a bootable CD or DVD and it is useful if you're unable to boot into the System Recovery options but you want to access the command prompt in the Windows RE. You can create a system repair disk from the Backup and Restore Center applet. Of course, you'll need to create it on an operational system but once you create it, you can use it on any computer to boot into the Windows RE.

- **Pre-installation environments** A pre-installation environment is a basic operating system with a command prompt and no graphical interface. As an example, the Windows RE is a pre-installation environment that has been modified with additional troubleshooting tools. You can also create your own pre-installation environment for other troubleshooting issues. For example, you can create a bootable CD with a Windows pre-installation environment and add antivirus tools. You can use this as an offline scanning kit for infected systems.

   MORE INFO Microsoft has published the Infrastructure Planning and Design Malware Response document. Appendix C of that document includes steps that you can use to create an offline scanning kit. You can access the download here: *http://go.microsoft.com/fwlink/?LinkId=93108.*

- **Emergency repair disk** An emergency repair disk (ERD) is a specific tool used in Windows 2000 and some earlier operating systems. It isn't supported in Windows XP, Windows Vista, or Windows 7 but there are similar tools. The Automated System Recovery (ASR) tool available in Windows XP is used instead of an ERD. You must create an ASR backup before the system fails. If you have an ASR backup, you can perform an ASR restore to recover the system. On Windows Vista, you can use the Windows Complete PC Backup and Restore tool instead of an ERD, and on Windows 7 you can create a System Image from the Backup and Restore applet instead of an ERD.

   MORE INFO Chapter 17 of the CompTIA A+ Training Kit (Exam 220-801 and Exam 220-802), ISBN-10: 0735662681, is focused on troubleshooting Windows operating systems. It provides more depth on the common symptoms that you're likely to see and the tools that you can use to resolve these problems.

Can you answer these questions?

You can find the answers to these questions at the end of this chapter.

1. What command would you use in Windows XP to repair a boot sector, and where can you execute this command?
2. What tool is used to read information recorded in the Windows System log?
3. How can you remove incompatible drivers if these drivers prevent you from booting into Windows normally?

Objective 4.7: Given a scenario, troubleshoot common security issues with appropriate tools and best practices

In this objective, you're expected to recognize many of the common symptoms that indicate a system has a security issue. This objective builds on the knowledge from the Security domain of the 220-802 exam covered in Chapter 7 of this book. You're expected to be aware of the common threats to computers and what tools are available and how to use them. The majority of security issues in this objective relate to malware, so you should also know the best practices used to remove malware.

Exam need to know...

- Common symptoms
  For example: What is an indication of browser redirection caused by malware?

- Tools
  For example: What is updated within antivirus software to ensure that it can detect new viruses?

- Best practices for malware removal
  For example: What is the easiest way to isolate an infected computer?

Common symptoms

This section includes many of the common symptoms caused by security issues, with a focus on malware infections. User systems can often be infected without the user's knowledge, but the system will usually give some indication of the problem. When you recognize that the problem is from malware, you can start using the tools to remove it.

True or false? Malware can cause a system to go to a different website than requested by a user.

Answer: *True.* Browser redirection occurs when a user attempts to access one Internet site but the browser is redirected to a different site.

Browser redirection is caused by malware and normally attempts to take a user to a malicious website. In large organizations, a proxy server will often block the user from visiting the malicious website. Instead, the proxy server sends an error to the user indicating that access to the site is blocked by the proxy server's content filter. Some malware also tries to modify the proxy server settings in the web browser to bypass the proxy server.

Malicious websites often have malicious code that they try to download onto a system when a user visits. When successful, it's referred to as a drive-by download. Some antivirus software monitors websites and will warn users when they attempt to visit a site with suspicious code. If the user ignores the warning and clicks through to the site anyway, the antivirus software might block the malicious download or the malware might get through. It's best to avoid malicious websites whenever possible.

EXAM TIP Browser redirection caused by malware redirects a browser Internet request from a legitimate website to a malicious website. Proxy servers in larger organizations will often block access to malicious websites and instead give a message to the user indicating that the site is blocked. This error is often the first indication of browser redirection. Some malware tries to change the proxy server settings in a web browser to bypass the proxy server.

True or false? When a user hears from friends that they are receiving emails from the user that the user never sent, it indicates that the user's email account has likely been hijacked.

Answer: *True*. Attackers attempt to learn the password of email accounts, and when successful, they can hijack the account and use it to send out spam and other malicious email.

If an account has been hijacked, the best solution is for the user to change the password. When the attacker no longer knows the password, they can't use it to send malicious email. Along these lines, users should be encouraged to use strong passwords and not use the same password for all their accounts.

It is also possible for an attacker to impersonate a user by modifying the name displayed in the email address or by modifying the From address with a bogus email address. This is sometimes referred to as spoofing the name or email address. For example, I recently received an email with my sister's name displayed but from an email address that my sister never used. It included a greeting with a link, but the words and punctuation in the email didn't match my sister's style. I double-checked with my sister and learned that she didn't send it and never used that email address. If I had clicked the link, it would have taken me to a website listed as suspicious and known to have hosted malicious software recently. Thankfully, I didn't click, but many people are fooled by this type of email spoofing.

EXAM TIP Attackers attempt to learn the password for email accounts, and when successful, they hijack the account and can send email using this account. The solution is to change the password and use a different strong password for different accounts. Attackers sometimes try to impersonate the user and simply send emails using someone else's name. Users often hear from their friends when this occurs, and it indicates that their account has been hijacked or that an attacker is using their name in emails.

True or false? If malware can successfully update the lmhost file in a Windows-based system, it can prevent the system from retrieving Windows updates.

Answer: *False*. The lmhost file is used only for NetBIOS names, but host names are used on the Internet. Modifying the lmhost file will not affect any Internet access.

However, the true/false statement is true if you change *lmhost* to *host*, and it indicates a common symptom of a malware infection. If a system cannot obtain updates from a Windows update site, it might be infected with malware that has modified the host file. Known malware has added entries into the host file of a Windows-based system, giving it a bogus IP address for the Windows update site. Each time the system tries to get an update, it fails because it is using the incorrect IP address.

EXAM TIP   A system that cannot obtain updates from Windows update sites might be infected with malware. A known method to prevent updates is by modifying the host file.

Additional symptoms you might see that indicate a malware infection include:

- **Pop-ups**   Pop-ups are additional Windows that appear with and without user interaction. They are frequently used on Internet websites to provide useful information but if they're appearing without the user taking action, they indicate a possible malware infection. You should ensure that the pop-up blocker in the web browser is enabled. On Internet Explorer you can enable it on the Privacy tab of the Internet Options applet. Next, you should run up-to-date antivirus software to check the system for malware.

- **Rogue antivirus**   Criminals have created fake antivirus software (also known as rogue antivirus software, rogueware, scareware, and ransomware) and regularly trick unsuspecting users into installing it. As one example, when a user goes to a malicious site, a pop-up appears informing the user that a virus has been detected, and encouraging the user to download and install free antivirus software. It's free but it installs malware on the user's system. After a fake scan, it reports finding multiple viruses but will only remove them if the user pays an additional fee such as $69.95. To resolve this, you need to first uninstall the rogue antivirus software and then scan the system with legitimate antivirus software. You often need to run antivirus software from safe mode or from a pre-installation CD with antivirus software installed to ensure the malware is completely removed.

- **Security alerts**   A security alert is from the operating system or from antivirus software and informs the user of a specific security issue. These should be investigated and resolved. The biggest warning with this is that criminals have become proficient at making rogue antivirus alerts look like legitimate security alerts. You need to ensure the security alert is valid.

- **PC locks up**   Malware can often cause a system to randomly lock up preventing the system from responding to mouse or keyboard inputs. Other times, the system reboots or stops with a stop error. A virus scan using up-to-date antivirus software can detect if the system is infected and remove the malware. These symptoms could also be caused from overheating, a failing power supply, or RAM damaged from electrostatic discharge.

- **Files disappearing** Malware sometimes deletes or modifies files so if you see files disappearing, it might be due to malware. Most often the files that you'll notice disappearing are system files. The operating system will report errors when a system file is no longer available.

- **File permission changes** Some malware will modify permissions on files or folders. This is often done so that the malware has full rights and permissions to the files. For example, some malware will change permissions on system files and folders so that it can easily manipulate them.

- **Access denied** An access denied error message can also indicate an infection from malware, or an attempt by malware to infect a system. For example, a drive-by download occurs when an unsuspecting user visits a malicious website. When the user visits, the website attempts to download and install the malware onto the user's system. If the user is logged on with a standard user account or User Access Control (UAC) is enabled, the installation fails and the user will see a pop-up indicating access is denied. Similarly, if a system is already infected, the malware might try to install additional malware and the user might see this error.

Tools

Antivirus software is the obvious tool used to remove malware. However, there are times when you need to take steps beyond just running antivirus software to remove it.

Anti-malware software is another name for antivirus software. Most antivirus software is able to detect more than just viruses. It can detect multiple types of malware including viruses, worms, and Trojans.

True or false? From within safe mode, you can often remove malware that cannot be removed while the system is booted normally.

Answer: *True*. Malware often takes extra steps to protect itself after it starts running, and these protection methods are not active in safe mode.

When you start a system in safe mode, only the basic services and drivers are started. More importantly, malware processes are not started in safe mode, so they aren't able to protect the malware files. If you run antivirus software after booting the system into safe mode, it has a better chance of successfully removing some malware.

> **EXAM TIP** Antivirus software is the primary tool used to remove malware. You can use it to remove malware while a system is running normally. Occasionally, you'll need to start the system in safe mode to remove some malware. It's best to update the antivirus definitions before starting the system in safe mode. You might be able to update them while the system is running normally or copy them from another system.

If you are unable to boot into safe mode due to an infection, you can use a pre-installation environment configured with up-to-date antivirus software. A pre-installation environment with antivirus software is also referred to as an offline scanning kit and was described earlier in this objective.

True or false? You can ensure that all malware is removed from a disk by performing a low level format of the disk.

Answer: *True.* A low level format (also known as a zero fill program) will securely erase all data on a disk.

In some situations, antivirus software is unable to securely erase malware from a disk. In these circumstances, the best chance at removing the malware is by performing a low level format. A standard format might erase the malware, but a quick format definitely will not erase it.

> **EXAM TIP** A low level format provides the highest level of assurance that all data (including any malware) has been overwritten. A quick format does not provide any assurances that the data or malware has been overwritten. A standard or full format might overwrite the data and malware, but it isn't as secure as a low level format.

> **MORE INFO** Chapter 6 of this book compares a quick format with a full or standard format. Chapter 7 of this book compares a low level format with a standard format.

True or false? You can remove a serious malware infection from a single disk system with the factory restore CD or DVD.

Answer: *True.* The factory restore media will restore the system to the state it was in when the system was purchased, and this will remove malware from the existing system.

Using the factory restore media can be used as a last ditch effort to restore a system after a serious infection. It will erase all existing data on the system's disk, including any user data. If you have to use this method, you should first try to back up any user data that you can back up. Before restoring the user data on the restored system, you should scan it with up-to-date antivirus software.

> **EXAM TIP** You can eliminate serious malware infections by using the factory restore media. This method will also obliterate all user data on the system disk, so it should be backed up first, if possible.

True or false? If a system is returned to service after a lengthy repair, you should update the operating system and antivirus signatures as soon as possible.

Answer: *True.* Keeping Windows operating systems and antivirus signature files up to date is an important best practice to keep them protected.

Patch management programs will keep systems up to date with current updates for Windows operating systems, applications, and antivirus signatures. However, if a system has not been operational, it hasn't received these updates and it could be vulnerable to some significant threats. Updating the operating system, applications, and antivirus software should be a priority before returning a system back to service.

Best practices for malware removal

CompTIA has listed several best practices you should follow when removing malware, and you're expected to know what they are. Many of these best practices are followed by both large and small organizations to help limit the adverse effects of malware.

True or false? After discovering that a networked computer is infected with a virus, you should isolate it as soon as possible by turning it off.

Answer: *False*. You should isolate a networked computer as soon as possible when you discover that it is infected, but the best method is by disconnecting the NIC cable or turning off the wireless NIC.

There are times when you or a security expert needs to gather information about the malware. However, if the system is turned off, it deletes information in the system cache that might be useful.

True or false? You should create a new restore point just before removing a virus and disable System Restore after removing the virus.

Answer: *False*. It is recommended that you disable System Restore before removing the virus and that you create a restore point after cleaning the system of all malware.

By disabling System Restore, you prevent the system from recording the changes that cleaned the system in a new restore point. If you don't, a user could inadvertently restore the system to this infected restore point by selecting it. By creating a new restore point after removing the malware, you are creating a point in time when the system is known to be free of malware.

True or false? Educating the user is the first step a technician should take when resolving a problem related to malware.

Answer: *False*. Educating the user is important, but CompTIA lists this as the last step a technician should take after resolving a malware infection.

There are several steps you can take when removing malware from Windows-based systems. The following steps include all of the items specifically listed by CompTIA as "best practices for malware removal":

- **Identify malware symptoms** This includes symptoms listed in the "Common symptoms" section within this objective.

- **Quarantine infected system** You quarantine a system by isolating it from other systems. A simple way to do so is by unplugging the network cable.

- **Disable System Restore** You should disable System Restore before removing malware. This ensures that the system changes that are removing the malware aren't recorded and can't be accidentally restored at a later time.

- **Remediate infected system** Often, this simply means running antivirus software with up-to-date signature files to remove the malware. In some cases, you need to use other system tools, such as safe mode, or one of the recovery environments like the Window Recovery Console in Windows XP or the Windows RE in Windows Vista and Windows 7.

- **Schedule scans and updates** Ideally, antivirus software will catch malware before it infects your system. However, some malware can get through. For example, a new virus might not be recognized by the current signature files in the antivirus software. However, if you regularly update the signature files and schedule system scans, the new virus will be detected after the antivirus vendor updates its signature files to include it.

- **Enable System Restore and create restore point** If you disable System Restore prior to removing malware, you should enable it and create a current restore point.

- **Educate end user** After a user's system has been infected, they are often more receptive to information about common threats and steps that they can take to prevent a reoccurrence. After resolving the problem, it's valuable to let the user know how crafty criminals can be and some of the common ways that they try to trick users into infecting their systems.

NOTE When educating a user about a problem, it's valuable to let them know that anyone can be tricked. As a knowledgeable technician, you probably know what to avoid, and it's easy to fall into the trap of thinking everyone knows about a certain risk. If you come across as though you're ridiculing the user for making a mistake, they aren't likely to listen to the information that you're giving them.

EXAM TIP Know the items in the "Best practices for malware removal" list. They are listed specifically in the objectives, and CompTIA is known for asking questions specifically related to lists like this.

Can you answer these questions?

You can find the answers to these questions at the end of this chapter.

1. What should be done if an email account is hijacked?

2. What should be done with antivirus software to ensure that it can detect new viruses?

3. What are the best practices (and the correct order) specified by CompTIA for serious malware infections?

Objective 4.8: Given a scenario, troubleshoot, and repair common laptop issues while adhering to the appropriate procedures

This objective expects you to know about many of the common symptoms related to laptop issues and how to resolve them. You're also expected to know about some best practices related to disassembling laptops. Many of the topics within this objective build on the Laptops domain from Exam 220-801, which was 11 percent of that exam and was covered in Chapter 3, "Laptops," of this book. Some of these topics also build on wireless networking topics covered in Chapter 2 of this book.

Exam need to know...

- Common symptoms
  For example: What are some common function keys included on laptops, and what are their purposes?
- Disassembling processes for proper reassembly
  For example: What should be done with screws as they are removed from a laptop?

Common symptoms

This section expects you to know about many of the common symptoms related to laptops and the cause of these symptoms. Some symptoms can easily be resolved by simply toggling keys on the keyboard, while others require technicians to have a deeper knowledge of laptops.

True or false? The easiest way to enable an output to an external monitor on a laptop is by toggling the appropriate key on the keyboard.

Answer: *True.* Most laptops have a key designated for dual displays, and by toggling this key, you can enable different display modes.

Laptops often include an extra Fn key, which is used with the function keys to give them an alternate purpose. For example, the F1 key is normally used for help but it can be used to toggle the display mode when used with the Fn key on some laptops. There isn't a standard for which function key to use for different alternate purposes, so you might see the F1 key used for dual displays on one laptop but another laptop might use the F2 key instead. By toggling this key, you can select one of the following choices on most laptops:

- External display only
- Primary laptop display only
- Duplicate desktop on primary display to external display
- Extend desktop from primary display onto external display

You can also enable the secondary video output by using the Display applet from within Windows. However, it is much easier to enable the secondary video output by simply toggling the appropriate key on the keyboard.

True or false? Users can increase and decrease the brightness of their display on a typical laptop by using the keyboard.

Answer: *True.* Laptops commonly have a function key that controls the brightness of the display when combined with the Fn key.

When troubleshooting problems, the easiest solution should be considered first. In this case, if a user complains of a dim display, you can suggest that they simply toggle the brightness key to see whether they can get the brightness they want.

True or false? The Caps Lock key on some laptops results in numbers being displayed when specific letter keys are pressed.

Answer: *False.* The Caps Lock key causes letters to be displayed in uppercase. However, the Num Lock key on some laptops can cause the behavior described in this true/false question.

When a laptop doesn't have room for a separate numeric keypad, it will often include a pseudo numeric keypad over some of the letter keys. When the Num Lock key is selected, pressing these letters causes numbers to be displayed instead of letters.

True or false? If wireless access suddenly stops on a single laptop computer, the most likely reason is a faulty wireless card.

Answer: *False.* The most likely reason is that the wireless switch or wireless key has disabled wireless for the laptop.

Most laptops include wireless capabilities, and these can often be enabled or disabled by pressing one of the keys or toggling a switch on the laptop. Users can accidentally disable the wireless capability without realizing how they did it. This is the easiest thing to check and the most obvious in this situation.

EXAM TIP Laptops have limited space for the keyboard and often have alternate uses of different keys. When users don't understand these keys, they often perceive it as a problem and ask for help. PC technicians who understand these keys can quickly resolve the problem with just a keystroke or two. These keys are often included to configure dual displays, enable and disable wireless, modify the screen brightness, and modify the volume.

MORE INFO Objective 3.3, "Compare and contrast laptop features," of Exam 220-801 specifically addresses many of the special keys found on laptops and is covered in Chapter 3 of this book. Chapter 8 of the CompTIA A+ Training Kit (Exam 220-801 and Exam 220-802), ISBN-10: 0735662681, covers laptops in depth and includes special function keys commonly found on laptops.

The primary types of display monitors that you'll see on laptop computers are LED or liquid crystal display (LCD)–based monitors. CRT monitors are much too big and bulky to be used with today's laptops, and plasma monitors generate too much heat.

Both LCD and LED-type monitors use LCDs within the display, but they use different types of backlights. LCD-based monitors use a cold cathode fluorescent lamp (CCFL) as a backlight, and LED monitors use LEDs for the backlight. CCFLs often fail, but it's rare for the LED's backlight to fail.

If the display is barely perceptible and the laptop is using a traditional LCD monitor, it's likely that the CCFL has failed. One way to verify that the CCFL has failed is by shining a flashlight into the display. If you can see the screen with the flashlight, it indicates that the CCFL has failed. If it is completely dark, it indicates that the display has failed and needs to be replaced.

NOTE In many cases, it is not cost effective to replace the display screen on a laptop. Organizations commonly have specific guidelines related to the replacement cost and the repair cost. For example, if the cost to repair a laptop is 50 percent of the cost of a new laptop, an organization will often choose to replace the laptop instead of repair it.

True or false? You can modify the Power Options of a laptop to cause it to hibernate when the lid is closed.

Answer: *True.* The Power Options in the Control Panel can be modified to change the laptop's behavior when the lid is closed.

It's common to configure a laptop to hibernate when the lid is closed. When configured this way, the user doesn't need to wait for a logical shutdown but can instead just close the lid when they are done. Later, they can simply open the lid and it will return to the same state it was in when they shut the lid. It's also possible to configure this action to put the computer to sleep or completely turn it off.

EXAM TIP The Power Options applet can be used to modify the behavior of the power button on desktop computers and to specify what happens when the lid is closed.

MORE INFO Chapter 6 of this book covers the Power Options applet in more depth. It includes the differences between sleep and hibernate.

True or false? You should replace laptop batteries that cannot accept a full charge.

Answer: *True.* Laptop batteries often need to be replaced, and a common symptom is that the laptop shuts down shortly after switching over to battery power.

The battery will normally charge while the laptop is on AC power. If you remove the AC power and the system shuts down after a short period of time, it indicates that the battery either cannot be fully charged or cannot hold the charge. The best solution is to replace the battery. For example, a new laptop might be able to run on battery power for five hours, but a couple of years later, it might be able to run on battery power for only 30 minutes or less. This is a clear indication that the battery needs to be replaced.

NOTE Some batteries are susceptible to a problem known as *memory effect*, which causes the run time of a battery to become shorter and shorter. The new battery might run for five hours, but the user might never use battery power for more than 30 minutes before recharging it. After a period of time, the battery "remembers" that it needs to last for only 30 minutes, and that's as long as it lasts. This can be resolved in some batteries, but for a typical battery used in laptops, you'll need to replace it.

True or false? Intermittent wireless connectivity on a single laptop can be caused by a loose antenna connection.

Answer: *True.* If the antenna is not properly attached to the wireless card, it can result in intermittent wireless access.

The antenna won't typically come loose during normal operation. However, when performing other hardware maintenance on a laptop, it's possible to jiggle this loose or not secure it properly when reassembling the laptop.

Systems can often still connect when the antenna isn't connected. However, the signal received from the WAP will be weak, resulting in intermittent connections.

True or false? You can resolve interference problems from other wireless networks by changing from the default channel 6 to channel 3 or 9.

Answer: *False.* Interference on channel 6 from other wireless networks will also affect channels 3 and 9.

You can often get better performance by changing from the default channel 6 to channel 1 or 11. This is often useful in areas where multiple wireless networks are operating, such as in an apartment building.

Another problem that can cause intermittent connectivity is from interference. Wireless routers and wireless access points should be located away from sources of interference such as fluorescent lights.

EXAM TIP Intermittent wireless connectivity on a laptop can be caused by a loose connection with the antenna. This is most likely to occur after the laptop has been opened and disassembled for repair. It can also be caused by interference from multiple wireless networks using the same channel.

Some additional symptoms you might see on laptops are:

- **No display** If you don't see anything displayed when the laptop is powered on, a good check is to shine a flashlight into the display. If you can see Windows with the light shining in, it indicates that the backlight is not working. On LCD systems, the backlight is a CCFL so it might have failed, or the inverter that provides power to the CCFL might have failed. If you don't see any display at all when you shine the flashlight into the display, it indicates the display itself has probably failed.

- **Flickering display** A flickering display on a laptop indicates a loose connection. The solution is to open it up and secure the connections. You might remember that flickering can be caused by the refresh rate being set too low on a CRT display, but CRTs are not used with laptops.

- **Sticking keys** The most common cause of sticking keys is from food or beverages being spilled into the keyboard. The best solution is to clean it with compressed air.
- **Ghost cursor** Users can accidentally manipulate the cursor by touching the touchpad or the pointing stick embedded in the keyboard. The result is that the cursor seems to jump around on its own, even though the user isn't touching the mouse. If the user is not using the touchpad or pointing stick, you can disable them to eliminate the problem. If they are being used, you can modify the sensitivity of the device in the Control Panel Mouse applet.
- **No power** The most obvious reason why a laptop doesn't have power is because it isn't plugged into an AC source and the battery is dead. Laptops use power adapters that convert commercial AC power to DC power needed by the laptop. Many of these have LEDs that indicate when they are receiving power. If that LED is available and lit, check the LED where the power adapter plugs into the laptop's DC jack. If these LEDs aren't lit, but the adapter is plugged into a good power source, the adapter is probably faulty. The next choice is a faulty DC jack. When a laptop is plugged in, the battery should be charging so you should be able to remove the power adapter and the system should stay on. If it can't run on battery power at all, either the DC jack is faulty preventing the battery from charging, or the battery is faulty.

Disassembling processes for proper reassembly

You often need to disassemble laptops when they need to be repaired or upgraded. In some cases, this is rather simple and requires you only to remove a couple of screws for an access panel on the bottom of the laptop. In other cases, it can be very complex. There are several actions that PC technicians can take to prevent problems and ensure that the system can be returned to full service.

True or false? As a best practice, PC technicians should label screws as they remove them from a laptop while disassembling it.

Answer: *True.* CompTIA lists this specifically as a best practice in this objective.

When you label the screws as you remove them, you have a better chance of getting the proper screw back into the same location.

The full list of best practices related to disassembling a laptop in the CompTIA objectives is as follows:

- **Document and label cable and screw locations** This can be simplified by taking pictures with a smartphone during the disassembly.
- **Organize parts** While disassembling the laptop, it's best to organize the parts as you remove them. For example, some screws used to secure access panels in place are slightly different in size. By organizing them as you remove them, you'll ensure that the proper screw is returned to the proper location.

- **Refer to manufacturer documentation** The manufacturer's manual is the best source for learning the proper methods of disassembling a laptop.
- **Use appropriate hand tools** Common screws are removed with screwdrivers. When prying open the case or removing plastic covers, you should use plastic wedges or plastic shims. These help prevent damage when the case and covers are removed.

EXAM TIP The CompTIA objectives list specific steps that a PC technician should follow when disassembling laptops. When specifics are listed like this, CompTIA often asks questions directly related to them, so you should know them before taking the exam.

Can you answer these questions?

You can find the answers to these questions at the end of this chapter.

1. What can a user do to increase the brightness of a laptop?
2. What can cause intermittent wireless connectivity for a laptop?
3. What specific actions are recommended by CompTIA when disassembling a laptop?

Objective 4.9: Given a scenario, troubleshoot printers with appropriate tools

This objective expects you to be able to recognize common symptoms with printers and resolve them with appropriate tools. This objective builds on knowledge from the Printers domain of the 220-801 exam covered in Chapter 4, "Printers," of this book. As a reminder, the Printers domain comprises 11 percent of the 220-801 exam, and it has a heavy focus on laser printers. You can also expect this objective to have a heavy focus on laser printers.

Exam need to know...

- Common symptoms
  For example: What would cause toner to fall off the printed page? What stage of a laser printer puts toner onto the page?
- Tools
  For example: What is used to clean up spilled toner?

Common symptoms

Many of the common symptoms of printer problems are related to the quality of the output. If you understand how the printer works normally, you'll have a better chance of identifying the likely cause of the problem.

True or false? If a laser printer is printing blank sheets, you should check the fusing stage.

Answer: *False*. The fusing stage melts the toner onto the paper, so if this stage has problems, the toner falls off but the sheets are not blank.

Toner is applied to the paper in the development stage, so if the paper is completely blank, it is most likely because it is not receiving any toner.

The seven stages of the laser imaging process are mentioned specifically in the 220-801 exam. Understanding each stage in the process is important when troubleshooting laser printers. The seven stages are as follows:

- **Processing**   The image is converted to a raster image by the raster image processor (RIP) and stored in the printer's memory.
- **Charging**   The imaging drum is charged with a high negative voltage (between -500 and -1000 VDC) with a primary charge roller or a corona wire. This prepares the drum to accept the image from the laser.
- **Exposing**   The laser writes the raster image onto the drum in this stage. The electrical potential of the drum is changed where the laser shines onto the drum, and this change of electrical potential allows the toner to be electrically attracted to the drum.
- **Developing**   The toner is applied to the drum during this stage. It sticks to the drum but only where the laser has drawn the image onto the drum.
- **Transferring**   During this stage, the paper is moved through the printer. The paper is electrically charged so that the toner is transferred from the drum onto the paper.
- **Fusing**   The fuser assembly melts the toner onto the paper.
- **Cleaning**   Excess toner is scraped off the drum, and an erase lamp is used to remove the charge from the drum.

EXAM TIP   Ensure that you are aware of each stage of the laser printing process and what components are used during each of these stages. Even though the laser printing process isn't listed in the 220-802 exam objectives, you'll find that you can answer many questions if you understand the laser printing process.

MORE INFO   Chapter 4 of this book covers printers in depth and includes more detailed information about each of these stages. Additionally, Chapter 7 of the CompTIA A+ Training Kit (Exam 220-801 and Exam 220-802), ISBN-10: 0735662681, covers printers in depth.

True or false? Network printers have link lights similar to any NIC.

Answer: *True*. If a printer has connectivity problems, you can check the link light to verify that it is connected to the network.

Most NICs have LEDs used to indicate when the NIC is connected to another system and when data is being transferred over the connection. Link lights are usually solid green to show a connection. Data activity lights will typically blink to show activity.

True or false? An error from a printer saying "load letter" indicates that the printer is out of paper.

Answer: *True*. The error indicates that the printer is out of letter-sized paper.

Some printers give clear errors, such as "printer out of paper." Printers with multiple trays often indicate what type of paper needs to be loaded, such as letter-sized paper or legal-sized paper.

True or false? You can usually resolve ghost image or shadow image problems on a laser printer by replacing the toner.

Answer: *False*. Replacing the toner will not resolve ghost image or shadow image problems on a laser printer.

Ghost image problems are often related to what was printed previously or to a problem with the drum. For example, if you print a very dark image on a laser printer, the next page might have a residual image. You can confirm this by printing blank pages after a dark image or reducing the resolution of the dark image to eliminate the problem. Problems related to the drum indicate that the cleaning scraper might need to be replaced or that the drum itself might need to be replaced.

Some of the other errors that you might come across, including the steps to resolve them, are as follows:

- **Streaks**   Streaks on a laser printer are most likely the result of scratches on the imaging drum, especially if they are occurring in the same location on the printed page. The only solution is to replace the drum. Streaks on an inkjet printer can be caused by dirty or misaligned print heads. You can clean inkjet print heads with software tools provided by the manufacturer.
- **Faded print**   This indicates that you're low on toner or ink. Replacing the toner, ink cartridge, or ink ribbon should eliminate this problem.
- **Toner not fused to the paper**   The fuser assembly fuses the toner to the paper. Replace the fuser to resolve the problem.
- **Creased paper**   Printers often crease the paper as it is fed through the paper path, but it should not be noticeable unless you're using a heavier bond paper. A solution is to send the paper through the feeder rather than through the paper tray.
- **Paper not feeding**   Pickup rollers are used to pull paper through a printer. You can clean them or replace them to resolve this problem.

- **Paper jam**   This occasionally occurs, and after removing the paper jam, you won't see it again for a long time. However, if a printer is regularly jamming, it might be because of low-quality paper or paper that has been exposed to high humidity. Replace the paper to see whether this resolves the problem. It's also possible that the pickup and separator rollers are worn. Replacing the rollers with a maintenance kit might resolve the problem.

- **Garbled characters on paper**   The most likely reason for this is the wrong print driver. Double-check the driver to ensure that the correct driver is installed, and if necessary, update the driver. This symptom might also indicate a problem with the cable. For example, the maximum distance of a USB 2.0 cable is 5 meters (about 16 feet), and using a longer cable can result in a garbled output. Reseating the cable will ensure that you don't have a loose connection.

- **Vertical lines on page**   A clogged toner cartridge on a laser printer can cause this symptom. The solution is to remove the cartridge and shake it or to replace the cartridge. This symptom can also be caused by a scratched or dirty drum, requiring the drum to be replaced. On inkjet printers, dirty or misaligned print heads can cause this symptom, but it can be resolved by cleaning and aligning them.

- **Backed up print queue**   Print jobs will stop printing if the print spooler service has been paused. The simple solution is to resume the Print Spooler service. If you're unable to get jobs in the queue to start, you can restart the Print Spooler service from the Services applet and send the jobs to the printer again.

- **Low memory errors**   The RIP stores the raster image in the printer's memory before it is sent to the printer. If the image is too large or the printer doesn't have enough onboard memory, you'll see memory errors. The solution is to either reduce the resolution of the print job or add additional memory.

- **Access denied**   An access denied error indicates that a user doesn't have adequate permissions to use the printer. Typically, the Everyone group is assigned Allow Print permission so that anyone can print, but this is changed on printers when administrators don't want all users to be able to send print jobs to a printer.

- **Printer will not print**   As with many troubleshooting problems, you should check the basics first. Ensure that the system is plugged in, turned on, and properly connected. If the computer has an online/offline button, ensure that it is online. In some cases, turning the printer off and back on will resolve the problem.

- **Color prints in wrong print color**   You might see this symptom if the ink cartridges or color toner cartridges are inserted in the wrong location. The solution is to put them into the correct locations. However, it might take time before the colors return to normal because of residual ink left over in the printer.

- **Unable to install printer**   Users need to be in the Power Users or Administrators group to install a printer on a Windows XP–based system. You might see this permission if the user doesn't have adequate permissions on Windows XP. Regular users can install printers on Windows 7.
- **Error codes**   Error codes can be cryptic numbers such as "error 3F" or plain words such as "out of paper." If the error code isn't clear, you can identify the meaning of the code from the manufacturer's printer manual.

EXAM TIP   Exam questions might refer to a specific brand or model of a printer. Don't let this distract you. The exam is vendor-neutral, and the question is typically asking a generic question that could be applied to any printer of the same type.

Tools

When working with printers, there are some specific tools that you should know about. Some tools, such as compressed air, can be used in other maintenance situations. Other tools, such as a laser printer maintenance kit, are used only with printers.

Many printer manufacturers provide software tools that you can use with their printers. These are very valuable, and you should know about them, but they are not mentioned specifically in this objective. However, they are useful for resolving some of the common symptoms related to printers mentioned in the previous objective. For example, many inkjet printers have software tools that you can use to align or clean the print heads.

True or false? Toner should be vacuumed up with a regular vacuum cleaner as soon as possible.

Answer: *False.* Toner is an extremely fine powder of carbon and plastic particles, and they will pass through a regular vacuum.

Spilled toner can be vacuumed with a special toner vacuum cleaner that will capture all of the particles. If a toner vacuum isn't available, you should consult the Material Safety Data Sheet (MSDS) to determine the best way to clean it. One method often recommended by MSDS documentation is to remove it with cool, damp cloth towels. Do not rub or use hot water, because the friction or heat can melt the resin, making it much more difficult to remove.

EXAM TIP   Spilled toner can be cleaned up with a toner vacuum, but a regular vacuum cleaner should not be used. You can also clean it up with cool, damp cloth towels.

True or false? A "service required" message on a laser printer typically means that it is out of paper.

Answer: *False.* A "service required" message typically means that you need to apply the maintenance kit for the printer.

Most laser printers track how many pages are printed. When a specific number of pages have been printed, the printer gives a message such as "service required" or "Perform printer maintenance." These messages indicate that routine maintenance should be performed. Laser printer maintenance kits include items such as replacement pickup and separator rollers, transfer rollers, and fuser assemblies. They also provide instructions for cleaning specific components within the printer.

EXAM TIP Laser printers have maintenance kits that should be periodically applied to printers. A maintenance kit includes replacement components and cleaning instructions.

True or false? You should restart the Print Spooler service if a print job doesn't print and cannot be deleted.

Answer: *True.* Restarting the Print Spooler service will clear out print jobs that are hung up in the print queue.

Windows-based systems send print jobs to the print spooler, which then sends the jobs to the print device. The Print Spooler service manages this activity, but it can sometimes get hung up. You should first try to delete jobs that are stuck, but if this doesn't work, you can restart the Print Spooler service from the Services applet. This will clear out the print queue, and all jobs will need to be sent to the printer again.

EXAM TIP The print queue for a printer is managed by the Print Spooler service. You can clear out the print queue by restarting the Print Spooler service from the Services applet.

True or false? Compressed air can be used to blow out paper dust from impact printers.

Answer: *True.* Compressed air cans are often used by technicians to clean out the inside of some printers, such as impact printers and thermal printers.

Compressed air is not recommended for laser printers. The air can blow dust into the imaging drum, causing damage.

Can you answer these questions?

You can find the answers to these questions at the end of this chapter.

1. What should you use to clean up spilled toner?
2. What should be repaired or replaced if toner falls off the printed page?
3. What should you do if a print job doesn't print and it cannot be deleted from the print queue?

Answers

This section contains the answers to the "Can you answer these questions?" sections in this chapter.

Objective 4.1: Given a scenario, explain the troubleshooting theory

1. The six CompTIA troubleshooting steps in their proper order are as follows:
   a. Identify the problem
   b. Establish a theory of probable cause (question the obvious)
   c. Test the theory to determine cause
   d. Establish a plan of action to resolve the problem and implement the solution
   e. Verify full system functionality and, if applicable, implement preventive measures
   f. Document findings, actions, and outcomes
2. Technicians should establish a plan of action to resolve a problem after confirming a theory.
3. If a theory cannot be confirmed, a PC technician should either establish a new theory or escalate the problem.
4. The last step in the CompTIA troubleshooting theory process is documentation. Technicians should document their findings, actions, and outcomes.

Objective 4.2: Given a scenario, troubleshoot common problems related to motherboards, RAM, CPU and power with appropriate tools

1. The most likely result from a broken heat sink clamp is an overheated CPU, causing unexpected shutdowns and system lockups. The heat sink is designed to draw heat away from the CPU. If the clamp breaks off, the heat sink won't have a tight connection with the CPU and won't effectively draw heat away.
2. Common hardware reasons for unexpected shutdowns and system lockups of a computer include overheating (due to dust buildup or failing cooling components), faulty or failing RAM, and faulty or failing power supply. Malware is a software cause of the same symptoms.
3. Power supply testers are used to measure voltages in a power supply that isn't installed in a computer. A multimeter is used to measure voltages for a power supply that is connected to a computer.

Objective 4.3: Given a scenario, troubleshoot common problems related to motherboards, RAM, CPU and power with appropriate tools

1. Two PATA drives in the same IDE channel should be configured with one as the master and one as the slave, or you can configure both with cable select and use a compatible cable.

2. RAID-0 does not provide any fault tolerance and requires you to restore the data after you rebuild the array. RAID-1, RAID-5, and RAID-10 can tolerate a single failed drive without losing data.

3. The chkdsk command-line tool or the Check Disk Windows Explorer tool is used to check the integrity of a disk.

Objective 4.4: Given a scenario, troubleshoot common video and display issues

1. If a monitor has power but is not displaying video from a computer, you should ensure that the video cable is connected to the correct port on the computer. You should also ensure that the cable is securely connected to both the computer and the monitor.

2. A dead pixel is a dot on the screen that can't change colors, and it is typically white or black, depending on the type of monitor.

3. If the video card was recently upgraded, you should check to ensure that it has power. If the incorrect driver is used for a video card, you'll see degraded video on the monitor. In some cases, Windows might stop with a fatal stop error, or Windows might refuse to use the driver and default to VGA mode.

Objective 4.5: Given a scenario, troubleshoot wired and wireless networks with appropriate tools

1. If you lower power levels on a WAP, it can result in intermittent connectivity for some of the wireless clients.

2. You can create a twisted-pair cable with wire strippers and a crimper. You can test the cable with a cable tester.

3. Lower power levels from the WAP or wireless router can cause intermittent connectivity for the clients. If the network is overloaded from too many users (authorized or unauthorized), it reduces the performance of the network. If a single system is having problems, it might be due to out-of-date drivers for the wireless NIC.

Objective 4.6: Given a scenario, troubleshoot operating system problems with appropriate tools

1. The **fixboot** command is used in Windows XP to repair a boot sector. It is executed from the recovery console.
2. The Event Viewer is used to read Windows logs, including the Windows System log.
3. If Windows won't boot normally due to an incompatible driver, you can boot the computer into safe mode and use Device Manager to roll back or uninstall the driver.

Objective 4.7: Given a scenario, troubleshoot common security issues with appropriate tools and best practices

1. A hijacked email account is one where an attacker has discovered the password and is now sending spam or other emails using this account. The solution is for the user to replace the current password with a strong password.
2. Antivirus software should be updated regularly with new signature definitions to ensure that it can detect new viruses.
3. CompTIA lists the following best practices for malware removal:
   a. Identify malware symptoms
   b. Quarantine infected system
   c. Disable System Restore
   d. Remediate infected systems
   e. Schedule scans and updates
   f. Enable System Restore and create restore point
   g. Educate end user

Objective 4.8: Given a scenario, troubleshoot, and repair common laptop issues while adhering to the appropriate procedures

1. Laptops commonly have function keys that can be pressed to increase the brightness. It's also possible to use the Display applet in the Control Panel to increase the brightness.
2. Intermittent wireless connectivity is most often caused either by a loose antenna connection after a repair or from interference from other wireless networks on the same channel.
3. CompTIA recommends the following actions when disassembling a laptop as methods of ensuring that it can be properly reassembled and returned to full service:
   a. Document and label cable and screw locations
   b. Organize parts
   c. Refer to manufacturer documentation
   d. Use appropriate hand tools

Objective 4.9: Given a scenario, troubleshoot printers with appropriate tools

1. The best choice to clean up spilled toner is a toner vacuum. A regular vacuum cleaner should not be used, because the toner particles will pass through the vacuum cleaner and be sent into the air.

2. The fuser assembly melts the toner onto the paper, and if the toner is falling off the printed page, it indicates that the fuser assembly isn't functioning properly and should be replaced.

3. You can restart the Print Spooler service if a print job is stuck in the queue and cannot be deleted.

Index

N

Nano-ITX, 13
NAS (Network Attached Storage), 35, 113–114
National Television System Committee (NTSC), 32
native resolution, 60
NAT (Network Address Translation), 100, 111
nbtstat command, 202, 323
netstat command, 202, 323
Net Use command, 224
Network Address Translation (NAT), 100, 111
Network Attached Storage (NAS), 35, 113–114
Networking tab, Task Manager tool, 210
network interface card (NIC). See NIC (network interface card)
networks
 cables
  coaxial, 79–80, 82
  fiber, 78, 80–81
  overview, 80
  required knowledge, 78, 80
  twisted-pair, 78–79, 81–82
 command line tools for, 200–202
 devices
  access points, 112–113
  bridges, 113
  firewalls, 114
  hubs, 110
  Internet appliance, 115
  modems, 113
  NAS, 113–114
  overview, 109
  required knowledge, 109–110
  routers, 111–112
  switches, 110–111
  VoIP phones, 114–115
 Internet connections
  cable and fiber, 102–103
  cellular, 105
  overview, 102
  phone lines, 103–104
  satellite, 104
  WiMAX, 105
 ports, 91–92
 protocols, 92
 SOHO routers
  built-in networking services, 99–100
  MAC filtering, 97–98

 overview, 97
 port forwarding, 98–99
 port triggering, 98–99
 required knowledge, 97
 wireless channels, 98
 wireless security, 100–101
 TCP/IP
  APIPA, 85–86
  client-side DNS, 87
  DHCP, 87–88
  gateway, 89–90
  IP classes, 83–84
  IPv4 vs. IPv6, 84–85
  overview, 83
  public vs. private addresses, 85–86
  required knowledge, 83
  static vs. dynamic addresses, 87
  subnet mask, 88–89
 TCP vs. UDP, 93–94
 tools
  cable tester, 117
  crimper, 116
  loopback plug, 118
  multimeter, 116–117
  overview, 115
  punchdown tool, 118
  required knowledge, 115–116
  toner probe, 117
 troubleshooting
  common symptoms, 318–320
  overview, 318
  required knowledge, 318
  tools for, 321–323
 types of
  LAN, 106
  MAN, 107
  overview, 106
  PAN, 107
  required knowledge, 106
  topologies, 108–109
  WAN, 107
 virtual machine requirements, 241–242
 for Windows clients
  alternative IP address, 228
  connections for, 224
  file & printer sharing, 222–223
  firewall settings, 225
  homegroup, 222–223
  Home vs. Work vs. Public network settings, 227–228
  network card properties, 228–229

About the author

DARRIL GIBSON, A+, Network+, Security+, CASP, SSCP, CISSP, MCT, CTT+, MCSE, MCITP is founder and CEO of Security, Consulting, and Training, LLC. Darril has written or co-written more than 25 books, including several on security and security certifications. He regularly posts articles on *http://blogs.GetCertifiedGetAhead.com* and can be reached at *darril@GetCertifiedGetAhead.com*.

What do you think of this book?

We want to hear from you!
To participate in a brief online survey, please visit:

microsoft.com/learning/booksurvey

Tell us how well this book meets your needs—what works effectively, and what we can do better. Your feedback will help us continually improve our books and learning resources for you.

Thank you in advance for your input!